Mitchell Symons was born in 1957 in London and educated at Mill Hill School and the LSE where he studied Law. Since leaving BBC TV, where he was a researcher and then a director, he has worked as a writer, broadcaster and journalist. He was a principal writer of early editions of the board game Trivial Pursuit and has devised many television formats. Currently, he writes a weekly column for the *Sunday Express*.

Also by Mitchell Symons

Non-fiction:
Forfeit!
The Equation Book of Sports Crosswords
The Equation Book of Movie Crosswords
The You Magazine Book of Journolists
    (four books, co-author)
Movielists (co-author)
The Sunday Magazine Book of Crosswords
The Hello! Magazine Book of Crosswords
    (three books)
How To Be Fat: The Chip And Fry Diet (co-author)
The Book of Criminal Records
The Book of Lists
The Book of Celebrity Lists
The Book of Celebrity Sex Lists
The Bill Clinton Joke Book
National Lottery Big Draw 2000 (co-author)
That Book
This Book
The Other Book
Why Girls Can't Throw
Where Do Nudists Keep Their Hankies?
Don't Get Me Started

Fiction:
All In
The Lot

THE
ULTIMATE
LOO BOOK

THE ULTIMATE LOO BOOK

MITCHELL SYMONS

CORGI BOOKS

TRANSWORLD PUBLISHERS
61-63 Uxbridge Road, London W5 5SA
A Random House Group Company
www.rbooks.co.uk

THE ULTIMATE LOO BOOK
A Corgi Book: 9780552159869

This anthology was previously published as THIS, THAT AND THE OTHER by
Corgi Books in 2007
Previously published in three separate volumes:
THAT BOOK originally published by Bantam Press 2003 Copyright © Mitchell
Symons 2003
THIS BOOK originally published by Bantam Press 2004 Copyright © Mitchell
Symons 2004
THE OTHER BOOK originally published by Bantam Press 2005 Copyright ©
Mitchell Symons 2005

First published as the *The Ultimate Loo Book* for Marks and Spencer P.L.C. in
2008
Corgi edition published 2009

Copyright © Mitchell Symons 2007

The quotation from *On the Waterfront* by Budd Schulberg is reproduced by
permission of Faber & Faber.

This book is a work of non-fiction

A CIP catalogue record for this book is available from the British Library

Addresses for Random House Group Ltd companies outside the UK can be
found at: www.randomhouse.co.uk
The Random House Group Ltd Reg. No. 954009

The Random House Group Limited supports The Forest Stewardship
Council (FSC), the leading international forest certification organisation.
All our titles that are printed on Greenpeace approved FSC certified paper
carry the FSC logo. Our paper procurement policy can be found at:
www.rbooks.co.uk/environment

Printed in the UK by CPI Bookmarque, Croydon
10 9 8 7 6 5 4 3 2 1

To my darling wife, Penny,
and to our wonderful sons,
Jack and Charlie

THAT
BOOK

FATHERS

Uma Thurman's father was the first American to be ordained a Buddhist monk

Nicholas Parsons's GP father delivered Margaret Thatcher

Stephen King's father went out for a packet of cigarettes and never returned

Julianna Margulies's father wrote the 'plop, plop, fizz, fizz' jingle for Alka-Seltzer

Laura Dern was bullied at school because her father – Bruce Dern – was 'the only person to kill John Wayne in the movies'

Rachel Weisz's father invented the artificial respirator

Vic Reeves's father and grandfather share his birthday – and his real name of Jim Moir

Bob Marley had a white Liverpudlian father

Elvis Costello's father sang the 'I'm A Secret Lemonade Drinker' jingle for R. White's lemonade

Eminem, Eartha Kitt, Lance Armstrong, Sir Charlie Chaplin, Bill Clinton, Evander Holyfield (whose father had 27 children), Vanilla Ice, Eric Clapton, Naomi Campbell and Mike Tyson never knew their fathers

The fathers of Peter O'Toole, Sir Albert Finney, Mel Smith and Frances Barber were all bookmakers, while Sir Jimmy Savile's father was a bookmaker's clerk

The fathers of George Michael and Yusuf Islam (Cat Stevens) were both Greek restaurateurs

The fathers of Sir Roger Moore, Selina Scott, Julian Clary, Burt Reynolds, Terry Waite, Queen Latifah, Ross Kemp, Arnold Schwarzenegger and Eddie Murphy were all policemen

The fathers of Gordon Brown, Otis Redding, Jane Austen, Sir David Frost, Alice Cooper, John Hurt, Ike Turner, Denzel Washington, Rita Coolidge, Aretha Franklin, Lord Laurence Olivier, Tori Amos, Nina Simone, Frances McDormand and Jessica Simpson were all clergymen

The fathers of Fred Perry, Sir James Goldsmith, Emma Soames, Captain Marryat, Bertrand Russell, Malcolm Muggeridge, Lord Montagu of Beaulieu, Susie Orbach and Elizabeth David were all MPs

The fathers of Harry Houdini, Erich Segal, Jackie Mason and Isaac Asimov were all rabbis

The fathers of Glenn Close, Roger Black, Pamela Stephenson, Katharine Hepburn, Mike Oldfield, Jacqueline Bisset, Brian de Palma, Tony Blackburn, Jane Seymour, Bill Pullman, Edvard Munch, William Roache, Willem Dafoe, Kate Bush, W.H. Auden, Mike Leigh, Dame Judi Dench, Sir Nigel Hawthorne, Sir Tom Stoppard, Humphrey Bogart, Stephen Hawking, Sir Ben Kingsley, Hillary Clinton and Gavin Rossdale were all doctors

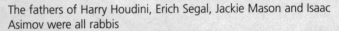

Lucy Davis (Jasper Carrott), Emilio Estevez (Martin Sheen), Jennifer Jason Leigh (Vic Morrow) and Norah Jones (Ravi Shankar) all have/had famous fathers but found fame themselves with different surnames

People whose fathers died in World War One: Dame Barbara Cartland, Alfred Shaughnessy, David Niven, Lord Killanin, Lord Longford, Dame Ninette de Valois, Albert Camus

People whose fathers died in World War Two: Bill Cash, Norman Stone, Leslie Thomas, Nick Raynsford, Sir Ludovic Kennedy, Dame Norma Major, Henry Cecil, Tim Rathbone, Roy Walker, John Phillips, Leonard Rossiter, John Ehrlichman, Robert Kilroy-Silk, Screaming Lord Sutch, The Duke of Kent, Gerhard Schroeder, Roger Waters

The fathers of Ricky Gervais, Julie Walters, Jean Shrimpton, Glenda Jackson, Bill Wyman and Boy George all worked in the building trade

The fathers of David Bailey, Harvey Goldsmith, Edwina Currie and Steve Wright were all tailors

The fathers of Michael Parkinson, Gareth Edwards and Robson Green were all miners while Bryan Ferry's father tended pit ponies

The fathers of Melvyn Bragg, Malcolm McDowell and Jamie Oliver were all publicans

The fathers of Dennis Waterman, Alexei Sayle, Dudley Moore and Paul Merton all worked on the railways

The fathers of Jim Carrey and Jeremy Irons were both accountants

The fathers of Barbara Windsor and George Harrison were both bus drivers

The fathers of Alan Bennett and George Cole were both butchers

The fathers of Jerry Hall, Sir Sean Connery and Zandra Rhodes were all lorry drivers

The fathers of Faye Dunaway and Christina Aguilera were both US Army sergeants

The fathers of Rupert Everett and Elizabeth Hurley were both British Army majors

The fathers of Mick Jagger and Ewan McGregor were both PE teachers

The fathers of Robert Redford, Sting and Emma Bunton were all milkmen

The fathers of Sarah Lancashire and Victoria Wood were both writers who wrote episodes of Coronation Street

The fathers of Russell Crowe and Patricia Hodge were both hoteliers

The fathers of Olivia Newton-John and Noel Edmonds were both headmasters

The fathers of Robert Duvall and Jim Morrison were admirals in the US Navy while Kris Kristofferson's father was a US Air Force general

Rufus Sewell's father was an animator who worked on *Yellow Submarine*

Anthony Quinn (81), Sir Charlie Chaplin (73), Clint Eastwood (66), Sir John Mortimer (61), Cary Grant (62), Yves Montand (67), Marlon Brando (65), Pablo Picasso (68), Arthur English (61),

Francisco de Goya (68), Saul Bellow (84), Lord Snowdon (68), James Doohan (80), David Jason (61) and James Brown (67) all became fathers past the age of 60

Sylvia Plath, Charlotte Brontë and Gloria Vanderbilt all had father fixations

The fathers of Judy Garland, Jacqueline Onassis, Liza Minnelli and Anne Heche were all gay

The fathers of Sir Michael Redgrave, Pat Phoenix, Lord Jeffrey Archer and Patrick Mower were all bigamists

'To be a successful father there's one absolute rule: when you have a kid, don't look at it for the first two years' (Ernest Hemingway); 'Fathers should neither be seen nor heard. That is the only proper basis for family life' (Oscar Wilde); 'The most important thing a father can do for his children is to love their mother' (Theodore Hesburgh); 'The fundamental defect of fathers is that they want their children to be a credit to them' (Bertrand Russell)

'My father told me all about the birds and the bees. The liar – I went steady with a woodpecker till I was 21.' (Bob Hope)

'It's a wonderful feeling when your father becomes not a god but a whole man. When he comes down from the mountain and you see this man with weaknesses. And you love him as this whole being – not just a figurehead.' (Robin Williams)

'When I was a boy of fourteen, my father was so ignorant I could hardly stand to have the old man around. But when I got to twenty-one, I was astonished at how much he had learned in seven years.' (Mark Twain)

'My dad was always there for me and I want my kids to have the same.' (Kevin Costner)

'My dad is a lot smarter than I am and his line of integrity is to a fault.' (George Clooney)

'My father was frightened of his mother. I was frightened of my father and I'm damned well going to make sure that my children are frightened of me.' (King George V)

'I looked up to my father too much to really open my heart to him. We were almost formal. I did not tell him I loved him. All I can do is hope that he would have known.' (Hugh Laurie)

'My father was the great influence on me. At home he was always building something and we'd always be down with him in his workshop at night. He encouraged me to use my hands and eyes – to be observant and inquisitive. He taught me about beautiful objects.' (Viscount Linley)

'My father made me feel I could do anything a boy could do.' (Esther Rantzen)

'I knocked on his door and was told to wait so I stood around for a while and eventually my father came down and told me to go away. I said, "If I do, I will never see you again," and he said that was what he wanted. So I did go away and I never saw him again.' (Sir Norman Wisdom)

MOTHERS

Eric Clapton, Dame Catherine Cookson, Jack Nicholson and Bobby Darin had mothers whom the rest of the world thought were their sisters; indeed, Darin was 32 before he discovered that his 'mother' was actually his grandmother and that his 'sister' was his mother

Charlton Heston's mother's maiden name was Charlton

When Sir Michael Caine was a child, his mother pasted his ears to his head to stop them sticking out

Victoria Principal's mother's maiden name was Ree Veal

Jarvis Cocker's mother made him wear lederhosen at school, which caused the other children to laugh at him

Jeremy Clarkson's mother made her fortune from Paddington Bear merchandise

David Schwimmer's mother is the attorney who handled Roseanne's first divorce

Telly Savalas and Tommy Lee both had mothers who won the Miss Greece beauty contest

Ryan Giggs, Shirley Maclaine, Marilyn Monroe, Sally Jessy Raphael, Jean Harlow, Lauren Bacall, Pablo Picasso, Shelley Winters and Catherine Deneuve all used their mother's maiden name instead of their father's surname

Priscilla Presley and Claudia Cardinale both became mothers again after becoming grandmothers

Uma Thurman's mother had been married to Timothy Leary before marrying Uma's father

Baroness Shirley Williams (Vera Brittain), Liza Minnelli (Judy Garland), Caron Keating (Gloria Hunniford), Joely Richardson (Vanessa Redgrave), Emma Forbes (Nanette Newman), Mia Farrow (Maureen O'Sullivan), Jennifer Ehle (Rosemary Harris), Carrie Fisher (Debbie Reynolds), Melanie Griffith (Tippi Hedren), Gaynor Faye (Kay Mellor), Kate Hudson (Goldie Hawn) and Sophie Ellis-Bextor (Janet Ellis) all have/had famous mothers but found fame themselves with different surnames

James Cagney, Adolf Hitler, D.H. Lawrence, Marcel Proust, Liberace, Gustav Mahler, Sir J.M. Barrie, Sigmund Freud, Elvis Presley, Peter Tchaikovsky, Harry Houdini, Frank Lloyd Wright and Sir Isaac Newton all had mother fixations

The mothers of Oscar Wilde, Peter O'Toole, Ernest Hemingway, General Douglas MacArthur, Bill Tilden and Franklin D. Roosevelt dressed their sons as girls for the first few years of their lives

The mothers of Sarah Bernhardt, Richard Pryor and Clara Bow were prostitutes

The mothers of Patrick Macnee and Jodie Foster were both lesbians

Dame Cleo Laine's mother was a bigamist

'My mother was an incredible character who was very funny and would outride any storm.' (Sir Michael Caine)

'My mother was consumed with her own interest, which was gambling. She was really very self-centred.' (Michael Winner)

'I look so much like my mum, especially when I dress up as a woman.' (Terry Jones)

'The mother is the one who tells you you are beautiful. The mother is the one who keeps reassuring you during those times of insecurity, who keeps your chin up. And I didn't have that.' (Mick Hucknall, whose mother left when he was three)

'My mother is a wonderful, eccentric lady who has no concept whatever of interior monologue. We'll be driving along in the car and she'll suddenly say, "Ants don't like cucumbers, you know. And roaches don't like cinnamon. Do you want some cheese, Michael? Rembrandt was the Lord of the day."' (Mike Myers)

'My mother's death was the most painful thing, because I was so close to her. When you lose someone dear it really encourages you to seize every day, you know, because no one knows how long they've got.' (Ronan Keating)

'There are only two things a child will share willingly – communicable diseases and his mother's age.' (Benjamin Spock)

'My mother loved children – she would have given anything if I had been one.' (Groucho Marx)

'I modelled Tootsie on my mother who was a great character. Sadly she didn't live to see it as she died while I was making the movie but she's in it.' (Dustin Hoffman)

'When I told my mother I was going to marry a Catholic, she couldn't hear me because her head was in the oven.' (Mel Brooks)

'My mum was a great feminist and always said, "Hold your head high – no matter what happens. It's fine, as long as you know you've conducted yourself properly."' (Nicole Kidman)

'My mother gave me two pieces of advice: "Never talk about the movies you didn't do and never talk specifically about men."' (Gwyneth Paltrow)

'My mother's best advice to me was: "To thine own self be true." She often thought Polonius was much maligned. She is the smartest woman I know, with a mind like a steel trap.' (Ben Affleck)

'My mom's a tough bird and one of my best friends in the world. She told me when I was very young, "Don't ever take any crap off anybody, ever." All through my teens and to this day, I don't.' (Johnny Depp)

'My life has been a whirlwind but my mother always helps me to put things in perspective.' (Claire Sweeney)

'There's nothing I won't tell my mother. Nothing. We talk every day on the telephone.' (Claudia Schiffer)

'When I was growing up, the biggest influence in my life was my mother. She made great sacrifices to send me to private school and I will always be grateful for that.' (Naomi Campbell)

Stewardesses is the longest word that is typed with only the left hand

WORDS

The only 15-letter word that can be spelled without repeating a letter is uncopyrightable

Hull City is the only British league football team that hasn't got any letters you can fill in with a biro

If you mouth the word 'colourful' to someone, it looks like you are saying, 'I love you'

'Knightsbridge' is the place with the most consonants in a row

There is no Albanian word for headache

Just 1,000 words make up 90 per cent of all writing

No word in the English language rhymes with orange, silver or month

The Hawaiian alphabet has only 12 letters

'Dreamt' is the only English word that ends in the letters 'mt'

The Frying Squad, The Cod Father, Codswallop, Fryer Tuck, Flash in the Pan, Our Plaice and Rock & Sole are all genuine names of fish and chip restaurants

Hairport, Fringe Benefits, Cutting Time, The Clip Joint, Short & Curlers, Power Cuts, Hairs & Graces and Millionhairs are all genuine names of hairdressing salons

Spoonerisms

'Kinquering congs their titles take'

'Let us drink to the queer old dean'

'The Lord is a shoving leopard'

'That is just a half-warmed fish'

'The cat popped on its drawers'

'Is the bean dizzy?'

'Please sew me to another sheet'

'You will leave by the next town drain'

The human condition

Only one person in two billion will live to be 116 or older

The human body grows the equivalent of a new skeleton every seven years

A newborn baby's heart beats twice as fast as an adult's

The average person's heart beats 36 million times a year

Adult humans have 206 bones. At birth, an infant has 350 bones. As the child grows, many bones fuse with other bones

A quarter of the 206 bones in the human body are in the feet

As a child grows, the body part that grows least is the eye. While the rest of an adult body is 20 times bigger than it was at birth, the eye is only three and a quarter times bigger

Women get more migraines than men

The average person is a quarter of an inch taller at night

Fingernails grow four times faster than toenails

The average person sleeps for about 220,000 hours (or just over 25 years) in a lifetime

It takes just one minute for blood to travel through the whole human body

People who live in the city have longer, thicker nose hairs than people who live in the country

The first of the five senses to go with age is smell

More boys than girls are born during the day; more girls are born at night

Your stomach has to produce a new layer of mucus every two weeks otherwise it will digest itself

The human sneeze travels at 600mph

The strongest muscle in the body is the tongue

You can't kill yourself by holding your breath

Right-handed people live, on average, nine years longer than left-handed people do

Humans are the only animals that cry

AROUND THE WORLD

Disneyworld is bigger than the world's five smallest countries

The Danish flag – dating back to the thirteenth century – is the world's oldest unchanged national flag

Italy's national flag was designed by Napoleon

There is a city called Rome in every continent

There are three American towns named Santa Claus

Istanbul is the only city in the world to be in two continents (Europe and Asia)

Los Angeles's full name is: 'El Pueblo de Nuestra Señora la Reina de los Angeles de Poriuncula' and can be abbreviated to 3.63 per cent of its size: 'LA'

Mongolians put salt in their tea instead of sugar

Americans on average eat 18 acres of pizza every day

All the continents are wider in the north than in the south

You could drive a car round the world four times with the amount of fuel in a jumbo jet

If the population of China walked past you in single file, the line would never end because of the rate of reproduction

China has more English speakers than the United States

Ten per cent of the Russian government's income comes from the sale of vodka

The glue on Israeli postage stamps is certified kosher

The highest point in Pennsylvania is lower than the lowest point in Colorado

The Dead Sea is really a lake

'Q' is the only letter that doesn't appear in the names of any of the fifty states of the US

There isn't a (real) river in the whole of Saudi Arabia

If all the Antarctic ice melted, the ocean level would rise nearly 250 feet, and 25 per cent of the world's land surface would be flooded

Antarctica is the only continent without snakes or reptiles

ANIMALS

A pig's orgasm lasts for 30 minutes

It takes a male horse only 14 seconds to copulate

The elephant is the only mammal that can't jump

A skunk will not bite and throw its scent at the same time

Cats have over one hundred vocal sounds; dogs have only about ten

The female nutria, a furry rodent,
is the only mammal with nipples along
its backbone

A donkey will sink in quicksand but a mule won't

Pigs can become alcoholics

Tigers have striped skin, not just striped fur

The reindeer is the only female animal with antlers

Polar bears can smell a human being from 20 miles away

Most dinosaurs were no bigger than chickens

Wombats can run up to 40kph and stop dead in half a stride. They kill their prey this way – the prey runs into the wombat's bum-bone and smashes its face

When hippopotamuses get upset, their sweat turns red

Of all the mammal species in the world, almost a quarter are bats

No new animals have been domesticated in the last 4,000 years

The world's biggest frog is bigger than the world's smallest antelope

An angry gorilla pokes its tongue out

INSECTS ETC

A male spider's reproductive organ is located at the end of one of his legs

The average caterpillar has 2,000 muscles in its body (we humans have 656)

Tarantulas can go for up to two years without eating

Anteaters can stick out their tongues up to 160 times a minute

Mother tarantulas kill 99 per cent of the babies they hatch

Queen bees only ever use their stingers to kill other queen bees

Queen termites can live for up to 100 years

The most poisonous spider is not the black widow but the wingless daddy longlegs – but its fangs can't pierce human skin and so it poses no threat

A cockroach can live for several weeks after being decapitated

The snail is the only insect with retractable antennae

Gram for gram, a bumblebee is 150 times stronger than an elephant

An ant can survive for two weeks underwater

The house fly hums in the middle octave key of F

Hmmmmmmmm

The male gypsy moth can 'smell' the virgin female gypsy moth from 1.8 miles

Snails can sleep for three years without eating

The ant can lift 50 times its own weight and can pull 30 times its own weight

The praying mantis is the only insect that can turn its head without moving its body

A bee is more likely to sting you on a windy day

FISH ETC

Starfish don't have brains

The catfish has over 27,000 taste buds (more than any other creature on the planet)

Goldfish kept in a darkened room eventually turn white

The baby blue whale gains ten pounds in weight per hour

Whale songs rhyme

The male rather than the female seahorse carries the eggs

The starfish is the only creature on the planet that can turn its stomach inside out

A goldfish has a memory span of three seconds

The giant squid has the largest eyes in the world

A pregnant goldfish is called a twit

The oldest recorded age reached by a goldfish is 41

The white shark is the only sea creature with no natural enemies

Dolphins sleep with one eye open

A blue whale's tongue weighs more than an elephant

BIRDS ETC

The longest recorded flight of a chicken is thirteen seconds

Female canaries can't sing

The ptarmigan turns completely white in the winter

The average ostrich's eye is the size of a tennis ball and bigger than its brain

There is the same number of chickens in the world as humans

The waste produced by one chicken in its lifetime could supply enough electricity to run a 100-watt bulb for five hours

The most common bird in the world is the starling

The hummingbird is the only bird that can fly backwards

The average lifespan of a parrot is 120 years

The golden eagle can spot a rabbit from nearly two miles away

The penguin is the only bird that walks upright (it is also the only bird that can swim but not fly)

Ostriches yawn in groups before going to sleep

Owls are the only birds that can see the colour blue

Pigeons are the only birds that can drink water without having to raise their heads to swallow

Bats always turn left when leaving a cave

Flamingoes can only eat with their heads upside down

HISTORY

Each king in a deck of playing cards represents a great king from history: Spades – King David; Clubs – Alexander the Great; Hearts – Charlemagne; Diamonds – Julius Caesar

The only painting Vincent Van Gogh sold in his lifetime was *The Red Vineyard*

The Roman Emperor Nero 'married' his male slave Scotus

Michelangelo's cook was illiterate so he drew her a shopping list – which today is priceless

Spiral staircases in medieval castles ran clockwise so that attacking knights climbing the stairs couldn't use their right hands – their sword hands – while the defending knights coming down could. And left-handed men, believed to descend from the devil, couldn't become knights

The shortest war in history was between Zanzibar and England in 1896: Zanzibar surrendered after 38 minutes

February 1865 is the only month in recorded history not to have a full moon

Pirates wore earrings in the belief that it improved their eyesight

The architect who built the Kremlin had his eyes gouged out by Ivan The Terrible so that he'd never be able to design another building like it

In Ancient Egypt, priests plucked every hair from their bodies, including their eyebrows and eyelashes

THINGS THAT STARTED IN THE 1950S

Rock 'n' roll, X-certificate films, the singles charts, CND, nuclear submarines, telephone weather forecasting service, the Planetarium at Madame Tussaud's, televising of Rugby League matches, credit cards, the EEC, NATO, duty-free booze for holidaymakers, the Mini, the Miss World contest, Angry Young Men (in literature and in the theatre), kitchen-sink dramas, Teddy Boys, *This Is Your Life*, teabags, the frisbee, *Carry On* films, Wimpy Bars, ABTA, Luncheon Vouchers, *Andy Pandy*, tranquillizers, parking meters, Disneyland, *The Guinness Book of Records*, space travel, fluoride toothpaste, Lego, transistor hearing aids, ITV (and, therefore, TV commercials), Cinemascope, diet soft drinks (no-cal ginger ale), the Eurovision Song Contest, Yellow Pages, Barbie dolls, comprehensive schools, fishfingers, automatic electric kettles, television detector vans, TV situation comedies, heart pacemakers, yellow no-parking lines, typewriter correction fluid, microwave ovens, the hovercraft, TV party political broadcasts, the Velcro fastener, *Blue Peter*, zebra crossings, Premium Bonds, *The Mousetrap*, Polyfilla, British motorways, trunk calls, life peers, postcodes, non-stick saucepans, Club Med, the Moonies, supermarket chains, go-karts, polio vaccines, Beatniks, kidney transplants, roll-on deodorants, boutiques, Legal Aid, disposable nappies

MANIACS

Kleptomaniac (person obsessed with stealing)

Chionomaniac (snow)

Ablutomaniac (bathing)

Timbromaniac (stamps)

Pyromaniac (fire)

Nudomaniac (nudity)

Cynomaniac (dogs)

Ailuromaniac (cats)

Ichthyomaniac (fish)

Oniomaniac (buying)

Arithomaniac (counting)

Philopatridomaniac (homesickness)

Bruxomaniac (grinding teeth)

Klazomaniac (shouting)

Catapedamaniac (jumping from high places)

Onychotillomaniac (picking nails)

Cresomaniac (personal wealth)

Phagomaniac (food)

Titillomaniac (scratching)

Erythromaniac (blushing)

Dromomaniac (travelling)

THINGS THAT MONEY CAN'T BUY

Membership of the MCC or Glyndebourne (long waiting-lists that you can't leapfrog no matter how rich you are)

The affection of a dog (they either love you or they don't – irrespective of how wealthy you are)

A handgun (at least not legally)

A swan (all swans are owned by the Queen)

Any freehold property in Grosvenor Square (the Duke of Westminster owns Grosvenor Square and they have a policy of never selling freeholds)

An entry in *Who's Who*

An Aztec bar (Cadbury's don't make them any more)

A full driving licence

The *Mona Lisa* (like all paintings kept in museums, it's simply not for sale)

Entry to the Royal Enclosure at Royal Ascot

A cure for a cold

A new Citroën 2CV car

The skeleton of the Elephant Man (it's in the London Hospital, from whom Michael Jackson tried to buy it – offering millions – to no avail)

'Rude' number plates

A place at a British university

A private beach in mainland England (you can buy a private road giving you private access to the shore but you can't buy the beach itself)

Fellowship of the Royal Society

Immunity from the law

A Cuban Red Macaw (the last one disappeared in 1894)

A ticket for a PanAm flight (at least not since 3 December 1991)

Entry to a British Playboy Club (the last one closed in 1988)

A planet (there's an international agreement which prohibits any country or individual from buying one)

A Nobel prize

Money can't buy a wild donkey (no such animal now exists)

Murphy's Law

Anything that can go wrong will go wrong

The first place to look for something is the last place you would expect to find it

When someone says, 'It's not the money, it's the principle', nine times out of ten it's the money

Whenever you make a journey by bicycle, it's always more uphill than downhill

As soon as you mention something:
a) if it's good, it goes away;
b) if it's bad, it happens

You never find something until you replace it

When the train you are on is late, the bus to take you home from the station will be on time

If an experiment works, something has gone wrong

It always rains when you've just washed your car but washing your car to make it rain won't work

When you dial a wrong number, it's never engaged

Cheques get lost in the post but bills never do

In a supermarket, the other queues always move faster than yours

Illnesses always start on a Friday evening … but end on a Monday morning

Friends come and go but enemies accumulate

The odds of the bread falling butter-side down are directly proportional to the value of the carpet

The severity of an itch is inversely proportional to how easy it is to scratch

If during a month only three enjoyable social activities take place, they will all happen on the same evening

The only way to get a bank loan is to prove you don't need one

SINGULAR PEOPLE

Samuel L. Jackson was Bill Cosby's stand-in for three years on *The Cosby Show*

Kate Beckinsale won the W.H. Smith Young Writers Competition for prose and poetry – two years running

Chuck Berry invented his duck walk initially to hide the creases in his suit

John Wayne once won the dog Lassie from its owner in a poker game

Jack Nicholson was in detention every day for a whole school year

Olivia Newton-John is president of the Isle of Man Basking Sharks Society

Mariah Carey's vocal range spans five octaves

Nick Nolte ate real dog food in the film *Down And Out In Beverly Hills* (when he was showing the dog how to eat from a dog bowl)

When Paul Gambaccini was at Oxford at the same time as Bill Clinton, it was he who was voted The American Most Likely To Succeed

Melissa Joan Hart can recite the mathematical expression 'pi' to 400 decimal places

Nicolas Cage ate a live cockroach for *Vampire's Kiss*

Sir Winston Churchill smoked an estimated 300,000 cigars in his lifetime

Tom Cruise has saved three lives – in Santa Monica, off the island of Capri and in London

Ben Stiller was taught how to swim by The Pips (as in Gladys Knight & the Pips)

Amanda Peet can recite all the lines from *Tootsie* and *A Chorus Line*

Richard Gere, even in his worst mood, never swears. If a visitor in his house swears, even by mistake, they're asked to leave

Pierce Brosnan bought the typewriter of James Bond creator Ian Fleming for £52,800

As a teenager, Colin Farrell put Smarties under his pillow to lure Marilyn Monroe from the dead

Isaac Asimov is the only author to have a book in every Dewey-decimal category except Philosophy

Florence Nightingale used to travel everywhere with a pet owl in her pocket

THE WORKER'S PRAYER

'Grant me the serenity to accept the things I cannot change, the courage to change the things I cannot accept and the wisdom to hide the bodies of those people I had to kill today because they pissed me off, and also help me to be careful of the toes I step on today as they may be connected to the butt that I might have to kiss tomorrow.'

FRIDAY THE 13TH

The fear of the number 13 – or 'triskaidekaphobia' as it's technically known – goes back a long way. According to Scandinavian mythology, there was a banquet in Valhalla into which Loki (the God of Strife) intruded – thereby making thirteen guests – where Balder (the God of Light) was murdered. In Christian countries, this superstition was confirmed by the Last Supper.

Meanwhile, Friday is considered unlucky because it was the day of the Crucifixion and because Adam and Eve ate the forbidden fruit on a Friday and also died on a Friday. Some Buddhists and Brahmins (high caste Hindus) also consider Friday to be unlucky. In combining superstitions about both Friday and the number thirteen, Friday the 13th is feared as being twice as frightful.

Sir Winston Churchill, the former British Prime Minister, never travelled on a Friday the 13th unless it was absolutely essential.

Graham Chapman, the late member of the Monty Python team, actually *liked* Friday the 13ths. Indeed, he arranged to be buried on the 13th hour of Friday, 13th October 1989.

Good things that have happened on a Friday the 13th include: John Betjeman was knighted (June 1969), *The Third Man* (one of the greatest films of all time) received its premiere (January 1950), the Allies recaptured Tobruk (November 1942) and Alfred Dreyfus was restored to the French army and promoted to major (July 1906).

Notable things that have happened on a Friday the 13th include: the first condom commercial was screened by the BBC (November 1987), Viv Richards took his score to 291 against England at the Oval (August 1976) and Harold Macmillan dismissed a third of his Cabinet (July 1962).

Bad things that have happened on a Friday the 13th include: a violent earthquake in Turkey killed more than a thousand people (March 1992), a hurricane in Britain left nine people dead (January 1984) and a plane crash left survivors stranded in the Andes without food and compelled to turn to cannibalism to stay alive (October 1972).

Months that begin on a Sunday will always have a Friday the 13th.

People who were born on a Friday the 13th include Steve Buscemi, Sara Cox, Zoe Wanamaker, Peter Scudamore, Samuel Beckett, Craig Bellamy, Julia Louis-Dreyfus, Samantha Morton, Mary-Kate and Ashley Olson, Danus Rucker, Georges Simenon, Peter Tork, Darius Vassell, Suggs, Howard Keel, Christopher Plummer and Robin Smith.

People who have died on a Friday the 13th include Benny Goodman, Arnold Schoenberg, Tupac Shakur, Sir Henry Irving and former US Vice-President Hubert Humphrey.

BEDS AND SLEEP

We spend something like a third of our lives in bed

An adult sleeping with another adult in a standard bed – 4 foot 6 inches wide and 6 foot 2 inches long – has less personal space than a baby in a cot

When the Hays Office censored Hollywood films, there was a series of rules concerning what could and could not be shown on screen: for example, couples – even married couples – could not be shown in a bed together unless both the man and the woman had at least one foot on the floor

Sian Phillips solved the problem of sharing a bed: 'In the past I had an arrangement where I had a large double bed and my partner had a single bed.'

When the playwright Kay Mellor was first married, she and her husband Anthony lived in his mother's home in a single bed

Gary Barlow, the singer and songwriter, lost his virginity at the age of 14 in a single bed; Shane Richie, the TV presenter and actor, lost his virginity at the age of 12 in a single bed

Hans Christian Andersen, the Danish writer of fairytales, died falling out of bed (actuarially, the chances of dying by falling out of bed are one in two million in a year)

In Tallin, Estonia, couples are not allowed to play chess in bed while making love

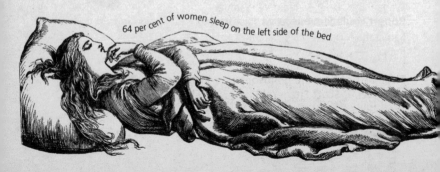

64 per cent of women sleep on the left side of the bed

Not only is homosexuality banned in Albania, but two people of the same sex are also banned from sharing a bed – even if they're not homosexual

A bed is the third most popular luxury chosen by castaways on the radio programme *Desert Island Discs* (a piano is first and 'writing materials' are second)

The expression 'to get out of bed on the wrong side' comes from the nineteenth-century superstition that there was a 'right' side (the right) for getting out of bed and a 'wrong' side (the left), based, of course, on the traditional fear of anything 'left' ('sinister' being the Latin word for left)

King Louis XI of France started the practice of French kings receiving their courtiers and ministers in bed by introducing *lit de justice* (bed of justice), a ceremonial appearance before his parliament of the king lying in bed, with his princes on stools, and with great officials standing and lesser ones kneeling

Mark Twain wrote large parts of *Huckleberry Finn* and *The Adventures of Tom Sawyer* in bed, though he pointed out that working in bed must be very dangerous as so many deaths occur there

Mae West did all her writing in bed, remarking, 'Everybody knows I do my best work in bed.'

Robert Louis Stevenson wrote most of *Kidnapped* in bed

Sir Winston Churchill habitually dictated letters and went through his red boxes in bed

Thomas Hobbes, the philosopher, and the writers Edith Wharton, F. Scott Fitzgerald and Marcel Proust all worked in their beds

W.C. Fields's cure for insomnia was: 'Get plenty of sleep.'

When John Denver lost his temper with his then wife, Annie (made famous in *Annie's Song*), he sawed their bed in half

Peter Stringfellow, the nightclub owner, shared a single bed with his three younger brothers when he was growing up

More than 600,000 Americans each year are injured on beds and chairs

The shortest recorded time taken by one person to make a bed is 28.2 seconds by Wendy Wall of Sydney, Australia in 1978; the record time for two people to make a bed is 14 seconds by Sister Sharon Stringer and Nurse Michelle Benkel at London's Royal Masonic Hospital at the launch of the 1994 edition of *The Guinness Book of Records*

George Burns once said: 'You have to have something to get you out of bed. I can't do anything in bed anyway.'

The United States has many sleepy towns: Sleepy Eye (Minnesota), Sleepy Creek (Oregon), Sleeping Beauty Peak (Arizona), Sleepers Bend (California)

According to the philosopher Friedrich Nietzsche: 'Sleeping is no mean art. For its sake one must stay awake all day.'

Max Kauffmann reckoned that 'the amount of sleep required by the average person is about five minutes more', while Fran Lebowitz decided: 'Sleep is death without the responsibility.'

Insomnia is defined as 'a chronic inability to fall asleep or to enjoy uninterrupted sleep' and it affects nearly everyone at some stage. Worse than insomnia is the extremely rare condition chronic colestites, a form of total insomnia that renders its victims incapable of definable sleep – sometimes for years.

Famous insomniacs include David Baddiel, Dame Elizabeth Taylor, Winona Ryder, Baroness Margaret Thatcher, Robbie Williams, Gwyneth Paltrow, Daryl Hannah, Renée Zellweger, Hillary Clinton, Mariah Carey (who claims that she sleeps for just three hours a night) and Michelle Pfeiffer (who can't sleep at all some nights)

Famous people in history who were insomniacs include Samuel Beckett, Abraham Lincoln, Marilyn Monroe, Spencer Tracy, Vincent Van Gogh, Napoleon Bonaparte, Charles Dickens, Cary Grant, Caligula, Joseph Conrad, Marlene Dietrich, W.C. Fields, F. Scott Fitzgerald, Galileo, Hermann Goering and Rudyard Kipling

Sleepwalking, or somnambulism, is no joke. In 1987, an 11-year-old American boy, Michael Dixon, was found 100 miles away from his home after sleepwalking to a freight train and travelling on it from Illinois to Indiana

Snoring is also no joke – especially for the sleeping partners of sufferers. Great snorers in history have included Beau Brummell, Abraham Lincoln, King George II and Benito Mussolini. 'Laugh and the world laughs with you; snore and you sleep alone,' declared Anthony Burgess, while Mark Twain wondered why 'there ain't no way to find out why a snorer can't hear himself snore'.

ACRONYMS USED BY DOCTORS AND NURSES

TMB – Too Many Birthdays

NFN – Normal for Norfolk

GOK – God Only Knows

GROLIES – Guardian Reader Of Limited Intelligence In Ethnic Skirt

SIG – Stroppy Ignorant Girl

TEETH – Tried Everything Else, Try Homoeopathy

TFBUNDY – Totally Fucked But Unfortunately Not Dead Yet

PFO – Pissed and Fell Over

TUBE – Totally Unnecessary Breast Examination

FLK, FLP – Funny Looking Kid, Funny Looking Parents

FORD – Found On Road Drunk

FTF – Failure To Fly (of attempted suicide)

ADASTW – Arrived Dead And Stayed That Way

TFBUNDY

WOFTAM – Waste of Fucking Time And Money

OAP – Over-Anxious Patient

LTBB – Lucky To Be Breathing

OTHER MEDICAL EXPRESSIONS USED IN HOSPITALS

Ash Cash – money paid for signing cremation forms

Ash Point – where you collect the Ash Cash

Code Brown – incontinence-related emergency

Cold Tea Sign – the several cups of cold tea on the bedside cabinet beside a geriatric patient indicating that he/she is deceased

Crumblie – a geriatric patient

Departure Lounge – geriatric ward

Digging For Worms – varicose vein surgery

Eternal Care – intensive care

Guessing Tube – stethoscope

Handbag Positive – an old lady lying in her hospital bed clutching her handbag, indicating that she's confused and disorientated

House Red – blood

Sieve – a doctor who admits every patient he sees

Treat 'n' Street – quick patient turnaround

Wall – a doctor who resists admitting patients at all costs

HONOURS

Winston Churchill turned down the Order of the Garter after losing the 1945 General Election, saying, 'I could not accept the Order of the Garter from my sovereign when I have received the order of the boot from the people,' but he did accept it eventually

Graham Greene turned down a knighthood: apparently he read the letter offering him one, passed it to his secretary and asked her to 'refuse in the normal way'

Other men who rejected knighthoods include Alastair Sim, J.B. Priestley, Augustus John, Henry Moore, Francis Bacon, T.S. Eliot, Michael Faraday, E.M. Forster and Paul Scofield (twice)

George Bernard Shaw turned down an earldom as well as a knighthood, saying, 'Being Bernard Shaw is sufficient honour for any man – anyway, if I want to satirise the Establishment and all of its rituals, I must be free to do so.' He also said, 'Titles distinguish the mediocre, embarrass the superior and are disgraced by the inferior.'

John Lennon returned his MBE in 1969 citing three reasons: the UK's involvement in Vietnam, the war in Biafra and because *Cold Turkey* (his latest record) was slipping down the charts

Men who were stripped of their honours for committing crimes include Sir Roger Casement (before being hanged for treason in 1916), Lester Piggott (his OBE, after being sent to prison for tax evasion in 1988) and Lord Michael Spens (his MBE, after being jailed for theft in 1975)

Other men who were stripped of their honours include the Italian dictator, Benito Mussolini (Order of the Bath in 1940), and the spies

Kim Philby (OBE in 1965) and Anthony Blunt (Knight Commander of the Royal Victorian Order in 1979)

Pele (1997), Henry Kissinger (1995), Norman Schwarzkopf (1991), Kurt Waldheim (1969), J. Edgar Hoover (1947), Sidney Poitier (1974), André Previn (1996), Colin Powell (1993), President Mitterrand (1984), Alistair Cooke (1973), Magnus Magnusson (1989), Bob Geldof (1986), Douglas Fairbanks Jr (1949), Lech Walesa (1991), Bill Gates (2005), Elie Wiesel (2006), Simon Wiesenthal (2004), Steven Spielberg (2001), Spike Milligan (2001), James Galway (2001) and Rudolph Giuliani (2002) are among the people who have received honorary knighthoods (as non-British citizens they can't put 'Sir' before their name)

As everyone knows, honours are handed out to civil servants with, so to speak, their payslips. Within the Civil Service certain honours are known by these initials: CMG (Call Me God); KCMG (Kindly Call Me God) and GCMG (God Calls Me God)

People who have been honoured with university doctorates include Liam Neeson (Ulster), Mark Knopfler (Leeds), Joanna Lumley (Kent), Dame Kiri Te Kanawa (Durham), Sting (Northumbria), Sean Bean (Sheffield Hallam), Sir Alex Ferguson (Robert Gordon University in Aberdeen), Paul Scofield (Sussex), Sir David Attenborough (Bristol), Victoria Wood (Lancaster), Sir Sean Connery (Heriot-Watt), Kenneth Branagh (Belfast), Dame Maggie Smith (London), Sir Anthony Hopkins (University of Wales), Dame Judi Dench (Oxford), J.K. Rowling (D. Litt, Exeter), Delia Smith (John Moores and East Anglia), Lulu (Westminster), Robson Green (Newcastle), Lennox Lewis (North London University), Geena Davis (Boston), Matt Damon (Harvard), Arnold Schwarzenegger (Wisconsin), Tom Selleck (Pepperdine, Malibu), Robert De Niro (New York)

Tony Blair is an honorary member of the Dennis the Menace Fan Club

Johnny Vaughan is an honorary Butlin's Redcoat

LOSING US PRESIDENTIAL AND VICE-PRESIDENTIAL CANDIDATES

Year:	Presidential Candidate	Vice-Presidential Candidate
2004:	John Kerry	John Edwards
2000:	**Al Gore**	**Joseph Lieberman**
1996:	Robert Dole	Jack Kemp
1992:	**George Bush**	**Dan Quayle**
1988:	Michael Dukakis	Lloyd Bentsen
1984:	**Walter Mondale**	**Geraldine Ferraro**
1980:	Jimmy Carter	Walter Mondale
1976:	**Gerald Ford**	**Robert Dole**
1972:	George McGovern	Sargent Shriver
1968:	**Hubert Humphrey**	**Edmund Muskie**
1964:	Barry Goldwater	William Miller
1960:	**Richard Nixon**	**Henry Cabot Lodge**

THE LEADER OF THE PARTY THAT CAME SECOND IN GENERAL ELECTIONS

Michael Howard (Conservative; 2005)

William Hague (Conservative; 2001)

John Major (Conservative; 1997)

Neil Kinnock (Labour; 1992)

Neil Kinnock (Labour; 1987)

Michael Foot (Labour; 1983)

James Callaghan (Labour; 1979)

Edward Heath (Conservative; October 1974)

Edward Heath (Conservative; February 1974)

Harold Wilson (Labour; 1970)

Edward Heath (Conservative; 1966)

Sir Alec Douglas-Home (Conservative; 1964)

Hugh Gaitskell (Labour; 1959)

NUMBER-ONE RECORDS AT THE TIME OF ALL GENERAL ELECTIONS SINCE RECORD CHARTS BEGAN

5 May 2005: 'Is This The Way To Amarillo?' (Tony Christie feat. Peter Kay).

7 June 2001: 'Do You Really Like It' (DJ Pied Piper and the Master of Ceremonies)

1 May 1997: 'I Believe I Can Fly' (R Kelly)

9 April 1992: 'Stay' (Shakespear's Sister)

11 June 1987: 'I Wanna Dance With Somebody (Who Loves Me)' (Whitney Houston)

9 June 1983: 'Every Breath You Take' (The Police)

3 May 1979: 'Bright Eyes' (Art Garfunkel)

10 October 1974: 'Kung Fu Fighting' (Carl Douglas)

28 February 1974: 'Devil Gate Drive' (Suzi Quatro)

18 June 1970: 'In The Summertime' (Mungo Jerry)

31 March 1966: 'The Sun Ain't Gonna Shine Anymore' (The Walker Brothers)

15 October 1964: 'Oh Pretty Woman' (Roy Orbison)

8 October 1959: 'Only Sixteen' (Craig Douglas)

26 May 1955: 'Stranger In Paradise' (Tony Bennett)

THINGS FROM ABROAD

Danish pastry, German measles, Brazil nuts, Mexican stand-off, Dutch elm disease, Chinese whispers, Russian salad, Indian gift, French leave, Russian roulette, Swiss roll, Hong Kong flu, Cuban heels, Mexican wave, Greek urn, Singapore sling, Dutch uncle, Turkish delight, Indian tonic water, French bread, Maltese cross, Italian vermouth, Panama hat, Spanish omelette

THINGS THAT ARE BRAND NAMES

Tannoy, Li-Lo, Jiffy Bag, Optic, Plasticine, Biro, Crimplene, Hoover, Fibreglass, Babygro, Sellotape, Cellophane, Portakabin, Catseyes, Rawlplug, Jacuzzi, Spam, Perspex, Calor Gas, Formica, Yo-Yo, Tarmac

THE LAST WORDS OF MEN ABOUT TO BE EXECUTED

GEORGE APPEL (1928) As Appel was being strapped into the electric chair, he said to the witnesses, 'Well, folks, you'll soon see a baked Appel.'

THOMAS GRASSO (1995) Before he was given his lethal injection, he complained, 'I did not get my Spaghetti-O's, I got spaghetti. I want the press to know this.'

SIR WALTER RALEIGH (1618) 'So the heart be right, it is no matter which way the head lieth.' And then he was beheaded.

JAMES FRENCH (1966) On his way to the chair, he said to a newspaper reporter, 'I have a terrific headline for you in the morning: "French Fries".'

FRANCIS CROWLEY (1931) 'You sons of bitches. Give my love to Mother.' Then he was electrocuted.

NEVILLE HEATH (1946) Just before being hanged, his last request was for a whisky. 'In the circumstances,' he added, 'you might make that a double.'

JOHNNY FRANK GARRETT (1992) Before being lethally injected, he said, 'I'd like to thank my family for loving me and taking care of me. And the rest of the world can kiss my ass.'

ERSKINE CHILDERS (1922) He called out to the firing squad, 'Take a step forward, lads. It will be easier that way.'

ROBERT DREW (1994) Before being given his lethal injection, he said, 'Remember, the death penalty is murder.'

FREDERICK WOOD (1963) When Wood was in the electric chair, he said to the assembled company, 'Gentlemen, you are about to see the effects of electricity upon wood.'

NED KELLY (1880) The notorious Australian bushwacker's last words as he stood on the scaffold awaiting his hanging were: 'Ah well, I suppose it had to come to this. Such is life.'

JIMMY GLASS (1987) said, 'I'd rather be fishing.' Then he was electrocuted.

GERALD CHAPMAN (1926) Just before he was hanged, he said, 'Death itself isn't dreadful, but hanging seems an awkward way of entering the adventure.'

GARY GILMORE (1977) Having campaigned for the right to die, he just said, 'Let's do it!' – and the firing squad duly did.

ROBERT ALTON HARRIS (1992) Before being gassed, he said, 'You can be a king or a street sweeper, but everyone dances with the Grim Reaper.'

DR WILLIAM PALMER (1856) The British serial killer stood on the gallows and asked the officials, 'Are you sure this thing is safe?'

BEATLES SONGS AND WHO OR WHAT INSPIRED THEM

'A Day In The Life'

This song was about lots of things but the line 'He blew his mind out in a car' was inspired by the death in a car of Tara Browne, an Irish heir (he was male, despite the name) who was related to the Guinness family. Browne was friendly with Paul and other members of the rock aristocracy.

'Things We Said Today'

Written by Paul for Jane Asher. 'We'll go on and on.' Alas not.

'We Can Work It Out'

Once again for Jane Asher. 'Try to see it my way,' begged Paul, but she wouldn't.

'You've Got To Hide Your Love Away'

Supposedly written by John 'for' Brian Epstein. The love that Epstein had to hide was, of course, his homosexuality.

'She's Leaving Home'

Paul read a story in the papers about teenage runaway Melanie Coe. Her father was quoted as saying, 'I cannot imagine why she should run away. She has everything here,' which has its echo in Paul's line: 'We gave her everything money could buy.' Amazing coincidence: unknown to Paul, he had actually met the young girl when he had presented her with a competition prize on *Ready Steady Go* four years earlier.

'She Said She Said'

Written by John during his acid phase. John got the line 'I know what it's like to be dead' when he overheard the actor Peter Fonda talking to George about a near-death childhood experience.

'I Saw Her Standing There'

Like the girl in the song, Iris Caldwell was just 17 when Paul met her while she was dancing in a nightclub. Iris, whose brother was Liverpool musician Rory Storm, went out with Paul for two years.

'Sexy Sadie'

Famously written by John for the Maharishi Mahesh Yogi, who, John reckons, 'made a fool of everyone' by pretending to be pure when really he was a bit of a lech.

'Dear Prudence'

Written to encourage Prudence Farrow (Mia Farrow's younger sister) to stop meditating so much – 'won't you come out to play?' – during The Beatles' time in India.

COUPLES WHO DIVORCED AND THEN REMARRIED

Dame Elizabeth Taylor & Richard Burton

Melanie Griffith & Don Johnson

Elliott Gould & Jenny Bogart

Sarah Miles & Robert Bolt

Baroness Ruth Rendell & Don Rendell

Alexander Solzhenitsyn & Natalya Reshtovskaya

Art & Jean Carney

Eminem & Kimberley Scott

Richard Pryor & Jennifer Lee

Richard Pryor & Flynn BeLaine

Mick Fleetwood & Jenny Boyd

Robert Wagner & Natalie Wood

Dorothy Parker & Alan Campbell

George Peppard & Elizabeth Ashley

Jane Wyman & Fred Karger

Dionne Warwick & Bill Elliott

Paul Hogan & Noelene Edwards

Kurt Weill & Lotte Lenya

José Ferrer & Rosemary Clooney

George C. Scott & Colleen Dewhurst

Dennis Wilson & Karen Lamm

Milton Berle & Joyce Matthews

Billy Rose & Joyce Matthews

Neil & Diane Simon

Andy & Kate Summers

Note also: Cher's parents married and divorced each other three times

MEN WHO FELL IN LOVE WITH THEIR WIFE'S SISTER

Stavros Niarchos, Charles Dickens, George Sanders (after divorcing Zsa Zsa Gabor he married her sister Magda), Peter Paul Rubens (did it the other way round – marrying the sister, Helena, of Suzanne, his former mistress), Peter Bogdanovich (also did it the other way round – marrying the sister, Louise, of his murdered lover Dorothy Stratton), King Henry VIII (also did it the other way round – marrying the sister, Anne Boleyn, of his erstwhile lover Mary), Wolfgang Mozart, Sigmund Freud, Robert Southey, Daniel Massey

PEOPLE WHO MARRIED THEIR COUSIN

James Boswell, Franklin D. Roosevelt, Albert Einstein, Lewis Carroll, Mary, Queen of Scots, Queen Victoria, Satyajit Ray, Charles Darwin, Saddam Hussein, King Olav V of Norway, Karen Blixen, Catherine the Great, André Gide, H.G. Wells, Rose Tremain, Edgar Allan Poe (whose bride was just 13), Jerry Lee Lewis (whose bride was also just 13), Rudy Giuliani, Werner Von Braun, Jesse James

PEOPLE WHO WERE BETROTHED VERY QUICKLY

Muhammad Ali – in 1964 he met Sonji Roi and proposed to her on the same day; they married 42 days later

Michael Douglas – in 1977 he met Diandra Luker at Jimmy Carter's presidential inauguration. They spent two days in his Washington hotel room, he proposed after nine days and they married six weeks later

Peter Noone – in 1967 he married Mireille six weeks after they met

Marco Pierre White – in 1992 he proposed to Lisa Butcher three weeks after they met

Pamela Anderson – in 1995 she and Tommy Lee decided to marry after a five-day courtship

Leslie Ash – in 1982 she married Jonathan Weston after a two-week courtship

Charlie Sheen – in 1995 he married Donna Peele after a six-week courtship

Julia Roberts – in 1993 she married Lyle Lovett after a three-week romance

Kate Jackson – in 1978 she married Andrew Stevens after a six-week courtship

Drew Barrymore – in 1994 she married Jeremy Thomas after a six-week courtship

Shannen Doherty – in 1993 she married Ashley Hamilton after a two-week romance

John Major – in 1970 he and Norma Wagstaff decided to marry after just three weeks

Lord David Owen – in 1968 he and Debbie Schabert were married after a 26-day courtship

Jim Davidson – he and Alison Holloway were married after a three-week courtship

Judy Geeson – in 1985 she and Kristoffer Tabori were married eight weeks after they met

Raine, Countess Spencer – in 1993 she was proposed to by Count Jean-François de Chambrun 33 days after they met

Mike Oldfield – in 1978 he married Diana Fuller who ran the Exegesis course he'd been on; the marriage lasted one month

COUPLES WHO HAD OPEN MARRIAGES

Aneurin Bevan & Jennie Lee

Harold & Grace Robbins

Bertrand Russell & Dora Black

Carl & Emma Jung

John F. & Jacqueline Kennedy

Leonard & Virginia Woolf

William & Jane Morris

Salvador & Gala Dalí

**Lord Louis & Lady Edwina
Mountbatten**

Dmitri & Nina Shostakovich

Gary & Veronica (Rocky) Cooper

Sir William & Lady Emma Hamilton

Horatio & Fanny Nelson

Marlene Dietrich & Rudolf Sieber

Lyndon & Lady Bird Johnson

PEOPLE WHO COMMITTED BIGAMY

Rudolph Valentino, George Gissing, King George III, Anaïs Nin, Judy
Garland (unwittingly married Mark Herron in 1964 when she was still
married to Sid Luft) and Sidney Reilly (the Ace of Spies)

**It is also claimed that John F. Kennedy married a Palm Beach
socialite in 1947 and was still married to her in 1953 when he
married Jacqueline Bouvier**

MEN WHO MARRIED THEIR SECRETARY

Bertrand Russell, Jorge Luis Borges, Lord Hailsham, T.S. Eliot, Burt Lancaster, Lord Douglas Hurd, Fyodor Dostoevsky, Robin Cook, Lord Woodrow Wyatt, Sir James Goldsmith, Thomas Hardy, Sir Peter Hall, Jimmy Hill, Sir Henry Wood, Bryan Gould, John Stonehouse, Lord John Wakeham

PEOPLE WHO NEVER MARRIED

Greta Garbo, Sir Isaac Newton, Florence Nightingale, Ludwig van Beethoven, Cecil Rhodes, Frederic Chopin, Dame Flora Robson, Queen Elizabeth I, Henri de Toulouse-Lautrec, Jane Austen, Louisa May Alcott, Christabel Pankhurst, Giacomo Casanova, Alma Cogan, Alexander Pope, Lillian Gish, P.L. Travers, George Gershwin, Juan Fangio, Tessie O'Shea, Lilian Baylis, Helene Hanff, David Hume, John Locke, Jean-Paul Sartre, Rene Descartes, Immanuel Kant, Friedrich Nietzsche, Philip Larkin, Patricia Highsmith, Adam Smith, A.L. Rowse, Edgar Degas, Rory Gallagher, Maria Montessori, Edward Lear, Benny Hill, Stendhal, Johannes Brahms, Rupert Brooke, Voltaire, Mack Sennett, Coco Chanel, Vitas Gerulaitis, Stephane Grappelli, Frank Richards, Screaming Lord Sutch, Irma Kurtz, Sir Edward Heath, Julie Christie, Sir Cliff Richard, Valerie Singleton, Selina Scott, Sir Jimmy Savile, Dame Mary Peters, Baroness Betty Boothroyd, Celia Imrie, Zandra Rhodes, Harold 'Dickie' Bird, Celia Hammond, Gloria Steinem, Ralph Nader, Lynsey De Paul, Jean Alexander, Ann Widdecombe, Patricia Routledge, Sir Patrick Moore, Marcelle D'Argy Smith, Kate Adie, Eleanor Bron, Leonard Cohen, Lorraine Chase, Sir Cyril Smith

PEOPLE WHO MARRIED NINE TIMES

Mike Love, Pancho Villa, Zsa Zsa Gabor

PEOPLE WHO MARRIED EIGHT TIMES

Dame Elizabeth Taylor (twice to the same man), Marie
McDonald, Mickey Rooney, Alan Jay Lerner, Artie Shaw

PEOPLE WHO MARRIED SEVEN TIMES

Lana Turner, Richard Pryor, Barbara Hutton, Claude Rains, Stan Laurel
(three times to the same woman), Jennifer O'Neill, Larry King

PEOPLE WHO MARRIED SIX TIMES

Sir Rex Harrison, Johnny Weissmuller, Gloria Swanson, Hedy Lamarr,
Norman Mailer, King Henry VIII, Robert Evans, Harold Robbins, Steve
Earle, Jerry Lee Lewis, David Merrick (twice to the same woman)

PEOPLE WHO MARRIED FIVE TIMES

Tony Curtis, Danielle Steel, James Cameron, Billy Bob Thornton,
Martin Scorsese, Jan Leeming, Joan Collins, Stavros Niarchos,
David Lean, Ernest Borgnine, George C. Scott (twice to the same
woman), George Peppard (twice to the same woman), John Huston,
J. Paul Getty I, Roy Boulting, Ginger Rogers, Rue McClanahan, Victor
Mature, Eva Gabor, Judy Garland, Henry Fonda, Jane Wyman (twice
to the same man), George Foreman, Rita Hayworth, Ingmar Bergman,
Tammy Wynette, Clark Gable, Veronica Lake, Dick Emery, Richard
Burton (twice to the same woman), John Osborne, Brigitte Nielsen

PEOPLE WHO MARRIED FOUR TIMES

Frank Sinatra, Stockard Channing, Jason Robards, Ethel Merman, Doris Day, André Previn, Jim Davidson, Merle Oberon, Keith Floyd, Dennis Hopper, Janet Leigh, Ernest Hemingway, Barry Humphries, John Derek, David Soul, Donald Pleasence, Liza Minnelli, Bertrand Russell, Sir Peter Hall, Sir Charlie Chaplin, George Sanders, Paulette Goddard, Peggy Lee, Bette Davis, Al Jolson, Jane Seymour, Michael Crichton, Peter Sellers, Christina Onassis, Lawrence Durrell, Kim Philby, Yul Brynner, Leslie Charteris, Bertolt Brecht, Lionel Barrymore, Melanie Griffith (twice to the same man), Joan Fontaine, Erica Jong, Humphrey Bogart, Cary Grant, Christie Brinkley, Madeleine Carroll, William Shatner, Andy McNab, Joan Crawford, Connie Francis, Mao Tse-Tung, Lindsay Wagner, Dinah Sheridan, Brigitte Bardot, Dudley Moore, David Bailey, Eddie Fisher, Burgess Meredith, Janet Street-Porter

MEN WHO MARRIED OLDER WOMEN

Robert Browning (his wife, Elizabeth Barrett, was 6 years older than him)

Raymond Chandler (his wife, Pearl Bowen, was 17 years older than him)

Clark Gable (both of his first wives were considerably older than him – his first wife Josephine Dillon was 17 years older)

Benjamin Disraeli (his wife, Mary Wyndham Lewis, was 12 years older than him)

William Shakespeare (his wife, Anne Hathaway, was 7 years older than him)

Sir Roger Moore (his second wife, Dorothy Squires, was 12 years older than him)

WOMEN WHO MARRIED YOUNGER MEN

Sarah Bernhardt (her only husband was 11 years younger than her)

Martha Raye (married a man, Mark Harris, 23 years younger than her)

Colette (her third husband was 17 years younger than her)

Dame Elizabeth Taylor (married a man, Larry Fortensky, 20 years younger than her)

Edith Piaf (married a man, Theo Sarapo, 20 years younger than her)

Merle Oberon (married a man, Robert Wolders, 25 years younger than her)

Jennie Churchill (married George Cornwallis-West who was 20 years younger than her and Montagu Porch who was 23 years younger than her)

Marti Webb (married Tim Flavin who was 15 years younger than her and Tom Button who is 23 years younger than her)

Sian Phillips (married Robin Sachs who is 17 years younger than her)

Jenny Lind (married Otto Goldschmidt who was 9 years younger than her)

Kate Jackson (she twice married men who were 6 years younger than her)

Joanna Lumley (her husband Stephen Barlow is 8 years younger than her)

Ruth Gordon (her husband, Garson Kanin, was 16 years younger than her)

Isadora Duncan (her husband, Sergei Esenin, was 17 years younger than her)

Janet Street-Porter (her fourth husband, David Solkin, was 22 years younger than her)

Millicent Martin (her second husband, Norman Eshley, was 11 years younger than her)

Helena Rubenstein (her husband, Prince Artchil Gourielli-Tchkonia, was 20 years younger than her)

Kate O'Mara (her husband, Richard Willis, was 18 years younger than her)

Vivienne Westwood (her husband Andreas Kronthoaler is 25 years younger than her)

Joan Collins (her husband Percy Gibson is 32 years younger than her)

Madonna (her husband Guy Ritchie is 10 years younger than her)

Demi Moore (her husband Ashton Kutcher is 15 years younger than her)

PEOPLE WHO MARRIED AT THE AGE OF 13

Josephine Baker, Loretta Lynn, Mahatma Gandhi, June Havoc

PEOPLE WHO MARRIED AT THE AGE OF 14

Marie Antoinette, Jerry Lee Lewis, Janet Leigh (eloped – the marriage was later annulled)

PEOPLE WHO MARRIED AT THE AGE OF 15

Mary, Queen of Scots, Eva Bartok, Annie Oakley, Fanny Brice, Aaliyah, Stella Stevens

PEOPLE WHO MARRIED AT THE AGE OF 16

Dolores del Rio, Sophie Tucker, Marti Caine, Kay Mellor, Placido Domingo, Marilyn Monroe, Catherine The Great, Ellen Terry, Beverley Callard, Joan Bennett, Sandra Dee, Tom Jones, Doris Day, Linda Thorson, Josephine Cox

COUPLES WHO MARRIED IN LAS VEGAS

Ursula Andress & John Derek

John & Bo Derek

Melanie Griffith & Don Johnson (the first time)

Samantha Janus & Mauro Mantovani

Noel Gallagher & Meg Mathews

Sheena Easton & Tim Delarm

George Clooney & Talia Balsam (by an Elvis impersonator)

Paul Newman & Joanne Woodward

Clint Eastwood & Dina Ruiz

Paula Yates & Bob Geldof

Caroline Aherne & Peter Hook

Jason Connery & Mia Sara

Ruby Wax & Trevor Walton

Frank Sinatra & Mia Farrow

Natasha Henstridge & Damian Chapa

Ross Boatman & Sophie Camara

Sir Michael Caine & Shakira Baksh

Nicolas Cage & Patricia Arquette

Joan Collins & Peter Holm

Richard Gere & Cindy Crawford

Demi Moore & Bruce Willis

Caroline Goodall & Derek Hoxby

Dinah Sheridan & Aubrey Ison

Gabriel Byrne & Ellen Barkin

Sylvia Kristel & Alan Turner

Dudley Moore & Brogan Lane

Elvis Presley & Priscilla Beaulieu (but not by an Elvis impersonator)

Jonathan Ross & Jane Goldman

Richard & Sally Burton

Brigitte Bardot & Gunther Sachs

Jane Russell & Robert Waterfield

Milla Jovovich & Luc Besson

Bette Midler & Martin Von Haselburg (by an Elvis impersonator)

Chris Evans & Billie Piper

Angelina Jolie & Billy Bob Thornton

ENGAGEMENTS THAT DIDN'T LEAD TO MARRIAGE

Brad Pitt & Gwyneth Paltrow

Audrey Hepburn & Lord James Hanson

Jimmy Connors & Chris Evert

Lauren Bacall & Frank Sinatra

Julia Roberts & Kiefer Sutherland

Sir David Frost & Diahann Carroll

Lucille Ball & Broderick Crawford

King George V (when he was Duke of York) & Hon. Julia Stonor
(because she was a Catholic)

Naomi Campbell & Adam Clayton

Greta Garbo & John Gilbert (the engagement ended on the wedding
day – she stood him up at the altar)

Sir Paul McCartney & Jane Asher

Brian Cox & Irina Brook

Claudia Schiffer & David Copperfield

Johnny Depp & Winona Ryder

Liza Minnelli & Desi Arnaz Jnr

Roger Vadim & Catherine Deneuve

Bryan Ferry & Jerry Hall

Ruthie Henshall & John Gordon Sinclair

Scott Baio & Pamela Anderson

Ben Stiller & Jeanne Tripplehorn

Alyssa Milano & Scott Wolf

Cameron Diaz & Jared Leto

Demi Moore & Emilio Estevez

Sean Penn & Elizabeth McGovern

Sela Ward & Peter Weller

Laura Dern & Jeff Goldblum

Minnie Driver & Josh Brolin

MARRIAGE PROPOSALS THAT WERE TURNED DOWN

Ernest Hemingway's proposal to Gertrude Stein

The Duke of Westminster's proposal to Coco Chanel

Howard Hughes's proposal to Susan Hayward

James Stewart's proposal to Olivia de Havilland

Kenneth Williams's proposal for a celibate marriage to Joan Sims

PEOPLE WHO MARRIED THEIR EX-SPOUSE'S RELATION

Cleopatra married Ptolemy XIII and then when he died his brother Ptolemy XIV

George Sanders married the Gabor sisters, Zsa Zsa and Magda

Dame Barbara Cartland married the McCorquodale cousins

Gloria Grahame's second husband was the film director Nicholas Ray; her fourth husband was his son, Tony

Joseph Chamberlain married the Kenrick cousins, Harriet and Florence

THE THREE GERMAN REICHS

The First Reich was The Holy Roman Empire (962–1806)

The Second Reich was The German Empire (1871–1918)

The Third Reich was The Nazi Empire (1933–1945)

WAYS IN WHICH BRITAIN IS ON TOP OF THE WORLD

Highest (joint) percentage of the population that is literate

Highest proportionate number of botanical gardens and zoos in the world

In Queen Victoria, the longest-reigning queen the world has ever known

Top Air Ace of World War One (Edward Mannock – 73 kills)

More public lending libraries than any other country in the world

The three most published authors of all time are British: William Shakespeare, Charles Dickens and Sir Walter Scott

The busiest international airport in the world in London Heathrow

London has the longest underground railway network in the world

We publish more books than any other country in the world

Highest (joint) percentage of the population that has access to sanitation services

The longest-running show in the world – *The Mousetrap*, since 1952

THINGS THAT BRITAIN GAVE TO THE WORLD

The Mariner's Compass (1187)

The Slide Rule (1621)

The Pressure Cooker (1679)

The Match (1680)

The Kitchen Range
(seventeenth century)

Vasectomy (seventeenth century)

The Machine-Gun (1718)

The Chronometer (1735)

The Sandwich (1760)

Modern Flush Toilet (1775)

The Power Loom (1785)

Gas Lighting (1792)

The Piggy Bank (eighteenth century)

Clothes Washer and Dryer (1800s)

The Locomotive (1804)

Photographic Lens (1812)

The Electromagnet (1824)

Modern Rainwear (1830)

The Lawn Mower (1830)

The Computer (1835)

Photography (on paper) (1838)

The Postage Stamp (1840)

The Bicycle (1840)

The Travel Agency (1841)

Ship's Metal Hull and Propeller (1844)

The Pneumatic Tyre (for coaches) (1845)

The Glider (1853)

Steel (Production) (1854)

The Refrigerator (1855)

Linoleum (1860)

Colour Photography (1861)

The Telegraph (Transatlantic Cable) (1866)

The Stapler (1868)

The Electric Light (1878)

The Vending Machine (1883)

The Pneumatic Tyre (for bicycles) (1888)

The Thermos (1892)

The Loudspeaker (1900)

The Electric Vacuum Cleaner (1901)

Car Disc Brakes (1902)

The Telephone Booth (1903)

The Geiger Counter (1908)

Stainless Steel (1913)

The Tank (1916)

The Turbojet (1928)

The Decompression Chamber (1929)

The Food Processor (1947)

The Integrated Circuit (1952)

The Hovercraft (1955)

Acrylic Paint (1964)

The CAT Scanner (1972)

Test-Tube Babies (1978)

Genetic Fingerprinting (1987)

Note also: Football, the Railway, Tennis, Sell-by Dates on food, the Disposable Nappy, Airline Meals, the Underground, the custom of embracing under the mistletoe, Package Tours, Garden Cities, the Hearse, Christmas Cards, the Mini-Skirt, Punk Rock, Cricket

THINGS INVENTED BY THE FRENCH

The suit (eighteenth century), the tie (seventeenth century), aluminium ware (early nineteenth century), aspirin (1853), the coffee pot (1800), the handkerchief (fifteenth century), the Christmas cracker (nineteenth century), the sewing machine (1830), Teflon utensils (1954), wallpaper (fifteenth century)

GENUINE PRODUCTS

Sor Bits (Danish mints), Krapp (Scandinavian toilet paper), Grand Dick (French red wine), Nora Knackers (Norwegian biscuits), Moron (Italian wine), Mukki (Italian yoghurt), Cock (French deodorant), Plopp (Swedish toffee bar), Bum (Turkish biscuits), Donkee Basterd Suker (Dutch sugar), Zit (Greek fizzy drink), Bimbo Bread (South America), Craps Chocolate (France), Darkie Toothpaste (Taiwan), Pschitt (French fizzy drink), Homo-Milk (Canada)

FIRSTS

The world's **first** traffic island was installed – at his own expense – by Colonel Pierrepoint outside his London club; he was killed crossing over to it

The **first** ready-to-eat breakfast cereal was Shredded Wheat in 1893 (it beat Kellogg's Corn Flakes by just five years)

The **first** scientifically planned slimming diet was devised in 1862 by Dr Harvey, an ear specialist, for an overweight undertaker (incidentally, dieting was initially something that only men tended to do – women didn't start to do it until they stopped wearing figure-altering corsets)

The **first** dry cleaning was in 1849 by a Monsieur Jolly-Bellin of France, who discovered the process by mistake when he upset a lamp over a newly laundered tablecloth and found that the part that was covered with spirit from the lamp was cleaner than the rest

The **first** ice lolly dates back to 1923 when lemonade salesman Frank Epperson left a glass of lemonade with a spoon in it on a windowsill one very cold night: the next morning, the ice lolly was born

The **first** ever guest on *This Is Your Life* – in Britain – was Eamonn Andrews (and, of course, he went on to host the show)

Steven Seagal was the **first** non-Asian to successfully open a martial arts academy in Japan

Paddy Ashdown's grandfather was the **first** man in Ireland to buy a car

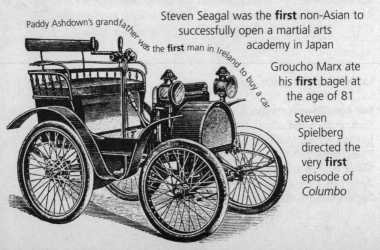

Groucho Marx ate his **first** bagel at the age of 81

Steven Spielberg directed the very **first** episode of *Columbo*

The **first** presenter of *A Question of Sport* (in 1970) wasn't David Coleman but David Vine

Courteney Cox was the **first** person on US TV ever to use the word 'period' – in an ad for Tampax

Harry Houdini was the **first** man to fly a plane in Australia – in 1910

Jimmy Carter was the **first** president to have been born in a hospital

The **first** man to fly over the North Pole – and indeed the South Pole – was called Dickie Byrd

The **first** Englishman to be killed in an aviation accident was Mr Rolls of Rolls-Royce fame

Soft toilet paper was sold for the **first** time in Britain in 1947 and was only available in Harrods

Gustav Mahler composed his **first** piece of music at the age of four, Sergei Prokofiev composed his **first** piece of music aged five and Wolfgang Mozart was just eight when he composed his **first** symphony

The **first** song Bruce Springsteen ever learned to play on the guitar was The Rolling Stones's 'It's All Over Now'

The **first** person in Britain to own a video phone was Jeremy Beadle (the second was Alan Minter)

Peter Snow and Peter Hobday co-presented the **first** edition of *Newsnight* in 1980

Barbra Streisand's **first** performance was as a chocolate chip cookie

Peter Sellers was the **first** male to feature on the cover of *Playboy*; he also provided the voices for the **first** PG Tips chimps ad – for which he was paid £25

The **first** duplicating machine was invented by James Watt, the inventor of the steam engine, in 1778 (patented in 1780) to help him with all the copying he had to do for his steam-engine business

Britain's **first** National Lottery was in 1567 to pay for public works. There were 400,000 tickets at ten shillings each (though these could be subdivided 'for the convenience of the poorer classes'). The top prize was £5,000, of which £3,000 was paid in cash, £700 in plate and the rest in good tapestry, etc.

The **first** member of the Royal Family ever to leave home for a haircut was the Queen: it was in Malta back in the days when she was a princess and she is said to have enjoyed the experience

Cuba Gooding Jr's **first** job was as a dancer for Lionel Richie at the 1984 Los Angeles Olympics

Harrison Ford's **first** film role was as a bellboy in the 1966 film *Dead Heat On A Merry-Go-Round* and he had to say, 'Paging Mr Ellis' (Ellis being James Coburn)

PROVERBS THAT ARE CLEARLY NOT TRUE

An apple a day keeps the doctor away

You can't judge a book by its cover

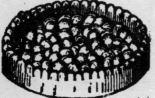

You can't have your cake and eat it

The best things in life are free

Every cloud has a silver lining

Ask no questions and you will be told no lies

Barking dogs seldom bite

There is no accounting for taste

The race is not to the swift

It never rains but it pours

PEOPLE WHO WERE BORN ON SIGNIFICANT DAYS IN HISTORY

Grandmaster Flash – the day that the EEC came into being

Cuba Gooding Jr – the day that Christiaan Barnard performed his second heart transplant

Barry John – the day that the Battle of the Bulge ended

Mark Lamarr – the day of the first transmission of the first episode of *The Forsyte Saga*

Michael Crawford – the day that Burma was invaded by the Japanese

Stefan Edberg – the day that Indira Gandhi became Indian Prime Minister

Emma Bunton – the day that Concorde made its first commercial flight (to Bahrain)

Frank Skinner – the day that Prince Charles started prep school

Jean Simmons – the day that Leon Trotsky was expelled from the USSR

Terry Jones – the day that Vidkun Quisling became Prime Minister of Norway

Alice Cooper – the day that Ceylon gained its independence

Natalie Imbruglia – the day that Edward Heath resigned as leader of the Conservative Party

Carole King – the day that soap rationing began in Britain

Robbie Williams – the day that Alexander Solzhenitsyn was expelled from the USSR

John McEnroe – the day that Fidel Castro became Prime Minister of Cuba

Seal – the day that the USSR stood down in the Cuban Missile Crisis

Alan Rickman – the day that the Indian navy mutinied

Lee Evans – the day that Muhammad Ali first became world heavyweight champion

Sir Peter O'Sullevan – the day that Germany and Russia signed the Treaty of Brest-Litovsk

Lord Douglas Hurd – the day that Mahatma Gandhi began his campaign of civil disobedience

Mickey Spillane – the day that Moscow became the capital of Russia

Olivia de Havilland – the day that the first Battle of the Somme began

Pamela Anderson – the day that BBC2 began regular colour broadcasts

Kenneth Clarke – the day that the Vichy Government was set up in France

Tom Cruise – the day that French rule in Algeria ended

Shane Lynch – the day that Israeli commandos rescued hostages in a raid on Entebbe airport

O J Simpson – the day that Princess Elizabeth's engagement to Prince Philip was announced

Gaby Roslin – the day that the communications satellite *Telstar* was launched

Nelson Mandela – the day that the second Battle of the Marne was fought

Raymond Chandler – the day that John Dunlop applied to patent a pneumatic tyre

Salvador Allende – the day that the FBI was created

Dame Helen Mirren – the day that the Labour Party came to power in the 1945 General Election

Geri Halliwell – the day that Idi Amin ordered the expulsion of 50,000 Asians from Uganda

Steve Martin – the day that Japan surrendered (VJ Day)

Jenny Hanley – the day that India and Pakistan both achieved independence

Lily Tomlin – the day that Germany invaded Poland

Siegfried Sassoon – the day that Johannesburg was founded

Kate Adie – the day that William Joyce was sentenced to death

Larry Hagman – the day that Britain abandoned the Gold Standard

Keith Duffy – the day that the Watergate trial started

Anneka Rice – the day that the first transatlantic jet service started

Vaclav Havel – the day that the Jarrow Hunger March started

Kate Winslet – the day that Niki Lauda became world motor racing champion

Matthew Pinsent – the day that Fiji became independent

Eminem – the day that the Queen made the first ever visit by a British monarch to a communist state (Yugoslavia)

Joan Plowright – the day of the Wall Street Crash

Yasmin Le Bon – the day that Tanganyika and Zanzibar combined to make Tanzania

Tom Watt – the day that Nikita Krushchev denounced Stalin at the communist Party Conference

Stubby Kaye – the day that World War One ended

Leonardo DiCaprio – the day that the new Covent Garden fruit market opened at Nine Elms

Imran Khan – the day that *The Mousetrap* opened in London

Sir Geoff Hurst – the day that the US and Britain declared war on Japan

Frank Sinatra – the day that the Germans built the first all-metal aeroplane

PEOPLE WHO HAD BAD ADOLESCENT ACNE

Dustin Hoffman, Victoria Beckham, Jennifer Capriati, Chris Morris, Jim Henson, Jack Nicholson, Janis Joplin, Mike Myers, F. Murray Abraham, Siena Guillory, Vanessa Redgrave, Rob Brydon ('professional acne'), Charlotte Salt, Trinny Woodall, Sir Derek Jacobi, Elvis Presley, Ricky Martin, Tim Vincent

PEOPLE WHO ARE FLUENT IN FOREIGN LANGUAGES

Mira Sorvino (Mandarin Chinese)

Imogen Stubbs (French)

Tim Roth (French and German)

Orlando Bloom (French)

Condoleezza Rice (Russian)

Roger Lloyd-Pack (German, Italian and French)

Eddie Izzard (French)

Kate Beckinsale (French and Russian)

Geena Davis (Swedish)

Davina McCall (French)

Rachel Weisz (German)

Helena Bonham Carter (French)

Rupert Everett (French and Italian)

Kate Adie (Swedish)

Alan Bennett (Russian)

Prunella Scales (French)

Gabriel Byrne (Spanish)

Edward Norton (Japanese)

Natalie Portman (Hebrew)

PEOPLE WHO READ THEIR OWN OBITUARIES

Dave Swarbrick

Mark Twain

Wild Bill Hickok

Bob Hope

The Queen Mother

Harold Macmillan

Max Jaffa

Alfred Nobel

Ian Dury (heard it)

Bertrand Russell

P.T. Barnum

Daniel Boone

PEOPLE WHO SURVIVED PLANE CRASHES

Clint Eastwood, Sir Bobby Charlton, Yasser Arafat, Dame Elizabeth Taylor, Peter Snow, David Coulthard, Frankie Dettori, Patrick Swayze, Sting, Luciano Pavarotti, Rowan Atkinson, Brian Blessed

PEOPLE WHO HAD HIPS REPLACED

Murray Walker, Maeve Binchy, Dave Prowse, Dame Elizabeth Taylor, Oscar Peterson, Peter Vaughan, Anita Pallenberg, Charlton Heston, Sir Jimmy Young, John Cleese, Gerd Muller, Bob Wilson, Tony Britton, Liza Minnelli (twice), The Duke of Kent, Nicholas Soames, Jack Nicklaus (twice)

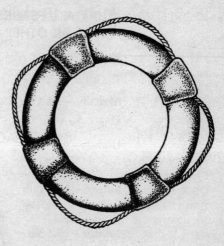

THE FIRST TEN CASTAWAYS ON *DESERT ISLAND DISCS*

First broadcast 29 January 1942

Vic Oliver (comedian)

James Agate (critic)

Commander Campbell (mariner and explorer)

C.B. Cochran (showman)

Pat Kirkwood (actress)

Jack Hylton (bandleader)

Captain Dingle (explorer)

Joan Jay (glamour girl)

The Reverend Canon W.H. Elliott (precentor of the Chapels Royal)

Arthur Askey (comedian)

WHAT A 10-STONE PERSON WOULD WEIGH ON OTHER PLANETS

Pluto – 7lb

The Moon – 1st 10lb

Mercury – 3st 11lb

Mars – 3st 11lb

Uranus – 9st 1lb

Venus – 9st 11lb

Saturn – 10st 11lb

Neptune – 11st 12lb

Jupiter – 25st 5lb

MPs WHO WERE THE BABY OF THE HOUSE OF COMMONS

Tony Benn (Labour; 25 in 1950)

David Steel (Liberal; 26 in 1965)

Stephen Dorrell (Conservative; 27 in 1979)

John Profumo (Conservative; 25 in 1940)

Charles Kennedy (SDP; 23 in 1983)

Paul Channon (Conservative; 23 in 1959)

Malcolm Rifkind (Conservative; 27 in 1974)

Matthew Taylor (Liberal; 24 in 1987)

WELL-KNOWN SONGS BASED ON CLASSICAL MUSIC

'Lady Lynda' (The Beach Boys) – based on Bach's *Jesu Joy of Man's Desiring*

'I Believe In Father Christmas' (Greg Lake) – based on Prokofiev's *Lieutenant Kije Suite*

'It's Now Or Never' (Elvis Presley) – based on De Capua's *O Sole Mio*

'Stranger In Paradise' (Tony Bennett) – based on Borodin's *Polotsvian Dances*

'Sabre Dance' (Love Sculpture) – based on Aram Khachaturian's ballet *Gayaneh*

'More Than Love' (Ken Dodd) – based on Beethoven's *Pathetique Sonata*

'Could It Be Magic' (Barry Manilow) – based on Chopin's *Prelude In C Major*

'Joybringer' (Manfred Mann's Earth Band) – based on Holst's *The Planets*

'A Lover's Concerto' (The Toys) – based on Bach's *Minuet In G*

'All By Myself' (Eric Carmen) – based on Rachmaninov's *Piano Concerto No. 2*

'Who's Afraid of The Big Bad Wolf' (1933) – based on Johann Strauss's 'Champagne Song' from *Die Fledermaus*

'Lullaby of Broadway' (1935) – based on Brahms's *Hungarian Dances* and Offenbach's 'Barcarolle' from *Tales of Hoffman*

'Where Did You Get That Hat' (1888) – based on Wagner's *Lohengrin* and *Die Meistersinger*

WELL-KNOWN SONGS BASED ON OTHER SONGS

'Love Me Tender' (1956) – based on George Poulton's 'Aura Lee' (1861)

'El Condor Pasa' (1933) – based on a Peruvian folksong

'Waltzing Matilda' (1903) – based on Robert Tannahill's 'Craigielea'

'Those Were The Days' (1968) – based on a traditional East European tune

'Don't Sit Under The Apple Tree' (1942) – based on 'Long Long Ago' (1833)

'It's All In The Game' (1951) – based on 'Melody' by Dawes (1912)

'She'll Be Comin' Round The Mountain (When She Comes)' (1899) – based on the hymn 'When The Chariot Comes'

'Hello Dolly' (1964) – based on 'Sunflower' by Mack David (1948)

'Midnight In Moscow' (1962) – based on the Russian song 'Padmas Koveeye Vietchera'

'My Sweet Lord' (1971) – based on Ronald Mack's 'He's So Fine' (1962)

FAMOUS RELATIVES OF OLYMPIC COMPETITORS

Grace Kelly (her father, John Kelly, Rowing 1920)

Roddy Llewellyn (his father, Sir Harry Llewellyn, Showjumping 1952)

Jean Simmons (her father, Charles Simmons, Gymnastics 1952)

Jonathon Porritt (his father, Arthur Porritt, 100 metres 1924)

Bobby Davro (his father, Bill Nankeville, 1500 metres 1948)

Charlotte Rampling (her father, Godfrey Rampling, 4x400 metres 1936)

Prince Rainier (his son, Prince Albert, Bobsleigh 1988)

Sir Rex Harrison (his son, Noel, Alpine Skiing 1952)

Tara Palmer-Tomkinson (her father, Charles Palmer-Tomkinson, Skiing 1964)

Andre Agassi (his father, Mike Agassi, Boxing 1948 and 1952 for Iran)

Hugh Laurie (his father, Ran Laurie, Rowing – Gold Medal winner – 1948)

Lindsay Davenport (her father, Volleyball 1968)

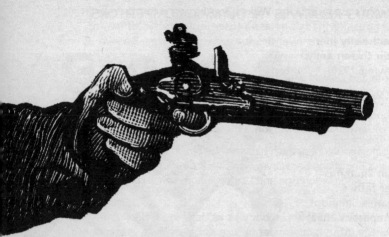

THE SPOOKY LINCOLN–KENNEDY COINCIDENCES

Lincoln was elected President in 1860 (having been elected to Congress in 1846); Kennedy was elected President in 1960 (having been elected to Congress in 1946)

Both presidents were directly concerned in civil rights for black people

Lincoln had a secretary named Kennedy; Kennedy had a secretary named Lincoln

Both presidents were shot in the head (from behind) and both presidents were with their wives when they were assassinated

Both wives had lost children while living at the White House

Both assassinations took place on a Friday and both presidents were warned that they might be assassinated but both refused to change their schedules

Lincoln was shot in a theatre by a man who hid in a warehouse; Kennedy was shot from a warehouse by a man who hid in a theatre

Kennedy was riding in a Lincoln when he was shot

Lincoln's assassin (John Wilkes Booth) was a Southerner in his twenties; Kennedy's assassin (Lee Harvey Oswald) was a Southerner in his twenties (both assassins were known by their three names)

Booth and Oswald were both shot before they could be tried

Lincoln was succeeded by his vice-president, Andrew Johnson, who was born in 1808; Kennedy was succeeded by his vice-president, Lyndon Johnson, who was born in 1908

Lincoln and Kennedy each had seven letters in their names; John Wilkes Booth and Lee Harvey Oswald each had 15 letters in their names; Andrew Johnson and Lyndon Johnson each had 13 letters in their names

NB A month before Lincoln was assassinated, he was in Monroe, Maryland; a year before Kennedy was assassinated, he was in Marilyn Monroe

PEOPLE WHO ENTERED COMPETITIONS TO IMITATE OR IMPERSONATE THEMSELVES AND LOST

David Bellamy (he was driving to an engagement one day, listening to a local radio station in his car. The station was running a 'Phone in and give us your David Bellamy impersonation' competition. He stopped at a telephone box, phoned in to take part – and came third)

Dolly Parton

Graham Greene (entered a competition to parody his style in the *Spectator* – came third)

Charlie Chaplin

Jason Donovan (sent in a tape to *Stars In Their Eyes* but was turned down)

Elvis Presley (entered an Elvis lookalike contest in a US burger joint but came third)

THE LAST LINES OF CLASSIC MOVIES

'The horror, the horror.' (*Apocalypse Now*)

'Madness. Madness.' (*The Bridge On The River Kwai*)

'That's right, that's right – attaboy, Clarence.' (*It's A Wonderful Life*)

'I used to hate the water – I can't imagine why.' (*Jaws*)

'The old man was right, only the farmers won; we lost, we'll always lose.' (*The Magnificent Seven*)

'Eliza? Where the devil are my slippers?' (*My Fair Lady*)

'Why, she wouldn't even harm a fly.' (*Psycho*)

'Well, Tillie, when the hell are we going to get some dinner?' (*Guess Who's Coming To Dinner*)

'We saw her many times again, born free and living free, but to us she was always the same, our friend Elsa.' (*Born Free*)

'Hello, everybody, this is Mrs Norman Maine.' (*A Star Is Born*)

'I haven't got a sensible name, Calloway.' (*The Third Man*)

'Thank you, thank you, I'm glad it's off my mind at last.' (*The 39 Steps*)

'Good, for a minute I thought we were in trouble.' (*Butch Cassidy And The Sundance Kid*)

'All right, Mr De Mille, I'm ready for my close-up.' (*Sunset Boulevard*)

'I now pronounce you men and wives.' (*Seven Brides For Seven Brothers*)

'Louis, I think this is the beginning of a beautiful friendship.' (*Casablanca*)

'Oh, Aunt Em, there's no place like home.' (*The Wizard of Oz*)

'The way we're swimming, old girl.' (*The African Queen*)

'Mediocrities everywhere, I absolve you, I absolve you, I absolve you, I absolve you. I absolve you all.' (*Amadeus*)

'Cool Hand Luke, hell, he's a natural born world-shaker.' (*Cool Hand Luke*)

'I guess we all died a little in that damn war.' (*The Outlaw Josey Wales*)

WOMEN WHO HAD GRANDFATHERS WHO WON 1954 NOBEL PRIZES

Olivia Newton-John (Max Born, won for Physics)

Mariel Hemingway (Ernest Hemingway, won for Literature)

OSCAR ONLYS

The **Only** role to garner two Oscars is Vito Corleone: Marlon Brando won the Best Actor Oscar in this role for *The Godfather* (1972), while Robert De Niro won the Best Supporting Actor Oscar in the same role for *The Godfather Part II* (1974). This film is also the **Only** sequel to win an Oscar as Best Film

The **Only** actor to win an Oscar for less than ten minutes' work: Anthony Quinn, who was on screen for only nine minutes in *Lust For Life* (1956)

The **Only** actress to win an Oscar for less than ten minutes' work: Dame Judi Dench, who was on screen for only eight minutes in *Shakespeare In Love* (1998)

The **Only** Oscar to win an Oscar: Oscar Hammerstein II (Best Song: 1941 and 1945)

The **Only** actress to win an Oscar for playing an Oscar nominee: Maggie Smith in *California Suite* (1978)

The **Only** silent film to win Best Picture: *Wings* (1927)

The **Only** actor to win a Best Actor Oscar when nominated alongside four previous Oscar winners: Adrien Brody for *The Pianist* (2003)

The **Only** actor to win a Best Actor Oscar in a foreign language film: Roberto Benigni for *Life Is Beautiful* (1998); note also that Robert De Niro's performance in *The Godfather Part II* was mostly in Italian

The **Only** actress to win a Best Actress Oscar in a foreign language: Sophia Loren for *Two Women* (1961)

The **Only** actress to win a Best Supporting Actress Oscar for playing the title role in a film: Vanessa Redgrave for *Julia* (1977)

The **Only** films in which all the members of the cast have been nominated for Oscars: *Who's Afraid of Virginia Woolf?* (four cast members 1966), *Sleuth* (two cast members 1972) and *Give 'em Hell Harry* (one cast member 1975)

The **Only** family in which three generations have won Oscars – the Hustons: Walter for *The Treasure of The Sierra Madre* (1948), John for *The Treasure of The Sierra Madre* and Anjelica for *Prizzi's Honor* (1985). Walter and John Huston are also the only father and son to win acting Oscars for the same film. The Coppolas: Carmine for *The Godfather, Part II* (1974), his son Francis for *The Godfather, Part II* (1974) etc. and Sofia for *Lost in Translation* (2004). In addition, Francis's nephew (and Sofia's cousin) Nicolas Cage won the Best Actor Oscar for *Leaving Las Vegas* (1995)

The **Only** mother and daughter to be nominated for Oscars in the same year: Diane Ladd and her daughter Laura Dern for *Rambling Rose* (1991)

The **Only** films to win 11 Oscars: *Ben-Hur* (1959) and *Titanic* (1997) and *Lord of the Rings: The Return of the King* (2003), which is also the **Only** film to win 11 Oscars and win in every category for which it was nominated

The **Only** films to get 11 Oscar nominations but not a single Oscar: *The Turning Point* (1977) and *The Color Purple* (1985)

The **Only** sisters to win Best Actress Oscars: Joan Fontaine for *Suspicion* (1941) and Olivia de Havilland for *To Each His Own* (1946). And they didn't speak to each other!

The **Only** twins to win Oscars: Julius J. Epstein and Philip G. Epstein (with Howard Koch) for *Casablanca* (1943)

The **Only** Oscar sold for more than half a million dollars: Vivien Leigh's for *Gone With The Wind*, which fetched $510,000 at auction in 1994

The **Only** posthumous acting Oscar was won by Peter Finch for *Network* (1976)

The **Only** actor to get two posthumous Oscar nominations: James Dean, for *East of Eden* (1955) and *Giant* (1956)

The **Only** animation film nominated for Best Film: *Beauty And The Beast* (1991)

The **Only** actress to win four Oscars: Katharine Hepburn, for *Morning Glory* (1932–33), *Guess Who's Coming To Dinner?* (1967), *The Lion In Winter* (1968) and *On Golden Pond* (1981). Jack Nicholson (two Best Actor and one Best Supporting Actor) and Walter Brennan (all as Best Supporting Actor) hold the record for the most Oscars for actors with three

The **Only** Best Supporting Actor winner to perform one-armed push-ups when he received his award: Jack Palance when he won for *City Slickers* (1991)

The **Only** father to win a Best Actor Oscar after his daughter had already won two Best Actress Oscars: Henry Fonda (*On Golden Pond*, 1981) after Jane Fonda had won for *Klute* (1971) and *Coming Home* (1978)

The **Only** daughter of a Best Actor winner to win an Oscar for Best Supporting Actress: Angelina Jolie for *Girl Interrupted* (1999); she is the daughter of Jon Voight, who won for *Coming Home* (1978)

The **Only** actors to get seven acting nominations without winning a single Oscar: Peter O'Toole and Richard Burton

The **Only** actress to get six acting nominations without winning a single Oscar: Deborah Kerr

The **Only** two actresses to compete against each other in both the Best Actress and the Best Supporting Actress categories in the same year: Holly Hunter and Emma Thompson in 1993

The **Only** actors to refuse Oscars: George C. Scott, *Patton* (1970) and Marlon Brando, *The Godfather* (1972)

The **Only** actor nominated as both Best Actor and Best Supporting Actor in the same year: Al Pacino (1992)

The **Only** octogenarian to win a Best Actress Oscar: Jessica Tandy for *Driving Miss Daisy* (1989)

The **Only** octogenarian to win a Best Supporting Actor Oscar: George Burns for *The Sunshine Boys* (1975)

The **Only** person to open the Oscar envelope to find his own name on the card: Irving Berlin (Best Song, 'White Christmas', 1942)

The **Only** man to be nominated for producer, director, writer and actor on the same film – twice – was Warren Beatty for *Heaven Can Wait* (1978) and *Reds* (1981)

The **Only** film in which the Best Director Oscar was shared by two men: *West Side Story* (Robert Wise and Jerome Robbins in 1961)

The **Only** women nominated as Best Director: Lina Wertmuller, *Seven Beauties* (1976), Jane Campion, *The Piano* (1994) and Sofia Coppola, *Lost in Translation* (2004)

The **Only** foreign language films nominated for Best Picture: *Grand Illusion* (1938, France), *Z* (1969, Algeria), *The Emigrants* (1972, Sweden), *Cries And Whispers* (1973, Sweden), *Il Postino* (*The Postman*; 1995, Italy), *Life Is Beautiful* (1998, Italy), *Crouching Tiger, Hidden Dragon* (2000, Taiwan)

The **Only** actors to win consecutive Oscars: Spencer Tracy (1937 and 1938), Jason Robards (1976 and 1977) and Tom Hanks (1993 and 1994)

The **Only** actresses to win consecutive Oscars: Luise Rainer (1936 and 1937) and Katharine Hepburn (1967 and 1968)

The **Only** actresses to get acting nominations five years running: Bette Davis (1938–42) and Greer Garson (1941–45)

The **Only** actors to get acting nominations four years running: Marlon Brando (1951–54) and Al Pacino (1972–75)

The **Only** films to win Best Actor and Best Actress Oscars: *It Happened One Night* (1934), *One Flew Over The Cuckoo's Nest* (1975), *Network* (1976), *Coming Home* (1978), *On Golden Pond* (1981), *The Silence of The Lambs* (1991) and *As Good As It Gets* (1997)

The **Only** films to win Oscars for Best Picture, Best Director, Best Actor, Best Actress and Best Screenplay: *It Happened One Night* (1934), *One Flew Over The Cuckoo's Nest* (1975) and *The Silence of The Lambs* (1991)

HEAD BOYS AT SCHOOL

Ian Hislop (Ardingly)

Hugh Dennis (University College School)

Sir Peter Hall (The Perse School)

Jonah Lomu (Wesley College)

Frank Bruno (Oak Hall)

Simon MacCorkindale (Haileybury)

Peter Jay (Winchester)

John Fowles (Bedford)

Lord William Rees-Mogg (Charterhouse)

Lord Douglas Hurd (Eton)

Lord David Owen (Mudd House Preparatory School)

Boris Johnson (Eton)

Nicholas Serota (Haberdashers' Aske's)

Steven Norris (Liverpool Institute)

Richard Curtis (Harrow – 'a freakish head of school')

Sir Ian McKellen (Bolton Grammar)

Alan Duncan MP (Beechwood Park Prep and Merchant Taylors')

Terry Jones (Royal Grammar School, Guildford)

Stuart Hall (Glossop Grammar)

Omar Sharif (Victoria College)

Peter Tatchell (Mount Waverley High School)

Simon Hughes MP (Christ College, Brecon)

Sir Tom Courtenay (Kingston High School)

HEAD GIRLS AT SCHOOL

Sarah, Duchess of York (Hurst Lodge)

Dame Norma Major (Peckham Comprehensive)

Baroness Margaret Thatcher (Kesteven and Grantham Girls' School)

Mo Mowlam (Coundon Court Comprehensive)

Dame Thora Hird (Morecambe Preparatory School)

Joan Bakewell (Stockport High School for Girls)

Gillian Shephard (North Walsham High School for Girls)

Kate Winslet (Redroofs Theatre School)

Baroness Lynda Chalker (Roedean)

Emma Nicholson (St Mary's, Wantage)

Baroness Sarah Hogg (St Mary's Convent, Ascot)

Francine Stock (St Catherine's, Guildford)

Kate Dimbleby (St Paul's)

Kate Hoey (Belfast Royal Academy)

Jill Dando (Broadoak Sixth-form Centre)

Minette Walters (Godolphin)

J.K. Rowling (Wyedean Comprehensive in Chepstow)

Esther McVey (Belvedere Girls' School, Liverpool)

Princess Beatrice (St George's School, Ascot)

SOME GENUINE AILMENTS

Lumpy Jaw (bacterial infection of the jaw with weeping sores)

Barbados Leg (elephantitis)

Painter's Colic (lead poisoning)

Iliac Passion (enduring pain in the lower three-fifths of the small intestine)

Parrot Disease (illness caused by inhaling dust contaminated by the droppings of infected birds)

Crab Yaws (tropical disease resembling syphilis with lesions on the foot)

Mad Staggers (often fatal gastric paralysis in horses)

Farmer's Lung (allergic reaction to fungi growing on hay, grain or straw)

Derbyshire Neck (enlargement of the thyroid gland visible as swelling on the neck)

Soldier's Heart (stress-related palpitations)

THE BBC'S ONLY FEMALE SPORTS PERSONALITIES OF THE YEAR

Anita Lonsborough (1962)

Dorothy Hyman (1963)

Mary Rand (1964)

Ann Jones (1969)

Princess Anne (1971)

Mary Peters (1972)

Virginia Wade (1977)

Jayne Torvill (with Christopher Dean) (1984)

Fatima Whitbread (1987)

Liz McColgan (1991)

Paula Radcliffe (2002)

Dame Kelly Holmes (2004)

Zara Phillips (2006)

FAMOUS PEOPLE WITH FAMOUS GODPARENTS

Winona Ryder (Timothy Leary)

Whitney Houston (Aretha Franklin)

Bertrand Russell (John Stuart Mill)

Jennifer Aniston (Telly Savalas)

Peter Scott (Sir J.M. Barrie)

Jonathan Aitken (Queen Juliana)

Mia Farrow (George Cukor and Louella Parsons)

Robert Cummings (Orville Wright)

Martin Amis (Philip Larkin)

Drew Barrymore (Steven Spielberg)

Earl Spencer (The Queen)

Andrew Parker Bowles (The Queen Mother)

Bridget Fonda (Larry Hagman)

Jeremy Thorpe (Megan Lloyd George)

Angelina Jolie (Jacqueline Bisset)

Sophie Dahl (Babs Powell)

THE WORLD'S GREATEST URBAN MYTH

Good Luck, Mr Gorsky: On 20 July 1969, Neil Armstrong, commander of Apollo 11, was the first person to set foot on the moon. His first words – 'That's one small step for man, one giant leap for mankind' – were heard by millions. He then said: 'Good luck, Mr Gorsky.' People at NASA thought he was talking about a Soviet cosmonaut, but it turned out there was no Gorsky in the Russian space programme. Over the years Armstrong was frequently asked what he had meant by 'Good luck, Mr Gorsky', but he always refused to answer for fear of offending the man. When Mr Gorsky died, Neil Armstrong finally felt able to tell the story. When he was a kid playing in his back yard, he once had to fetch his ball from the neighbours' yard. As he dashed in, he overheard his neighbour Mrs Gorsky shouting at Mr Gorsky: 'Sex! You want sex? You'll get sex when the kid next door walks on the moon!'

Alas, not only is the story untrue, but Neil Armstrong never even uttered the words 'Good luck, Mr Gorsky'. This story is an urban myth that has gathered currency on the internet. It's a prime example of the old saw that a lie can be halfway round the world before the truth has even got its boots on.

WONDERFULLY NAMED CHARACTERS FROM THE WORLD OF BERTIE WOOSTER

Barmy Fotheringay-Phipps, Stilton Cheesewright, Pongo Twistleton-Twistleton, Gussie Fink-Nottle, Biscuit Biskerton, Stiffy Stiffham, Catsmeat Potter-Pirbright, Dogface Rainsby, Oofy Prosser, Freddie Fitch-Fitch

STATISTICALLY THE MOST LANDED UPON MONOPOLY SQUARES

In order:

Trafalgar Square

Go

Marylebone Station

Free Parking

Marlborough Street

Vine Street

King's Cross Station

Bow Street

Water Works

Fenchurch Street Station

PEOPLE WHO GUESTED IN THE *BATMAN* TV SERIES

Shelley Winters (Ma Parker)

Ethel Merman (Lola Lasagne)

Tallulah Bankhead (Mrs Max Black)

Anne Baxter (Olga, Queen of the Cossacks)

Bruce Lee (Kato)

Glynis Johns (Lady Penelope Peasoup)

Jock Mahoney (Leo, one of Catwoman's accomplices)

James Brolin (Ralph Staphylococcus)

Michael Rennie (The Sandman)

George Sanders (Mr Freeze)

Zsa Zsa Gabor (Minerva)

**Roddy McDowall
(The Bookworm)**

Art Carney (The Archer)

Joan Collins (The Siren)

Vincent Price (Egghead)

Liberace (Chandell)

Cliff Robertson (Shame)

**Eartha Kitt
(Catwoman)**

Julie Newmar
(Catwoman)

**Lee Meriwether
(Catwoman)**

Edward G. Robinson
(cameo role)

George Raft (cameo role)

Phyllis Diller (cameo role)

Jerry Lewis (cameo role)

Gypsy Rose Lee (cameo role)

Rob Reiner (cameo role)

Sammy Davis Jr. (cameo role)

**Note: Robert F. Kennedy, Frank Sinatra, Jose Ferrer, Yul
Brynner, Dame Elizabeth Taylor, Gregory Peck, Mae West,
Gloria Swanson and Cary Grant all wanted to appear but no
parts could be found for them**

FAMOUS PEOPLE BORN ON THE VERY SAME DAY AS OTHER FAMOUS PEOPLE DIED

Donald Trump and John Logie Baird – 14.6.46

Jason Donovan and Helen Keller – 1.6.68

Graham Chapman and Lord Baden-Powell – 8.1.41

Yoko Ono and Gentleman Jim Corbett – 18.2.33

Donna Summer and Sir Malcolm Campbell – 31.12.48

Adam Ant and Henri Matisse – 3.11.54

Michael Stipe and Albert Camus – 4.1.60

Frank Zappa and F. Scott Fitzgerald – 21.12.40

Sir James Savile and Harry Houdini – 31.10.26

Johnny Rotten and A.A. Milne – 31.1.56

Victoria Principal and William Joyce (Lord Haw Haw) – 3.1.46

Janet Jackson and Randolph Turpin – 16.5.66

Billy Ocean and George Orwell – 21.1.50

Germaine Greer and W.B. Yeats – 29.1.39

Suzanne Danielle and Humphrey Bogart – 14.1.57

Patrick Ewing and Marilyn Monroe – 5.8.62

Roberta Flack and Pope Pius XI – 10.2.39

Jacqueline Bisset and William Heath Robinson – 13.9.44

James Gandolfini and Dag Hammarskjöld – 18.9.61

Richard Carpenter and Hermann Goering – 15.10.46

Winona Ryder and Duane Allman – 29.10.71

k.d. lang and James Thurber – 2.11.61

Art Carney and Wilfred Owen – 4.11.18

Kelly Brook and Merle Oberon – 23.11.79

David Mamet and Ernst Lubitsch – 30.11.47

Dennis Wise and Walt Disney – 15.12.66

Oscar de la Renta and Florenz Ziegfeld – 22.7.32

COMIC BOOK SUPERHEROES AND THEIR CONCEALED IDENTITIES

Spiderman (Peter Parker)

Superman (Clark Kent)

Batman (Bruce Wayne)

Robin (Dick Grayson)

The Green Hornet (Britt Reid)

Supergirl (Linda Lee Danvers)

Batgirl (Babs Gordon)

The Incredible Hulk (Bruce Banner)

Captain Marvel (Billy Batson)

Wonder Woman (Diana Prince)

WOMEN WHO HAD SONGS WRITTEN FOR THEM

Marilyn Monroe – 'Candle In The Wind' (Elton John/Bernie Taupin)

Dame Elizabeth Taylor – 'Emotionally Yours' (Bob Dylan)

Christie Brinkley – 'Uptown Girl' (Billy Joel)

Joni Mitchell – 'Our House' (Graham Nash)

Billie-Jean King – 'Philadelphia Freedom' (Elton John/Bernie Taupin)

Joan Baez – 'It Ain't Me Babe' (Bob Dylan)

Kylie Minogue – 'Suicide Blonde' (Michael Hutchence)

Marianne Faithfull – 'Wild Horses' (Mick Jagger)

Geri Halliwell – 'Eternity' (Robbie Williams)

Nicole Appleton – 'Songbird' (Liam Gallagher)

Patti Boyd – 'Layla' (Eric Clapton)

Jenny Boyd – 'Jennifer Juniper' (Donovan)

Rita Coolidge – 'Delta Lady' (Leon Russell)

Judy Collins – Suite: 'Judy Blue Eyes' (Stephen Stills)

GREAT COUNTRY & WESTERN TITLES

'You're The Reason Our Kids Are Ugly' (Loretta Lynn)

'I Cheated Me Right Out of You' (Moe Bandy)

'You're Out Doing What I'm Here Doing Without' (Gene Watson)

'The Lord Knows I'm Drinkin'' (Cal Smith)

'She Got The Goldmine (I Got the Shaft)' (Jerry Reed)

'Now I Lay Me Down To Cheat' (David Allan Coe)

'You Just Hurt My Last Feeling' (Sammi Smith)

'She's Actin' Single (I'm Drinkin' Doubles)' (Gary Stewart)

'I'm Gonna Hire A Wino To Decorate Our Home' (David Frizzell)

'Divorce Me C.O.D.' (Merle Travis)

'Heaven's Just A Sin Away' (The Kendells)

'I Forgot More Than You'll Ever Know' (The Davis Sisters)

'I'm The Only Hell (Mama Ever Raised)' (Johnny Paycheck)

PAIRS OF FAMOUS PEOPLE WHO DIED ON PRECISELY THE SAME DAY

Freddie Mercury (rock star) and Klaus Kinski (actor) – 24.11.91

Maria Callas (opera singer) and Marc Bolan (rock star) – 16.9.77

Fred Perry (tennis player) and Donald Pleasence (actor) – 2.2.95

Ben Travers (playwright) and Alexei Kosygin (former Soviet premier) – 18.12.80

G.K. Chesterton (writer) and Maxim Gorky (writer) – 14.6.36

Ronnie Kray (gangster) and Arthur English (comic actor) – 17.3.95

Woody Guthrie (folk singer) and Sir Malcolm Sargent (orchestral conductor) – 3.10.67

Rudolf Nureyev (ballet dancer) and Dizzy Gillespie (jazz musician) – 6.1.93

Sir P.G. Wodehouse (writer) and Sir Julian Huxley (scientist) – 14.2.75

Gilbert Harding (broadcaster) and Clark Gable (film star) – 16.11.60

Marvin Gaye (soul singer) and Rene Cutforth (broadcaster) – 1.4.84

Jim Laker (England cricketer) and Otto Preminger (film director) – 23.4.86

Orson Welles (film director and actor) and Yul Brynner (actor) – 10.10.85

Cecil Day-Lewis (poet) and Dame Margaret Rutherford (actress) – 22.5.72

Orville Wright (aviation pioneer) and Mahatma Gandhi (Indian leader) – 30.1.48

David Niven (actor and author) and Raymond Massey (actor) – 29.7.83

Sir Anthony Eden (former British prime minister) and Peter Finch (actor) – 14.1.77

Lord Bernard Miles (actor and producer) and Dame Peggy Ashcroft (actress) – 14.6.91

Sammy Davis Jr. (entertainer) and Jim Henson (the man behind the Muppets) – 16.5.90

River Phoenix (actor) and Federico Fellini (film director) – 31.10.93

Earl Spencer (Princess Diana's father) and Paul Henreid (actor) – 29.3.92

John F. Kennedy (US President) and Aldous Huxley (writer) – 22.11.63

General Leopoldo Galtieri (former Argentinian dictator) and Maurice Gibb (musician) – 12.1.2003

MEN WHO WERE THE SEVENTH SONS OF SEVENTH SONS

Glen Campbell

Perry Como

EXTRAORDINARY BEQUESTS

In 1987, Bob Fosse, the choreographer and film director (he won an Oscar for *Cabaret*), left $378.79 to each of 66 people to 'go out and have dinner on me'; these included Liza Minnelli, Janet Leigh, Elia Kazan, Dustin Hoffman, Melanie Griffith, Neil Simon, Ben Gazzara, Jessica Lange and Roy Scheider

In 1974, Philip Grundy, a dentist, left his dental nurse £181,000 on condition that she didn't wear any make-up or jewellery or go out with men for five years

In 1955, Juan Potomachi, an Argentinian, left more than £25,000 to the local theatre on condition that they used his skull when performing *Hamlet*

In 1765, John Hart left his brother a gun and a bullet 'in the hope that he will put the same through his head when the money is spent'

Mr John Bostock left in his will £100 to the manager of the local Co-op for the provision, 'until the fund be exhausted', of a two-ounce bar of chocolate every week for each child under the age of five in the parish of Westgate-in-Weardale

An unnamed Irishman left £1500 in his will to the Department of Health and Social Security (as it then was) to repay the money he had received while on the dole

In 1950, George Bernard Shaw left a considerable portion of his estate for the purpose of replacing the standard English alphabet of 26 letters with a more efficient alphabet of at least 40 letters – it was never achieved

The British dramatist Richard Brinsley Sheridan told his son that he was cutting him out of his will with just a shilling. His son's reaction was, 'I'm sorry to hear that, sir. You don't happen to have the shilling about you now, do you?'

In 1856, Heinrich Heine, the German poet, left everything to his wife on the condition that she remarried 'so that there will be at least one man to regret my death'

In 1937, F. Scott Fitzgerald drew up a will in which he specified 'a funeral and burial in keeping with my station in life'. Three years later, just before his death, a much poorer Fitzgerald amended this provision to read 'cheapest funeral … without undue ostentation or unnecessary expense' – his funeral cost precisely $613.25

The longest will in the world was one drawn up for Frederica Cook, an American woman – when it was proved at London's Somerset House in 1925, it consisted of four bound volumes totalling 95,940 words. Amazingly, she didn't have all that much to leave

The shortest valid British will – which was contested but eventually passed after the 1906 case Thorne v. Dickens – consisted of three words: 'All for mother'. What caused the confusion was that the testator didn't mean his mother but his wife

William Shakespeare bequeathed to his wife, Anne, 'my second best bed'. This has been interpreted as a snub. In fact, his 'second best bed' was probably the one most used by the two of them and it was therefore a sentimental gesture. His best bed went to the male heirs of his elder daughter

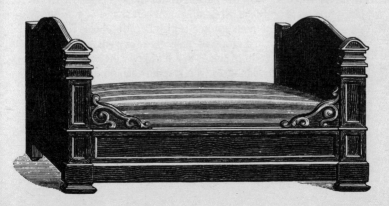

An unnamed Scotsman bequeathed each of his two daughters her weight in £1 notes. The elder, slimmer daughter received £51,200, while her younger, fatter sister got £57,433

In 1975, Edward Horley, a former Mayor of Altrincham, instructed his solicitors to buy a lemon, cut it in two and send one half to the income tax inspectorate and the other half to the tax collector with the message, 'Now squeeze this'

In 1997, Robert Brett, a Californian who wasn't allowed to smoke at home, left his entire fortune to his wife provided that she smoked four cigars a day for the rest of her life

A wealthy American banker left a codicil in his will cutting out two members of his family: 'To my wife and her lover, I leave the knowledge I wasn't the fool she thought I was. To my son, I leave the pleasure of earning a living. For twenty-five years he thought the pleasure was mine'

Charles Millar, a strait-laced Canadian lawyer who died in 1928 at the age of 73, had a bizarre sense of humour. He wondered how much people would do in the pursuit of money. To a preacher and a judge, who were both against gambling, he left shares in a racetrack that would make both men automatic members of a horse racing club. Both accepted. To a group of ministers who were anti-alcohol, Millar left $50,000 worth of shares in a brewery – they all accepted bar one. To three acquaintances who loathed each other, Millar bequeathed a holiday home in Jamaica which they were obliged to share – which they did. Most controversially, Millar bequeathed more than $500,000 to the Toronto woman who 'has given birth to the greatest number of children at the expiration of ten years from my death'. Millar's relatives tried – but failed – to overturn the will and, ten years later, four women who had each had nine children in the ten years shared the money

ANAGRAMS

'TO BE OR NOT TO BE: THAT IS THE QUESTION, WHETHER TIS NOBLER IN THE MIND TO SUFFER THE SLINGS AND ARROWS OF OUTRAGEOUS FORTUNE' is an anagram of: 'IN ONE OF THE BARD'S BEST-THOUGHT-OF TRAGEDIES, OUR INSISTENT HERO, HAMLET, QUERIES ON TWO FRONTS ABOUT HOW LIFE TURNS ROTTEN'

NEIL ARMSTRONG: 'THAT'S ONE SMALL STEP FOR A MAN, ONE GIANT LEAP FOR MANKIND' is an anagram of: 'THIN MAN RAN; MAKES A LARGE STRIDE, LEFT PLANET, PINS FLAG ON MOON! ON TO MARS!'

Eric Clapton (NARCOLEPTIC), Andi Peters (PEDESTRIAN) and Britney Spears (PRESBYTERIANS) all have names that can be anagramatized into single words

WORKABLE CARAMEL LIPS – Camilla Parker Bowles

ECCENTRIC MOUTH, MAN – Martine McCutcheon

LARGE FAT NOISE – Gloria Estefan

MANURE PLOT – Paul Merton

NOT ARENA KING – Ronan Keating

'ONLY JERK!' SCREAM – Jeremy Clarkson

HIM ALL SPOTTY – Timothy Spall

GROAN MADLY – Gary Oldman

HER ILLEGAL CHARM SALE – Sarah Michelle Gellar

MOANS LYRIC – Carly Simon

BLAME, COMPLAIN – Naomi Campbell

I'M AS CHEAP BENEATH – Stephanie Beacham

DOCILE OR PARANOID – Leonardo DiCaprio

NO NEAR SHOTS – Sharon Stone

ADULT ACTORS WHO PLAYED CHILDREN

Colin Welland *et al* (*Blue Remembered Hills*)

Richard Attenborough (*The Guinea Pig*)

Keith Barron (*Stand Up, Nigel Barton*)

Denholm Elliott *et al* (*School Play*)

Ginger Rogers (*The Major And The Minor*)

Joan Fontaine (*Letter From An Unknown Woman*)

Cary Grant (*Monkey Business*)

Bette Davis (*Payment On Demand*)

HOW ROCK GROUPS GOT THEIR NAMES

Abba From the initials of the four members of the band: Agnetha, Björn, Benny and Anni-Frid. Anni-Frid, however, is now known as Frida. This means that the ABBA Fan Club is now known as the ABBF Fan Club.

The Beatles All The Beatles were fans of Buddy Holly and The Crickets and so John decided to call his band The Beetles. Then he changed it to 'Beatles' as they were a *beat* band.

Blue Oyster Cult From an anagram of Cully Stout Beer, which the band's manager and producer were drinking when they were trying to come up with a name for the band.

Crowded House Chose the name because of the cramped living conditions in their rented house.

Deacon Blue From a song by Steely Dan, 'Deacon Blues'.

Dire Straits A friend, noting their perilous financial position, suggested the name.

The Doobie Brothers 'Doobie' was Californian slang for a marijuana joint.

The Doors Taken from a line written by Aldous Huxley, 'All the other chemical Doors in the Wall are labelled Dope …'

Duran Duran From the name of the villain – played by Milo O'Shea – in the Jane Fonda film *Barbarella*.

Eurythmics Named after an early twentieth-century form of dance and mime ('Eurhythmics') based on Greek methods of teaching children music through movement.

Everything But The Girl Took their name from a second-hand shop where everything was for sale except for the people who worked there.

Fine Young Cannibals Took their name from a 1960 film *All The Fine Young Cannibals*, which starred Robert Wagner and Natalie Wood.

Green Day Took their name from their own slang expression 'good marijuana' (it's a green day)

Frankie Goes To Hollywood Took their name from a newspaper cutting about Frank Sinatra going into films.

Happy Mondays Named after the Blue Order song, 'Blue Monday'.

Iron Maiden After a medieval torture device (consisting of a metal form with spikes on the inside).

Led Zeppelin From the Keith Moon (then drummer with The Who) line – which he often used – 'That went down like a lead zeppelin.' The band later dropped the 'a' in lead.

Level 42 Took their name from *The Hitchhiker's Guide To The Galaxy* by Douglas Adams, in which the number 42 is the answer to the 'meaning of life'.

The Lovin' Spoonful From the words of a Mississippi John Hurt song, 'Coffee Blues'; this is bluesmen's slang for what a man gives a woman during sex.

Lynyrd Skynyrd Named themselves after Leonard Skinner, a disliked gym teacher at their high school.

Mungo Jerry From T.S. Eliot's *Old Possum's Book of Practical Cats*.

Oasis The name came from a sports centre in Swindon.

Pink Floyd They named themselves after legendary bluesmen, Pink Anderson and Floyd Council.

The Pogues Short for the Gaelic *pogue mahone*, which means 'kiss my arse'.

Prefab Sprout As a child, singer Paddy McAloon had misheard the words 'pepper sprout' in a Nancy Sinatra song as 'prefab sprout', and that's the name he always wanted to give his band.

The Pretenders After the Sam Cooke song, 'The Great Pretender'.

Radiohead From the Talking Heads song, 'Radiohead'.

The Righteous Brothers When the duo performed at black clubs, they were praised with the words, 'That's righteous, brother.'

The Rolling Stones Named themselves after a Muddy Waters song, 'Rollin' Stones'.

The Searchers Named themselves after the John Ford classic that starred John Wayne and Natalie Wood.

Simple Minds From the lyrics of the David Bowie song 'Jean Genie'.

The Small Faces They chose the name 'Faces' because, in Mod terms, they were all 'faces' (cool dudes). The word 'Small' came from the fact that all four members of the band were under 5 foot 6.

Soft Machine Took their name from a novel by William Burroughs (see also Steely Dan).

Steely Dan From the William Burroughs novel *Naked Lunch* in which Steely Dan was a steam-powered dildo.

The Teardrop Explodes Taken from a caption in a comic book.

Thin Lizzy Named after a robot in the *Beano* comic named Tin Lizzie. The band inserted the 'h' in Thin on the basis that it wouldn't be sounded in Ireland and might be worth a chuckle when it confused people.

Three Dog Night From the Australian slang for a freezing night (in the outback, a man would need to sleep with one dog to keep warm on a cold night, two dogs on a very cold night and three dogs on the coldest night).

The Velvet Underground Taken from the title of a pornographic book about sado-masochism.

Wet Wet Wet Took their name from words in a Scritti Politti song, 'Getting, Having And Holding'.

Z.Z. Top Billy Gibbons, the band's vocalist, was inspired by the Z beams on a pair of open hay-loft doors.

EXTRAORDINARY EXECUTIONS AND NON-EXECUTIONS

In the eighteenth and nineteenth centuries, people – including children – were hanged for incredibly trivial offences. In 1819, Thomas Wildish was hanged for letter-stealing; in 1750, Benjamin Beckonfield was hanged for the theft of a hat; in 1833, an unnamed nine-year-old boy was hanged for stealing a pennyworth of paint from a shop; in 1782, a 14-year-old girl was hanged for being found in the company of gypsies.

In 1948, William John Gray was sentenced to hang for the murder of his wife. However, he was reprieved after medical examiners ruled that hanging would cause him too much pain. This was based on the extent of injuries to his jaw. It was explained that if he were hanged, the noose wouldn't dislocate his neck and that he would either die of strangulation or he would be decapitated altogether, as his injured jawbone was too weak to hold the rope around his neck.

In 1679, Messrs Green, Berry and Hill were hanged at Tyburn for a murder they committed on … Greenberry Hill

On 16 August 1264 at precisely nine o'clock in the morning, Inetta de Balsham was hanged. The King's messenger arrived a few seconds later with a reprieve. The hangman ran up the stairs and cut the rope with a sword. The victim's face had already turned blue but she survived.

Similarly, in 1705, John Smith was hanged for burglary at Tyburn Tree. After he had been hanging for fifteen minutes, a reprieve arrived and he was cut down. He was revived and managed to recover. As a result of his experience, he became known as John 'Half-Hanged' Smith.

In 1736, Thomas Reynolds was hanged for robbery at Tyburn Hill. He was cut down and placed in a coffin. However, as the hangman's assistant was nailing down the coffin lid, the lid was pushed away and the assistant's arm was grabbed from within. Reynolds was then taken out of the coffin and to a nearby house, where he vomited three pints of blood and died.

In 1650, charged with the murder of her newborn baby (a crime that only ceased to be a capital offence in 1922), Ann Green was hanged at Oxford Gaol. After an hour, she was cut down but was seen to be twitching. One person jumped on her stomach and a soldier struck her on the head with his musket. Her body was then passed on to a professor of anatomy who was preparing to cut her open when he heard a noise from her throat. She was put into a warm bed and her breathing restarted. By the next day she was almost fully recovered and she was eventually pardoned.

On 23 February 1885, John Lee was due to be hanged at Exeter Gaol for the murder of his employer (on thin circumstantial evidence). However, after the hangman put the noose around his neck, the scaffold's drop wouldn't respond to the lever. Lee was returned to his cell while the hangman tested the drop with weights until it worked perfectly. A second attempt was made but, once again, the drop didn't work. When Lee stood on the scaffold for the third time, it again proved impossible. Lee was returned to his cell and later given a reprieve by the Home Secretary. He became famous as 'The Man They Couldn't Hang'.

Being a hangman was no insurance against being hanged. Four English hangmen were hanged: Cratwell in 1538 for robbing a booth at St Bartholomew's Fair; Stump-leg in 1558 for thieving; Pascha Rose in 1686 for housebreaking and theft, and John Price in 1718 for murdering an old woman.

Postscript: Albert Pierrepoint was Britain's last executioner. He hanged more than 400 people. After his retirement, he campaigned for abolition saying, 'I do not now believe that any of the hundreds of executions I carried out has in any way acted as a deterrent against future murder. Capital punishment, in my view, achieved nothing except revenge.'

PEOPLE AND THEIR TATTOOS

Davina McCall: alien on her bottom, rose on her wrist and a devil's horn on each hip

Kerry Katona: soaring bird on the base of her spine

Anna Kournikova: a sun on her bottom

Kelly Osbourne: small heart on her hip and a small etching on the back of her neck

Colin Farrell: ex-wife Amelia Warner's name on his finger and 'Carpe diem' on his forearm

Sarah Michelle Gellar: Chinese character for integrity on her lower back

David Beckham: sons' names across his back

Robbie Williams: lion on his shoulder with 'Born To Be Mild' underneath; on his other arm he has a Maori design. Also has the Alcoholics Anonymous Serenity Prayer tattooed on his arm, but has replaced the word 'God' with 'Elvis'

Eminem: 'Slit me' on his wrists; the name of his wife Kim on his stomach with a tombstone and the inscription 'Rot In Flames'; an Indian tribal tattoo on his forearm

Charlize Theron: fish – her mother has a matching tattoo

Jude Law: 'Sexy Sadie' on his arm

Angelina Jolie: a tattoo on her belly which reads 'Quod me nutrit me destruit' – 'What feeds me destroys me'

Roseanne: pink rose on left foot; ex-husband Tom Arnold's name on shoulder and bottom now replaced with flowers and fairies

Gerard Depardieu: star on arm

Ulrika Jonsson: devil on bottom

Mel C: Celtic band on arm, huge phoenix on back and Chinese dragon running the length of her calf

Mick Hucknall: federal symbol of Europe on arm

Cher: flower on bottom

Alexander McQueen: Japanese fish symbol on chest

Vanilla Ice: leaf on stomach

Drew Barrymore: butterfly and flower sprig on bottom

Ringo Starr: half moon on arm

Vinnie Jones: 'Leeds Utd' on leg

Sean Bean: '100% Blade' on arm

Madonna: 'MP' – standing for 'Madonna's Property' – and Marilyn Monroe's face on bottom

Julia Roberts: red heart with a Chinese character meaning 'strength of heart' on shoulder

Sir Sean Connery: 'Scotland Forever' and 'Mum and Dad' on arms

Björk: Icelandic rune on shoulder

Melanie Griffith: pear on bottom

Geri Halliwell: sundial design on top of back and jaguar further down

Marianne Faithfull: bird on hand

Chrissie Hynde: dolphin on arm

Dame Helen Mirren: pair of crosses on hand

FAMOUS NOVELS ORIGINALLY REJECTED BY PUBLISHERS

The Time Machine (H.G. Wells)

***The Mysterious Affair At Styles* (Agatha Christie)**

Harry Potter And The Philosopher's Stone (J.K. Rowling)

***The Razor's Edge* (W. Somerset Maugham)**

The Good Earth (Pearl Buck)

***The Picture of Dorian Gray* (Oscar Wilde)**

Moby Dick (Herman Melville)

***The Naked And The Dead* (Norman Mailer)**

Northanger Abbey (Jane Austen)

***Barchester Towers* (Anthony Trollope)**

The Ginger Man (J.P. Donleavy)

***Catch-22* (Joseph Heller)**

The Wind In The Willows (Kenneth Grahame)

***A Time To Kill* (John Grisham)**

The Rainbow (D.H. Lawrence)

***The Spy Who Came In From The Cold* (John Le Carré)**

Animal Farm (George Orwell)

***Tess of The D'Urbervilles* (Thomas Hardy)**

Lord of The Flies (William Golding)

GREAT NOVELS AND THEIR ORIGINAL TITLES

Lady Chatterley's Lover (D.H. Lawrence): *Tenderness*

Roots (Alex Haley): *Before This Anger*

The Postman Always Rings Twice (James M. Cain): *Bar-B-Q*

The Mill On The Floss (George Eliot): *Sister Maggie*

Portnoy's Complaint (Philip Roth): *A Jewish Patient Begins His Analysis*

A Portrait of The Artist As A Young Man (James Joyce): *Stephen Hero*

East of Eden (John Steinbeck): *The Salinas Valley*

The Time Machine (H.G. Wells): *The Chronic Argonauts*

Valley of The Dolls (Jacqueline Susann): *They Don't Build Statues To Businessmen*

Catch-22 (Joseph Heller): *Catch-18*

Treasure Island (Robert Louis Stevenson): *The Sea-Cook*

Jaws (Peter Benchley): *The Summer of The Shark*

War And Peace (Leo Tolstoy): *All's Well That Ends Well*

Moby Dick (Herman Melville): *The Whale*

Of Mice And Men (John Steinbeck): *Something That Happened*

The Great Gatsby (F. Scott Fitzgerald): *The High-bouncing Lover*

Gone With The Wind (Margaret Mitchell): *Ba! Ba! Black Sheep*

Frankenstein (Mary Shelley): *Prometheus Unchained*

BOOK TITLES AND THEIR LITERARY ORIGINS

From Here To Eternity (James Jones): taken from Rudyard Kipling's Gentlemen Rankers

Brave New World (Aldous Huxley): taken from William Shakespeare's *The Tempest*

For Whom The Bell Tolls (Ernest Hemingway): taken from John Donne's Devotions

The Moon's A Balloon (David Niven): taken from e.e. cummings's *& N &*

Now Voyager (Olive Higgins Prouty): taken from Walt Whitman's Leaves of Grass

Under The Greenwood Tree (Thomas Hardy): taken from William Shakespeare's *As You Like It*

Paths of Glory (Humphrey Cobb): taken from Thomas Gray's Elegy In A Country Churchyard

Of Mice And Men (John Steinbeck): taken from Robert Burns's *To A Mouse*

A Confederacy of Dunces (John Kennedy Toole): taken from Jonathan Swift's Thoughts On Various Subjects

Gone With The Wind (Margaret Mitchell): taken from Ernest Dowson's *Cynara*

The Grapes of Wrath (John Steinbeck): taken from Julia Ward Howe's The Battle Hymn of The American Republic

Tender Is The Night (F. Scott Fitzgerald): taken from John Keats's *Ode To A Nightingale*

The Dogs of War (Frederick Forsyth): taken from William Shakespeare's Julius Caesar

EXTRAORDINARY EVENTS THAT (ALMOST) DEFY EXPLANATION

DOUBLE PROOF A pair of identical American twin boys were separated at birth in 1940 and adopted by different people who didn't know each other. Each boy was named James, each boy married a woman named Linda, had a son named James Alan, and was then divorced. When they eventually met up at the age of 39, they found that their hobbies, experiences and tastes had been and were remarkably similar.

BABY LUCK Some coincidences are just too extraordinary. In 1975 in Detroit, a baby fell out of a building 14 storeys up. Fortunately, it landed on a man named Joseph Figlock and so survived. A year later, another baby fell from the same building and survived by falling on … Joseph Figlock.

LIVE MUSHROOMS A nun at a convent in Clwyd tried but failed to grow mushrooms in the convent grounds. She died at the age of 79 in 1986, and a decent crop of mushrooms has grown on her grave every autumn since. Nowhere else in the convent do mushrooms grow.

SPONTANEOUS COMBUSTION In 1938, Phyllis Newcombe, 22, combusted spontaneously at a dance hall during a waltz. Many people witnessed this unexplained phenomenon, which has parallels with the combustion of a British pensioner, Euphemia Johnson, who died after suddenly bursting into fire during her afternoon tea.

A GOLDEN SHEEP In 1984, a Greek Orthodox priest was cooking a sheep's head when he discovered that the sheep had a jaw composed of 14-carat gold (worth some £4,000). The sheep had come from a herd owned by the priest's own brother-in-law and he couldn't come up with any plausible explanation – nor could the Greek ministry of agriculture when they looked into the case.

LET IT RAIN In 1986, American judge Samuel King was annoyed that some jurors were absent from his Californian court because of heavy rain, so he issued a decree: 'I hereby order that it cease raining by Tuesday.' California suffered a five-year drought. So in 1991 the judge decreed, 'Rain shall fall in California beginning February 27.' Later that day, California had its heaviest rainfall in a decade.

DEAD AGAIN In Bermuda, two brothers were killed precisely one year apart at the age of 17 by the same taxi driver carrying the same passenger on the same street. The two boys had each been riding the same moped.

A TIME TO DIE It is said that when a person dies their spouse often dies soon afterwards, but this is exceptional. Charles Davies died at 3.00 in the morning at his sister's house in Leicester. When his sister phoned his home in Leeds to tell his wife, she discovered that Charles's wife had also just died … at 3.00 in the morning.

SOME THINGS TO KNOW ABOUT US PRESIDENTS

Herbert Hoover (1929–33) and his wife both spoke fluent Chinese. Hoover was also the first president to have a telephone on his desk in the White House.

When Calvin Coolidge (1923–29) was being driven in a car, he would always insist that the driver didn't exceed 16mph.

Andrew Jackson (1829–37) once killed a man in a duel because he had insulted his wife.

Ulysses S. Grant (1869–77) was tone-deaf and once said: 'I only know two tunes. One of them is "Yankee Doodle" and the other isn't.'

George Washington (1789–97) had wooden false teeth.

James Garfield (1881) could simultaneously write in Greek with one hand while writing in Latin with the other.

At up to 24 stones, William Taft (1909–13) was the heaviest president and once had the misfortune of getting stuck in the White House bathtub. At just over seven stones, James Madison (1809–17) was the lightest president.

Jimmy Carter (1977–81) developed the knack of reading at speed and was once tested and found to have 95 per cent comprehension at a reading rate of 2,000 words a minute.

Ronald Reagan (1981–89) was the first – and so far only – president to have been divorced.

George Bush (1989–93), a chubby toddler, was nicknamed 'Fatty McGee McGaw' by his father.

James Buchanan (1857–61) was the first – and so far only – bachelor to become president. He also suffered from an unfortunate nervous twitch that caused his head to jerk frequently.

When he was young, Rutherford Hayes (1877–81) suffered from a strange phobia: the fear of going insane.

The first president to leave the US while in office was Theodore Roosevelt (1901–09): in 1906 when he visited the Panama Canal zone. He was also the first president to be a master of jujitsu.

Calvin Coolidge (1923–29) was famous for being a man of few words. At a White House dinner, a female guest told him that her father had bet her she wouldn't be able to get more than two words out of the president. 'You lose' were the only words he spoke to her.

PEOPLE WHO DIED ON THEIR BIRTHDAYS

Raphael (6 April 1483–1520 – and for good measure both days fell on Good Friday)

Shakespeare (23 April 1564–1616, though there is some doubt over his precise date of birth)

Frans Francken (6 May 1581–1642)

Joe Mercer (9 August 1914–1990)

Ingrid Bergman (29 August 1915–82)

Keith Boyce (11 October 1943–96)

Betty Friedan (4 February 1921–2006)

Famous people who were adopted

Bill Clinton, Anna Ryder Richardson, Kate Adie, John Thomson, Ray Liotta, Nicky Campbell, George Cole, Eric Clapton, Gerald Ford, Daley Thompson, Dame Kiri Te Kanawa, Rob Newman, Debbie Harry, Mike McShane, Axl Rose, James Michener, Bo Diddley, Michael Denison, Michael Medwin, Helen Rollason, Wincey Willis, Frances McDormand, Michael Gore, Nicole Richie, Roman Abramovic, KT Tunstall, Jim Bowen, Andy McNab

Famous women who adopted children

Nicole Kidman, Dame Julie Andrews, Jamie Lee Curtis, Frances McDormand, Sharon Stone, Calista Flockhart, Drew Barrymore, Diane Keaton, Honor Blackman, Michelle Pfeiffer, Mia Farrow, Dawn French, Dame Shirley Bassey, Jilly Cooper, Dame Kiri Te Kanawa, Kirstie Alley, Penelope Keith, Angelina Jolie, Madonna

WOMEN WHO PUT THEIR BABIES UP FOR ADOPTION

Clare Short, Roseanne, Pauline Collins, Joni Mitchell, Sheila Mercier, Kate O'Mara, Linda Lovelace

ONLY CHILDREN

Shannon Elizabeth, Marilyn Manson, Craig David, Adrien Brody, Dale Winton, Teri Hatcher, Alan Bleasdale, David Essex, Barbara Windsor, Sir Elton John, Mick Hucknall, Bob Hoskins, Ulrika Jonsson, Uri Geller, Cherie Lunghi, Lord Melvyn Bragg, David Gower, Penelope Keith, Robert De Niro, Terry Venables, Clive James, Lester Piggott, Harold Pinter, Sir Peter Hall, Miriam Margolyes, Charlotte Church, Dame P.D. James, Vanessa-Mae, Jean-Paul Gaultier, Dame Ruth Rendell, Jacques Chirac, Frederick Forsyth, Sarah Michelle Gellar, Nick Faldo, Barbara Taylor Bradford, Chris Tarrant, Paul Merton, Dr David Starkey, Sir John Mortimer, Michael Parkinson, Ken Hom, David Copperfield, Ruby Wax, Aled Jones, Martina Hingis, Sam Mendes, Harry Enfield, Burt Bacharach, Sir Anthony Hopkins, Sir Peter Ustinov, Sam Torrance, Julie Burchill, Noel Edmonds, Lauren Bacall

KINGS AND THEIR UNFORTUNATE NICKNAMES

King Rudolf **The Sluggard**
(King Rudolf III of Burgundy from 993 to 1032)

King Malcolm **The Maiden**
(King Malcolm IV of Scotland from 1153 to 1165)

King Louis **The Fat**
(King Louis VI of France from 1108 to 1137)

King Ferdinand **The Fickle**
(King Ferdinand I of Portugal from 1367 to 1383)

King Charles **The Mad**
(King Charles VI of France from 1380 to 1422)

King Ivan **The Terrible**
(King Ivan IV of Russia from 1547 to 1584)

King Louis **The Stubborn**
(King Louis X of France from 1314 to 1316)

King Charles **The Bad**
(King Charles II of Navarre from 1349 to 1387)

King Henry **The Impotent**
(King Henry IV of Castile from 1454 to 1474)

King Ethelred **The Unready**
(King Ethelred II of England from 978 to 1016)

KINGS AND THEIR *FORTUNATE* NICKNAMES

King Louis **The Just**
(King Louis XIII of France from 1610 to 1643)

King William **The Good**
(King William II of Sicily from 1166 to 1189)

King Philip **The Handsome**
(King Philip of Castile in 1506; he was
married to Joan The Mad)

King Charles **The Victorious**
(King Charles VII of France from
1422 to 1461)

King Henry **The Saint**
(King Henry II of Germany from
1014 to 1024)

King Richard **The Lionheart**
(King Richard I of England from
1189 to 1199)

King Philip **The Fair**
(King Philip IV of France from 1285 to 1314)

King Ferdinand **The Great**
(King Ferdinand I of Castile from
1035 to 1065)

King Charles **The Wise**
(King Charles V of France from
1364 to 1380)

King Louis **The Well-Beloved**
(King Louis XV of France from
1715 to 1774)

PEOPLE WITH ROSES NAMED AFTER THEM

Anna Ford, Penelope Keith, Sir Paul McCartney, Clive Lloyd, Geoffrey Boycott, Pam Ayres, Dame Vera Lynn, Prince Philip, Tina Turner, Jane Asher, Princess Michael of Kent, Sir Jimmy Savile, Sue Lawley, Dame Julie Andrews, Sir Bobby Charlton, Anne Diamond, Arthur Scargill, Jimmy Greaves, Michael Crawford, Sir Cliff Richard, Angela Rippon, Felicity Kendal, Maureen Lipman, Hannah Gordon, Joanna Lumley, Charlie Dimmock, Whoopi Goldberg

REAL PEOPLE MENTIONED IN BEATLES SONGS

The Queen ('Penny Lane' and 'Mean Mr Mustard')

Edgar Allan Poe ('I Am The Walrus')

Harold Wilson and Edward Heath ('Taxman')

B.B. King, Doris Day and Sir Matt Busby ('Dig It')

Charles Hawtrey ('Two of Us')

Mao Tse-tung ('Revolution')

Sir Walter Raleigh ('I'm So Tired')

Peter Brown ('The Ballad of John And Yoko')

Bob Dylan ('Yer Blues')

THE INFINITE WISDOM OF MARK TWAIN

'There are several good protections against temptation, but the surest is cowardice.'

'Always do right. This will gratify some people, and astonish the rest.'

'When angry, count to four; when very angry, swear.'

'A flea can be taught everything a Congressman can.'

'It takes your enemy and your friend – working together – to hurt you to the heart: the one to slander you and the other to get the news to you.'

'I can live for two months on a good compliment.'

'I was born modest. Not all over but in spots.'

'I am opposed to millionaires – but it would be dangerous to offer me the position.'

'Fewer things are harder to put up with than the annoyance of a good example.'

'Man is the only animal that blushes – or needs to.'

'If you tell the truth you don't have to remember anything.'

'I must have a prodigious quantity of mind; it takes me as much as a week, sometimes, to make it up.'

'Man: a creature made at the end of the week's work when God was tired.'

'Such is the human race, often it seems a pity that Noah didn't miss the boat.'

'Education is what you must acquire without any interference from your schooling.'

'Familiarity breeds contempt ... and children.'

'The public is the only critic whose opinion is worth anything at all.'

THE ADVENTURES OF BARRY HUMPHRIES

Before finding fame as Dame Edna Everage, Humphries was a Dadaist who performed a series of stunts in the name of art.

On his frequent flights between Australia and Britain, Humphries would pass the time by surreptitiously putting some Russian (or vegetable) salad in a sick bag and then, when other passengers were watching, he would pretend to throw up into the bag. He would then proceed to eat its contents. Humphries didn't restrict this 'gag' to aeroplanes but also performed it to a wider public. He would put some Russian salad on the pavement and then return to it later and eat it with a spoon. Once, in Fleet Street in the 1960s, a policeman approached him but was so sickened that he started retching. Humphries took the opportunity to disappear.

One of his favourite tricks was to get a female co-conspirator to dress up as a schoolgirl. The two of them would start kissing and when a policeman showed up to ask him what he was doing with a 'minor', he would flourish her birth certificate proving that she was, in fact, over 18.

One particularly unpleasant stunt was performed – like many of his others – on a train. His friend would board a train pretending to be blind with his leg in plaster and wearing a neck brace. Humphries would then get on board pretending to be a German and start abusing his friend, physically and verbally. Humphries was never challenged by other passengers. Meanwhile, after he got off, his friend would sit there saying, 'Forgive him, forgive him.'

For another stunt, Humphries would fill a public dustbin with rubbish and then, just before it reached the top, he would put in some really expensive food – smoked salmon, cooked chicken, Champagne – and cover this with a layer of rubbish. When people arrived, Humphries, dressed as a tramp, would astonish them by rummaging in the bin and pulling out fabulous delicacies.

In 1968, when the cinema was infested with a plague of ludicrous *avant-garde* films, Humphries invented a 'film director' named Martin

Agrippa, who had supposedly been working with the Blind Man's Cinema and who had made a film which had won the 'Bronze Scrotum' in Helsinki. Together with the (genuine) film director Bruce Beresford, he made a spoof film which was subsequently exhibited at several Festivals of Underground Cinema where it was taken entirely seriously.

With a group of friends, Humphries used to go to a shop every day at the same time and pay for a bar of Lux soap but never take the soap away. They would sometimes get strangers to do the same thing. Each time, the shopkeeper would say, 'You've forgotten your soap,' to which Humphries & Co. would respond, 'We don't want the soap, we just want to buy it!' Eventually, Humphries took the soap out of the shop but returned saying, 'I'm sorry, I forgot to leave the soap.' The shopkeeper eventually moved to another part of town.

One of Humphries's greatest stunts was performed while he was a university student. He took his seat on a Melbourne commuter train. At the first stop, one of his pals boarded the train and served him a grapefruit. At the next stop, another pal took away the grapefruit and gave him cornflakes. And so on – through the eggs and bacon and the coffee – until he had been served a full breakfast.

Humphries invented a 'film director' who had supposedly been working with the Blind Man's Cinema

FORMER WARM-UP MEN

Clive Anderson (*After Midnight*)

Mark Lamarr (*Harry Enfield*)

Michael Barrymore (*Larry Grayson's Generation Game*)

Brian Conley (*Wogan* – but was fired for being 'too funny')

Phill Jupitus (to touring bands – as Porky The Poet)

Rowland Rivron (for Ruby Wax)

Mike Myers (for Timmy Mallett)

Daniel Kitson (*The 11 O'Clock Show*)

Victor Borge (*Bing Crosby's Kraft Music Hall*)

Neil Innes (briefly for *Monty Python*)

Lee Hurst (*Have I Got News For You?*)

Gary Glitter (*Ready Steady Go*)

Peter Kay (*Parkinson*)

Bill Pertwee (*Beggar My Neighbour*)

Jeremy Beadle (Mouthtrap – hosted by Don Maclean)

FAMOUS PEOPLE WITH FAMOUS ANCESTORS

Mike Myers – William Wordsworth

Patricia Cornwell – Harriet Beecher Stowe

Gena Lee Nolin – Sir Isaac Newton

Kyle MacLachlan – Johann Sebastian Bach

Cate Blanchett – Louis Blériot

Tom Hanks – Abraham Lincoln

Glenn Ford – President Martin Van Buren

Prince Philip – Queen Victoria

Helena Bonham Carter – Herbert Asquith

**Judy Garland – President General
Ulysses S. Grant**

Dame Barbara Cartland – Robert The Bruce

Joyce Grenfell – Nancy Astor

David 'Kid' Jensen – Robert Louis
Stevenson

**William Holden – President
Warren G. Harding**

General Colin Powell –
King Edward I

**Basil Rathbone – King
Henry IV**

Richard Nixon – King
Edward III

FAMOUS PEOPLE BORN ON THE VERY SAME DAY AS OTHER FAMOUS PEOPLE

Keith Chegwin and Paul Merton (17.1.57)

Richard Dunwoody and Jane Horrocks (18.1.64)

Charles Darwin and Abraham Lincoln (12.2.1809)

Jerry Springer and Stockard Channing (13.2.44)

Sir Alan Bates and Barry Humphries (17.2.34)

Yoko Ono and Sir Bobby Robson (18.2.33)

Prince Andrew and Leslie Ash (19.2.60)

Douglas Bader and Eddie Waring (21.2.10)

Prince Edward and Jasmine Guy (10.3.64)

Sir Michael Caine and Quincy Jones (14.3.33)

Damon Albarn and Michael Atherton (23.3.68)

Tommy Hilfiger and Peter Powell (24.3.51)

John Major and Vangelis and Eric Idle (29.3.43)

Marlon Brando and Doris Day (3.4.24)

Francis Coppola and Sir David Frost (7.4.39)

Jimmy Osmond and Nick Berry (16.4.63)

Harold 'Dickie' Bird and Jayne Mansfield (19.4.33)

Sachin Tendulkar and Gabby Logan and Lee Westwood (24.4.73)

Andre Agassi and Uma Thurman (29.4.70)

Sir Albert Finney and Glenda Jackson (9.5.36)

Maureen Lipman and Donovan (10.5.46)

Bono and Merlene Ottey (10.5.60)

Ian Dury and Pam St Clement (12.5.42)

Brian Jones and Dino Zoff (28.2.42)

Jackie Mason and Giorgio Armani (9.6.34)

William Hague and Leigh Bowery (26.3.61)

Diana, Princess of Wales and Carl Lewis (1.7.61)

Pam Shriver and Neil Morrissey (4.7.62)

Sylvester Stallone and President George W. Bush (6.7.46)

Dame Diana Rigg and Natalie Wood (20.7.38)

Stanley Kubrick and Bernice Rubens (26.7.28)

Kate Bush and Daley Thompson (30.7.58)

Jason Robinson and Hilary Swank (30.7.74)

Angela Bassett and Madonna (16.8.58)

Robert De Niro and John Humphrys (17.8.43)

Christian Slater and Edward Norton (18.8.69)

Sir Donald Bradman and Lyndon B. Johnson (27.8.08)

Lenny Henry and Michael Jackson (29.8.58)

Chrissie Hynde and Julie Kavner (7.9.51)

Goran Ivanisevic and Stella McCartney (13.9.71)

Tommy Lee Jones and Oliver Stone (15.9.46)

Jarvis Cocker and David Seaman (19.9.63)

Hansie Cronje and Catherine Zeta Jones (25.9.69)

Chris Tarrant and Charles Dance (10.10.46)

Amanda Burton and Fiona Fullerton (10.10.56)

Dannii Minogue and Snoop Dogg (20.10.71)

Hillary Rodham Clinton and Jaclyn Smith (26.10.47)

Robert Jones and Sean Hughes (10.11.65)

Daryl Hannah and Julianne Moore (3.12.60)

Keith Floyd and Richard Whiteley (28.12.43)

John Denver and Sir Ben Kingsley (31.12.43)

NON-PROFESSIONAL GOLFERS WHO SCORED HOLES-IN-ONE IN GOLF

Jimmy Tarbuck, Mike Reid, Richard Nixon, Graham Gooch, Bob Hope, Bing Crosby, Sir Henry Cooper, Michael Lynagh, Sir Bobby Charlton, Johnny Mathis (five times), Joan Fontaine, Sandi Toksvig, Piers Morgan, Joel Cadbury

PEOPLE WHO APPEARED IN BRITISH SOAPS AS THEMSELVES

Paula Yates (*Brookside*)

Lily Savage (Brookside)

The Nolan Sisters (*Brookside*)

Michael Parkinson (Brookside)

Linda Lusardi (*Hollyoaks*)

Ian Botham (Emmerdale)

Eamonn Holmes (*Brookside*)

Lorraine Kelly (Brookside)

Sarah Greene (*Brookside*)

Zandra Rhodes (The Archers)

Sir Terry Wogan (*The Archers*)

Chris Moyles (*The Archers*)

Alan Titchmarsh (The Archers)

Anneka Rice (The Archers)

Loyd Grossman (*Brookside*)

Freddie Trueman (*Emmerdale*)

Bernard Manning (*Coronation Street*)

Russell Grant (*Brookside*)

Princess Margaret (*The Archers*)

Chris Lowe (*Neighbours*)

Harold Macmillan (*The Archers*)

Martin Offiah (*Emmerdale*)

Bruce Grobbelaar (*Brookside*)

Carol Smillie (*Brookside*)

Graham Norton (*Brookside*)

Prince Charles (*Coronation Street*)

Marti Pellow (*Emmerdale*)

PEOPLE WHO MADE GUEST APPEARANCES IN SITUATION COMEDIES

Linda McCartney (*Bread*)

John Cleese (*Cheers*)

Vincent Hanna (*Blackadder The Third*)

Roy Hattersley (*Chef*)

Lulu (*Absolutely Fabulous*)

Kylie Minogue (*The Vicar of Dibley*)

George Hamilton (*Birds of A Feather*)

Larry King (*Spin City*)

Midge Ure (*Filthy, Rich & Catflap*)

Noel Edmonds (*The Detectives*)

Rolf Harris (*Goodnight Sweetheart*)

Sir Ludovic Kennedy (*Yes Minister*)

Carol Smillie (*2Point4 Children*)

Jenny Agutter (*Red Dwarf*)

Ainsley Harriott (*Red Dwarf*)

Timothy Spall (*Red Dwarf*)

Koo Stark (*Red Dwarf*)

Esther McVey (*Goodnight Sweetheart*)

Sean Bean (*The Vicar of Dibley*)

Jeremy Paxman (*The Vicar of Dibley*)

Twiggy (*Absolutely Fabulous*)

Laurence Llewelyn-Bowen (*The League of Gentlemen*)

Tamzin Outhwaite (*Men Behaving Badly*)

Leslie Ash (*Get Fit With Brittas*)

REAL PEOPLE WHO APPEARED IN *THE BEANO*

Chris Evans (with Dennis The Menace)

Geri Halliwell (with Minnie The Minx)

Linford Christie (with Billy Whizz)

Ronan Keating (with Plug from The Bash Street Kids)

Alan Shearer (with Ball Boy)

Michael Owen (with Ball Boy)

Ken Dodd (with Dennis The Menace's dog Gnasher)

Tony and Cherie Blair (with Ivy The Terrible)

David Jason as Del Boy Trotter (with Roger The Dodger)

Rowan Atkinson as Mr Bean (with Calamity James)

COLLECTORS OF ...

Old photographs (Brian May)

Dolls' houses and furniture (Dame Judi Dench)

1940s typewriters (Tom Hanks)

Ornamental ducks (Josie Lawrence)

Comics (Jonathan Ross)

Old radios (Steve Wright)

Bird and animal skulls (Vic Reeves)

Porcelain pigs (Janet Jackson)

Old tin-plate toys (Michael Barrymore)

***Planet of The Apes* memorabilia (Shane Richie)**

Shirley Temple memorabilia (Melissa Joan Hart)

Antique toys (Dustin Hoffman)

Antique books (John Simpson)

Old fruit machines (Sid Owen)

Literary autographs (Sir Tom Stoppard)

Art – particularly Victorian nudes (Ozzy Osbourne)

Beanie babies (Nick Carter)

Garden gnomes (Cerys Matthews)

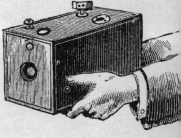

Vintage Polaroid cameras (Brendan Fraser)

Dried insects – which she paints and frames (Claudia Schiffer)

Antique watches (Nicolas Cage)

Loo seats (Prince Charles)

American comic books (Lenny Henry)

Chairs (Brad Pitt)

Puppets (David Arquette)

Medical prosthetics such as eyes and limbs; vintage metal lunchboxes (Marilyn Manson)

Inflatable ducks (Kim Basinger)

Coat hangers (Penelope Cruz)

Snakes (Slash)

Thimbles (José Carreras)

PEOPLE WHO LAUNCHED THEIR OWN FRAGRANCES

Linda Evans – Forever Krystle

Dame Elizabeth Taylor – White Diamonds

Englebert Humperdinck – Release Me

Omar Sharif – Omar Sharif

Sophia Loren – Sophia

Björn Borg – Signature

Cynthia Lennon – Cynthia Lennon's Woman

Joan Collins – Scoundrel

Luciano Pavarotti – Luciano Pavarotti Parfum For Men

Catherine Deneuve – Deneuve

Naomi Campbell – Naomi

Jennifer Lopez – J-Lo

Christina Aguilera – Fetish

Isabella Rossellini – Manifesto

PEOPLE WHO LAUNCHED THEIR OWN PRODUCTS

Burt Reynolds – jewellery

Joan Collins – jeans

Paul Newman – salad dressing

Jerry Hall – swimwear

Pepsi and Shirlie – girls' clothes

Princess Stephanie – swimwear

Ken Kercheval – popcorn

Joan Rivers – jewellery

Denise Van Outen – T-shirts

Iman – Iman cosmetics

Bo Derek – shampoos, conditioners and fragrances for dogs (the brand name is Bless The Beast)

Kelly LeBrock – Kelly LeBrock's Homeopathic Remedy Kit For Kids

Jaclyn Smith – perfume and clothing

Clint Eastwood – Pale Rider Ale

Elle Macpherson – designer lingerie

Ted Nugent – beef jerky

Jay-Z – Roc-a-Wear clothing

Marie Osmond – cosmetics, porcelain dolls and clothing patterns

Christina Aguilera – cosmetics

Sadie Frost – Frost French clothing

Jennifer Lopez – clothing ($10 million deal with Tommy Hilfiger's younger brother)

Carlos Santana – shoes that 'radiate rhythm, passion and energy'

Loyd Grossman – pasta sauces

Chaka Khan – range of chocolates called Chakalates

Kylie Minogue – lingerie range called Love Kylie

Missy Elliott – lipstick: Misdemeanor Lipstick

Busta Rhymes – clothing range called Bushi

Jane Seymour – clothing range

PEOPLE WHO INSURED PARTS OF THEIR BODY

Michael Flatley – legs for £25 million

Bruce Springsteen – voice for £3.5 million

Dolly Parton – bust for £2 million

Ken Dodd – teeth for £4 million

Jamie Lee Curtis – legs for £700,000

Keith Richards – third finger of left hand for £1 million

Mark King – hands for £1 million

Jennifer Lopez – body for $1 billion (£660 million)

Tina Turner – lips for $1 million and breasts for $750,000 (£5 million overall)

Mariah Carey – body for £1 billion

Jenny Frost – body for £1 million

GUEST EDITORS OF FRENCH *VOGUE*

The Dalai Lama, Sir Alfred Hitchcock, Nelson Mandela, Federico Fellini, Joan Miró, Princess Caroline of Monaco, Salvador Dalí, Orson Welles, David Hockney, Martin Scorsese, Marc Chagall, Mikhail Baryshnikov, Roman Polanski

GUEST EDITORS

Lord Snowdon – *Country Life*

Cherie Blair – *Prima*

Mario Testino – *Visionaire*

Damien Hirst – *The Big Issue*

Joan Collins – *Marie Claire* (UK)

Jenny Eclair – *Loaded*

Isabelle Huppert – *Cahiers Du Cinema*

Gwyneth Paltrow – *Marie Claire* (US)

Jennifer Saunders & Joanna Lumley – *Marie Claire* (UK)

Sir Terence Conran – *Country Life*

Susan Sarandon – *Marie Claire* (US)

Roseanne – *New Yorker, National Enquirer*

Geri Halliwell – *New Woman*

Victoria Wood – *Radio Times*

Jerry Springer – *Chat*

Leonardo DiCaprio – *National Geographic* children's magazine

PEOPLE WITH FAMOUS AUNTS

Nigel Havers – Dame Elizabeth Butler-Sloss

Jemma Redgrave – Vanessa Redgrave

Macaulay Culkin – Bonnie Bedelia

Alessandra Mussolini – Sophia Loren

Bridget Fonda – Jane Fonda

Jodie Kidd – Vicki Hodge

George Clooney – Rosemary Clooney

N.B. Paris Hilton's great aunt is Zsa Zsa Gabor

PEOPLE WITH FAMOUS UNCLES

Alan Howard – Leslie Howard

Judge Jules – Rick Stein

Sir Bobby Charlton – Jackie Milburn

Ewan McGregor – Denis Lawson

Nicolas Cage – Francis Coppola

Harriet Walter – Christopher Lee

Jack Davenport – Jonathan Aitken

Penelope Wilton – Bill Travers

PARENTS OF TWINS

Ben Elton, Donald Sutherland, Phil Silvers, Gordon Ramsay, George W. Bush, Denzel Washington, Al Pacino, Ally McCoist, Jeremy Paxman, Cheryl Baker, Robert De Niro, Earl Spencer, Ivan Lendl, Jane Seymour, Nigel Benn, Fern Britton, Mollie Sugden, James Galway, Michael Buerk, Gary Oldman, Dean Gaffney, Pele, Pat Cash, Graham Gooch, Sir Alan Bates, David Essex, Baroness Margaret Thatcher, Mel Gibson, Mark Knopfler, Judy Finnigan, Stan Boardman, Cybill Shepherd, James Stewart, Ingrid Bergman, Bing Crosby, Mia Farrow, Günter Grass

PARENTS OF TRIPLETS

Rodney Bewes

Tony O'Reilly

Richard Thomas (John-Boy in *The Waltons*)

Peter Barnes (playwright and director – at age of 71)

Jackie Clune

PEOPLE WITH A TWIN BROTHER/SISTER

Alanis Morissette (Wade)

Joseph Fiennes (Jake)

Vin Diesel (Paul)

Derek Thompson (Elaine)

Will Young (Rupert)

Matt Goss (Luke)

Alec Bedser (Eric)

Gayle Blakeney (Gillian)

Roger Black (Julia)

Reggie Kray (Ronnie)

Carol Thatcher (Mark)

Babs Beverley (Teddy)

Sir Henry Cooper (George)

Anthony Shaffer (Peter)

Isabella Rossellini (Ingrid)

Keith Chegwin (Jeff)

Alan Yentob (Robert)

John Sessions (Maggie)

Pier Angeli (Marisa)

John Boulting (Roy)

Tim Gullikson (Tom)

Elizabeth Carling (Laura)

Kiefer Sutherland (Rachel)

Jerry Hall (Terry – sister)

Lowri Turner (Catrin)

Benjamin Zephaniah (Velda)

MEN WHO HAD TWINS WHO DIED AT BIRTH OR IN CHILDHOOD

Elvis Presley, David Jason, Liberace, William Randolph Hearst, Ed Sullivan, Freddie Starr, Edgar Allan Poe, Leonardo da Vinci, Lewis Carroll, Oscar Wilde, Jay Kay, Justin Timberlake, Jim Broadbent, Philip K. Dick

Andy Garcia was born with a partly formed twin on his shoulder

PEOPLE WHO CAME FROM LARGE FAMILIES

Josephine Cox (one of 10 children)

Sol Campbell (one of 10 children)

Tim Allen (one of 10 children)

Rosie Perez (one of 10 children)

Mel Gibson (one of 11 children)

Richard Farleigh (one of 11 children)

Ms Dynamite (one of 11 children)

David Emanuel (one of 11 children)

Lucas Radebe (one of 11 children)

Benny Goodman (one of 11 children)

Lewis Carroll (one of 11 children)

Brian Lara (one of 11 children)

Glen Campbell (one of 11 children)

Dolly Parton (one of 12 children)

Sir Gordon Richards (one of 12 children)

Little Richard (one of 12 children)

George Burns (one of 13 children)

Perry Como (one of 13 children)

Little Eva (one of 13 children)

Richard Burton (one of 13 children)

Bud Flanagan (one of 13 children)

Nicolae Ceausescu (one of 13 children)

Me-One (one of 13 children)

Celine Dion (one of 14 children)

Charles Bronson (one of 15 children)

Billy Blanks (one of 15 children)

Chris Montes (the last of 20 children)

Sonny Liston (one of 25 children)

PEOPLE WHO HAVE/HAD FAMOUS FATHERS-IN-LAW

Gregor Fisher – Peter Vaughan

Woody Allen – André Previn

Jonny Lee Miller – Jon Voight

Barry Humphries – Sir Stephen Spender

Loyd Grossman – Sir David Puttnam

Anthony Quinn – Cecil B. De Mille

Axl Rose – Don Everly

Sir Charles Chaplin – Eugene O'Neill

Karen Dotrice – Wilfrid Hyde-White

Richard Wagner – Franz Liszt

Belinda Carlisle – James Mason

Sir David Frost – The Duke of Norfolk

John McEnroe – Ryan O'Neal

Vincent Hanna – Lord Gerry Fitt

W. Somerset Maugham – Dr Barnardo

Shannen Doherty – George Hamilton

Peter Lawford – Dan Rowan

Artie Shaw – Jerome Kern

Oskar Werner – Tyrone Power

Geraldo Rivera – Kurt Vonnegut Jr

W.H. Auden – Thomas Mann

Burt Lancaster – Ernie Kovacks

Wood Harrelson – Neil Simon

Sheryl Lee – Neil Diamond

David O. Selznick – Louis B. Mayer

Daniel Day-Lewis – Arthur Miller

P.J. O'Rourke – Sidney Lumet

Tony Blair – Anthony Booth

Boris Johnson – Charles Wheeler

Andrew Marr – Lord Jack Ashley

Lauren Holly – Anthony Quinn

Jeremy Irons – Cyril Cusack

George Clooney – Martin Balsam

Arnold Schwarzenegger – Sargent Shriver

Carl Wilson – Dean Martin

PEOPLE WHO HAVE/HAD FAMOUS MOTHERS-IN-LAW

Liam Neeson – Vanessa Redgrave

Sidney Lumet – Lena Horne

Simon Williams – Dame Celia Johnson

Janet Dibley – Janet Brown

Gary Oldman – Ingrid Bergman

Martin Scorsese – Ingrid Bergman

Cousins

Christopher Lee and Ian Fleming

Ginger Rogers and Rita Hayworth

Jon Snow and Peter Snow

Richard Briers and Terry-Thomas

Whitney Houston and Dionne Warwick

Peter Townsend (Princess Margaret's ex-lover) and Hugh Gaitskell

Natasha Richardson and Jemma Redgrave

Patrick Macnee and David Niven

Rip Torn and Sissy Spacek

Carole Lombard and Howard Hawks

Lauren Bacall and Shimon Peres

John Inman and Josephine Tewson

Ronald Harwood and Sir Antony Sher

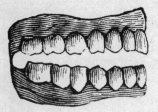

People who overcame stammers

Bruce Willis, Carly Simon, Sir Winston Churchill, Harvey Keitel, King George VI, Sam Neill, Frankie Howerd, James Earl Jones, Martyn Lewis, Paul Young, W. Somerset Maugham, Marilyn Monroe, Charles Darwin, Arnold Bennett, Lewis Carroll, Nicholas Parsons

THE FIRST 10 SONGS PLAYED ON RADIO 1

'Flowers In The Rain' (The Move)

'Massachusetts' (The Bee Gees)

'Even The Bad Times Are Good' (The Tremeloes)

'Fakin' It' (Simon and Garfunkel)

'The Day I Met Marie' (Cliff Richard)

'You Can't Hurry Love' (The Supremes)

'The Last Waltz' (Engelbert Humperdinck)

'Baby Now That I've Found You' (The Foundations)

'Good Times' (Eric Burdon and the Animals)

'A Banda' (Herb Alpert and the Tijuana Brass)

THE FIRST 10 SONGS PLAYED ON
TOP OF THE POPS

'I Only Want To Be With You' (Dusty Springfield)

'I Wanna Be Your Man' (The Rolling Stones)

'Glad All Over' (The Dave Clark Five)

'Stay' (The Hollies)

'Hippy Hippy Shake' (The Swinging Blue Jeans)

'Don't Talk To Him' (Cliff Richard and the Shadows)

'You Were Made For Me' (Freddie and the Dreamers)

'Twenty-four Hours From Tulsa' (Gene Pitney)

'She Loves You' (The Beatles)

'I Want To Hold Your Hand' (The Beatles)

WHAT FAMOUS PEOPLE DID IN WORLD WAR TWO

Sir Dirk Bogarde served as a captain in the Queen's Royal Regiment and saw action in France, Germany and the Far East. He also helped to liberate the Nazi concentration camp of Belsen.

Denholm Elliott served in the RAF until being shot down in a bombing mission over Denmark. He was captured and sent to a POW camp in Silesia for the last three years of the war. He gave a hugely praised performance as Eliza Doolittle in the camp production of *Pygmalion*.

Lord Denis Healey was a major in the Army and was the Beachmaster in the Anzio landings in Italy, for which he was mentioned in dispatches. He was also awarded a military MBE.

Tony Benn joined the RAF in 1943 at the age of 18. He got his wings just as Germany surrendered and so switched to the Fleet Air Arm to fight against Japan.

Kirk Douglas was a lieutenant in the US Navy and saw action in the Pacific before internal injuries suffered in combat led to an early discharge.

Paul Eddington joined ENSA but when he was called up registered as a conscientious objector. He was duly dismissed from ENSA but the war ended before his case (for being a conscientious objector) could be heard.

Sir Peter Ustinov served as a private in the Royal Sussex Regiment before being transferred to the position of David Niven's batman so that they could collaborate on the film *The Way Ahead*.

Hughie Green tried unsuccessfully to get into the RAF and so joined the Royal Canadian Air Force.

Richard Todd served with the Light Infantry, the Parachute Regiment and the 6th Airborne Division seeing action on (among others) D Day and in the Battle of the Bulge.

E.W. 'Jim' Swanton served as an acting major in the Royal Artillery before being captured in Singapore in 1942 and spending the rest of the war in a Japanese POW camp.

Enoch Powell rose through the ranks from private in the Royal Warwickshire Regiment to become a brigadier

Sammy Davis Jr. served in the US Army but was bullied by white southerners – five of whom once painted him white. However, he was taught to read by a black sergeant.

Sir Patrick Moore served in the RAF as a navigator with Bomber Command, reaching the rank of flight lieutenant.

Sheila Mercier served in the WAAF Signals, rising from section officer to adjutant.

Patrick Macnee served in the Royal Navy as a lieutenant, winning the Atlantic Medal.

Sir Ludovic Kennedy served in the Royal Navy (Volunteer Reserve) as a lieutenant and was also private secretary and ADC to the Governor of Newfoundland.

Sir Edmund Hillary served as a navigator in the Royal New Zealand Air Force in the Pacific.

Burt Lancaster served as a private in the American Fifth Army, having enlisted immediately after Pearl Harbor.

Ian Fleming served as assistant to the director of Naval Intelligence. After D Day, he was put in charge of Assault Unit No. 30, which was known as Fleming's Private Navy.

Kenneth Wolstenholme served as a bomber pilot in the RAF. He flew 100 missions over Germany and won the Distinguished Flying Cross (DFC) and Bar.

Walter Matthau served in the US Army in France (where he lost his virginity).

Tony Curtis served in the US Navy in the Pacific where he witnessed the Japanese surrender.

Jon Pertwee served as an officer in the Royal Navy (Volunteer Reserve). He served on HMS *Hood* and was lucky to be on shore leave when his ship was sunk by the *Bismarck* with only three survivors.

Ronald Searle was captured by the Japanese and was sent to the infamous Changi POW camp. He was also forced to work on the Burma–Siam railway.

Sir Kingsley Amis served as an officer in the Royal Corps of Signals and landed in Normandy three weeks after D Day.

Sir Michael Hordern was a Royal Navy officer and spent much of the war aboard the aircraft carrier *Illustrious* where he was also in charge of 'ship's entertainments'.

Donald Pleasence declared himself to be a conscientious objector at the start of the war and was sent to the Lake District to work as a forester. However, he had a change of heart and joined the RAF. He was shot down in France and spent the last year of the war in a German POW camp.

Sir Alec Guinness served in the Royal Navy in Combined Operations and captained a ship.

Marilyn Monroe worked in a Defense Plant while her then husband (James Dougherty) went into the Merchant Marines.

Audrey Hepburn starved in occupied Holland, living on two loaves of bread for one month.

Rod Steiger lied about his age to join the US Navy as a torpedoman on a destroyer in the South Pacific and saw action at Iwo Jima.

James Stewart saw active service as a pilot in the US Air Force with the rank of colonel.

Michael Foot was appointed acting editor of the London *Evening Standard*.

Dick Francis served as a pilot officer in the RAF, flying Lancaster and Wellington bombers.

Clive Dunn was captured and spent some of the war in a German POW camp.

Christopher Lee served in the RAF as a flight lieutenant and with Intelligence and Special Forces in the Western Desert, Malta, Sicily, Italy and Central Europe. He was mentioned in dispatches in 1944.

Jean Borotra was sports minister in the Vichy (pro-Nazi) French Government.

Bill Edrich was an RAF pilot who won the DFC for taking part in a daylight attack on Cologne in 1941. In one 48-hour period, he claims to have flown two bombing missions over occupied Europe, scored a century for Norfolk and made love to a local lass.

Tony Bennett served with the US Army in Europe as an infantryman.

Sir Jimmy Savile was sent down the mines as a Bevin Boy.

Murray Walker drove a tank.

PEOPLE WHO ATTENDED THE SAME SCHOOLS

Sir Ben Kingsley, Robert Powell, Michael Atherton and John Crawley (Manchester Grammar)

Sir Richard Branson and George Melly (Stowe)

Stephen Fry, Johnny Vaughan, Jonathan Agnew, Stephen Dorrell and John Suchet (Uppingham)

Sir Colin Cowdrey and Frederick Forsyth (Tonbridge)

Lord Brian Rix and A.J.P. Taylor (Bootham)

Bob Willis and Terry Jones (Royal Grammar, Guildford)

Kevin Whately, Rob Andrew, Rory Underwood and Craig Raine (Barnard Castle)

Peter Sissons and Steven Norris (Liverpool Institute High School For Boys)

Stewart Copeland, John Sergeant, John Standing, Tony Blackburn, Duncan Goodhew and Gareth Edwards (Millfield)

Mollie Sugden and Lord Denis Healey (Drake and Tonsons' Kindergarten)

Mick Fleetwood and Jeremy Irons (Sherborne)

Emile Heskey and Gary Lineker (City of Leicester School)

Jonathan King, David Dimbleby, Peter Gabriel and Nicky Henson (Charterhouse)

Bonnie Langford, Sarah Brightman and Nigel Havers (Arts Educational, London)

Sir P.G. Wodehouse, Raymond Chandler, Bob Monkhouse and Peter Lilley (Dulwich)

Jamie Theakston, Christopher Hampton, Sir Tim Rice and Tom Sharpe (Lancing)

Kelly Brook and Naomi Campbell (Italia Conti)

Chris Patten and Julian Clary (St Benedict's)

David Gilmour and Sir Peter Hall (The Perse School, Cambridge)

Ian Hislop and Terry-Thomas (Ardingly)

Imogen Stubbs, Shirley Conran, Harriet Harman, Celia Brayfield and Flora Fraser (St Paul's Girls)

Phil Tufnell, Bernard Jenkin, Barry Norman and Geoffrey Palmer (Highgate)

Beryl Reid and Judith Chalmers (Withington)

Nicky Campbell and Magnus Magnusson (Edinburgh Academy)

Peter Purves, Chris Lowe and Jimmy Armfield (Arnold)

Sir Malcolm Rifkind, Scott Hastings, Gordon Kennedy and Gavin Hastings (George Watson's)

Jeremy Paxman and Denholm Elliott (Malvern Boys)

Neil Diamond and Barbra Streisand (Erasmus Hall High, New York)

John Major and Raymond Briggs (Rutlish School, Merton)

Roger Lloyd Pack, Gyles Brandreth, Irina Brook and Amanda Craig (Bedales)

Rupert Everett, Michael Ancram, Lawrence Dallaglio, Edward Stourton and Piers Paul Read (Ampleforth)

Katherine Hamnett, Mary Archer, Nicola Horlick and Amanda Wakeley (Cheltenham Ladies)

Sir Stirling Moss, Sir Alan Ayckbourn, Sir Michael Bonallack, Gerald Harper and Simon MacCorkindale (Haileybury)

Chris de Burgh, Captain Mark Phillips, Ian Balding and Toby Balding (Marlborough)

Kyran Bracken, Bill Cash, Sir Arthur Conan Doyle and Charles Laughton (Stonyhurst)

Jeremy Clarkson, Nick Raynsford and Graeme Garden (Repton)

Kenneth Clarke and Leslie Crowther (Nottingham High School)

Dame Judi Dench and Margaret Drabble (The Mount, York)

Chubby Checker and Eddie Fisher (South Philadelphia High)

Des Lynam and Paul Scofield (Varndean Grammar)

Sir Alastair Burnet and Martin Bell (The Leys)

John Cleese, John Inverdale, Clive Swift, Simon Russell Beale and Chris Serle (Clifton)

Kenneth Cranham and Ken Livingstone (Tulse Hill Comprehensive)

Michael Winner and A.A. Gill (St Christopher, Letchworth)

John Gummer and Dinsdale Landen (King's, Rochester)

Peter Cook, Brough Scott and Ted Dexter (Radley)

Jools Holland and William G. Stewart (Shooters' Hill)

Robert Redford and Stacy Keach (Van Nuys High, California)

Andi Peters, Michael Aspel and Geoffrey Robinson (Emanuel)

Sir Ian McKellen and Nigel Short (Bolton Boys)

Jenny Agutter, Fiona Fullerton, Joanna David and Hayley Mills (Elmhurst)

Dame Maggie Smith and Miriam Margolyes (Oxford High)

Barry Cryer and Gerald Kaufman (Leeds Grammar)

Les Dennis and Sir Paul McCartney (Stockton Wood Primary)

Helena Bonham Carter, Angela Lansbury and Fay Weldon (South Hampstead High)

Rory Bremner, Christopher Lee, David Suchet, Peter Snow and Robin Oakley (Wellington College)

Michael Buerk and Johnnie Walker (Solihull)

Graham Greene and Michael Meacher (Berkhamsted)

Indira Gandhi, Claire Bloom and Dame Iris Murdoch (Badminton)

David Hockney and Adrian Moorhouse (Bradford Grammar)

Michael Fish and Michael Praed (Eastbourne)

Emma Thompson, Charlotte Coleman and Sue Carpenter (Camden School For Girls)

Tim Pigott-Smith, Lord Richard Attenborough, Sir David Attenborough and Mark Cox (Wyggeston Grammar)

Ann-Margret and Bruce Dern (New Trier High, Illinois)

Michael Palin and Sir Rex Harrison (Birkdale)

Hugh Grant, Simon Hughes, Alan Rickman, Keith Vaz and Mel Smith (Latymer Upper)

Mark Nicholas, Lord David Owen and Richard Adams (Bradfield)

Matthew Pinsent, Bamber Gascoigne and Patrick Macnee (Eton)

Keith Floyd and Lord Jeffrey Archer (Wellington, Somerset)

Esther Rantzen and Eleanor Bron (North London Collegiate)

Alan Bennett and John Craven (Leeds Modern)

Harold Pinter and Sir Michael Caine (Hackney Downs)

Salman Rushdie, Christopher Brasher, Alan Howarth, Andrew Rawnsley, Nicholas Winterton and Robert Hardy (Rugby)

Douglas Adams, Keith Allen, Jack Straw, Noel Edmonds and Griff Rhys-Jones (Brentwood)

Sir Peter Ustinov, Imogen Stubbs, Tony Benn, Shane MacGowan, Gavin Rossdale, Matthew Freud, Nigel Planer, Corin Redgrave and Lord Andrew Lloyd Webber (Westminster)

Baroness Lynda Chalker and Sarah Miles (Roedean)

Sir Tom Stoppard and Ade Edmondson (Pocklington)

Barry Davies and Brian Moore (Cranbrook)

John Patten and Paul Merton (Wimbledon College)

Samantha Bond, Nigella Lawson and Davina McCall (Godolphin and Latymer)

Tony Blair and Rowan Atkinson (Durham Choristers Preparatory School)

John Wayne, Cameron Diaz and Snoop Dogg (Long Beach Polytechnic High School)

Kerry Katona and Chris Evans (Padgate High School, Warrington)

CONVENT SCHOOLGIRLS

Dame Helen Mirren, Joanna Lumley, Barbara Windsor, Donna D'Errico, Caroline Aherne, Zoe Ball, Sue Barker, Samantha Fox, Patsy Kensit, Genevieve Bujold, Janet Dibley, Marianne Faithfull, Cherie Blair, Kathy Burke, Ann Widdecombe, Sarah Kennedy, Mia Farrow, Dillie Keane, Stephanie Beacham, Kristin Scott Thomas, Lisa Butcher, Andrea Corr, Caroline Corr, Sharon Corr

PEOPLE WHO WERE BULLIED AT SCHOOL

Gwyneth Paltrow (because she was 'gawky')

Harrison Ford (because he 'liked to hang out with girls')

Anthea Turner (because of her 'posh' accent)

Gillian Anderson (because of her 'independent' and 'bossy' attitude)

Prince Charles (because he was heir to the throne – was especially bullied during rugby games)

Marcella Detroit (because she was Jewish)

Mel Gibson (because of his American accent at his Australian school)

Sandra Bullock (because she was 'ugly')

Tom Cruise (because he 'was always the new kid in town')

Norman Pace (because he was so small)

Michelle Pfeiffer (because of her 'big lips')

Damon Albarn (because the other boys thought he was a 'gayboy')

Betty Boo (because she was a bookworm)

Sophie Dahl (by a boy who fancied her but whom she rejected)

Whitney Houston (because her 'hair was too straight' and her 'skin was too white')

Dannii Minogue (because she appeared on an Australian TV variety show at the age of ten)

Woody Allen (because of his name, Allen Konigsberg – 'I'd tell them my name was Frank, but they'd still beat me up')

Kate Winslet ('I was mentally bullied' – because of her weight)

Martin Clunes (taunted about his looks)

Patrick Swayze (because he liked to dance)

Ralph Fiennes ('for being a poof')

Joe Jackson (for being 'a bit of a misfit there, a sensitive kid who was into reading and classical music')

Jude Law (at a comprehensive in south-east London where suspects in the Stephen Lawrence murder were pupils; he moved to a private school where he was also bullied)

Dervla Kirwan (because she was shy)

Christina Aguilera (because she appeared on TV. In 2000, she got her own back on one of the bullies by driving in her sports car to the McDonald's where the girl worked. 'I heard you were working here and wanted to say hello,' she said)

Eminem (because his mum used to move all the time)

Victoria Beckham (because of her wealthy background; girls at school would push her around and swear at her in the playground and call her names because she had spots)

Ricky Martin (became the victim of a school bully called Manuel at the age of ten: 'He used to push me around and goad me into having a scrap, but I never fought back,' says Ricky)

Pierce Brosnan (for being Irish)

Kate Bush (for being skinny)

Gabrielle (because of a lazy eyelid on her right eye, which made her look different from the other children at school)

Robert Carlyle (because he had no shoes and long hair)

Winona Ryder (because of her androgynous look)

Bryan McFadden (because of his 'puppy fat')

Natalie Imbruglia ('for having big lips and big eyes')

Jodie Marsh ('for being what they call a boffin')

PEOPLE WHO WERE BULLIES (SELF-CONFESSED) AT SCHOOL

Stella McCartney, Jack Straw, David Schwimmer, Fiona Phillips, John Hegley, Charlie Drake

PEOPLE WHO WERE EDUCATED AT HOME

Dame Agatha Christie, Gerald Durrell, Molly Keane, C. S. Lewis, Sir Yehudi Menuhin, Alexander Graham Bell, Caitlin Moran, The Queen, George Bernard Shaw, Mary Wesley, Britney Spears, Joaquin Phoenix, The Everly Brothers

PEOPLE AND THEIR NICKNAMES FROM SCHOOLDAYS

Prince Andrew – The Sniggerer

Prince Edward – Jaws

Prince Philip – Flop

Prince William – Wombat

George Michael – Yog

Kate Moss – Mosschops

Cindy Crawford – Crawdaddy

Felicity Kendal – Fatty Foo

Beryl Bainbridge – Basher

Bob Geldof – Liver Lips

Kate Winslet – Blubber

Steven Spielberg – The Retard

Tony Robinson – Mighty Mouse

Sir Michael Caine – The Professor

Steve Wright – Concorde

Ronnie Wood – Cleopatra

Liam Gallagher – Weetabix

Noel Gallagher – Brezhnev

Sara Cox – Tefal (because of her high forehead) and Crazy Legs (because she was born with a clickyhip and has bent knees)

Michael Owen – Mincer

Cameron Diaz – Skeletor (because she was so skinny)

Alice Beer – Half-pint

Elle Macpherson – Smelly Elly

Rebecca Romijn-Stamos – Jolly Blonde Giant

Victoria Beckham – Acne Face

Ricky Martin – Kiki (this is also slang in Asia for 'pussy')

Geri Halliwell – Pancake (because of her flat chest)

Thom Yorke – Salamander (on account of his 'weird, wonky, reptile eyes')

Leonardo DiCaprio – The Noodle

Fiona Apple – Dog

Rowan Atkinson – Moon Man, Doopie and Zoonie

Puff Daddy – Born Sean Combs, he was given the nickname Puff because, as a child, he would huff and puff when angry

Sophia Loren – The Stick or Toothpick (because she was so thin)

Will Smith – The Prince (given to him by a teacher because of his regal attitude)

Denise Richards – Fish Lips

Kate Hudson – Hammerhead Shark (her brother's nickname because of the space between her eyes)

Charlie Dimmock – Charlie Bubbles (her headmaster's nickname for her because of her curls)

Jeff Goldblum – Bubwires ('because I had braces on my teeth when nobody else did and I think they were saying "barbed wires"')

Justin Timberlake – Brillo Pad (because of his curly locks)

Sophie Anderton – Thunder-thighs

Robert De Niro – Bobby Milk (because he was so white)

Nicole Kidman – Stalky

Kylie Minogue – Shorty

Davina McCall – Div

Gisele Bundchen – Oli (short for Olive Oyl because she was so tall and skinny)

Shane Filan – Shorty

Britney Spears – Boo-Boo

Elijah Wood – Little Monkey

PEOPLE WHO WERE EXPELLED FROM SCHOOL

Martin Amis (from Battersea Grammar for bunking off school at the age of 14 for a few months to play a part in the film *A High Wind In Jamaica*)

Roger Daltrey (from Acton Grammar School for smoking and refusing to wear school uniform)

Boy George (from Eltham Green School for – according to his headmaster – 'not coming to school and not working')

Jackie Collins (from Francis Holland School for smoking)

Jade Jagger (from St Mary's Calne for sneaking out on a date with her then boyfriend Josh Astor)

Stephen Fry (from Uppingham for theft)

Guy Ritchie (from Stanbridge Earls School near Andover for being in a girl's room or for snorting sulphate on Sports Day – depending on whether you listen to his dad or to him)

Macy Gray (from boarding school after, she says, reporting a dean who made improper physical contact)

Dan Aykroyd (from St Pius X Preparatory Seminary for committing acts of 'minor' delinquency)

Nicolas Cage (from elementary school for putting dead grasshoppers in the egg salad on picnic day)

Salma Hayek (from a Louisiana boarding school for setting alarm clocks back three hours)

Marilyn Manson (from a private conservative Christian school)

Kevin Spacey (from a military academy for hitting a classmate with a tyre)

Jeremy Clarkson (from Repton for many minor offences which his headmaster compared to being poked in the chest every day for five years)

Gabriel Byrne (from a seminary after being caught smoking in a graveyard)

Jeremy Beadle (from Orpington Secondary Modern for – among other things – hanging a pair of trousers on a flagpole)

Joshua Jackson (from two schools – one for poor attendance and the other for 'being mouthy')

Matthew Modine (from at least two high schools)

Jim Broadbent (from Leighton Park, just before his A-levels, for drinking)

PEOPLE WHO GOT FIRSTS AT UNIVERSITY

Imogen Stubbs (English, Cambridge)

Martin Bell (English, Cambridge)

David Baddiel (English, Cambridge)

Sir Roy Strong (History, Queen Mary College, London)

Arthur C. Clarke (Physics and Maths – in two years – King's College, London)

Lord Douglas Hurd (History, Cambridge)

Vanessa Feltz (English, Cambridge)

Michael Portillo (History, Cambridge)

Lord Maurice Saatchi (Economics, LSE)

Gordon Brown (History, Edinburgh)

Lord Denis Healey (Greats, Oxford)

Chris Smith (English, Cambridge)

Martin Amis (English, Oxford)

Laura Bailey (English, Southampton)

Louis Theroux (History, Oxford)

Cherie Blair (Law, LSE)

Chris Martin (Ancient History, UCL

Sally Phillips (Italian, Oxford)

Philippa Forrester (Ecology and Conservation, Birkbeck College)

PEOPLE WHO GOT THIRDS AT UNIVERSITY

Lord John Birt

Baroness Barbara Castle

Tariq Ali

Lord Home

W.H. Auden

Jack Higgins

Margaret Hodge

Johnny Vegas

Carol Vorderman

Richard Whiteley

Anthony Powell

Imran Khan

AMERICANS AND THEIR CLASSMATES' RATINGS

Billy Crystal – voted Wittiest Student In His Class

Tom Cruise – voted Least Likely To Succeed

Sylvester Stallone – voted Most Likely To End Up In The Electric Chair

Sandra Bullock – voted Most Likely To Brighten Your Day

Robin Williams – voted Least Likely To Succeed

Meg Ryan – voted Cutest Girl In Class

Gillian Anderson – voted Girl Most Likely To Go Bald (because of her hairstyles) and Most Likely To Be Arrested

Halle Berry – voted Prom Queen but was forced to share the title with a 'white, blonde, blue-eyed, all-American girl'

Matthew Fox – voted Most Likely To Appear On *Hee-Haw*

Eddie Murphy – voted Most Popular

Chris Tucker – voted Most Humorous

John Leguizamo – voted Most Talkative

Billy Crystal – voted Best Personality

Lorraine Bracco – voted Ugliest Girl

Sally Field – voted Class Clown

Heather Graham – voted Most Talented

James Gandolfini – voted Best Looking

PEOPLE WHO ENDOWED SCHOLARSHIPS AT THEIR OLD SCHOOLS

Hugh Grant (Latymer Upper)

Jeremy Irons (Sherborne)

PEOPLE WHO WENT TO FINISHING SCHOOL

Mary Wesley   Anne Robinson   **Zsa Zsa Gabor**

Camilla Parker-Bowles   **Minnie Driver (in Paris and Grenoble)**

FILM GAFFES

In *Charlie's Angels* (2000), when Drew Barrymore lifts up Lucy Liu to spin her around and kick the baddie, Drew calls out 'Lucy!' to get her attention – even though Lucy Liu's character's name is 'Alex'. See also *The Doors* (1991), when Meg Ryan calls Val Kilmer 'Val' instead of 'Jim', his character's name, and *The War of The Roses* (1989), in which Michael Douglas addresses Danny DeVito's character as 'DeVito'.

In *Rear Window* (1954), James Stewart has a cast on his leg for the whole film, which is fine except that in one scene the cast switches legs.

In *The Bible* (1966), the actor playing Adam has a belly button …

In *Spider-Man* (2002), Peter shoots his web at a lamp and pulls it across the room, smashing it, but seconds later it's back on the dresser in one piece.

In *Robin Hood: Prince of Thieves* (1991), the sheriff uses the expression '10.30'. Clocks didn't exist in the twelfth century.

In *Commando* (1985), the Porsche is wrecked on the left side – until Arnie drives it away and it's fine.

In *Harry Potter And The Philosopher's Stone* (2001), at the start-of-term feast Harry sits down on one side of the table next to Ron. When the food is served, Harry is on the other side of the table, next to Hermione.

In *Austin Powers In Goldmember* (2002), we learn that Austin Powers left school in 1959. This means that the family holiday in Belgium, when he was a baby, would have been between 1941 and 1944 when Belgium was occupied by the Nazis.

In *The Bridge On The River Kwai* (1957), Alec Guinness – who won an Oscar for his role – has his name spelt with just one 'n' in the final credits. Christopher Walken also had his name misspelled: in the credits of *Annie Hall* (1977).

In *The Perfect Storm* (2000), when the men are watching movies, there's a copy of *Blade Runner* (*Director's Cut*) on the table. The director's cut was released in 1992, but this movie is set in 1991.

In *Gladiator* (2000), in a battle scene, a chariot is turned over and a gas cylinder can be seen in the back.

In *The Maltese Falcon* (1941), as Sam Spade (Humphrey Bogart) slaps Joel Cairo (Peter Lorre), the latter's bow-tie changes from polka dots to stripes.

In *Speed* (1994), Harry (Jeff Daniels) is shot by Jack (Keanu Reeves) in the *left* leg but we later see him limping on the *right* leg.

In *The Wedding Singer* (1998), Julia's wedding was supposed to take place on Sunday, 5 August 1985. But in 1985, August 5th fell on a Monday.

In *The Last Temptation of Christ* (1988), you can see the label in Christ's robe.

In *It's A Wonderful Life* (1946), the old man's cigar disappears when he sends young George to deliver a prescription.

In *Spartacus* (1960), you can clearly see a vaccination scar on the arm of Spartacus (Kirk Douglas).

In *The Silence of The Lambs* (1991), Clarice Starling (played by Jodie Foster) has blue eyes, but the actress playing her as a child has brown eyes.

In *My Best Friend's Wedding* (1997), when Jules is trying on her dress she's wearing a white bra with a visible strap. Later, this becomes a black bra.

EXTRAORDINARY MIDDLE NAMES

Joan HENRIETTA Collins

Rowan SEBASTIAN Atkinson

Mel COLUMCILLE Gibson

Gene ALDEN Hackman

Woody TRACY Harrelson

Rob HEPLER Lowe

Joseph ALBERIC Fiennes

Geri ESTOLLE Halliwell

Quincy DELIGHT Jones

Kate GARRY Hudson

Jack SIEGFRIED Ryder

Leonardo WILHELM DiCaprio

Russell IRA Crowe

Mark FREUDER Knopfler

Bob PRIMROSE Wilson

John MARWOOD Cleese

Robson GOLIGHTLY Green

Jo VELDA O'Meara

Lawrence BRUNO NERO Dallaglio

Jeremy DICKSON Paxman

Uma KARUNA Thurman

Damon ERNEST DEVERAUX Hill

Hugh JOHN MUNGO Grant

Sir Terence ORBY Conran

Ben GEZA Affleck

Emile IVANHOE Heskey

FAMOUS WOMEN BORN WITH THE FIRST NAME MARY

Lauren Hutton, Dame Barbara Cartland, Dusty Springfield, Kathleen Turner, Christine Hamilton, Debbie Reynolds, Lily Tomlin, Dorothy Lamour, Sissy Spacek, Bo Derek, Meryl Streep, Debra Winger, Farrah Fawcett, Tipper Gore, Mae West

FAMOUS PEOPLE WHO USE THEIR MIDDLE NAMES AS FIRST NAMES

Barbara Jane Horrocks

David Jude Law

Laura Reese Witherspoon

Keith Rupert Murdoch

Marvin Neil Simon

Ruz Fidel Castro

Desmond John Humphrys

Mary Debra Winger

Olive Marie Osmond

Walter Bruce Willis

Charles Robert Redford

Roberta Joan (i.e. Joni) Mitchell

William Bradley Pitt

George Ivan (i.e. Van) Morrison

Gordon Angus Deayton

James Gordon Brown

Michael Terry Wogan

Henry Warren Beatty

Michael Sylvester Stallone

Dorothy Faye Dunaway

Christina Brooke Shields

John Richard Whiteley

Thomas Sean Connery

Rosalie Anderson (i.e. Andie) MacDowell

PEOPLE NAMED AFTER SOMEONE/SOMETHING FAMOUS

Halle Berry (after the Halle Brothers department store)

Christopher Walken (named Ronald – a first name he dropped – after the actor Ronald Colman)

Heath Ledger (after Heathcliff in *Wuthering Heights*)

John Leguizamo (after the actor John Saxon)

Natasha Richardson (after the heroine in Tolstoy's *War And Peace*)

Charisma Carpenter (after an Avon perfume)

Dido (after the African warrior queen)

Marilyn Monroe – born Norma Jean Baker (after the actress Norma Talmadge)

Dale Winton (after the actor Dale Robertson)

Dustin Hoffman (after the cowboy star of the silent movies Dustin Farnum)

Mariel Hemingway (after a bay in Cuba)

Gloria Hunniford (after the actress Gloria Swanson)

Glenn Hoddle (after the bandleader Glenn Miller)

Sugar Ray Leonard (after the musician Ray Charles)

Whitney Houston (after the American TV soap star Whitney Blake)

Shirley Maclaine and Shirley Jones (after Shirley Temple)

Chelsea Clinton (after the song 'Chelsea Morning')

Dame Thora Hird (after the song 'Thora, Speak To Me Thora')

Martina Hingis (after the tennis star Martina Navratilova)

Dennis Bergkamp (after the footballer Denis Law)

Bette Midler (after the actress Bette Davis)

Oprah Winfrey (after Orpah, from the Bible's Book of Ruth; it was misspelt on her birth certificate)

Gillian Taylforth (after the dancer Gillian Lynne)

PEOPLE WHOSE NAMES ARE USED IN COCKNEY RHYMING SLANG

George Best – guest

Jeremy Beadle – needle

Tommy Steele – eel

Melvyn Bragg – shag

Richard Todd – cod

Cilla Black – back

David Bowie – blowy (in the sense of windy)

Sir Michael Caine – pain

Sir Edward Heath – teeth

Gregory Peck – cheque

Jane Russell – mussel

Doris Day – way

Mickey Rooney – loony

CELEBRITIES WHOSE NAMES ARE USED IN NEW RHYMING SLANG

Giorgio Armani – sarnie

Niki Lauda – powder

Christian Slater – later

Roberta Flack – sack

Calvin Klein – fine

Thelonius Monk – skunk

Kate Moss – toss

Britney Spears – beers

Fat Boy Slim – gym

Ronan Keating – meeting

Gloria Gaynor(s) – trainers

Carmen Miranda – veranda

Axl Rose – nose

Ringo Starr – bar

Belinda Carlisle(s) – piles

Sylvester Stallone – phone

Unusual names famous people have given their children

Lennon – Liam Gallagher and Patsy Kensit

Keelin – Jerry Garcia

Pixie, Fifi Trixiebelle and Peaches – Bob Geldof and Paula Yates

Heavenly Hiraani Tiger Lily – Michael Hutchence and Paula Yates

Homer – Matt Groening

Kidatia – Quincy Jones

Rufus Tiger and Tiger Lily – Roger Taylor (of Queen)

Bria – Eddie Murphy

Happy – Macy Gray

Jaden Gil – Steffi Graf and Andre Agassi

Denim – Toni Braxton

Jermajesty (boy) – Jermaine Jackson

Moon Unit, Dweezil, Diva and Emuukha Rodan – Frank Zappa

Dandelion (now Angela) – Keith Richards

Rain – Richard Pryor

Elijah Blue and Chastity Sun – Cher

Dakota Mayi – Don Johnson and Melanie Griffith

Navarone – Priscilla Presley

Dog – Sky Saxon

Rumer Glenn, Scout Larue and Tallulah Belle – Bruce Willis and Demi Moore

Brooklyn (girl) – Donna Summer

Brooklyn and Romeo (boys) – Victoria and David Beckham

Missy – Damon Albarn

Satchel – Spike Lee

Satchel – Woody Allen

Piper Maru – Gillian Anderson

Willow – Gabrielle Anwar

Starlite Melody – Marisa Berenson

Memphis Eve and Elijah Bob Patricius Guggi Q – Bono

Zowie (now Joey) – David Bowie

Sailor Lee – Christie Brinkley

Phoenix Chi – Mel B

Free – Barbara Hershey and David Carradine

Kansas – David Carradine

Tyson – Neneh Cherry

Braison Chance and Destiny Hope – Billy Ray Cyrus

Morgana – Morgan Freeman

Skylar – Sheena Easton

Arrana and Blue Angel – The Edge

Colton Jack – Chris Evert

Atiana Cecilia – Oscar de la Hoya

Chiara-Charlotte – Catherine Deneuve and Marcello Mastroianni

Lily-Rose Melody – Johnny Depp and Vanessa Paradis

Mallory Loving – Rick Derringer

Gracie Fan – Danny DeVito and Rhea Perlman

Caleb – Jack Nicholson

Brawley King – Nick Nolte

Gulliver – Gary Oldman

Morgane – Roman Polanski

Maesa – Bill Pullman

Elettra-Ingrid – Isabella Rossellini

Justice – Steven Seagal

Sage Moonblood – Sylvester Stallone

Amadeo – John Turturro

Ocean and Sonnet – Forest Whitaker

Mercedes – Val Kilmer and Joanne Whalley

Chance Armstrong – Larry King

Samaria – LL Cool J

Rainie – Andie MacDowell

Arpad Flynn – Elle Macpherson

Speck Wildhorse – John Cougar Mellencamp

And also: George Foreman named five of his sons George and his daughter Georgetta

PEOPLE WHO CHANGED THEIR NAMES

Sir Elton John (Reginald Dwight)

Meg Ryan (Margaret Hyra)

Alice Cooper (Vincent Furnier)

P.J. Proby (James Smith)

Elkie Brooks (Elaine Bookbinder)

Ricky Martin (Enrique Morales)

Joan Rivers (Joan Molinsky)

Kiki Dee (Pauline Matthews)

Woody Allen (Allen Konigsberg)

Martin Sheen (Ramon Estevez)

Macy Gray (Natalie McIntyre)

Hammer (Stanley Burrell)

Engelbert Humperdinck (Gerry Dorsey)

Bono (Paul Hewson)

Bo Derek (Mary Cathleen Collins)

Calvin Klein (Richard Klein)

Harry Hill (Matthew Hall)

David Copperfield (David Kotkin)

Bill Wyman (William Perks)

Omar Sharif (Michael Shalhoub)

James Garner (James Baumgarner)

David Bowie (David Jones)

Vic Reeves (Jim Moir)

Cilla Black (Priscilla White)

Jodie Foster (Alicia Foster)

Pat Benatar (Patricia Andrejewski)

Sid Owen (David Sutton)

Barry Manilow (Barry Pincus)

Michael Keaton (Michael Douglas)

Theresa Russell (Theresa Paup)

Me-One (Erik Martin)

Carmen Electra (Tara Leigh Patrick – advised by Prince to change: Carmen after the opera and Electra after the goddess)

Eminem (Marshall Mathers III)

Queen Latifah (Dana Owens)

Tom Cruise (Thomas Cruise Mapother IV)

Ice Cube (O'Shea Jackson)

Donna Karan (Donna Faske)

Larry King (Lawrence Zeiger)

Nathan Lane (Joseph Lane)

Ralph Lauren (Ralph Lifshitz)

Spike Lee (Shelton Lee)

Courtney Love (Courtney Menely)

Toni Morrison (Chloe Wofford)

Ozzy Osbourne (John Michael Osbourne)

Bernadette Peters (Bernadette Lazzara)

Tim Allen (Tim Allen Dick)

Snoop Dogg (Cordozar Broadus)

Shania Twain (Eilleen Twain)

Wynonna (Christina Ciminella)

Puff Daddy (Sean Combs)

Marilyn Manson (Brian Warner – he named himself after Marilyn Monroe and Charles Manson)

Jay-Z (Shawn Carter)

Joaquin Phoenix (Joaquin Bottom – his surname was changed by his parents, which suggests that his older brother, the late actor River Phoenix, was once called River Bottom)

Sonique (Sonia Clarke)

Shaggy (Orville Burrell)

Norman Cook (Quentin Cook)

Stockard Channing (Susan Williams Antonia Stockard)

Ms Dynamite (Niomi Daley)

Eric Clapton (Eric Clapp)

Tina Turner (Annie Mae Bullock)

Doris Day (Doris Kapelhoff)

Axl Rose (William Bailey)

Michael Barrymore (Michael Parker)

Aliases

Mr Bellacon and Paul Cruise – Tom Cruise

Mr Dripnoodle – Johnny Depp

Tipsy McStagger and Phil S. Stein – Robbie Williams

Mr Hugh Jarse – George Michael

Miss Trixie Firecracker and Lili Paris – Geri Halliwell

Miss Flo Cha – Mel C

Mr Tyne and Mr Wear – Ant and Dec

Claris Norman – Madonna

Pussy Jones – Dannii Minogue

Peter Gunn – Eminem

Bobby Dee – Kevin Spacey

A.N. Other – Prince Edward (in an Austrian hotel)

Sir Humphrey Handbag – Sir Elton John

Miss R. Dynastar – Vanessa-Mae

Miss Cupcake – Mariah Carey

Doctor Frank'n'furter – Abs 5ive

Sabrina Duncan – Shirley Manson

Miss Honey – Nicole Kidman

Bambi Shots – Anastacia

Mary Black – Courtney Love

John Doe – Keanu Reeves

Tom Feral – Kevin Costner

Kate Fleming – Gwyneth Paltrow

Casey Cobb – Jessica Simpson

People with four initials

V.H.B.M. Bottomley (Virginia Bottomley)

J.P.M.S. Clary (Julian Clary)

N.K.A.S. Vaz (Keith Vaz)

K.P.T.F. Duffy (Keith Duffy)

C.P.A.G. Windsor (The Prince of Wales)

M.J.C.C. Rutherford (Mike Rutherford)

Sardines

The word SARDINE refers to any of several species of small food fish of temperate waters that are also known as pilchards – especially when adult. Sardines are shoaling fish that live near the surface feeding on plankton. This ends the encyclopaedia definition.

SARDINES are sensitive fish. They move away from their shoaling grounds and don't return for decades after naval battles.

SARDINES can improve your memory – according to a study of children in 1987. People with memory disorders have low levels of acetyl choline which certain foods – such as sardines – can mitigate.

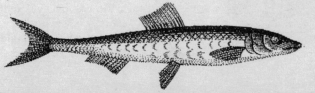

SARDINES can help cancer sufferers. Trials at Edinburgh Royal Infirmary showed that a fatty acid in sardine oils prevents patients losing weight by blocking a substance produced by tumours that destroys body tissue. This is important because about half of cancer patients lose weight – some so severely that it kills them.

In Alexandria, Minneapolis, no man is allowed to make love with the smell of SARDINES on his breath.

In Marseille, France, a 4,500 piece jigsaw depicting a two-acre SARDINE was laid out by thirty people in one week in 1992.

In 1995, millions of dead SARDINES were washed ashore along the Australian New South Wales coast when a mystery illness led to them suffocating after mucus blocked their gills.

In 1994, in Lima, Peru, 1,500 young people made a three-mile-long SARDINE sandwich in an attempt to get into the Peruvian *Guinness Book of Records*.

In Ipswich, Queensland, in Australia, SARDINES rained down from the sky in 1989. The fish were sucked up from the sea by a strong updraft of air and fell to the ground like hail. The local cats were said to be delighted.

There's the true story of the young boy who was told by his teacher to write about the harmful effects of oil on fish for his homework. He wrote, 'My mummy opened a tin of SARDINES. The sardines were covered in oil and they were all dead'.

The European Patents Office says that the most commonly requested item among its 31 million patent documents is SARDINE-flavoured ice cream. A spokesman says, 'No one believes that it actually exists until they've called it up and seen it themselves.'

PEOPLE WHO APPEARED IN ADVERTISEMENTS WHEN THEY WERE CHILDREN

Jonathan Ross (Rice Krispies)

Patsy Kensit (Birds Eye frozen peas)

Simon Le Bon (Persil)

Michael Portillo (Ribena)

Jodie Foster (Coppertone)

Martyn Lewis (Cow & Gate baby food)

B.B. King (Pepticon health tonic)

Keith Chegwin (Marathon)

Emma Bunton (Milky Bar)

Leslie Ash (Fairy Liquid)

Kate Winslet (Sugar Puffs)

Drew Barrymore (Gainsburgers)

Mike Myers (Datsun)

Sarah Michelle Gellar (Burger King; she couldn't say 'burger' and so needed a speech coach)

Melissa Joan Hart (Splashy – a bath toy)

Kirsten Dunst (a doll with bodily functions on US TV)

Yasmine Bleeth (was a Johnson & Johnson baby)

Jeff Daniels (McDonald's)

Rick Schroder (had appeared in about 60 adverts by the age of seven)

Brooke Shields (was the Ivory Snow baby at the age of 11 months)

Christian Bale (Pac-Man cereal)

Jessica Biel (Pringles crisps)

Danniella Westbrook (Asda)

FORMER FLATMATES

Tommy Lee Jones and Al Gore

Sir Michael Caine and Terence Stamp

Lauren Holly and Robin Givens

M. Emmet Walsh and William Devane

Ewan McGregor and Jude Law

Joel & Ethan Coen, Frances McDormand and Holly Hunter

Marilyn Monroe and Shelley Winters

David Baddiel and Frank Skinner

Charles Bronson and Jack Klugman

Charles Manson and Dennis Wilson

Peter Howitt and Kevin McNally

Cary Grant and Randolph Scott

Dustin Hoffman, Gene Hackman and Robert Duvall

Lesley Joseph and Maureen Lipman

David Niven and Errol Flynn

James Stewart and Henry Fonda

Michael Douglas and Danny DeVito

Mel Gibson and Geoffrey Rush

Ted Hughes and Peter O'Toole

Matt Damon and Ben Affleck

Zoe Ball and John Thomson

PEOPLE AND THE SPORTS THEY PLAYED

Shannon Elizabeth could have become a professional tennis player

Matthew Perry was ranked number 2 at tennis in Ottawa at the age of 13

Yanni was a member of the Greek national swimming team

Kurt Russell left acting in 1971 to pursue a career in minor league baseball

Hilary Swank swam in the Junior Olympics; she was also a top gymnast

Queen Latifah was a power forward on two state championship basketball teams in high school

Sonique 'could have competed on an international level' in the pentathlon as a teenager

Josh Hartnett turned to acting only after his soccer career ended

George Clooney once tried out for the Cincinnati Reds baseball team

Heath Ledger nearly became a professional ice hockey player but chose acting over sport when given an ultimatum

Gisele Bundchen originally wanted to be a professional volleyball player

Allison Janney wanted to be a competitive figure skater but a freak accident ended her chances

Dr Benjamin Spock won a rowing gold medal at the 1924 Olympics

Tommy Lee Jones is a champion polo player

Chevy Chase used to work as a tennis professional at a club

Paul Newman once achieved second place in the gruelling Le Mans 24 Hour Race

Richard Harris won a Munster Cup medal playing in the second row for Garryowen in 1952 and might well have gone on to play Rugby Union for Ireland had he not contracted TB

Richard Gere won a gymnastics scholarship to the University of Massachusetts

Keanu Reeves was the goalkeeper in his high school ice-hockey team, where he earned the nickname 'The Wall' and where he was voted MVP (Most Valuable Player)

Arnold Schwarzenegger was not only a bodybuilding champion but also won the Austrian Junior Olympic Weightlifting Championship

Julio Iglesias used to play in goal for Real Madrid's second team

Robert De Niro learned to box for his Oscar-winning role as Jake La Motta in *Raging Bull* and was so good that La Motta himself said that he could have taken it up professionally

Bill Cosby was good enough at American football to be offered a trial with the Green Bay Packers

William Baldwin was a good enough player to have originally considered a professional baseball career with the New York Yankees

Kirk Douglas once supplemented his meagre earnings with professional appearances in the ring as a wrestler

Billy Crystal attended college on a full baseball scholarship but decided not to pursue a career in the sport

Peter O'Toole 'distinguished himself on the rugby field' when he served in the navy in 1950–52

David Suchet played rugby union on the wing for Richmond RFC

Jim Brown embarked on an acting career only after having been a star at American football

Davy Jones was an apprentice jockey before joining The Monkees; however, it was only after he retired from singing and made a racing comeback that he had his first win as a jockey

Warren Beatty was offered scholarships as an American football player by several universities but turned them all down to concentrate on acting

Tom Cruise was an all-round sporting star at school but it was his wrestling that led to his acting career: he was in the school wrestling team but after injuring his knee turned to acting instead

Ian McShane could have followed his father into a career with Manchester United but he turned down the opportunity in order to pursue acting

Jack Palance worked as a professional boxer – which was how he got the broken nose that helped him to earn parts playing the heavy

Mickey Rourke had 26 amateur fights in the 1970s and then quit when his acting career took off; in recent years, he has returned to the ring with some success

Liam Neeson boxed for a local team from the age of nine until the age of 17 (in one early match his nose was broken and he had it set on the spot by his manager)

Jonathan Dimbleby was the 1964 showjumping champion of the south of England

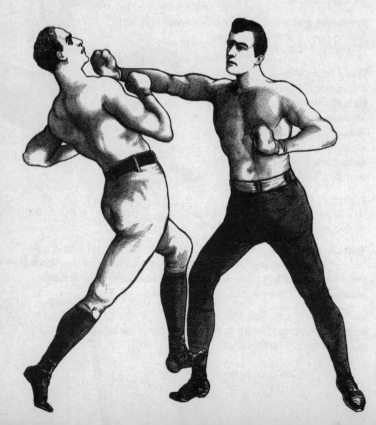

Roy Walker was a champion hammer thrower

Amanda De Cadenet trained four hours a day to become an Olympic gymnast (unsuccessfully)

Sheryl Crow was a competitive hurdler

Mel C ran for Cheshire county when she was a schoolgirl

Alanis Morissette takes part in triathlons

Sarah Michelle Gellar was a competitive figure skater for three years and was ranked third in New York State

Geena Davis tried in 1999 to qualify for the US Women's Olympic Archery team

Ellen DeGeneres considered becoming a professional golfer

Ross Davidson was an international water-polo player

Jonathan Cake won a Cambridge Blue for rugby after being drafted in at the last moment as a replacement, but gave up the game because there were only so many auditions he could go to with a bashed-in nose

Paul McGann was a junior triple-jump champion considered good enough to compete in a future Olympic Games

Rolf Harris was Junior Backstroke Champion of all Australia in 1946

Gabby Logan represented Wales at gymnastics in the 1990 Commonwealth Games

Kate Hoey was Northern Ireland's high jump champion in the 1960s

PEOPLE WHO PLAYED FOR – OR HAD TRIALS WITH – FOOTBALL CLUBS

Sir David Frost (Nottingham Forest)

David Essex (Leyton Orient)

The Duke of Westminster (Fulham)

Des O'Connor (Northampton Town)

Bradley Walsh (Brentford)

Eddie Large (Manchester City)

Stan Boardman (Liverpool)

Angus Deayton (Crystal Palace)

Rod Stewart (Brentford)

Gordon Ramsay (played twice for Rangers)

Stuart Hall (Crystal Palace)

Rick Savage (Sheffield United)

Gavin Rossdale (Chelsea)

Audley Harrison (Watford)

Lee Latchford-Evans (Wimbledon)

Nicky Byrne (Leeds United)

Ralf Little (Swindon and Millwall)

Andrew Murray (Glasgow Rangers)

Ricky Tomlinson was offered a trial by Scunthorpe United but didn't take it up

FORMER BEAUTY QUEENS

Joan Blondell (Miss Dallas 1926)

Dorothy Lamour (Miss New Orleans 1931)

Zsa Zsa Gabor (Miss Hungary 1936 – stripped of the title for being too young)

Veronica Lake (Miss Florida 1937 – stripped of the title for being too young: 'Being disqualified after you've won something is a pretty good way to lose.')

Lauren Bacall (Miss Greenwich Village 1942)

Cloris Leachman (Miss Chicago 1946)

Gina Lollobrigida (Miss Italy 1946)

Marilyn Monroe (Miss California Artichoke Queen 1947)

Vera Miles (Miss Kansas 1948)

Debbie Reynolds (Miss Burbank 1948)

Anita Ekberg (Miss Sweden 1950)

Sophia Loren (Miss Elegance 1950)

Shirley Jones (Miss Pittsburgh 1952)

Imelda Marcos (Miss Manila 1953)

Kim Novak (Miss Deepfreeze 1953)

Raquel Welch (Miss Photogenic 1953)

Dyan Cannon (Miss West Seattle 1957)

Elke Sommer (Miss Viarrego 1959)

Julie Ege (Miss Norway 1962)

Cybill Shepherd (Miss Teenage Memphis 1966)

Shakira Caine (Miss Guyana 1967)

Kim Basinger (Miss Junior Athens 1969)

Victoria Principal (Miss Miami 1969)

Oprah Winfrey (Miss Black Tennessee 1971)

Lynda Carter (Miss World USA 1973)

Michelle Pfeiffer (Miss Orange County 1976)

Sharon Stone (Miss Crawford County 1976)

Marla Maples (Miss Resaca Beach Poster Girl 1983)

Halle Berry (Miss USA 1986 – first runner-up)

Helena Christensen (Miss Denmark 1986)

Jeri Ryan (Miss Illinois 1989)

Ali Landry (Miss USA 1996)

PEOPLE WHO PLAY/PLAYED IN BANDS

Russell Crowe is in a band named 30 Odd Foot of Grunts

Kevin Bacon formed the Bacon Brothers with his older brother Michael

Joe Pesci was lead vocalist with Joey Dee and the Starlighters

Johnny Depp was in a series of garage bands, one of which (The Kids) opened for Iggy Pop; later he became a member of the band P (with Steve Jones of the Sex Pistols and Flea of the Red Hot Chilli Peppers)

Gary Sinise formed The Bonsoir Boys in 1997

Director Mike Figgis was once in a band with Bryan Ferry

Stephen King and Matt Groening are in a band called Rock Bottom Remainders

David Lynch plays bass in a heavy metal group called Blue Bob

Ricky Gervais sang in a band named Seona Dancing

Ruud Gullit used to play bass guitar in a band named Revelation Time

Richard Gere was the lead singer with The Strangers

Loyd Grossman was the singer and guitarist with a group called Jet Bronx and the Forbidden which got to number 49 in 1977 with 'Ain't Doin' Nothin''

Kevin Costner was the vocalist with the group Roving Boy

Melvyn Bragg was lead singer of a group named Memphis 5; he was also in a skiffle group playing tea-chest bass

Nigel Havers was in a pop group with his brother (they used to sing Herman's Hermits-type songs)

Diane Keaton sang with The Roadrunners

Leslie Ash was a backing singer in the group Smiley & Co

Tony Blair was the lead singer in a university band, The Ugly Rumours

Michelle Collins started her career as a backing singer with Mari Wilson

Damon Hill played guitar in a punk band named Sex Hitler and the Hormones (with fellow aspiring racing drivers)

Chevy Chase played drums for a college group that included Donald Fagen and Walter Becker of Steely Dan

Roger Black played bass guitar for the amateur punk group The Psychedelic Vegetables

Jeremy Vine used to play drums in a rock band called Flared Generation

Patsy Kensit sang with Eighth Wonder

PEOPLE WHO GUESTED ON RECORDS

Rick Wakeman played synthesizer on 'Space Oddity' (David Bowie)

Brian Jones played oboe on 'Baby You're A Rich Man' (The Beatles)

Peter Gabriel played flute on 'Lady D'Arbanville' (Cat Stevens)

Billy Joel played piano on 'Leader of The Pack' (The Shangri-Las)

Elton John played piano on 'He Ain't Heavy, He's My Brother' (The Hollies)

Jack Bruce played bass on 'Sorrow' (The Merseys)

George Harrison played guitar on 'Badge' (Cream)

Eric Clapton played guitar on 'While My Guitar Gently Weeps' (The Beatles)

Paul Weller played guitar on 'Champagne Supernova' (Oasis)

David Gilmour played guitar on 'Wuthering Heights' (Kate Bush)

Ritchie Blackmore played guitar on 'Just Like Eddie' (Heinz)

Phil Collins played drums on 'Puss 'N Boots' (Adam Ant)

Mark King played bass on 'If I Was' (Midge Ure)

Stevie Wonder played harmonica on 'I Feel For You' (Chaka Khan)

SOME PEOPLE AND THE SONGS ON WHICH THEY SANG BACKING VOCALS

David Bowie – 'It's Only Rock And Roll' (The Rolling Stones)

Sir Tim Rice – 'Lily The Pink' (The Scaffold)

Sheryl Crow – 'Silver Girl' (Fleetwood Mac)

Eric Clapton – 'All You Need Is Love' (The Beatles)

Rupert Everett – 'American Pie' (Madonna)

Britt Ekland – 'Tonight's The Night' (Rod Stewart)

George Michael – 'Nikita' (Elton John)

Donovan – 'Yellow Submarine' (The Beatles)

Mick Jagger – 'You're So Vain' (Carly Simon)

Paul Young – 'Black Coffee In Bed' (Squeeze)

Phil Spector – 'My Sweet Lord' (George Harrison)

Bruce Springsteen – 'Street Hassle' (Lou Reed)

Luther Vandross – 'Young Americans' (David Bowie)

Sir Paul McCartney – 'Mellow Yellow' (Donovan)

Jimmy Somerville – 'Suspicious Minds' (Fine Young Cannibals)

John Lennon – 'Fame' (David Bowie)

Eric Clapton – 'I Wish It Would Rain Down' (Phil Collins)

Kate Bush – 'Games Without Frontiers' (Peter Gabriel)

Sting – 'Money For Nothing' (Dire Straits)

Michael Douglas – 'When The Going Gets Tough (The Tough Get Going)' (Billy Ocean)

Billy Idol – 'Dancin' Clown' (Joni Mitchell)

David Beckham – 'Out Of Your Mind' (Victoria Beckham – he sang on the first take which, apparently, wasn't subsequently used)

Roger Daltrey – 'Bad Attitude' (Meat Loaf)

George Michael – 'The Last Kiss' (David Cassidy)

Belinda Carlisle – 'Pearl's Café' (The Specials)

Richard Ashcroft, Patsy Kensit and Meg Mathews – 'All Around The World' (Oasis)

Sting – 'Shape' (Sugababes)

WHAT THEY DID BEFORE BECOMING FAMOUS

Sir Michael Gambon – apprentice toolmaker

Geena Davis – live mannequin in a New York department store

Roy Walker – shipyard worker (and worked on the *QE2* in Belfast)

Phill Jupitus – press officer for The Housemartins

Charlie Dimmock – apple-picker, airport check-in clerk

Harvey Keitel – shoe salesman and court stenographer, having joined the US Marines at the age of 16 and served in the Lebanon

Paul O'Grady – social worker

Renée Zellweger – bartender assistant

Lucy Lawless – worked in a gold mine

Huey Lewis – slaughtered rabbits: he had to hit them over the head with a pipe, then skin them and gut them

Johnny Vaughan – grill chef, jewel courier, sales assistant, video shop manager

Beck – painted signs, moved refrigerators, took ID photos at the YMCA in New York, worked in a video store

Neve Campbell – ballerina

Hugh Grant – advertising account executive

Tom Clancy – insurance agent

George Clooney – sold insurance door to door, cut tobacco in Kentucky

Ellen DeGeneres – vacuum cleaner saleswoman

Dennis Franz – postman ('the worst postman in the history of the Post Office')

Whoopi Goldberg – bricklayer, bank teller, make-up artist for a funeral parlour

John Goodman – bouncer

Dustin Hoffman – toy seller at Macy's, attendant in a psychiatric institution

Russell Crowe – bingo caller

Vin Diesel – bouncer

Matthew Modine – electrician, macrobiotic chef

Kevin Richardson – played a Ninja Turtle at the Disney–MGM Studios theme park

J.K. Rowling – worked at the Amnesty International office in London and then at the Chamber of Commerce in Manchester

Meg Ryan – journalist

Mariella Frostrup – press officer for UB40

Davina McCall – singing waitress in Paris

Liam Neeson – forklift driver at the Guinness brewery in Belfast

Melinda Messenger – air stewardess

Björk – fish factory employee

Josh Hartnett – video store clerk

Chris Isaak – funeral parlour assistant

Sue Perkins – cleaned toilets for a hotel in Croydon for £1.50 an hour

Nathan Lane – police bail interviewer

Peter Gabriel – milliner

Elvis Costello – computer programmer at the Elizabeth Arden factory

Bob Geldof – meat packer

Tom Jones – glove cutter

Sir Ben Kingsley – penicillin tester

Madonna – worked in Burger King; also as a lifeguard and a lift operator

Robert Redford – pavement artist

Tina Turner – maid

Joe Cocker – plumber

Sir Elton John – messenger boy

Willem Dafoe – magazine binder at *Penthouse*, carpenter and electrician

Gloria Estefan – Spanish and French interpreter for customs at an American airport

Bill Withers – manufactured aeroplane loo seats

Tom Hanks – bellhop

Kylie Minogue – video shop worker

Jon Bon Jovi – served in Burger King

James Caan – rodeo rider

Kathy Bates – cashier in the gift shop in New York's Museum of Modern Art

Simon Le Bon – lumberjack

Mick Jagger – hospital porter

Cher – receptionist in a department store

Ozzy Osbourne – slaughterhouse labourer

Annie Lennox – fish filleter

Bob Hoskins – nightclub bouncer

Rod Stewart – grave digger

Vic Reeves – pig farmer

Warren Beatty – cocktail bar pianist

Jeremy Irons – social worker

Michelle Pfeiffer – supermarket assistant

Sir Sean Connery – french polisher

Dame Diana Rigg – coffee bar assistant

Julie Walters – nurse

DROVE TAXIS

Pierce Brosnan, Michael Keaton, Alan Alda, Oliver Stone

Note also: Stephen Fry, Prince Philip, Lord Andrew Lloyd Webber, Michael Jackson, John Wayne, Liberace and Keith Allen bought London cabs for their own personal use

FORMER TEACHERS

Sarah Kennedy, Sting, Bryan Ferry, Patricia Hodge, Jim Bowen, Sebastian Faulks, Gabriel Byrne, Dame Anita Roddick, Billy Crystal (substitute teacher), Luciano Pavarotti (elementary school), Dawn French, Oliver Stone (in Vietnam), Dan Brown, Anne Fine, Russell Harty, Archbishop Desmond Tutu, Michael Morpurgo

WORKED AS LION-CAGE CLEANERS

Clive James, Sylvester Stallone

WORKED AS WAITERS AND SERVED FAMOUS PEOPLE

Richard Gere (once served Robert De Niro)

Dido (once dropped 16 glasses of white wine and a tray on Stephen Fry when waitressing at Cafe Flo in London)

Mary Steenburgen (once served Jack Nicholson)

SERVED IN THE ISRAELI ARMY

Dr Ruth Westheimer, Uri Geller, Debra Winger, Vidal Sassoon

AUDITIONED UNSUCCESSFULLY FOR THE MONKEES

Charles Manson, Stephen Stills

FORMER HAIRDRESSERS

Chuck Berry, Lewis Collins, Alison Moyet, Mike McGear, Yazz, Danny DeVito, Sid James, Michael Barrymore (at Vidal Sassoon), Twiggy, Jayne Middlemiss, Delia Smith, Whoopi Goldberg, Tionne Watkins (shampooist), Richard Ashcroft (for just two days), Willy Russell, Sharleen Spiteri, Melanie Sykes

WHAT THEY ORIGINALLY INTENDED TO BE

Whitney Houston – vet

Alec Baldwin – lawyer

Rowan Atkinson – electrical engineer

Britt Ekland – vet

Paul Theroux – doctor

Eddie Izzard – accountant

Michael Palin – explorer

Jeremy Irons – vet

Gary Numan – airline pilot

Marilyn Monroe – schoolteacher

Dame Agatha Christie – professional musician

Lynn Redgrave – cook

Dennis Quaid – musician

George Lucas – racing driver

Pope John Paul II – actor

Patricia Routledge – headmistress

William H. Macy – vet

Bruce Dickinson – vet

Bruce Oldfield – teacher

Mel Gibson – chef

Angelina Jolie – funeral director

Charisma Carpenter – teacher

Julio Iglesias – lawyer

Tobey Maguire – chef

David Duchovny – a bathtub (he was six at the time)

Dustin Hoffman – concert pianist

Lisa Kudrow – doctor

Jennifer Lopez – hairstylist

J.C. Chasez – carpenter

Kathleen Quinlan – gymnastics teacher

Forest Whitaker – classical tenor

Lance Bass – astronaut (and passed the NASA exams)

Charlie Dimmock – forensic scientist

Morgan Freeman – fighter pilot

Liz McLarnon – lawyer

Janet Jackson – lawyer

Hannah Waterman – vet

Emma Bunton – a pony (she was a young child at the time)

Ricky Gervais – a vet (when he was seven) and a marine biologist (when he was ten)

Ethan Hawke – newsreader

Claudia Schiffer – lawyer

Eminem – comic-book artist

Colin Farrell – footballer

Julia Roberts – vet

Alan Rickman – graphic artist

Miranda Richardson – vet

Natalie Appleton – dentist

Angela Rippon – ballet dancer

Sue Perkins – ophthalmic surgeon

James McAvoy – missionary then sailor in the navy

STARTED OUT AS SECRETARIES

Cilla Black, Anneka Rice, Caroline Aherne, Su Pollard, Sarah, Duchess of York, Ulrika Jonsson, Belinda Carlisle, Shania Twain, Anne Robinson, Betty Boothroyd, Catherine Keener, Joan Allen

TRAINED AS BALLET DANCERS

Victoria Principal

Leslie Caron

Clare Francis

Morgan Freeman

Charlize Theron

Caroline Quentin

Rachel de Thame

Jane Seymour (danced with the London Festival Ballet at the age of 13)

Mira Sorvino (performed in a professional production of *The Nutcracker* at the age of 12)

Penelope Cruz

Jennifer Ellison (Under-10 World Ballet Champion, Senior Champion at 14)

Sarah Jessica Parker (was with the Cincinnati Ballet and the American Ballet Theater)

WORKED AS SINGING TELEGRAMS

Sinéad O'Connor, Carol Smillie, Julian Clary, Chris Evans (Tarzan-o-gram), Virginia Madsen, Michaela Strachan, Keith Duffy, Nathan Lane

TRAINED TO BE DOCTORS BUT DIDN'T FINISH

Neil Diamond, Giorgio Armani, Lew Ayres (who went on to play Dr Kildare), Robert Dole, Wim Wenders, Christopher Isherwood, Roger Black, Robin Givens, Ralf Little, Dustin Hoffman, Bill Murray, William Roache

EX-POLICEMEN

Christopher Dean, Lord Jeffrey Archer, Dave Dee (and as such attended the scene of the crash in which Eddie Cochran died), Ray Reardon, Geoff Capes, John Arlott, Josef Locke, John Savident

PEOPLE WHO LIVED IN THEIR CARS

Brad Pitt

Chris Tarrant

Lenny Kravitz (a Ford Pinto)

Hilary Swank (with her mother when she was a kid)

Bob Hoskins (in a jeep after an expensive divorce)

Jim Carey and his family lived out of their car/trailer at one point

GENUINE CAR BUMPER STICKERS

CAUTION: I drive just like you!

Don't Drink and Drive – you might spill some

This car is insured by the Mafia – you hit me, they hit you

Be careful – 90 per cent of people are caused by accidents

Sorry, I don't date outside my species

Rehab is for Quitters

Not all dumbs are blonde

I took an IQ test and the results were negative

I don't brake for pedestrians

If you lived in your car, you'd be home by now

Honk if you've been married to Elizabeth Taylor

If you think I'm a lousy driver, you should see me putt

Learn from your parents' mistakes – use birth control

Of course I'm drunk – what do you think I am, a stunt driver?

Eat Well, Stay Fit, Die Anyway

YOU! Out of the gene pool!

You can't drink all day long if you don't start first thing in the morning

If you don't like the way I drive, get off the pavement

How many roads must a man travel down before he admits he is lost?

My wife's other car is a broom

I'm not a complete idiot – some parts are missing

He who laughs last thinks slowest

Ex-Saudi Arabian shoplifter – no hand signals

Instant asshole, just add alcohol

Beer isn't just for breakfast

PERSONALIZED CAR NUMBER PLATES

COM 1C (Jimmy Tarbuck)

1 PRO (Ray Reardon)

HRH 1 (The Queen)

777 SM (Sir Stirling Moss)

1 CUE (Jimmy White)

K7 (Duke of Kent)

OFF 1A (Martin Offiah)

8 DEB (Paul and Debbie Daniels)

P17 TSY and PAT 5Y (Patsy Palmer)

RH 666 (Robert Hardy)

EH 1 (Engelbert Humperdinck)

BOX 1T (Barry McGuigan)

MOVE 1T (Sir Cliff Richard)

MCP 1 (Martin Pipe)

CSM 43 (Colin Montgomerie)

1 MB (Max Bygraves)

BJM LAF1 (Bernard Manning)

KD 11 (Ken Dodd)

D1 SCOX (Judge Jules)

D1 DDY (David Hamilton)

NW 1 (Sir Norman Wisdom)

M1 BAD (Roy Keane)

AL 9 (Alan Shearer)

COLE 5 (Andy Cole)

K8 YER (Kieron Dyer)

PN 2000 (Phil Neville)

L11 BOW (Lee Bowyer)

H6 WELL (Harry Kewell)

QUALIFIED PILOTS

John Travolta, Nicholas Lyndhurst, Greg Norman, The Prince of Wales, Niki Lauda, Kurt Russell, Gary Numan, Kris Kristofferson, Gore Vidal (got his licence at the age of 10), B.B. King, Treat Williams, Tom Cruise, Luke Goss, John Grisham, Harrison Ford, Angelina Jolie, Patrick Swayze, Martin Shaw, Gene Hackman, Sir Alan Sugar

TOILETS

Sir John Harington (1561–1612) invented the toilet for Queen Elizabeth I after she'd banned him from her court for circulating smutty stories. So she allowed him to return. Sir John's toilet did the job – up to a point – but there were unpleasant side effects.

The reason so many houses bear the legend 'Queen Elizabeth I stayed here' is because she used to move on every time the stench became too much to bear.

The Victorian plumber, Thomas Crapper, perfected the system we all know and use: the siphon flush which, by drawing water uphill through a sealed cistern, is both effective and hygienic. Crapper was born in the village of Thorne: an anagram of throne. He also invented (and patented) the stair tread.

TALKING TOILETS

In British English and its sister Englishes, we have a huge number of synonyms for the toilet, such as bathroom, biffy, bog, can, chamber of commerce, cloakroom, comfort station, convenience, cottage (public toilet), crapper (after dear Thos.), donicker, dunny (originally Australian), gents', the geography (American euphemism, as in 'Can you show me the *geography* of the house?'), head (nautical), jakes, john, johnny, karzy, ladies', latrine, lavatory (which is, strictly speaking, a vessel for washing), little boys'/girls' room, loo, men's/women's room, personal hygiene station, powder-room, privy (an outdoor toilet), rest-room, sanctum sanctorum, shot-tower, smallest room, throne, washroom and WC (water closet).

TOILET FACTS

The most impossible item to flush is a ping-pong ball

In a survey, it was discovered that 91 per cent of 30,000 British women surveyed won't sit down properly on public toilets but instead adopt a semi-sitting, squatting position

Psycho was the first Hollywood film that showed a toilet flushing – thereby generating many complaints

The first toilet air-freshener was a pomegranate stuffed with cloves

The idea of separate cubicles for toilets is a relatively modern invention; the Romans, for example, sat down together in large groups

In Victorian times, loo seats were always made of wood: the well-to-do sat on mahogany or walnut while the poor put up with untreated white pine

The Victorians gave their loos names such as Cascade, Optimus, Alerto, Pluvius, Deluge, Tornado, Aquarius, Niagara, Planetas and the Subito

The town council of Cheltenham Spa once voted to replace the words 'Men' and 'Women' on their public toilets with 'Ladies' and 'Gentlemen' in order 'to attract a better class of person'

In the Middle Ages, 'waste' from public latrines ran directly into the river or the sea

ROYALS ON THE THRONE

In 1988, Australian officials built a special toilet for the Queen at a cost of £35,000. Then they decided to build a second – at the same cost – in case Prince Philip needed to go at the same time. Neither toilet was used.

Prince Charles insists on having his own wooden toilet seat installed wherever he's going.

Just before the Queen opened the Westminster and Chelsea hospital of which she was to be patron, officials realized that the hospital's initials would be WC and quickly changed the name to Chelsea and Westminster.

When Queen Victoria visited Trinity College Cambridge, she looked down at the River Cam, which was basically an open sewer, and seeing the toilet paper asked Dr Whewell, the Master of Trinity, what were all those pieces of paper floating down the river. The Master replied, 'Those, ma'am, are notices that bathing is forbidden.'

The death of Queen Victoria's beloved Albert was as a direct result of poor sanitation – he died of typhoid in 1861 (in 1870, one in every 3,000 people in Britain died of typhoid).

King Edward VII bought a 'WC enclosure in the form of an attractive armchair upholstered in velvet' for his mistress, the actress Lily Langtry.

Toilets around the world

In a 1992 survey by Andrex Moist Toilet Tissue, British public toilets were voted among the worst in the world, just ahead of those in Thailand, Greece and France.

The Japanese have invented the Shower Toilet. Originally designed for invalids, it boasts a self-raising seat cover, a bidet, water jets, a heated seat, a hot-air dryer and a fan for the removal of smells, all operated with an infra-red control. The Japanese have also built toilets that resemble coffee shops, churches and space stations, one that speaks your weight, and one that is a bicycle.

In 1993, Juan Bernaus was sentenced to three years' jail in Argentina for switching the 'Ladies' and 'Gents' signs round on public toilets.

An American jeweller has built the world's most expensive toilet, made of gold, diamonds, rubies and emeralds, with a mink seat – it costs $175,000.

Toilet paper

Before the invention of toilet paper, people used shells or stones, bunches of herbs, or at best a bit of sponge attached to a stick which they rinsed with cold water.

The Victorians were so delicate they couldn't bring themselves to use the words 'toilet paper'; instead they said 'curl papers'.

In 1986, Nathan Hicks of St Louis, Missouri shot his brother Herbert dead because he used six toilet rolls in two days.

The French use less toilet paper (8½lb per person per year) than any other European people; the Swedes use the most (18½lb), while the British are sixth in the European loo roll table with 10lb. In total we use nearly 1.5 billion loo rolls, more than 200,000 tons a year.

American civil servants' pay checks are recycled to make toilet rolls.

Hermann Goering refused to use regulation toilet paper and used to bulk-buy soft white handkerchiefs instead.

American researchers spent $100,000 on making the discovery that three out of four people hang their toilet rolls so that the paper is pulled down to be torn off rather than up.

The world's oldest piece of toilet paper – thought to be 1,200 years old – was found buried under an Israeli garage.

An American toilet manufacturer in California has created loo rolls made from hay. It is not known whether this is the same Californian company that in 1992 started selling 'camouflage' toilet paper for hunters to use so that fellow hunters don't mistake them for whitetailed deer.

CELEBRITIES AND TOILETS

Judy Garland and Lenny Bruce both died on the loo; King George II died after falling off a loo.

In 1993, Barbra Streisand got stuck in a toilet at Liza Minnelli's apartment during a party; fellow guests Jack Nicholson and Michael Douglas couldn't break down the door and so the building's porter had to come up to release her.

Actor George Hamilton was once trapped in the toilet of a restaurant, but he was rescued after a few minutes.

Jack Nicholson has a dead rattlesnake embedded in the clear plastic seat of his toilet.

While Gerald Ronson was at Ford Prison, he had to clean toilets, a job also once performed by the singer Tasmin Archer (at a recording studio) before she became famous. By contrast, the late Little 'The Loco-Motion' Eva found herself cleaning toilets in police stations *after* her days of fame.

Sir Winston Churchill did not believe in using toilet seats. He had them for his guests but when his plumber asked him what sort of seat he would have on his own loo, he responded, 'I have no need of such things.'

Chuck Berry installed video cameras in the women's toilets of his restaurant (The Southern Air).

Marti Pellow, the lead singer of Wet Wet Wet, was born in a public toilet in Clydebank.

PEOPLE WHO HAVE BEEN PESTERED FOR AUTOGRAPHS IN TOILETS

Sandi Toksvig was sitting in a public toilet which had a broken lock. A woman burst in by mistake and shut the door. Two seconds later she came back and said, 'You're that Sandi Toksvig. Can I have your autograph?'

Joan Collins stopped giving autographs after someone slid a piece of paper under a loo door and asked her to sign it.

Minnie Driver was also asked to give an autograph after someone slid a piece of paper under a loo door but merely said, 'Could we do this outside?'

Andrea Corr was asked for an autograph while she was throwing up. 'I couldn't believe it. I told her it might be a good idea if I washed my hands first.'

Julia Roberts was asked for an autograph while she was on the loo. She said, 'I'm the tiniest bit busy.'

Pierce Brosnan was asked while using a urinal. He obliged but: 'I refused the guy's request to say "shaken not stirred".'

Paul Newman stopped signing autographs 'when I was standing at a urinal at Sardi's and a guy came up with a pen and paper. I wondered: do I wash first and then shake hands?'

TOILET QUOTES

'You must know that it is by the state of the lavatory that a family is judged' (Pope John XXIII)

'The biggest waste of water in the country by far. You spend half a pint and flush two gallons' (Prince Philip in a 1965 speech)

'Everything a man brings to his marriage is consigned to the downstairs loo' (Kelly Hoppen, an interior designer)

PEOPLE AND THE NAMES THEY GAVE THEIR PETS

Renée Zellweger: a dog (collie/retriever) named Woofer

Britney Spears: two Yorkshire terriers named Mitzy and Baby, a Rottweiler named Cane and a poodle named Lady

Jessica Simpson: a pig named Brutus

Cameron Diaz: a cat named The Little Man

Paul O'Grady: a dog (golden retriever) named Bruno

Natalie Imbruglia: a dog (King Charles spaniel) named Charlie

Ozzy Osbourne: dogs named Baldrick (a bulldog), Sugar, Sonny, Raider, Buster and Phoebe

Samantha Mumba: a dog (shih-tzu) named Foxy

Sarah Michelle Gellar: a dog (Maltese terrier) named Thor

Natalie Appleton: a dog (chihuahua) named Chiquita

Nicole Appleton: a dog (chihuahua) named Godzilla

Drew Barrymore: a dog named Flossie (once saved Drew's life by waking her in a house fire)

Sara Cox: a dog (basset hound) named Snoop (after Snoop Dogg)

Daniel Radcliffe: dogs (border collies) named Binka and Nugget

Tara Palmer-Tomkinson: a dog (Burmese mountain dog) named Wolfgang

Derren Brown: a parrot named Figaro

Courtney Love: a dog named Bob Dylan

Melissa Joan Hart: a duck named Flipper and dogs named Holly Ochola and Permani Pele

Axl Rose: a dog named Sumner (Sting's surname at birth)

Julia Roberts: a dog named Gatsby

Anna Carteret: a cat named Michael Jackson

Matt LeBlanc: a dog (Dobermann) named Shadow

Isabella Rossellini: a dog (dachshund) named Ferdinando

William Shatner: a dog (Dobermann pinscher) named Kirk

Uma Thurman: a dog (chow chow) named Muffy

Steve Martin: a cat named Dr Carlton B. Forbes

David Baddiel: a cat named Chairman Meow

Victoria and David Beckham: dogs (Rottweilers) named Puffy and Snoopy

Jennifer Jason Leigh: dogs named Bessie and Otis

Kirsten Dunst: cats named Inky, Taz and Zorro

Hilary Swank: dogs named Lucky and Tanner, a rabbit named Luna, a parrot named Seuss and a cat named Deuce

Brendan Fraser: a dog (chihuahua) named Lucy

Ralph Lauren: a dog (bearded collie) named Rugby

Valentino: dogs (pugs) named Molly and Maggie

Domenico Dolce and Stefano Gabbana: dogs (yellow Labradors) named Lola and Dali

Giorgio Armani: cats – a Blue Russian named Uli and three Persians: Nerone, Micia and Charlie

A.J. McLean: dogs (Yorkshire terriers) named Vegas and Jack Daniels

Dame Elizabeth Taylor: parrots named Dick and Liz

Leonardo DiCaprio: a dog (poodle) named Rufus

Jim Carrey: a dog (Labrador) named Hazel (who gets a professional massage three times a week and lives in a $20,000 three-room dog house, complete with plush sofa)

George Michael: a dog (Labrador) named Hippy

Robbie Williams: a cat named Our Lady Kid

Madonna: a dog named Pepito

Geri Halliwell: a dog (shih-tzu) named Harry

Adam Sandler has a bulldog named Meatball

FEARS & PHOBIAS

Flying Dennis Bergkamp, Whitney Houston, Aaron Spelling, The Dalai Lama, Lenny Kravitz, Mike Oldfield, Lesley Joseph, Bret Easton Ellis, Bob Newhart, Muhammad Ali, Joanne Woodward, Sam Shepard, Billy Bob Thornton, Whoopi Goldberg, Cher, Glenda Jackson, Aretha Franklin, Emily Mortimer, Sharleen Spiteri, Dina Carroll, John Peel, Justin Timberlake, Joaquin Phoenix, Patsy Palmer

Germs &/or Dirt Michael Jackson, Howard Hughes, Marlene Dietrich, Prince

Clowns Billy Bob Thornton, Puff Daddy/P. Diddy, Johnny Depp

The Dark Nancy Dell'Olio, Melinda Messenger, Christina Aguilera, Joan Collins, Baroness Margaret Thatcher, Stephen King, Melanie Sykes, Tracey Emin

Heights Prince, Tara Fitzgerald, Vic Reeves, Martin Clunes, Ann Widdecombe, Will Young

Snakes Sarah, Duchess of York, Madeleine Albright, Isla Blair, Ross Kemp, Stephen King

Needles &/or Injections Martine McCutcheon, Angela Griffin

Earthquakes Kevin Bacon, George Clooney

Cats Julius Caesar, Napoleon, King Henry II

Spiders Leo McKern, Stephen King, Claudia Winkleman

OTHER PEOPLE AND THEIR FEARS & PHOBIAS

Lee Evans (the colour green – he once freaked out when he was made to wear a green suit)

Rachel Weisz (frogs – she's been known to go without a bath rather than evict amphibian intruders from her ground-floor bathroom)

The Dalai Lama (caterpillars)

Billy Bob Thornton (antiques)

Kate Beckinsale (metaphobia – fear of throwing up)

Christina Ricci (gerbils)

Matthew McConaughey (tunnels and revolving doors)

Queen Christina of Sweden (fleas)

Ernest Hemingway (telephones – because of his fear of the American income tax office)

Sigmund Freud (train travel)

Caroline Quentin (rats)

Queen Elizabeth I (roses)

Princess Margaret (dolls)

Madonna (thunder)

Judy Garland (horses)

Sir Alfred Hitchcock (policemen – he refused to learn to drive for fear of being stopped by a policeman)

Graham Greene (blood and bats)

Robert Mitchum (crowds)

Sid Caesar (haircuts)

Robert De Niro (dentists)

Natalie Wood (water – she was to die by drowning)

Nicholas Lyndhurst (tall buildings)

Leslie Grantham (moths)

FAMOUS PEOPLE WHO BOUGHT HOUSES THAT HAD BELONGED TO OTHER FAMOUS PEOPLE

Brian Jones bought A.A. Milne's house, Cotchford Farm in Hartfield, West Sussex

Pete Townshend bought Alfred, Lord Tennyson's house in Twickenham

Pete Townshend also bought Ronnie Wood's house, the Wick in Richmond, Surrey (which he'd bought from John Mills)

Lord Jeffrey Archer bought Rupert Brooke's house, the Old Rectory in Grantchester, Cambridgeshire

Nick Mason bought Camilla Parker-Bowles's house in Corsham, Wiltshire

Engelbert Humperdinck bought Jayne Mansfield's house in Beverly Hills, California

Burt Reynolds bought Al Capone's ranch in Florida

Jacqueline Bisset bought Clark Gable and Carole Lombard's house in Benedict Canyon, California

Martin Clunes bought Field Marshal Montgomery's home, the Old Rectory in Beaminster, Dorset

Noah Wyle bought Bo Derek's ranch (for £1.6 million) in Santa Barbara, California

Robert Kilroy-Silk bought Ozzy Osbourne's house in Little Chalfont, Buckinghamshire

Paul O'Grady (aka Lily Savage) bought Vic Reeves's house in Aldington, Kent, which had once been owned by Sir Noël Coward

Davinia Murphy bought Noel Gallagher's house – Supernova Heights – in North London

Jerry Seinfeld bought Billy Joel's 30-acre Long Island beachfront estate in 2000

John Cleese bought Bryan Ferry's Holland Park, London house in 1977 (for £80,000); he sold it in 2001 for £5 million

Madonna bought Diane Keaton's Beverly Hills home for £4.4 million

Earl Spencer bought David Gilmour's West London house for £4.5 million

Vic Reeves bought Tom Baker's house near Maidstone in Kent

PEOPLE AND THE INSTRUMENTS THEY CAN PLAY

Piano Dustin Hoffman, Sir Anthony Hopkins, Clint Eastwood, Richard Gere, Rupert Everett, Elijah Wood, David Baddiel, Pope Benedict XVI, Jane Fisher, Lorcan Cranitch, Hugh Jackman, Roger Lloyd-Pack, Sean Bean

Clarinet Woody Allen, Ricki Lake (also flute, piano and piccolo)

Banjo George Segal, Ewan McGregor (can also play the French horn)

Guitar Renée Zellweger, Serena Williams, Michael Ancram, Tony Blair, Gary Sinise (bass)

Saxophone Bill Clinton, James Gandolfini (also plays the trumpet), Darius Danesh, Don Cheadle

Cello Prince Charles, Emily Watson

Tuba John Malkovich

Accordion Gabriel Byrne

Mandolin Nicolas Cage – for his role in *Captain Corelli's Mandolin*

Violin Russell Crowe – for his role in *Master And Commander*

PEOPLE WHO EXPERIENCED BAD STAGE FRIGHT

Sir Derek Jacobi avoided the theatre for two years after drying as Hamlet in 1980.

Lord Laurence Olivier went through a bout of terrible stage fright when he was running the National Theatre and playing Othello. Olivier said, 'All I could see were the exit signs and all I wanted to do was run off the stage each night towards them.'

Freddie Starr became addicted to Valium because of his stage fright.

The first time the Irish singer Enya appeared on stage she took fright, fled and had to be coaxed back by a psychologist.

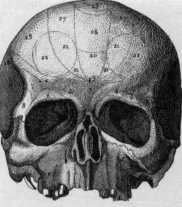

John Sessions fled the stage during a performance of *My Night With Reg* in 1995 because of stage fright, but he returned.

Barry Humphries suffers from stage fright 'every night' and has 'to overcome a tremendous reluctance to get on stage'.

Tim Roth started out as a stage actor on the fringe. Now he sticks to films because his stage fright leads him to having 'nightmares' about the theatre.

Marvin Gaye had such bad stage fright that he once tried to escape by climbing out of his dressing room.

Stephen Fry suffered such bad stage fright in *Cell Mates* (as well as other problems) that he left the country.

Dawn French was sick every night when she starred in *Then Again* in the West End. 'Every night I go on I'm knocking a couple of weeks off my life because of the stress.'

Barbra Streisand returned to the stage after stage fright put her off. On her return she said, 'It has taken me 2,700 hours and $360,000 worth of psychotherapy to be able to sing.' Streisand puts her stage fright partly down to a PLO death threat in 1967, which caused her to forget her lines on stage.

Elvis Presley's hip-wiggling started out as stage fright. According to Carl Perkins, 'Elvis was so nervous his legs would shake. One day he did it and the crowd went wild. He asked guitarist Scotty Moore, "What'd I do?" and Moore replied, "I don't know but do it again."'

In 1999, Paul McGann found the experience of performing at the Bush Theatre in Shepherd's Bush, London, so intimate that he vowed never to appear on stage again.

Uma Thurman has avoided stage work since 1996 after bursting into tears in an off-Broadway show.

Vanessa Redgrave was struck with panic while appearing in *The Prime of Miss Jean Brodie* and didn't perform on stage for another six years.

Tea Leoni had such bad stage fright while recording the pilot for *The Naked Truth* that she threw up five times.

In 2001, Robbie Williams announced he was going to take time off because he was suffering from stress and stage fright.

Judy Garland tried hypnosis but found that Irish whiskey worked better.

THINGS THAT NEW WORKERS ARE ASKED TO FETCH

A tub of elbow grease, invisible nails, a pair of rubber scissors, a dozen sky-hooks, a left-handed monkey-wrench, a glass hammer, a long weight, a horizontal ladder, a right-handed mug, a tin of striped paint

KISSING

The first kiss was supposedly delivered by God. According to Genesis, God breathed the 'spirit of life' into Adam. This has come to be interpreted symbolically as a kiss, which is why so many religious ceremonies include kissing.

A study by a Canadian anthropologist demonstrated that 97 per cent of women shut their eyes during a kiss but only 37 per cent of men did. The late actor Anthony Quinn had an explanation: 'Many a husband kisses with his eyes wide open. He wants to make sure his wife is not around to catch him.' Chico Marx (of the Marx Brothers) would have agreed. Chico was an habitual philanderer. When his wife caught him French kissing a girlfriend, he replied, 'I wasn't kissing her, I was whispering in her mouth.'

Kissing on the lips is something the Romans started. A husband returning from work would kiss his wife's lips to see if she'd been boozing during the day. The Romans had three different types of kiss: *basium*, the kiss on the lips; *osculum*, a friendly kiss on the cheek, and *suavium*, the full monty. In fact, the Romans were so keen on kissing that the Emperor Tiberius was obliged to ban the practice after an epidemic of lip sores. Until the Romans invaded, the British had no word for 'kissing'.

The French Kiss itself – tongues and all – was invented in the Brittany village of Pays de Mont as a substitute for sex because the population was growing too fast.

Kissing got a bad press because of Judas Iscariot, who used the kiss as a sign of betrayal. In exchange for 30 pieces of silver, Judas identified Jesus to his enemies in the Garden of Gethsemane by kissing him. This is probably the earliest known example of kiss and tell.

In writing – particularly in greetings cards and in love letters – we use XXXXs to represent kisses. The origins of this go back to the days when people who couldn't write signed their name with an X. To emphasize their sincerity, they would then kiss their mark – in the same way that they would have kissed a Bible when swearing an oath on it. This practice of kissing the X led to the X representing a kiss. The Romans also sealed the signing of contracts with a kiss.

Kissing under the mistletoe at Christmas is an English tradition that has been exported to other countries. It started with the Kissing Bough, which had mistletoe at its centre. When the Christmas Tree replaced the Kissing Bough, the mistletoe was salvaged and given its own unique position in the Yuletide ritual.

Human beings are not the only mammals that kiss. Polar bears and kangaroos kiss. Chimpanzees can and do French kiss. Sealions rub mouths, a male mouse licks the mouth of a female mouse and an elephant sometimes brushes its trunk against another elephant's lips.

Everyone knows that Lord Nelson said, 'Kiss me, Hardy.' However, some revisionists have claimed that what he really said was 'Kismet, Hardy', i.e. 'fate'. In fact, Hardy (an ancestor of Stan Laurel's partner, Oliver) understood him to say 'Kiss me' and that is what he duly did. Nelson said, 'Now I am satisfied,' and died about twenty minutes later, thanking God that he'd done his duty.

The Anti-Kissing League was formed in 1909 in America by people who considered kissing unhealthy.

How and where you kiss used to be a sign of where you stood in the social 'pecking' order. Equals kissed each other on the cheek. The lower you ranked to another person, the lower you had to kiss them. Thus a slave would kiss his master's feet, and a prisoner – not allowed even that close – would be obliged to kiss the ground near the foot, i.e. kiss the dirt.

Rodin's *The Kiss* is one of the world's most important pieces of sculpture. The figure – completed in 1886 – of two naked lovers kissing has not been entirely free from controversy. In the US in the last century, it was deemed to be too strong for the public and was exhibited in a special room.

The most kissed statue in the world is not The Kiss but a marble statue of Guidarello Guidarelli, a sixteenth-century Italian soldier. At the end of the nineteenth century, a rumour went around that any woman who kissed the statue would marry a fabulous man. Some five million kisses later, Guidarello's mouth is significantly redder than the rest of him.

One person who regretted kissing a work of art was Ruth van Herpen, who in 1977 was obliged to pay the restoration costs of a painting she had kissed and blighted with her red lipstick. In court, she declared that she 'only kissed it to cheer it up: it looked so cold'.

Alice Johnson, a 23-year-old American waitress, won a car in Santa Fe after kissing it for 32 hours and 20 minutes in a 1994 competition. She loosened four teeth in the process.

An American insurance company discovered that men were less likely to have a car accident on the way to work if they were kissed before they set off.

If you are late, you are said to have 'kissed the hare's foot'. Glandular fever is referred to as 'the kissing disease' (because that is how it is easily spread among adolescents). In the US a person who has been sacked is said to have been given the 'kiss-off'. A sailor who in olden times 'kissed the gunner's daughter' had been tied to the breech of a cannon and flogged. A person vomiting is said to be 'kissing the porcelain bowl'.

As all internet surfers know, the acronym KISS stands for 'Keep It Simple, Stupid'.

In Sicily, members of the Mafia have stopped kissing each other because the way they kissed was a dead giveaway to the police and mobsters were getting arrested.

SCREEN KISSES

The first film kiss was in, appropriately enough, the 1896 movie _The Kiss_. The protagonists were John C. Rice and May Irwin.

The film with the most kisses is the 1926 _Don Juan_, in which John Barrymore performed 191 kisses with different women. This was before the 1930 Hays Code, which banned 'excessive and lustful kissing'.

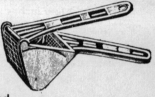

Greta Garbo didn't relish kissing scenes with Fredric March, her co-star in _Anna Karenina_, so she ate garlic before every such scene. Diana Rigg did the same before kissing George Lazenby in _On Her Majesty's Secret Service_. Julia Roberts hated kissing Nick Nolte while making _I Love Trouble_. At one point she sent a memo to the producer saying, 'If he puts his tongue in my mouth one more time I'm walking off the set.'

Nepal bans films featuring kisses by Nepalese actors. The same is true of Bangladesh and Macao.

The most famous kiss in a Hollywood film is probably that between Burt Lancaster and Deborah Kerr in _From Here To Eternity_.

The first genuine French kiss in a Hollywood movie was between Warren Beatty and Natalie Wood in the 1961 film _Splendor In The Grass_.

The first kiss in an Indian film didn't take place until the 1978 film _Love Sublime_, when Shashi Kapoor and Zeenat Aman embraced. An Indian minister described the kissing scenes as 'an insult' and called for a mass protest.

Bing Crosby – or so his co-stars claimed – had really bad breath, probably a result of his pipe-smoking. Clark Gable's bad breath wasn't improved by the whisky he regularly drank or the false teeth he wore, and Vivien Leigh hated having to kiss him in _Gone With The Wind_.

KISSING AROUND THE WORLD

Eskimos rub noses, as do a good many other peoples. Polynesians like a nose rub but also enjoy the *mitakuku*, which involves biting hairs from eyebrows. Trobriand islanders bite each other's eyelashes. In China, they touch each other's cheeks and then sniff. In the Pacific Islands, they inhale each other's breath. In Gambia, a man holds the back of a lover's hand against his nose. In Knightsbridge people put their cheeks a few inches apart from each other and say 'Mmmm'.

After World War Two, Americans were so keen to see the Japanese embrace the American way of life that during their occupation they ordered Japanese film makers to put kisses in their films. Some feat, in films that were invariably about Samurai warriors.

In Sorocaba, Brazil, they outlawed kissing in public places – specifically 'the cinematographic kiss, in which salivas mix to swell the sensuality'.

If you're in Scotland and are offered a 'Glasgow kiss', or in Liverpool a 'Kirby kiss', you'd better refuse unless you want a head butt.

Oliver Cromwell banned kissing on Sundays – even for married couples – on pain of a prison sentence.

In 1837, Thomas Saverland tried to kiss a woman who promptly bit off part of his nose. Saverland took her to court but lost, the judge commenting, 'When a man kisses a woman against her will, she is fully entitled to bite his nose, if she so pleases.'

In 1969, there was a mass kiss-in in the town of Inca on the island of Mallorca. Young lovers were being fined 500 pesetas for kissing in public, so a group of couples held a 'snogfest'. The police charged them and they were fined a total of 45,000 pesetas before being released.

KISSING AND HEALTH

The World Health Organization issued a warning against passionate kissing for World Aids Day 1991 – although current medical thinking is that you can't get AIDS from snogging.

Kissing is good for your teeth. According to dentists, kissing encourages saliva, which acts as a mouthwash that helps prevent tooth decay. However, a 1994 report by the German Dental Association claimed that French kissing could give you toothache on the basis that 'tongues can make holes in teeth'.

Kissing can prevent illness. When you absorb someone else's saliva, you also receive their enzymes, which gives you their immunities – a kind of antibiotic. Of course, kissing can pass on diseases too.

Kissing a frog doesn't necessarily get you a prince but it might get rid of your cold sore, thanks to a chemical secreted from frog skins.

A really tongue-twisting kissing session exercises 39 different facial muscles and can burn up 150 calories – more than a 15-minute swim. An ordinary peck uses up just three calories.

UNICEF AMBASSADORS

Sir Roger Moore, Julio Iglesias, Emmanuelle Béart, Sir Edmund Hillary, Imran Khan, Liam Neeson, George Weah, Lord Richard Attenborough, Liv Ullmann, Jane Seymour, Robbie Williams, Zinedine Zidane, Susan Sarandon, Nana Mouskouri, Martin Bell, Michael Jackson, Samantha Mumba

FAMOUS PEOPLE AND THEIR ALLERGIES

Tom Cruise (cats)

Beyonce Knowles (perfume)

Dannii Minogue (wheat, dairy products and yeast)

Lisa Faulkner (cats)

Sandra Bullock (horses)

Tony Robinson (cats and feathers)

Roger Cook (cucumbers)

Steve Wright (feathers)

Gaby Roslin (wheat)

Honor Blackman (cats)

Beverley Callard (avocados)

Andi Peters (chocolate)

Sue Townsend (monosodium glutamate)

Clint Eastwood (horses)

Susan Hill (wasps)

Nick Hancock (cats and dogs)

Bill Clinton (flowers)

Richard E. Grant (alcohol)

Donald Sutherland (cigarette smoke)

Drew Barrymore (garlic and coffee)

Naomi Campbell (tuna)

Sharon Stone (caffeine)

Iggy Pop (milk)

Trisha Goddard (lactose)

Lenny Henry (chicken)

CELEBRITIES AND WHO THEY CHOSE AS THEIR BEST MAN

GROOM	BEST MAN
Marco Pierre White	**Michael Winner**
Uri Geller (renewing vows)	**Michael Jackson**
Chris Evans	**Danny Baker**
Dennis Taylor	**Ian Woosnam**
David Bailey	**Mick Jagger**
Kenneth Clarke	**John Selwyn Gummer**
Jeremy Irons	**Christopher Biggins**
Bob Geldof	**Dave Stewart**
Kenneth Branagh	**Brian Blessed**
John McEnroe	**Björn Borg**
John Lennon	**Brian Epstein**
Viv Richards	**Ian Botham**
Tommy Steele	**Lionel Bart**
Jimmy Mulville	**Rory McGrath**
Martin Clunes	**Neil Morrissey**
David Seaman	**Bob Wilson**
Trevor Phillips	**Peter Mandelson**

Bungee jumpers

Davina McCall (over the Grand Canyon), Leonardo DiCaprio, Zara Phillips, Pat Rafter, Abs Breen, Andre Agassi, Ian Wright, Jeremy Guscott, Julian Lennon, Anna Walker, Chris Eubank, Debbie Harry, Jonathan Davies, Renny Harlin, Stuart Barnes, Joe McGann, Orlando Bloom, Dominic Monaghan, Jodie Marsh, Prince William, Richard Dunwoody, Robbie Williams

Vineyard owners

Sir Cliff Richard, Mick Hucknall, Sir Peter Ustinov, Francis Coppola, Gerard Depardieu, Jean Tigana, Sir Chay Blyth, Michel Roux, Sam Neill, The Dalai Lama, Greg Norman, Olivia Newton-John, Lorraine Bracco, Robin Williams

ACTORS AND THE ROLES THEY TURNED DOWN

Vin Diesel turned down Ben Affleck's role in *Daredevil*

Debra Winger turned down Glenn Close's role in *Fatal Attraction*

Diane Lane turned down Renée Zellweger's role in *Chicago*

John Travolta turned down Richard Gere's role in *Chicago*

Kevin Costner turned down Matthew Broderick's role in *War Games* (he did it to appear in *The Big Chill* but his role in that was left on the cutting-room floor)

George Segal turned down Dudley Moore's role in *10*

Robert Redford turned down Dustin Hoffman's role in *The Graduate*

Lee Marvin turned down George C. Scott's role in *Patton*

Sylvester Stallone turned down Eddie Murphy's role in *Beverly Hills Cop*

George Raft turned down Humphrey Bogart's role in *The Maltese Falcon*

Marlon Brando turned down Robert Redford's role in *Butch Cassidy And The Sundance Kid*

Eddie Cantor turned down Al Jolson's role in *The Jazz Singer*

Henry Fonda turned down Peter Finch's role in *Network*

Elvis Presley turned down Kris Kristofferson's role in *A Star Is Born*

Julia Roberts turned down Sharon Stone's role in *Basic Instinct*

Robert De Niro turned down Willem Dafoe's role in *The Last Temptation of Christ*

Richard Gere turned down Bruce Willis's role in *Die Hard*

CRICKET – AS EXPLAINED TO A FOREIGNER

You have two sides, one out in the field and one in.

Each man that's in the side that's in goes out, and when he's out he comes in and the next man goes in until he's out.

When a man goes out to go in, the men who are out try to get him out, and when he is out he goes in and the next man in goes out and goes in.

When they are all out, the side that's out comes in and the side that's been in goes out and tries to get those coming in, out.

Sometimes, there are men still in and not out.

There are two men called umpires who stay all out all the time and they decide when the men who are in are out.

When both sides have been in and all the men are out (including those who are not out) then the game is finished.

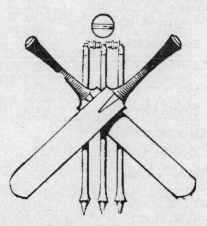

ALL THE BRITISH NEW TOWNS SINCE WORLD WAR TWO – AND WHEN THEY WERE NEW

Stevenage (1946)

Crawley (1947)

East Kilbride (1947)

Harlow (1947)

Hemel Hempstead (1947)

Newton Aycliffe (1947)

Glenrothes (1948)

Hatfield (1948)

Peterlee (1948)

Welwyn Garden City (1948)

Basildon (1949)

Bracknell (1949)

Cwmbran (1949)

Corby (1950)

Cumbernauld (1955)

Skelmersdale (1961)

Livingston (1962)

Redditch (1964)

Runcorn (1964)

Washington (1964)

Irvine (1966)

Milton Keynes (1967)

Newtown (1967)

Peterborough (1967)

Northampton (1968)

Telford (1968: known as Dawley from 1963 to 1968)

Warrington (1968)

Central Lancashire (1970 – based on Preston and Leyland)

Stonehouse (1973 – scrapped in 1976)

DISHES FROM AROUND THE WORLD

Pig's Organs In Blood Sauce (Philippines)

Baked Bat (Samoa)

Crispy Roasted Termites (Swaziland)

Roast Field Mice (Mexico)

Weaver Moths In Their Nests (Zaire)

Parrot Pie (actually twelve budgerigars) (Australia)

Bee Grubs In Coconut Cream (Thailand)

Guinea Pig In A Creole Style (Peru)

Queen White Ants (South Africa)

Calf Udder Croquettes (France)

Coconut Cream-marinated Dog (Indonesia)

Mice In Cream (Arctic)

Starling Stew With Olives (Turkey)

Stewed Cane Rat (Ghana)

Water Beetle Cocktail Sauce (Laos)

Turtle Ragout (Mexico)

Stuffed Bear's Paw (Romania)

Red Ant Chutney (India)

Baked Muskrat (Canada)

Raw Octopus (Hawaii)

Calf's Lung And Heart In A Paprika Sauce (Hungary)

Fox Tongues (Japan)

Pig's Face (Ireland)

Silkworm Pupae Soup (Vietnam)

Cajun Squirrel Ravioli (US)

Turtle Casserole (Fiji)

Lambs' Tails And Honey (Morocco)

Sun-dried Maggots (China)

PALLBEARERS FOR FAMOUS PEOPLE

Phil Everly, for Buddy Holly

Donald Dewar, for John Smith

Ben Crenshaw, for Harvey Penick

Jack Lemmon, for Rosalind Russell

John McEnroe, for Vitas Gerulaitis

Emerson Fittipaldi, for Ayrton Senna

James Stewart, for Clark Gable

Hubert de Givenchy, for Audrey Hepburn

Ian Botham, for Colin Milburn

Tom Mix, for Wyatt Earp

Joe Louis, for Sonny Liston

King Edward VII, for William Gladstone

Kenny Rogers, for Vincente Minnelli

Sir Bobby Charlton, Sir Tom Finney and Nat Lofthouse, for Sir Stanley Matthews

Tony Mortimer, for Reggie Kray

Rock Hudson, Frank Sinatra, Laurence Olivier, Gregory Peck, David Niven, Fred Astaire and Elia Kazan, for Natalie Wood

George Clooney, for Rosemary Clooney

Richard Madeley, for Caron Keating

Denis Law, Derek Dougan and Gerry Armstrong, for George Best

THIS
BOOK

PURE TRIVIA

Trivia was a Roman goddess to whom sacrifices were offered at crossroads. Because travellers often engaged in idle gossip at crossroads, Trivia's name (referring to three roads coming together) came to be associated with the sort of information exchanged in such places.

Offered a new pen to try, 97 per cent of people will write their own name.

The pitches that Babe Ruth hit for his last-ever home run and that Joe DiMaggio hit for his first-ever home run were thrown by the same man.

Donald Duck's middle name is Fauntleroy. Quackmore Duck is the name of Donald Duck's father.

Until the 18th century, India produced almost all the world's diamonds.

During US conscription for World War Two, there were nine documented cases of men with three testicles.

82 per cent of the Beatles music was about love.

The name Wendy was made up for the book *Peter Pan*.

All the clocks in *Pulp Fiction* are stuck on 4:20.

Every time Beethoven sat down to write music, he poured ice water over his head.

Venetian blinds were invented in Japan.

Alfred Hitchcock didn't have a belly button. It was eliminated when he was sewn up after surgery.

Windmills turn anti-clockwise.

The Nike swoosh was invented by Caroline Davidson back in 1971. She received $35 for making the swoosh.

The name of the character behind bars in the Monopoly board game is Jake the Jailbird.

Half the world's population has seen at least one James Bond movie.

Naturalists use marshmallows to lure alligators out of swamps.

There are three times as many households in the United States without telephones as there are without television sets.

The name Yucatan comes from the Maya for 'listen to how they speak' – which is what the Maya said when they first heard the Spanish.

M&Ms were developed so that soldiers could eat chocolate without getting their fingers sticky.

An ant lion is neither an ant nor a lion. It is the larval form of the lacewing fly.

The term 'the whole 9 yards' comes from World War Two. A .50-calibre machine-gun ammo belt measured exactly 27 feet (or 9 yards) before being loaded. If a fighter pilot fired all of it at once, the target was said to have received 'the whole 9 yards'.

The bark of the redwood tree is fireproof. Fires in redwood forests take place inside the trees.

Amethyst was once thought to prevent drunkenness.

50 per cent of Americans live within 50 miles of their birthplace.

20 per cent of all road accidents in Sweden involve an elk.

FIRSTS

The **first** time women and men used separate toilets was in 1739 at a Paris ball.

Ice-cream cones were **first** served at the 1904 World's Fair in St Louis.

Dubbed laughter was used on American television for the **first** time on 9 September 1950.

The **first** flushing toilet seen on US TV was on *Leave It To Beaver*.

Dr W.S. Halstead was the **first** to use rubber gloves during surgery in 1890.

The **first** sport to have a world championship was billiards in 1873.

Benjamin Franklin was the **first** person to suggest daylight saving.

Whoooooopi!

The **first** in-flight movie was shown on a Lufthansa flight on 6 April 1925.

The **first** couple to be shown in bed together on US prime time TV were Fred and Wilma Flintstone.

Austria was the **first** country to use postcards.

The **first** country to abolish capital punishment was Austria in 1787.

John Lennon's **first** girlfriend was named Thelma Pickles.

Whoopi Goldberg acquired her **first** name because she had a problem with flatulence.

The **first** product to have a bar code was Wrigley's gum.

Britain's **first** escalator was installed in Harrods in 1878.

The **first** plastic ever invented was celluloid in 1868. It's still used today to make billiard balls.

The **first** mosque in the US was built in 1893.

Sugar was **first** added to chewing gum in 1869 – by a dentist.

The **first** telegraph message tapped by its inventor, Samuel Morse, was: 'What hath God wrought?'

Iceland was the **first** country to legalize abortion in 1935.

The **first** words spoken on the telephone by its inventor, Alexander Graham Bell, were: 'Watson, come here, I need you.'

The **first** words spoken on the phonograph by its inventor, Thomas Edison, were: 'Mary had a little lamb.'

Captain Cook was the **first** man to set foot on all continents (except Antarctica).

In 1776, Croatia was the **first** country to recognize the United States.

Beethoven's Fifth was the **first** symphony to include trombones.

90 per cent of all new restaurants fail in the **first** year. Of the ones that survive, 90 per cent fail in the second year.

THE FIRST SINGLES THEY BOUGHT

Sue Perkins: 'My Camera Never Lies' (Bucks Fizz)

Brian May: 'Rock Island Line' (Lonnie Donegan)

Amanda Holden: 'I'm In The Mood For Dancing' (The Nolans)

Moby: 'Live And Let Die' (Wings)

Mick Hucknall: 'God Save The Queen' (The Sex Pistols)

Nicki Chapman: 'Killer Queen' (Queen)

Jordan: 'I Should Be So Lucky' (Kylie Minogue)

Jemma Redgrave: 'I'm The Leader of The Gang (I Am!)' (Gary Glitter)

Samantha Mumba: 'Sisters Are Doin' It For Themselves' (The Eurythmics and Aretha Franklin)

Sir Paul McCartney: 'Be-Bop-A-Lula' (Gene Vincent)

Beverley Callard: 'I'm A Believer' (The Monkees)

Dale Winton: 'I Only Want To Be With You' (Dusty Springfield)

Carol Vorderman: 'Sugar Baby Love' (The Rubettes)

Sophie Anderton: 'I Should Be So Lucky' (Kylie Minogue)

Pete Waterman: 'The Deadwood Stage' (Doris Day)

Paul Young: 'Fire And Water' (Free)

Zoë Ball: 'Merry Xmas Everybody' (Slade)

Arabella Weir: 'Daydream Believer' (The Monkees)

Steve Penk: 'Skweeze Me, Pleeze Me' (Slade)

Nicky Campbell: 'Alone Again (Naturally)' (Gilbert O'Sullivan)

Amanda Redman: 'MacArthur Park' (Richard Harris)

Paul O'Grady: 'Sugar Time' (Nancy Sinatra)

David 'Kid' Jensen: '(I Can't Get No) Satisfaction' (The Rolling Stones)

Frances Barber: 'Last Train To Clarksville' (The Monkees)

Kaye Adams: 'Ernie (The Fastest Milkman In The West)' (Benny Hill)

Jayne Middlemiss: 'Don't Stand So Close To Me' (The Police)

Philippa Forrester: 'Save Your Kisses For Me' (The Brotherhood of Man)

Griff Rhys Jones: 'I Want To Hold Your Hand' (The Beatles)

Roger Black: 'Knowing Me, Knowing You' (Abba)

Martine McCutcheon: 'Mickey' (Toni Basil)

Cilla Black: 'Why Do Fools Fall In Love' (Frankie Lymon And The Teenagers)

Mark Lamarr: 'Jake The Peg' (Rolf Harris)

Ardal O'Hanlon: 'Money, Money, Money' (Abba)

Rory McGrath: 'Don't Throw Your Love Away' (The Searchers)

BEGINNINGS

Leonardo da Vinci invented an alarm clock that woke the sleeper by rubbing his feet.

Kiwis lay the largest eggs (relative to body size) of any bird.

Human babies born in May are on average 200 grams heavier than babies born in other months.

The word 'sex' was coined in 1382.

From fertilization to birth, a baby's weight increases 5,000 million times.

Clark Gable was listed on his birth certificate as a girl.

One female mouse can give birth to 100 babies in a year.

When Harold Robbins was a child he used to run errands for Lucky Luciano.

Mel Gibson broke the school record for the most strappings in a week – 27.

Martine McCutcheon was shortlisted for the Pears Baby.

Bela Lugosi, the great screen Dracula, was actually born in Transylvania.

Roy Walker was in the Vienna Boys' Choir.

Numbering houses in London streets began only in 1764.

When a polar bear cub is born, it can't see or hear for the first month.

The first novel written on a typewriter was *The Adventures of Tom Sawyer*.

The ancient Greeks believed that boys developed in the right-hand side of the womb and girls in the left.

Paper was invented early in the 2nd century by a Chinese eunuch.

Bruce Oldfield didn't see an inside loo until the age of 12.

Carnegie Hall in New York City opened in 1891 with Tchaikovsky as guest conductor.

Pamela Anderson was Canada's Centennial Baby, having been the first baby born on the centennial anniversary of Canada's independence.

The drinking straw was invented in 1886.

Daryl Hannah was so shy as a child that at one point she was diagnosed as borderline autistic.

Carbonated soda water was invented in 1767 by Joseph Priestley, the discoverer of oxygen.

Screwdrivers were first used to help knights put on armour.

As a child Sheryl Crow used to pretend she was Stevie Wonder by playing the piano with the lights off.

The smoke detector was invented in 1969.

The wristwatch was invented in 1904 by Louis Cartier.

Dido, Emily Watson and Oliver Letwin were banned from watching TV as children.

Sylvester Stallone was kicked out of 14 schools in 11 years.

Jodie Foster was mauled by a lion when she was a child.

A newborn kangaroo is small enough to fit in a teaspoon.

WERE FOSTER CHILDREN

Vidal Sassoon, George Cole, Kathy Burke, Sylvester Stallone, Gary Glitter, Jane Lapotaire, Kriss Akabusi, Eartha Kitt, Neil Morrissey, Marilyn Monroe, Barbara Stanwyck, Shirley Anne Field (sent to a baby home and then to an orphanage), Seal (until his Nigerian mother reclaimed him), Rosie Perez, Paul Barber, Samantha Morton, Kerry McFadden

WERE BARNARDO'S BOYS

John Fashanu, Justin Fashanu, Leslie Thomas, Bruce Oldfield, Chris Armstrong

Born with a club foot

Dudley Moore, Josef Goebbels, Dr David Starkey, Mother Teresa, Emperor Claudius, Eric Richard, Lord Byron, Callan Pinckney

Born in india

Spike Milligan, Joanna Lumley, William Makepeace Thackeray, Angela Thorne, Sir Cliff Richard, Sir Basil Spence, Nigel Dempster, Lord Beveridge, Julie Christie, Kenneth Kendall, Engelbert Humperdinck, George Orwell, Lord Colin Cowdrey, Tiny Rowland, Kim Philby, Lindsay Anderson, John Aspinall, Margaret Lockwood, Googie Withers, Isla Blair, Vivien Leigh, Anna Carteret, Pete Best

Born in canada

Saul Bellow, David 'Kid' Jensen, William Shatner, k.d. lang, Joni Mitchell, Bryan Adams, Rick Moranis, Leonard Cohen, Greg Rusedski, Margot Kidder, Mary Pickford, Genevieve Bujold, Michael J. Fox, Donald Sutherland, Leslie Nielsen, Lou Jacobi, Mike Myers, Shania Twain, Jason Priestley, Michael Ondaatje, James Randi, Robbie Robertson, Lionel Blair, Natasha Henstridge, Alanis Morissette, Jim Carrey, Norman Jewison, Raymond Massey, Martin Short, Linda Thorson, Oscar Peterson, Christopher Plummer, Lynda Bellingham, Celine Dion, Norma Shearer, John Candy, David Cronenberg, Wayne Gretzky, Neil Young

BORN IN WALES

Ian Hislop, Heather Small, Carol Vorderman, Christian Bale, Ryan Giggs, The Edge, Dawn French, Jonathan Pryce, Paul Whitehouse, H, John Prescott, Anneka Rice, Neil Aspinall, Sir Stanley Baker, Michael Owen, Dame Shirley Bassey, Jessica Garlick, Keith Allen, Paula Yates, Julian Cope, John Humphrys, Gabby Logan, Doris Hare, Jeff Banks, Peter Greenaway, Ioan Gruffudd, Catherine Zeta-Jones, Jeremy Bowen, Tommy Cooper, Terry Jones, Ivor Novello, Michael Heseltine, Martyn Lewis, Helen Lederer, Timothy Dalton, Hywel Bennett, Ray Milland, David Broome, Leslie Thomas, T.E. Lawrence, Noel Sullivan, Patrick Mower, Roald Dahl, Me-One, Charlotte Church, Roger Rees, Griff Rhys Jones, Victor Spinetti, Christopher Timothy

BORN IN SCOTLAND

Sir Sean Connery, Alan Cumming, Sheena Easton, Carol Smillie, Tony Blair, Robbie Coltrane, David McCallum, Annie Lennox, Maxwell Caulfield, Hannah Gordon, Lulu, Ewan McGregor, Midge Ure, Donovan, Rory Bremner, Sharleen Spiteri, Stanley Baxter, Siobhan Redmond, Jimmy Somerville, Stephen Hendry, Fish, Andrew Marr, Matthew MacFadyen, Sylvester McCoy, John Sessions, Graeme Garden, John Hannah, Shirley Manson, Mark Knopfler, Ian Anderson, Barbara Dickson, Kaye Adams, Billy Connolly, Kenneth Cranham, Sir Jackie Stewart, Phyllida Law, Charles Kennedy, Jenni Falconer, Kirsty Gallacher, Ian McCaskill, Gail Porter, Tom Conti, Jack Bruce, Ronnie Corbett, Rhona Cameron, Sir Ludovic Kennedy, Jeff Stewart, Gordon Ramsay, Eddie Large, Ian Richardson, David Byrne, Sir Malcolm Rifkind, Marti Pellow, Irvine Welsh, Sally Magnusson, Lindsay Duncan, Robert Carlyle, Darius Danesh, John Gordon Sinclair, Jim Kerr, Annette Crosbie, Dame Muriel Spark, Nicky Campbell, Lorraine Kelly

BORN IN GERMANY

Ken Adam, John McEnroe, Andre Previn, Marsha Fitzalan, Charles Wheeler, Jackson Browne, Peter Alliss, Dominic Monaghan, Bruce Willis, Lucien Freud, Ruth Prawer Jhabvala, Henry Kissinger, Paul Ackford, Andrew Sachs, Gyles Brandreth, Jeri Ryan, Martin Lawrence, Pam Ferris, Peter Gilmore, Chris Barrie

BORN IN AFRICA

Nicola Pagett (Egypt)

Thomas Dolby (Egypt)

Fiona Fullerton (Nigeria)

Claudia Cardinale (Tunisia)

Derek Pringle (Kenya)

Glynis Barber (South Africa)

Stephanie Beacham (Morocco)

Patrick Allen (Nyasaland)

Moira Lister (South Africa)

Phil Edmonds (Zambia)

Debbie Thrower (Kenya)

William Boyd (Ghana)

Matthew Parris (South Africa)

BORN ELSEWHERE

Terry Butcher (Singapore)

Katie Boyle (Italy)

Chris De Burgh (Argentina)

Pamela Armstrong (Borneo)

Ted Dexter (Italy)

Fiona Bruce (Singapore)

Lisa Butcher (Singapore)

Minnie Driver (Barbados)

Louis Theroux (Singapore)

Dom Joly (Lebanon)

Eddie Izzard (Aden – now Yemen)

Robert Bathurst (Gold Coast – now Ghana)

Jenny Seagrove (Malaysia)

Dulcie Gray (Malaysia)

Sally Phillips (Hong Kong)

BORN PART-IRISH

Muhammad Ali, Joan Baez, Dolly Parton, Anthony Quinn, Emilio Estevez, Robert Mitchum, Valerie Harper, Don Ameche, Lucille Ball, Marlon Brando, James Clavell, Alex Haley, Kiri Te Kanawa, Robert De Niro, Freddie Prinze Jr, Lindsay Lohan

GYPSY BLOOD

Pat Phoenix, Elvis Presley, Eric Clapton, Vita Sackville-West, Django Reinhardt, Eric Cantona, David Essex, Bob Hoskins, Charlie Chaplin, Ava Gardner, Pablo Picasso, Nadja Auermann, Miguel de Cervantes, Yul Brynner

NATIVE AMERICAN BLOOD

Burt Reynolds (one-quarter Cherokee)

Johnny Depp (part Cherokee)

Waylon Jennings (part Cherokee and part Comanche)

Cher (part Cherokee)

Mike McShane

Tiger Woods

Johnny Cash (one-quarter Cherokee)

Lena Horne (one-eighth Blackfoot)

Jimi Hendrix (part Cherokee)

James Garner (part Cherokee)

Roy Rogers (part Choctaw)

Kim Basinger (part Cherokee)

Dolly Parton (one-eighth Cherokee)

Dennis Weaver (part Osage)

Quentin Tarantino (one-quarter Cherokee)

Billy Bob Thornton (one-quarter Choctaw)

Eartha Kitt (half Cherokee)

Farrah Fawcett (one-eighth Choctaw)

Sandy Duncan (part Cherokee)

Chuck Norris (half Cherokee)

John Phillips (half Cherokee)

Sally Field (part Cherokee)

Redd Foxx (one-quarter Seminole)

Joe Mantana (part Sioux)

Johnny Ray (part Blackfoot)

Oral Roberts (part Cherokee)

Will Rogers (part Cherokee)

Tommy Tune (part Shawnee)

Tori Amos (part Cherokee)

Jerry Hall (part Cherokee – her mother's father's grandmother was a Cherokee)

Val Kilmer (part Cherokee)

Jessica Biel (part Choctaw)

Hilary Swank

Sir Winston Churchill (one-sixteenth Iroquois)

Carmen Electra (part Cherokee)

Lou Diamond Phillips (one-eighth Cherokee)

Shannon Elizabeth (part Cherokee)

NB Benjamin Bratt's mother, a Peruvian Indian, is an activist for Native Americans

THE HUMAN CONDITION

If your body's natural defences failed, the bacteria in your gut would consume you within 48 hours, eating you from the inside out.

Only 4 per cent of babies are born on their due date.

People who smoke have 10 times as many wrinkles as people who don't smoke.

People who suffer from gum disease are twice as likely to have a stroke or heart attack.

We use 43 muscles to frown.

We use 17 muscles to smile.

The fastest-moving muscle in the human body is the one that opens and closes the eyelid.

14 million people were killed in World War One; 20 million died in the flu epidemic that followed it.

Women smile more than men do

Right-handed people tend to scratch with their left hand, and vice-versa.

It takes the typical person 7 minutes to fall asleep.

Every year, there are more births in India than there are people in Australia.

Someone who eats little is said to eat like a bird, even though many birds eat twice their weight in a day.

Men have on average 10 per cent more red blood cells than women do.

One square inch of human skin contains 625 sweat glands.

The Islands of Langerhans are a group of cells located in the pancreas.

Most people have lost 50 per cent of their taste buds by the time they reach 60.

15 million blood cells are produced and destroyed in the human body every second.

The human head is a quarter of our total length at birth, but an eighth of our total length by the time we reach adulthood.

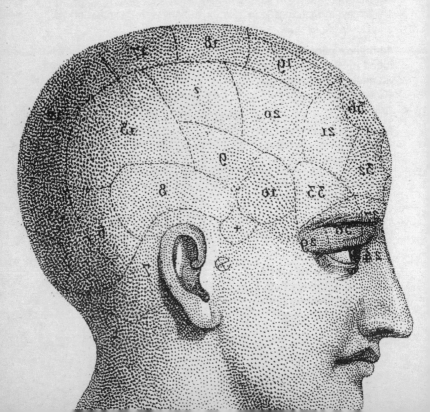

The hydrochloric acid in the human stomach is strong enough to dissolve a nail.

The foot is the most common part of the body bitten by insects.

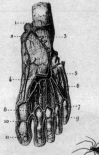

There are over 100 million light-sensitive cells in the retina.

The opposite of 'cross-eyed' is 'wall-eyed'.

We use 54 muscles every time we step forward.

The surface area of a human lung is equivalent to a tennis court.

Between the ages of 20 and 70, the typical person spends about 600 hours having sex.

Our hearing is less sharp after eating too much.

The hardest bone in the human body is the jawbone.

The largest cell in the human body is the ovum; the smallest is the sperm.

The most sensitive cluster of nerves is at the base of the spine.

By lying on your back and raising your legs slowly you can't sink in quicksand.

The longest-recorded tapeworm found in the human body was 33 metres in length.

Vegetarians live longer and have more stamina than meat-eaters, but they have a higher chance of getting blood disorders.

An eyelash lives about 5 months.

There are approximately 100 million acts of sexual intercourse each day.

In an average lifetime a person will walk the equivalent of three times around the world.

Men get hiccoughs more often than women do.

Every year 100 people choke to death on ballpoint pens.

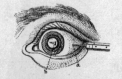

The colour red has been found to promote the hunger reflex in humans. This is why so many fast-food establishments use the colour in their logos and décor.

A human eyeball weighs an ounce.

Only 30 per cent of humans can flare their nostrils.

The average adult has about 18 square feet of skin.

A human being loses around 40 to 100 strands of hair a day.

A person will die from total lack of sleep more quickly than they will from starvation. Death will occur after about 10 days without sleep; starvation takes a few weeks longer.

If you go blind in one eye, you lose about a fifth of your vision, but all your sense of depth.

The human body contains enough iron to make a 3-inch nail.

Women have more genes than men, and because of this are better protected from things like colour blindness and haemophilia.

It takes about 200,000 frowns to make a permanent wrinkle.

The average nipple size is 0.27 inches for women and 0.22 for men.

The risk of a heart attack is higher on a Monday than on any other day of the week.

Intelligent people have more zinc and copper in their hair.

90 degrees below zero your breath will freeze in mid-air and fall to the ground.

Women are twice as likely as men to have panic attacks.

Schizophrenics hardly ever yawn.

The best way for a man to know whether he will go bald is to look at his mother's father.

An average pair of feet sweats a pint of perspiration a day.

There are twice as many left-handed men as there are left-handed women.

It takes about 150 days for a fingernail to grow from cuticle to fingertip.

Vision requires more brain power than the other four senses.

Women can detect smell better than men.

Men can read smaller print than women.

The average beard grows 5 inches a year.

The average newborn baby cries 113 minutes a day.

In one day an average person will take about 18,000 steps.

Women's hair is about half the diameter of men's

Women have a higher incidence of tooth decay than men.

The cartilage in the nose never stops growing.

The average person opens the fridge 22 times a day.

The average clean-shaven man will spend five months of his life shaving and will remove 28 feet of hair.

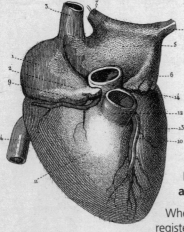

If you live to 70, your heart will have pumped 55 million gallons of blood.

In a lifetime, you eat around 35 tons of food.

The average reader can read 275 words per minute.

The vocabulary of the average person consists of 5,000 to 6,000 words.

In the adult human body, there are 46 miles of nerves.

When you stub your toe, your brain registers pain in 1/50th of a second.

The size of your foot is approximately the size of your forearm.

You burn 3.5 calories each time you laugh.

Women blink twice as often as men.

The kidneys use more energy than the heart (kidneys use 12 per cent of available oxygen; the heart uses 7 per cent).

The most common disease in the world is tooth decay.

You inhale about 700,000 of your own skin flakes each day.

83 per cent of people hit by lightning are men.

Human thighbones are as strong as concrete.

The thumbnail grows the slowest; the middle nail the fastest.

When you sneeze, your heart stops.

The average lifespan of a taste bud is 10 days.

According to medical experts, babies dream in the womb.

One out of every 200 women is endowed with an extra nipple.

Men are four times more likely than women to sleep naked.

The average person's eyes will be closed about 30 minutes a day because of blinking.

You'd have to walk 34 miles to melt away one pound of fat.

Women can hear better than men

Male patients fall out of hospital beds twice as often as female patients.

The body's largest internal organ is the small intestine, with an average length of 20 feet. The large intestine is only a sixth of the length of the small intestine.

The right lung takes in more air than the left (because the left lung is smaller to make room for the heart).

Women have a wider peripheral vision than men.

The average person grows up to 6 feet of nose hair in a lifetime.

It takes 25 muscles to swallow.

More people are allergic to cow's milk than any other food.

Teenagers are 50 per cent more susceptible to colds than people over 50.

The mouth produces 2 pints of saliva a day.

The vagina and the eye are self-cleaning organs.

While sleeping, one man in eight snores, and one in ten grinds his teeth.

It's harder to tell a convincing lie to someone you find sexually attractive.

The average person produces about 12,000 gallons of urine over the course of their lifetime.

Anthropologists know of no human society whose children don't play hide and seek.

Non-smokers dream more than smokers.

AIRLINE ACRONYMS

Aer Lingus
Arousing Erotic Randy Ladies In Nice Green Uniform Suits

Aeroflot
Aircraft Everywhere Run On Fuel Left Over by Tanks

Air India
An Interesting Ride, I'll Not Do It Again

Alitalia
Always Late In Transit, Always Late In Arrival

American
A Miracle Each Rider Is Currently Alive Now
Airline Meals Eaten Regularly Induce Cramps And Nausea

BWIA
But Will I Arrive?

Delta
Departures Extra-Late, Tardy Arrivals
Doesn't Even Leave The Airport

El Al
Every Landing Always Late
Everyone's Luggage Always Lost

Emirates
English Managed, Indian Run, A
Thousand Ex-pats Suffering

Finnair
Flies Ideally? Nah, Not Airborne In Reality

Garuda
Go And Relax Until Delay Announcement

Gulf Air
Get Used to Late Flights – Aircraft In Repair

KLM
Kamikaze Loving Maniacs

Liat
Luggage Is Always Tardy

Lot
Lots Of Trouble

Lufthansa
Let Us Fondle The Hostess And Not Say Anything

Olympic
Onassis Likes Your Money Paid In Cash

Qantas
Quick And Nasty Transportation, Australian Style
Quite A Neat Trick, Arriving Safely
Quits Air-travel, Next Time Approaches Ship

Ryanair
Running Your Ailing National Airline Into Receivership

Sabena
Such A Bad Experience – Never Again

SAS
Sex Always Supplied
Same As Sabena

Swissair
Sexy Women In Swissair Service Are
Incredibly Rare

United
Usually Not Inclined To Eliminate
Disasters

Virgin
Very Interesting Ride: Going
Into Nowhere

ANIMALS ETC.

An elephant's trunk can hold 2 gallons of water.

An adult lion's roar is so loud, it can be heard up to 5 miles away.

The word rodent comes from the Latin word 'rodere', meaning to gnaw.

A mole can dig over 250 feet of tunnel in a single night.

A cow's only sweat glands are in its nose.

When a horned toad is angry, it squirts blood from its eyes.

The average gorilla has a penis that is 2 inches long.

Bats have sex in the air.

Chameleons can move their eyes independently: one eye can look forward at the same time as the other looks back.

The pocket gopher, a burrowing rodent, can run backwards as fast as it can run forwards.

A chamois goat can balance on a point of rock the size of a £1 coin.

Frogs don't drink water – they absorb it through their skin.

A giraffe's erect penis is 4 feet long.

Bulls and crocodiles are colour-blind.

The ragdoll is the largest breed of domesticated cat in the world.

The sloth moves so slowly that green algae can grow undisturbed on its fur.

Male boars excite females by breathing on their faces.

The poison arrow frog has enough poison to kill 2,200 people.

Emus can't walk backwards.

Pigs can cover a mile in 7.5 minutes when running at top speed.

Iguanas can and do commit suicide.

The giraffe has the highest blood pressure of any animal.

A crocodile's tongue is attached to the roof of its mouth.

Crocodiles swallow stones to help them dive deeper.

Gorillas sleep for up to 14 hours a day.

Giraffes can't cough.

The last of a cat's senses to develop is its sight.

The ancient Egyptians trained baboons to wait at their tables.

A woodchuck breathes only 10 times during hibernation.

A python is capable of devouring a pig whole.

A rat can last longer without water than a camel can.

Rabbits have been known to reach a speed of 47 mph.

An iguana can stay under water for 28 minutes.

Brand-new baby giraffes are 6 feet tall and weigh almost 200 pounds.

Moose intercourse typically lasts about five seconds.

Giraffes rarely sleep more than 20 minutes a day.

A cat has 32 muscles in each ear.

Kangaroo means 'I don't understand' in Aborigine.

A polar bear's skin is black. Its fur is not white, but clear.

Polar bear liver contains so much vitamin A that it could be fatal to a human.

Minks have sex that lasts about 8 hours.

Cats can't taste sweet food.

Gorillas can't swim.

A rat can fall from a five-storey building without injury.

Greyhounds have the best eyesight of any dog.

When a giraffe is born, it has to fall around 6 feet to the ground.

The greater dwarf lemur in Madagascar always gives birth to triplets.

A giraffe's heart is 2 feet long.

Sheep are mentioned 45 times and goats 88 times in the Bible.

The placement of a donkey's eyes in its head enables it to see all four feet at one time.

Camels have three eyelids to protect themselves from blowing sand.

Frogs and toads never eat with their eyes open because they have to push food down into their stomach with the back of their eyeballs.

Hamsters blink one eye at a time.

A chameleon's tongue is twice the length of its body.

Brazil, Argentina, Australia and New Zealand all have more cattle than people.

Australia, Uruguay, Syria and Bolivia all have more sheep than people.

Somalia has more goats than people.

Denmark has twice as many pigs as people.

Alaska has almost twice as many caribou as people.

Paris is said to have more dogs than people.

Giraffes have no vocal cords.

A full-grown bear can run as fast as a horse.

The cheetah is the only cat that can't retract its claws.

A rodent's teeth never stop growing.

Beavers can hold their breath for 45 minutes.

Porcupines can float in water.

Deer sleep for only 5 minutes a day.

The skin of a hippopotamus is nearly bulletproof.

BIRDS ETC.

Lyre birds can imitate any sound they hear, from a car alarm to an electric chainsaw.

The owl can't move its eyes but it's the only creature able to turn its head in a complete circle.

Apart from chocolate and avocados, which are highly toxic to the parrot, pet parrots can eat most of the food we eat.

Kiwis are the only birds that hunt by smell.

Bluebirds can't see the colour blue.

Condors can fly 10 miles without flapping their wings.

A male emperor penguin spends 60 days or more protecting his mate's eggs, which he keeps on his feet, covered with a feathered flap. During this time he doesn't eat and loses about 25 pounds. When the chicks hatch, he feeds them a liquid from his throat. When the female penguin returns to care for the young, the male goes to sea to eat and rest.

A pigeon can't lay an egg

The smallest bird in the world is the bee hummingbird: it's 2.24 inches long and weighs less than a tiny coin.

The pouch under a pelican's bill holds up to 25 pounds of fish and water.

Geese often mate for life, and can pine to death at the loss of their mate.

The kiwi is the only bird with nostrils at the end of its bill.

Turkeys often look up at the sky during a rainstorm, and have been known to drown as a result.

Penguins are the only bird that can leap into the air like a porpoise.

The shell constitutes 12 per cent of an egg's weight.

Only the male nightingale sings.

The emu gets its name from the Portuguese word for ostrich.

An eagle can kill a young deer and fly away with it.

A pigeon can't lay an egg unless she sees another pigeon. If another pigeon isn't available, her own reflection in a mirror will do.

unless she sees another pigeon

There is a type of parrot in New Zealand that likes to eat the rubber strips that line car windows.

The fastest bird in the world is the peregrine falcon, which can fly faster than 200mph.

When the air force was conducting test runs and breaking the sound barrier, fields of turkeys dropped dead.

The bones of a pigeon weigh less than its feathers.

Ostriches stick their heads in the sand to look for water.

When the first duck-billed platypus arrived at the British Museum, the curators thought it was a fake and tried to pull its beak off.

A vulture will never attack a human or animal that is moving.

The albatross can sleep in flight.

Unlike humans, canaries can regenerate their brain cells.

It takes about 40 minutes to hard-boil an ostrich egg.

75 per cent of wild birds die before they reach 6 months old.

A woodpecker can peck 20 times a second.

Fish etc.

Nine out of every ten living things live in the ocean.

A male catfish keeps the eggs of his young in his mouth until they are ready to hatch.

Sharks will continue to attack, even when disembowelled.

A shark is the only fish that can blink with both eyes.

In order to mate, a male deep-sea anglerfish will bite a female and never let go – eventually merging his body into hers and spending the rest of his life inside her.

The red mullet only turns red after death.

Many male fish blow bubbles when they want to mate.

Whales increase their weight 30,000,000,000 times in their first 2 years.

A large whale needs more than 2 tons of food a day.

The closest relative to the manatee is the elephant.

A dolphin's hearing is so acute that it can pick up an underwater sound from 15 miles away.

When young, black sea basses are mostly female, but at the age of five many become male.

Whales can't swim backwards.

To change its line of sight, a whale must move its entire body.

The walking catfish can live on land.

A baby oyster is called a spat.

If a lobster loses an eye it can grow a new one.

If a mackerel stops swimming, it dies.

MACKEREL

A red sponge can be broken into a thousand pieces and still reconstitute itself.

The heart of a blue whale is the size of a small car.

The flounder, a flat fish, has both eyes on one side of its body.

One species of shark is so competitive that the babies fight each other within the womb, until only one is left to be born alive.

Bluefin tuna can swim at 50 miles per hour.

Sharks are immune to all known diseases.

A shark can grow a new set of teeth in a week.

Squids sometimes commit suicide by eating their own tentacles.

Oysters can change from one gender to the other and back again.

The female starfish produces 2 million eggs a year. 99 per cent of them are eaten by other fish.

The European freshwater mussel lives for at least 90 years.

5 piranha fish could chew a horse and rider up in 7 minutes.

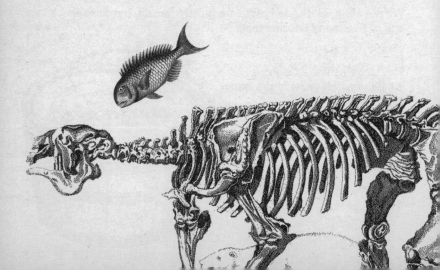

Sharks will eat anything except something in the vicinity of where they give birth. This is the only way nature protects them from accidentally eating their own babies.

To keep from being separated while sleeping, sea otters tie themselves together with kelp.

The shrimp's heart is in its head.

An octopus has 3 hearts.

A humpback whale's penis can be longer than 10 feet.

A whale can swim for 3 months without eating.

A whale's penis is called a dork.

85 per cent of all life on Earth is plankton.

Turtles can live for more than 100 years.

At 188 decibels, the whistle of the blue whale is the loudest sound produced by any animal.

All clams start out as males; some decide to become females at some point in their lives.

INSECTS ETC.

There are more insects in one square mile of rural land than there are human beings on Earth.

A queen bee lays about 1,500 eggs a day.

The only food cockroaches won't eat is cucumber.

Flies take off backwards.

A moth has no stomach.

The size of a mosquito penis is 1/100th of an inch.

Some ribbon worms will eat bits of themselves if they can't find any food.

The average bee yields only one-twelfth of a teaspoon of honey in its life.

Bees flap their wings 11,400 times a minute.

A female mosquito can produce 150,000,000 young in one year.

Mosquitoes are attracted to people who have recently eaten bananas.

Mosquitoes like the scent of oestrogen, so women get bitten by mosquitoes more than men do.

After eating, a housefly regurgitates its food and then eats it again.

A butterfly warms its body up to 81 degrees Fahrenheit before flying.

A typical bed houses over 6 billion dust mites.

A leech has 32 brains.

A greenfly born on Sunday can be a grandparent by Wednesday.

Insects shiver when they're cold.

The cicada spends 17 years of its life sleeping. In the 2 weeks it's awake, it mates and then dies.

Earthworms have 5 hearts.

The silkworm has 11 brains. But it uses only 5 of them.

Leeches can drink up to 5 times their weight in blood.

There are over 1,800 known species of flea.

The longest earthworm ever found was 22 feet long.

Mosquitoes are attracted to the colour blue twice as much as to any other colour.

A snail can crawl across a razor blade without getting injured because it excretes a protective slime.

Cockroaches can survive underwater for 15 minutes.

Australian termites have been known to build mounds 20 feet high and at least 100 feet wide.

Slugs have 4 noses.

If a cockroach breaks a leg it can grow another one.

A spider's web is a natural clotting agent; applied to a cut it quickly stops the flow of blood.

The aphid's reproductive cycle is so fast that females are born pregnant.

The world's termites outweigh the world's humans 10 to 1.

Stag beetles have stronger mandibles than humans.

More people are killed each year by bees than snakes.

ONLYS

Your tongue is the **only** muscle in your body that is attached at **only** one end.

'One' is the **only** number with its letters in reverse alphabetical order.

The **only** Dutch word to contain eight consecutive consonants is 'angstschreeuw'.

Only female mosquitoes bite, and only female mosquitoes buzz.

The **only** two people in the Baseball Hall of Fame who had nothing to do with baseball are Abbott and Costello.

No president of the United States was an **only** child.

If there were an ocean big enough, Saturn would be the **only** planet that could float because its density is lighter than that of water (it is mostly gas).

Goethe could write **only** if he had an apple rotting in the drawer of his desk.

The **only** bone not broken so far in a ski accident is one located in the inner ear.

The **only** person ever to decline a Pulitzer Prize for Fiction was Sinclair Lewis.

Hummingbirds are the **only** birds able to fly backwards.

Christopher Lee was the **only** member of the cast (and crew) of the *Lord of the Rings* movies to have met J.R.R. Tolkien.

New Zealand is the **only** country that contains every type of climate in the world.

Pierre, the capital of South Dakota, is the **only** US state capital name that shares no letters with the name of its state.

Earth is the **only** planet not named after a God.

Black lemurs are the **only** primates, other than humans, that might have blue eyes.

The Dutch town of Abcoude is the **only** town or city in the world whose name begins with ABC.

Maine is the **only** US state with just one syllable. Maine is also the only US state that borders only one other state.

Theodore Roosevelt was the **only** US president to deliver an inaugural address without using the word 'I'. (Abraham Lincoln, Franklin D. Roosevelt and Dwight D. Eisenhower tied for second place, using 'I' only once in their inaugural addresses.)

Only two US states have names beginning with double consonants: Florida and Rhode Island (if you don't count Wyoming).

Only two countries have borders on three oceans – the US and Canada.

Europe is the **only** continent without a desert.

The letter W is the **only** letter in the alphabet that has three – rather than one – syllables.

Sir Alec Douglas-Home is the **only** prime minister to have made it into *Wisden*, having played for Middlesex and, in 1926, toured Argentina with the MCC.

Samuel Beckett is the **only** Nobel prizewinner to have made it into *Wisden* – having played in a first-class fixture for Dublin University against Northamptonshire (scoring 18 and 12) in 1926.

Nauru is the **only** country in the world with no official capital.

Snails mate **only** once in a lifetime, but it can take up to 12 hours.

Lake Nicaragua boasts the **only** freshwater sharks in the world.

The **only** wild camels in the world are in Australia.

The polar bear is the **only** mammal with hair on the soles of its feet.

The **only** chancellor to have previously worked for the Inland Revenue is James Callaghan.

Pecans are the **only** food that astronauts can take untreated into space.

A Dalmatian is the **only** dog that can get gout.

Devon is the **only** county in Great Britain to have two coasts.

A bowling pin has to tilt **only** 7.5 degrees to fall down.

General Robert E. Lee is the **only** person ever to have graduated from the West Point military academy without a single demerit.

Only two female mammals possess hymens: humans and horses.

Only two male mammals possess prostates: humans and dogs.

Bruce Forsyth, Brenda Fricker, Kerry Packer and Steven Spielberg have **only** one kidney each. (NB Mel Gibson has a horseshoe kidney – two kidneys fused into one.)

Early Greek and Roman physicians believed the **only** way to grow a good crop of basil was to curse while scattering the seeds.

PURE TRIVIA

Amber was once thought to be solidified sunshine or the petrified tears of gods.

1,929,770,126,028,800 different colour combinations are possible on a Rubik's Cube.

Cleopatra used pomegranate seeds for lipstick.

The decibel was named after Alexander Graham Bell.

'Honcho' comes from the Japanese word meaning 'squad leader'.

A cat falling from the seventh floor of a building has a 30 per cent smaller chance of surviving than if it falls off the twentieth floor. It takes about eight floors for the cat to realize what's going on and prepare itself.

English soldiers of the Hundred Years' War were known to the French as 'Les Goddamns' because of their propensity to swear.

Hydrangeas produce pink and white flowers in alkaline soil and blue ones in acidic soil.

Rabbits love licorice.

Malaria was originally believed to be caused by the vapours rising from swamps (the name comes from 'bad air').

Portland, Oregon was named in a coin-toss in 1844. Heads Portland, tails Boston.

50 per cent of all marshmallows consumed in the US have been toasted.

One superstition to get rid of warts is to rub them with a peeled apple and then feed the apple to a pig.

The 'live long and prosper' sign by *Star Trek*'s Mr Spock is the sign that Jewish priests (Cohenim) used while saying certain prayers.

St Cassian was a schoolmaster whose pupils stabbed him to death with their pens.

Mel Blanc, the voice of Bugs Bunny, was allergic to carrots.

According to the ancient Chinese, swinging your arms cures headache pain.

Syphilis was known as the French disease in Italy and the English disease in France.

Pliny believed that the souls of the dead resided in beans.

Coffee drinkers have sex more frequently and enjoy it more than non-coffee drinkers.

Ham radio operators got the term 'ham' coined from the expression 'ham-fisted operators', a term used to describe early radio users who sent Morse code (i.e. pounded their fists).

Traditionally, a groom must carry a bride over the threshold to protect her from being possessed by the evil spirits that hang around in doorways.

Apples are more effective at keeping people awake in the morning than caffeine.

Lipstick contains fish scales.

Kidney stones come in any colour from yellow to brown.

A stretched-out Slinky is 87 feet long.

The hundred-billionth Crayola crayon was Periwinkle Blue.

A can of Spam is opened every 4 seconds.

Pinocchio was made of pine.

More people are killed annually by donkeys than in aeroplane crashes.

Maine is the toothpick capital of the world.

New Jersey has a spoon museum with over 5,400 spoons.

There was once a town in West Virginia called '6'.

The colder the room you sleep in, the more likely you are to have a bad dream.

The Gulf Stream would carry a message in a bottle at an average of 4 miles per hour.

The monkey wrench was invented by Charles Moncke.

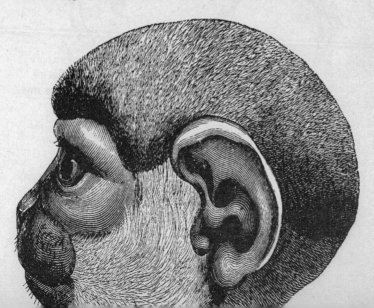

BEFORE FAME

Noel Gallagher used to be a roadie for the Inspiral Carpets (and Liam got the name Oasis from an Inspiral Carpets poster).

Shirley Williams screen-tested for the lead role in *National Velvet*.

Catherine Zeta-Jones broke into showbusiness as a teenage Shirley Bassey impersonator. Her father drove her around the working men's clubs to perform.

Geena Davis has an elbow that bends the wrong way (and when she was young, she'd do things like stand in a lift and the doors would close and she'd pretend that her arm had got caught).

Fidel Castro was voted Cuba's best schoolboy athlete (in 1944).

Simon Le Bon has taken part in the Whitbread Round-The-World yacht race.

Peter Snow auditioned to be James Bond (in the late 1960s) but was too tall.

Axl Rose used to earn $8 an hour for smoking cigarettes (for a science experiment at UCLA).

Michael Crichton handed in a paper written by George Orwell to see if his college professor had a down on him. He scored a B minus.

Billie Piper made her TV debut impersonating Posh Spice.

Emma Bunton played one of the bridesmaids catapulted onto a giant wedding cake in a Halifax Building Society TV commercial. Tina Barrett appeared in the same commercial.

Matt Damon used to break dance for money in Harvard Square.

Michelle Pfeiffer used to be a clerk at Von's grocery store in California where she learned to tie cherry stems in knots with her tongue.

Oprah Winfrey once approached Aretha Franklin as she got out of a limo and convinced the singer that she was abandoned. Aretha gave her $100, which she used to stay in a hotel.

FORMER ALTAR BOYS

Pierce Brosnan, Stephen Tompkinson, Phil Donahue, Jimmy Wray, Sir Michael Gambon, Frankie Fraser, Nigel Pivaro, Neil Jordan, Martin Scorsese, Louis Farrakhan, Bob Guccione, Paul McGann, Patric Walker, Tony Monopoly, Ron Todd, Bernhard Langer, Oliver North, Frank Bough, Danny La Rue, Engelbert Humperdinck, Eamonn Andrews, Charles Kennedy, Philip Treacy, Bernard Manning

DROPPED OUT OF COLLEGE

Ben Affleck (two colleges), Beau Bridges, Vin Diesel, Bill Murray, Dennis Quaid, Steven Spielberg, Stephen Stills, Eric Stoltz, Paula Abdul, Courteney Cox, Rosie O'Donnell, Marisa Tomei, Richard Dreyfuss, Carly Simon, David Gower, Bill Cosby, Jon Snow, Michael Douglas, Warren Beatty, Mick Jagger, Jane Fonda, Candice Bergen, Matt Damon, Christie Brinkley, Kate Beckinsale, Richard Stilgoe, Darius Danesh, Dave Gorman, Jake Gyllenhaal

SPENT PART OF THEIR CHILDHOOD IN A BROTHEL

James Brown

Louis Armstrong

Chico Marx (played piano in one)

Harpo Marx (also played piano but only knew two songs which he played over and over again at different speeds)

Edith Piaf (her grandmother was the cook. She also lived in one as an adult during the German occupation because it was one of the few buildings in Paris that was heated)

Richard Pryor (his grandmother was the owner)

NB Henri de Toulouse-Lautrec lived in a brothel as an adult

TEENAGE RUNAWAYS

Courtney Love, Oprah Winfrey, Bob Dylan, Daniel Day-Lewis, Billy Connolly, Errol Flynn, Roy Walker, Pierce Brosnan, Hazel O'Connor, Cary Grant, Ella Fitzgerald, Clare Higgins

ATTENDED ART SCHOOL

Robbie Coltrane, Charles Dance, Trevor Eve, Ralph Fiennes, Bob Holness, Jonathan Pryce, Alexei Sayle, Bryan Ferry, David Byrne, John Lennon, Sofia Coppola, Fran Healey, Muriel Gray, Vic Reeves, Jim Broadbent, Jada Pinkett-Smith, Sean Bean

RHODES SCHOLARS

Bill Clinton, Bryan Gould, Bill Bradley, Kris Kristofferson, Bob Hawke, Terrence Malick, Naomi Wolf, David Kirk, Dom Mintoff, Edward de Bono, Carl Albert, J. William Fulbright, Robert Penn Warren, Dean Rusk, General Wesley Clark

ATTENDED THE SORBONNE

Alan Alda, Jean-Luc Godard, Sam Waterston, Jacqueline Kennedy Onassis, Rose Tremain, Verity Lambert, Spencer Batiste, Michael Bogdanov, Dale Campbell-Savours, Lord Killanin, Prue Leith, Magnus Linklater, Sir Julian Critchley, Christian Lacroix, Clare Balding, Liza Minnelli

FORMER CHEERLEADERS

Reese Witherspoon, Meryl Streep, Paula Abdul, Madonna, Sally Field, Raquel Welch, Carly Simon, Jerry Lewis, Angela Bassett, Sandra Bullock, Renée Zellweger (star cheerleader), Cameron Diaz, Charisma Carpenter (for the San Diego Chargers), Steve Martin, Alicia Silverstone, Calista Flockhart, Jack Lemmon, Sela Ward, Teri Hatcher (for the San Franciso 49ers)

NB Uma Thurman abandoned her dreams of becoming a cheerleader at the age of ten after a bad experience at summer camp. 'The players were kind of embarrassed. We certainly didn't turn them on.'

FORMER (BOY) SCOUTS

Rolf Harris, Bill Clinton, David Bellamy, Sir Bobby Robson, Mark Spitz, Russell Grant, Georgie Fame, Richard Gere, Trevor Brooking, Sir Derek Jacobi, Frank Bough, Neil Armstrong, President Jacques Chirac, Sir David Attenborough, Leslie Thomas, Lord Brian Rix, Michael Parkinson, Lord Jeffrey Archer, Jason Donovan, Roger Rees, Brian Clough, Sir Stirling Moss, Tony Benn, Sir Norman Wisdom, Danny La Rue, James Stewart, Lord Richard Attenborough, Sir Richard Branson, Edward Woodward, Keith Richards, Michael Barrymore, George Michael, Lord Melvyn Bragg, Ken Dodd, John Major, Sir Paul McCartney, Jim Davidson, Ronnie Corbett, Sir Cliff Richard, Chris Tarrant

FORMER (GIRL) GUIDES

Janet Street-Porter, Mo Mowlam, Angela Rippon, Dame Anita Roddick, Helen Sharman, Björk, Michelle Gayle, Linda Robson, Sally Magnusson, Clare Short, Penny Junor, Emma Forbes, Emma Thompson, Diana Quick, Baroness Thatcher, Ann Widdecombe, Belinda Lang, Mariah Carey, Princess Margaret, Teresa Gorman, Venus Williams, Alice Beer, Glenda Jackson, The Princess Royal, Pauline Quirke, Susan Tully, Mandy Rice-Davies, Carol Vorderman, Anneka Rice, Delia Smith, Kim Wilde, Carol Smillie, Cherie Blair, The Queen, Cat Deeley, Lorraine Kelly, Sarah Kennedy, Davina McCall, Gail Porter, Kate Hoey, Claire Rayner, Jenni Murray, Sandi Toksvig, Lysette Anthony, Natasha Richardson, Hillary Clinton, Belinda Carlisle, Lesley Garrett, Kate Moss

HOMECOMING QUEENS

Rosie O'Donnell, Sela Ward, Caprice, Meryl Streep, Sissy Spacek, Meg Ryan, Lynne Cheney, Barbara Bush (Dubya's daughter), Kay Hartenstein, Tori Amos, Elizabeth Dole, Nicole Brown (O.J. Simpson's ex-wife), Sharon Tate

ACHIEVEMENTS BEFORE THE AGE OF 10

At the age of 3, Elizabeth Taylor danced in front of King George V.

At the age of 3, the 19th-century English philosopher John Stuart Mill was able to read Greek.

At the age of 4, Lulu sang in public for the first time.

At the age of 5, Natalie Wood appeared in her first film.

At the age of 5, Tori Amos won a scholarship to study piano in a Baltimore conservatory (but was kicked out by the age of 11).

At the age of 6, Shirley Temple was awarded an honorary Oscar 'in grateful recognition of her outstanding contribution to screen entertainment during the year 1934'.

At the age of 7, Fred Astaire was performing in vaudeville.

At the age of 8, Jamie Oliver was cooking in his father's pub.

At the age of 9, Ruth Lawrence passed A-level maths.

At the age of 9, Macaulay Culkin was cast as the lead character in *Home Alone*, the movie that made him famous.

WASHED DISHES FOR A LIVING

Ronald Reagan, Jacques Chirac, Burt Reynolds, Roseanne, Little Richard, Eddie 'The Eagle' Edwards, Sir Roger Moore, Steve Collins, Chrissie Hynde, Uma Thurman, Warren Beatty, Dustin Hoffman, Carlos Santana, Robert Duvall

TRAINED AS COMMERCIAL ARTISTS

Lynsey De Paul, David Bowie, Bob Hoskins, Roy Hudd, Sir Dirk Bogarde, Gene Hackman, Ian Hunter, Len Deighton, Pete Townshend, Leo Sayer

TOOK PART IN UNIVERSITY CHALLENGE AS COMPETITORS

David Mellor (Christ's College, Cambridge)

Clive James (Pembroke College, Cambridge)

Sebastian Faulks (Emmanuel College, Cambridge)

Miriam Margolyes (Magdalene College, Cambridge)

Alastair Little (Downing College, Cambridge)

John Simpson (Magdalene College, Cambridge)

Stephen Fry (Queens' College, Cambridge)

Andrew Morton (Sussex)

Malcolm Rifkind (Edinburgh)

WORKED AS USHERS/USHERETTES

Sylvester Stallone, Barbra Streisand, Marianne Jean-Baptiste, Charlene Tilton, George Michael, Elizabeth Garvie, George Segal, Nadia Sawalha, Jayne Irving, Kirk Douglas, Heather Graham, Al Pacino

WORKED AS MODELS

Joaquin Phoenix, Sharon Stone, Jessica Biel, Penelope Cruz, Bijou Phillips, Denise Richards, Chloe Sevigny, Mena Suvari, Christopher Walken, Emily Watson (for Laura Ashley, aged 4), Carol Smillie, Paul Marazzi, Rachel Stevens, Sophie Ellis-Bextor, Ralf Little, Willem Dafoe, Ashton Kurcher, Brooke Shields, Jacqueline Bisset, Sylvia Kristel, President Gerald Ford, Ali MacGraw, Charlotte Rampling, George Lazenby, Ellen Burstyn, Richard Jobson, Burt Reynolds, Jessica Lange, Dyan Cannon, Courteney Cox, Ted Danson, Susan Dey, Farrah Fawcett, Tom Selleck, Cybill Shepherd, Antonio Banderas, Cameron Diaz, Nick Nolte, Lindsay Lohan

STARTED OUT AS EXTRAS

Dustin Hoffman, Marilyn Monroe, Ronald Reagan, Clint Eastwood, Donald Sutherland, John Wayne, Robert De Niro, Bill Cosby, Clark Gable, Robert Duvall, Gary Cooper, Marlene Dietrich, Paulette Goddard, Stewart Granger, Jean Harlow, Sophia Loren, David Niven, Rudolph Valentino, Cate Blanchett (when she was 18, in a boxing movie filmed in Egypt where she was holidaying. She appeared in a crowd scene cheering for an American boxer who was losing to an Egyptian; she hated it so much she walked off the set), Gary Sinise (in *General Hospital*), Phil Collins (in *A Hard Day's Night*), Ben Affleck & Matt Damon (in *Field of Dreams*).

SERVED IN KOREA

Neil Armstrong, Sir Michael Caine, Frank Gorshin (as an entertainer), James Garner, Ty Hardin, Screamin' Jay Hawkins, Lee Hazlewood, Ed McMahon, Chaim Potok (as an army chaplain), Jamie Farr (Corporal Klinger in the TV series M*A*S*H – the only member of the cast to have served in Korea), Faron Young, P.J. Kavanagh, Berry Gordy Jr, Charlie Rich, Link Wray, John Mayall, Leonard Nimoy, John Wells, Robert Duvall

SERVED IN VIETNAM

Oliver Stone, Al Gore, Steve Kanaly (awarded the Purple Heart for the injuries he suffered there), Charles Lindbergh (as a brigadier-general), Oliver North, Colin Powell (two tours; awarded the Purple Heart), Dennis Franz (11 months in an elite airborne division), Brian Dennehy (was in the Marines for over five years and served eight months in Vietnam before returning home with shrapnel wounds and concussion), General Wesley Clark (was shot; awarded Silver Star for bravery), James Avery, Troy Evans

Stephen King failed the medical on four counts: flat feet, limited vision, high blood pressure and a punctured eardrum.

Roger Ebert went to the draft for the Vietnam War but was rejected for being overweight. He was 26 years old and weighed 206 pounds.

Micky Dolenz was drafted to serve in the US Army in 1967 despite medical grounds for deferment – trouble with Perthese disease in childhood had left him with one leg shorter than the other. Dolenz was eventually excused from military service for being underweight. Davy Jones was also drafted, but was excused as his family's sole source of support.

CONSCIENTIOUS OBJECTORS

Bill Clinton, Paul Eddington, Sir Michael Redgrave, Carl Wilson, Muhammad Ali, Lord Soper, Dom Mintoff, Donald Swann, Richard Dreyfuss, Harold Pinter, Lew Ayres, Fritz Weaver, Benjamin Britten

Mickey mouse club 'mouseketeers' on us tv

Justin Timberlake, Christina Aguilera, Britney Spears, J.C. Chasez, Keri Russell

Studied to be architects

Art Garfunkel, Rifat Ozbek, Janet Street-Porter, Queen Noor of Jordan, Justine Frischmann, Carla Bruni, Alan Plater, Lord Snowdon, Chris Lowe, Roger Waters, Ronnie Barker

Butlins redcoats

Ted Rogers, Des O'Connor, Roy Hudd, Michael Barrymore, Russell Grant, Darren Day, Jimmy Tarbuck, Ken Dodd, William G. Stewart, Dave Allen, Sir Cliff Richard, Johnny Ball, H (formerly from Steps), Bill Maynard, Duncan James

Qualified (medical) doctors

Graeme Garden, Che Guevara, David Owen, Harry Hill, Rob Buckman, W. Somerset Maugham, Lady Isobel Barnett, J.P.R. Williams, Graham Chapman, Sir Jonathan Miller, Anton Chekhov, Michael Crichton

WORKED IN THE CIRCUS

Pierce Brosnan (fire-eater in his teens)

Roberto Benigni (clown)

Christopher Walken (assistant lion tamer)

Harry Houdini (escapologist)

Burt Lancaster (acrobat)

Bob Hoskins (fire-eater)

Rupert Graves (clown)

Jack Higgins (odd jobs)

**W.C. Fields
(elephant attendant)**

Jeremy Beadle (ringmaster)*

Charlie Dimmock (trapeze artist)*

Cantinflas (prizefighter)

**Graham Cripsey (rode the wall
of death)**

Trevor Baylis (underwater
stunt in the Berlin Circus)

Yul Brynner (trapeze artist)

*After finding fame

LEFT-HANDED

Sarah Jessica Parker, Jean-Paul Gaultier, Angelina Jolie, Drew Barrymore, Charlie Dimmock, Eminem, Bruce Willis, Demi Moore, Rik Mayall, Goldie Hawn, Sir Bobby Charlton, Shirley MacLaine, Sir Henry Cooper, Phil Mickelson, Steve Ovett, Michael Crawford, Diane Keaton, Robert De Niro, Emma Thompson, Nicholas Lyndhurst, William Roache, Matthew Broderick, Paul Nicholas, Cheryl Baker, Ringo Starr, George Michael, Tom Cruise, Julia Sawalha, Syd Little, Loyd Grossman, Richard Dreyfuss, Robert Redford, Bob Geldof, Mark Spitz, Jennifer Saunders, Jean Shrimpton, Tony Robinson, Ruud Gullit, Phil Collins, Oprah Winfrey, Magnus Magnusson, Julian Clary, Julia Roberts, Michael Parkinson, Ross Kemp, Ryan O'Neal, Prince William, Bill Clinton, Uri Geller, George Bush, Sir Paul McCartney, Esther Rantzen, Terence Stamp, Seal

UNFORTUNATELY NAMED PRODUCTS AND CAMPAIGNS

Sharwoods launched its Bundh sauces – without realizing that, in Punjabi, the word 'bundh' is perilously close to a word meaning 'arse'.

Parker Pens' slogan, 'Avoid embarrassment – use Quink', when translated into Spanish came out as: 'Avoid pregnancy – use Quink'.

Plessey and **GEC** had a joint company in France called GPT. When this is pronounced in French, it comes out as Jay-Pay-Tay, which sounds like 'J'ai pété', meaning 'I have farted'.

Mitsubishi launched its Pajero 4WD without realizing that 'pajero' is Spanish for 'wanker'.

The computer company **Wang** ran an Australian TV commercial that contained the slogan, 'Wang cares'. It ran for just the one day.

KFC's 'finger-lickin' good' slogan was translated into China as 'eat your fingers off'.

Ford's car, the Pinto, couldn't be sold in Brazil because the word 'pinto' is slang for a small penis.

Electrolux was obliged to abandon its slogan 'Nothing sucks like Electrolux'.

The lager **Coors** had a slogan 'turn it loose' which, when translated into Spanish, became 'suffer from diarrhoea'.

Pepsi-Cola had a slogan 'Come alive with the Pepsi generation' which, when translated into Chinese, became 'Pepsi brings your ancestors back from the grave'.

Similarly, the name **Coca-Cola** was, at first, Ke-kou-ke-la in Chinese until the company discovered that the phrase means 'bite the wax tadpole' or 'female horse stuffed with wax', depending on the dialect.

The **Rolls-Royce** Silver Mist range had to be renamed for the German market because 'mist' means 'dung' in German.

Puffs tissues didn't sell well in Germany because 'puff' in German means 'brothel'.

The German hardware store chain **Götzen** opened a mall in Turkey but had to change the name as 'göt' means 'bum' in Turkish.

The Italian mineral water **Traficante** means 'drug dealer' in Spanish.

Honda launched its new car the Fitta in Scandinavia – only to find that 'fitta' was a slang word for vagina in Swedish, Norwegian and Danish.

Ford's Comet was called the Ford Caliente in Mexico, but although 'caliente' literally means hot (as in temperature), it's also used colloquially as 'horny'. Ford had a similar problem in Latin American countries with their Fiera, which means 'ugly old woman' there.

When **Mazda** launched the Laputa they didn't take into account the fact that 'puta' is the Spanish word for prostitute. The ads claiming that 'Laputa is designed to deliver maximum utility in a minimum space while providing a smooth, comfortable ride' took on a new meaning.

A **Nike** TV commercial for hiking shoes was shot in Kenya using Samburu tribesmen, one of whom was caught mouthing – in native Maa – 'I don't want these. Give me big shoes.'

Nissan launched the Moco before discovering that 'moco' is the Spanish for 'mucus'.

Frank Perdue's Chicken was advertised in Mexico with the slogan, 'It takes a tough man to make a tender chicken.' When translated into Spanish, this became: 'It takes a hard man to make a chicken aroused.'

The American slogan for **Salem** cigarettes, 'Salem – Feeling Free', was translated into Japanese as: 'When smoking Salem, you feel so refreshed that your mind seems to be free and empty.'

Hunt-Wesson introduced its Big John products in French Canada as Gros Jos before discovering that this is a slang expression for 'big breasts'.

Samarin, a Swedish remedy for upset stomachs, ran an ad that was a series of three pictures. The first was of a man looking sick, the second was of him drinking a glass of Samarin and the third was of him smiling. The company ran the ad in Arabic newspapers – where people read from right to left.

Toyota launched its MR2 model without realizing that, in France, it would be pronounced 'em-er-deux', which sounds very similar to 'merde', meaning 'shit'.

Bacardi brought out a fruit drink which they named 'Pavian' to suggest French chic, but, alas, 'pavian' means 'baboon' in German.

When **Gerber** first started selling baby food in Africa, they used their standard packaging with the cute baby on the label. Unfortunately, they were obliged to change it when they discovered that, in Africa, the standard practice is to put pictures of the contents on foods.

Jolly Green Giant translated into Arabic means 'Intimidating Green Ogre'.

When **Braniff** boasted about its seats in Spanish, what should have read 'Fly in leather' became 'Fly naked'.

SLOGANS SEEN OUTSIDE CHURCHES

No God – No Peace. Know God – Know Peace

Free Trip to heaven. Details Inside!

Try our Sundays. They're better than Baskin-Robbins

Have trouble sleeping? We have sermons – come and hear one!

God so loved the world that He did not send a committee

When down in the mouth, remember Jonah. He came out all right

Sign broken. Message inside this Sunday

How will you spend eternity – Smoking or Non-smoking?

Dusty Bibles lead to Dirty Lives

Come work for the Lord. The work is hard, the hours are long and the pay is low. But the retirement benefits are out of this world

It is unlikely there will be a reduction in the wages of sin

Do not wait for the hearse to take you to church

If you're headed in the wrong direction, God allows U-turns

Forbidden fruit creates many jams

In the dark? Follow the Son

If you can't sleep, don't count sheep. Talk to the Shepherd

GEOGRAPHY

Tasmania has the cleanest air in the inhabited world.

The furthest point from any ocean would be in China.

There are no public toilets in Peru.

The Red Sea is not red.

China uses 45 billion chopsticks per year.

The Pacific Ocean covers 28 per cent of the Earth's surface.

The poorest country in the world is Mozambique. (Switzerland is the richest.)

At the nearest point, Russia and America are less than 4 km apart.

Alaska is the most northern, western and eastern state; it also has the highest latitude, the most eastern longitude and the most western longitude, and could hold the 21 smallest states.

Birmingham has 22 more miles of canal than Venice.

The coastline of Alaska is longer than the entire coastline of the rest of the US (excluding Hawaii).

If an Amish man has a beard, he's married.

The people of Iceland read more books per capita than any other people in the world.

La Paz in Bolivia is so high above sea level there is barely enough oxygen in the air to support a fire.

Antarctic means 'opposite the Arctic'.

Fewer than 1 per cent of the Caribbean Islands are inhabited.

The volume of water in the Amazon river is greater than the next eight largest rivers in the world combined.

There is no point in England more than 75 miles from the sea.

Seoul, the South Korean capital, means 'the capital' in the Korean language.

Despite having a land mass over 27 times smaller, Norway's total coastline is longer than the US's.

Coca-Cola is Africa's largest private-sector employer.

Parsley is the most widely used herb in the world.

The Coca-Cola company is the largest consumer of sugar in the world.

In Albania nodding the head means 'no' and shaking the head means 'yes'.

The Coca-Cola company is the largest consumer of vanilla in the world.

Everything weighs 1 per cent less at the equator.

The East Alligator River in Australia's Northern Territory harbours crocodiles, not alligators.

Mongolia is the largest landlocked country.

More redheads are born in Scotland than in any other part of the world.

Eskimos use refrigerators to keep their food from freezing.

Two-thirds of the world's aubergines are grown in New Jersey.

28 per cent of Africa is wilderness; 38 per cent of North America is wilderness.

The University of Alaska covers four time zones.

Approximately 20 per cent of Americans have passports.

Canada has more lakes than the rest of the world combined.

One third of all the fresh water on Earth is in Canada.

10 per cent of the salt mined in the world each year is used to de-ice the roads in America.

Own/owned islands

Marlon Brando (Tetiaroa)

Sir Richard Branson (Necker)

Carla Lane (St Tedwell's East)

Charles Haughey (Inis Mhicileain)

Lord Peter Palumbo (Ascrib)

Björn Borg (Kattilo)

Malcolm Forbes (Lacaula)

Nick Faldo (Bartrath)

Björk (Ellidaey – given to her by the Icelandic government)

Leonardo DiCaprio (Blackadore Caye)

HISTORY

The first-known contraceptive was crocodile dung, used by Egyptians in 2000BC.

Armoured knights raised their visors to identify themselves when they rode past their king. This custom has become the modern military salute.

Nobody knows where Mozart is buried.

In the latter part of the 18th century, Prussian surgeons treated stutterers by snipping off portions of their tongues.

From 1807 till 1821, the capital of Portugal was moved to Rio de Janeiro, Brazil (at the time a colony of Portugal), while Portugal was fighting France in the Napoleonic Wars.

Abdul Kassem Ismael, the Grand Vizier of Persia in the 10th century, carried his library with him wherever he went. The 117,000 volumes were carried in alphabetical order by 400 camels.

Ethelred the Unready, King of England in the 10th century, spent his wedding night in bed with his wife and his mother-in-law.

The lance ceased to be an official battle weapon in the British Army in 1927.

The Toltecs, 7th-century native Mexicans, went into battle with wooden swords so as not to kill their enemies.

China banned the pigtail in 1911 as it was seen as a symbol of feudalism.

During World War One, the future Pope John XXIII was a sergeant in the Italian army.

Emperor Caligula once decided to go to war against the Roman god of the sea, Poseidon, and ordered his soldiers to throw their spears into the water.

The Pentagon has twice as many toilets as necessary because in the 1940s, when it was built, Virginia still had segregation laws requiring separate facilities for blacks and whites.

All 18 of Queen Anne's children (including 13 miscarriages) died before she did.

Mexico once had three presidents in one day.

Between 1839 and 1855, Nicaragua had 396 different rulers.

The Wright brothers' first flight was shorter than the wingspan of a 747.

Lady Macbeth had a son called Lulach the Fatuous.

Sultan Murad IV inherited 240 wives when he assumed the throne of Turkey in 1744. He put each wife into a sack and tossed them one by one into the Bosphorus.

During World War Two, it was against the law in Germany to name a horse Adolf.

Napoleon constructed his battle plans in a sandbox.

Ancient Egyptians slept on pillows of stone.

Richard the Lionheart spent just four months of his life in England

The Egyptians thought it was good luck to enter a house left foot first.

Mark Twain was born on a day in 1835 when Haley's Comet came into view. When he died in 1910, Haley's Comet came into view again.

Leonardo da Vinci could write with one hand and draw with the other at the same time.

Louis XIV took just three baths in his lifetime (and he had to be coerced into taking those).

George I, King of England from 1714 to 1727, was German and couldn't speak a word of English.

In ancient Greece, tossing an apple to a girl was a traditional proposal of marriage. Catching it meant she accepted.

In the 1500s, one out of 25 coffins was found to have scratch marks on the inside.

Gold

There is 200 times more gold in the world's oceans than has ever been mined.

All the gold ever mined would be as big as a 3-bedroom house; all the gold that's still to be mined (on land) would only be big enough to make the garage.

Gold is the only metal that doesn't rust – even if it's buried in the ground for thousands of years.

India is the world's largest consumer of gold.

There are just 6 grams of gold in an Olympic Gold medal.

NB In the original story of Cinderella, her slippers were made of gold, not glass. And her stepsisters were beautiful on the outside – their ugliness lay within.

PURE TRIVIA

The oldest known vegetable is the pea.

To strengthen a Damascus sword, the blade was plunged into a slave.

Catherine the Great relaxed by being tickled.

A coward was originally a boy who took care of cows.

There are 2,598,960 possible hands in a five-card poker game.

Cows can be identified by noseprints.

82 per cent of the workers on the Panama Canal suffered from malaria.

60 per cent of all US potato products originate in Idaho.

The Forth railway bridge in Scotland is a metre longer in summer than in winter as a result of thermal expansion.

In the Andes, time is often measured by how long it takes to smoke a cigarette.

Brazil got its name from the nut, not the other way around.

It would take about 2 million hydrogen atoms to cover the full stop at the end of this sentence.

Dirty snow melts quicker than clean snow.

The model ape used in the 1933 film *King Kong* was 18 inches tall.

Rodin's *The Thinker* is a portrait of the Italian poet Dante.

Johann Sebastian Bach once walked 230 miles to hear the organist at Lübeck in Germany.

After retiring from boxing, ex-World heavyweight champion Gene Tunney lectured on Shakespeare at Yale University.

The Beatles' song 'A Day In The Life' ends with a note sustained for 40 seconds.

Miss Piggy's measurements are 27–20–32.

In 1517, the *Mona Lisa* was bought by King Francis I of France to hang in a bathroom.

Salvador Dalí once arrived at an art exhibition in a limousine filled with turnips.

'Mary, Mary, Quite Contrary' was based on Mary, Queen of Scots.

There are 256 semihemidemisemiquavers in a breve.

There are two independent nations in Europe smaller than New York's Central Park: Vatican City and Monaco.

If the world's total land area were divided equally among the world's people, each person would get 8.5 acres.

Seattle, like Rome, was built on seven hills.

The Dutch town of Leeuwarden can be spelled 225 different ways.

The geographical centre of North America is in North Dakota.

The only city whose name can be spelled completely with vowels is Aiea in Hawaii.

John Wilkes Booth's brother once saved the life of Abraham Lincoln's son.

A GUIDE TO 'STRINE (AUSTRALIAN SLANG)

Bend the elbow (to) = have a drink (as in 'g'day, sport, fancy bending the elbow?')

Bonza or **beaut** = wonderful, great

Chook = chicken (as eaten on a 'barbie')

Crook = unwell (as in 'strewth, I'm crook')

Dead as a dead dingo's donga = in a parlous condition

Drink with the flies (to) = to drink alone (as in 'That cobber's drinking with the flies!')

Dunny = toilet

Fair dinkum = the real thing (sometimes uttered in spite of oneself, as in, 'Fair dinkum, that Pom can bat')

Fair go = Good chance (as in 'Shane's got a fair go of taking a wicket against these pommie bastards')

Godzone – God's own country (i.e. Australia)

Grog = booze ('BYOG' on an invitation means bring your own grog)

Hit your kick = open your wallet (as in 'come on, blue, hit your kick and pay for those tinnies')

Hooly dooly = I say! (as in 'Hooly dooly, have you seen the state of that dunny?')

Ripper = super

A sausage short of a barbie = not in possession of all (his) faculties

She'll be right = No problem (as in 'I'll be there at the cricket, she'll be right')

Spit the dummie (to) = lose one's cool (as in 'I think that poofter's spitting the dummie')

Spunky = good-looking (as in 'That Kylie sure is spunky')

True blue = honest or straight (said approvingly as in 'he may be an ocker but he's true blue' see also 'good as gold')

Tucker = food

Wowser = killjoy, spoilset

WORDS

The longest one-syllable word is SCREECHED.

ALMOST is the longest word in the English language with all the letters in alphabetical order. APPEASES, ARRAIGNING, HOTSHOTS, SIGNINGS and TEAMMATE all have letters which occur twice and only twice.

The syllable -OUGH can be pronounced nine different ways – as evidenced by the following sentence: 'A rough, dough-faced, thoughtful ploughman emerged from a slough to walk through the streets of Scarborough, coughing and hiccoughing.'

The sentence 'He believed Caesar could see people seizing the seas' contains seven different spellings of the 'ee' sound.

In English, only three words have a letter that repeats six times: DEGENERESCENCE (six Es), INDIVISIBILITY (six Is) and NONANNOUNCEMENT (six Ns).

The French equivalent of 'the quick brown fox jumps over the lazy dog', a sentence containing every letter of the alphabet (useful when learning to type), is 'allez porter ce vieux whisky au juge blond qui fume un Havane', which translates as 'go and take this old whisky to the fair-haired judge smoking the Havana cigar'.

The word QUIZ was allegedly invented in 1780 by a Dublin theatre manager, who bet he could introduce a new word of no meaning into the language within 24 hours.

***Alice in Wonderland* author Lewis Carroll invented the word CHORTLE – a combination of 'chuckle' and 'snort'.**

Dr Seuss invented the word NERD for his 1950 book *If I Ran the Zoo*.

The word GIRL appears just once in the Bible.

The word QUEUEING is the only English word with five consecutive vowels.

WEDLOCK is derived from the old English words for pledge ('wed') and action ('lac').

DIXIE is derived from the French word for 10 – *dix* – and was first used by a New Orleans bank that issued French-American $10 bills. Later the word expanded to represent the whole of the southern states of the US.

The shortest English word that contains the letters A, B, C, D, E, and F is FEEDBACK.

The word FREELANCE comes from a knight whose lance was free for hire.

The word SHERIFF comes from 'shire reeve'. In feudal England, each shire had a reeve who upheld the law for that shire.

The Sanskrit word for 'war' means 'desire for more cows'.

SOS doesn't stand for 'Save Our Ship' or 'Save Our Souls' – it was chosen by a 1908 international conference on Morse Code because the letters S and O were easy to remember. S is dot dot dot, O is dash dash dash.

The word CORDUROY comes from the French 'cord du roi' or 'cloth of the king'.

AFGHANISTAN, KIRGHISTAN and TUVALU are the only countries with three consecutive letters in their names.

RESIGN has two opposed meanings depending on its pronunciation ('to quit' and 'to sign again').

The word SET has the highest number of separate definitions in the Oxford English Dictionary.

In Chinese, the words 'crisis' and 'opportunity' are the same.

UNDERGROUND and UNDERFUND are the only words in the English language that begin and end with the letters 'und'.

The Chinese ideogram for 'trouble' shows 'two women living under one roof'.

Only three words in the English language end in 'dous': TREMENDOUS, HORRENDOUS, HAZARDOUS.

The tennis player, GORAN IVANISEVIC, has the longest name of a celebrity that alternates consonants and vowels.

UNITED ARAB EMIRATES is the longest name of a country consisting of alternating vowels and consonants.

TARAMASALATA (a type of Greek salad) and GALATASARAY (name of a Turkish football club) each have an A for every other letter.

TAXI is spelled the same way in English, French, German, Swedish, Spanish, Danish, Norwegian, Dutch, Czech and Portuguese.

The word THEREIN contains thirteen words spelled with consecutive letters: the, he, her, er, here, I, there, ere, rein, re, in, therein, and herein.

SWIMS is the longest word with 180-degree rotational symmetry (if you were to view it upside-down it would still be the same word and perfectly readable).

UNPROSPEROUSNESS is the longest word in which no letter occurs only once.

www as an abbreviation for 'World Wide Web' has nine spoken syllables, whereas the term being abbreviated has only three spoken syllables.

You look different

In French, OISEAU (bird) is the shortest word containing all five vowels.

ULTRAREVOLUTIONARIES has each vowel exactly twice.

FACETIOUS and ABSTEMIOUS contain the five vowels in alphabetical order.

SUBCONTINENTAL, UNCOMPLIMENTARY and DUOLITERAL contain the five vowels in reverse alphabetical order.

The shortest sentence in the English language is 'Go!'

PLIERS is a word with no singular form. Other such words are: ALMS, CATTLE, EAVES and SCISSORS.

ACCEDED, BAGGAGE, CABBAGE, DEFACED, EFFACED and FEEDBAG are seven-letter words that can be played on a musical instrument.

The word DUDE was coined by Oscar Wilde and his friends. It is a combination of the words 'duds' and 'attitude'.

'Hijinks' is the only word in common usage with three dotted letters in a row.

EARTHLING is first found in print in 1593. Other surprisingly old words are SPACESHIP (1894), ACID RAIN (1858), ANTACID (1753), HAIRDRESSER (1771), MOLE (in connection with espionage, 1622, by Sir Francis Bacon), FUNK (a strong smell, 1623; a state of panic, 1743), MILKY WAY (ca. 1384, but earlier in Latin) and MS (used instead of Miss or Mrs, 1949).

EWE and YOU are pronounced exactly the same, yet share no letters in common.

The words BORSCHTS, LATCHSTRING and WELTSCHMERZ each have six consonants in a row.

Ewe too!

TONGUE TWISTERS

Six sharp smart sharks

The sixth sick sheik's sixth sheep's sick

If Stu chews shoes, should Stu choose the shoes he chews?

Rory the warrior and Roger the worrier were wrongly reared in a rural brewery

Black-back bat

Sheena leads, Sheila needs

Wunwun was a racehorse, Tutu was one too. Wunwun won one race, Tutu won one too.

*Lesser leather
never weathered
wetter weather better*

A box of biscuits, a batch of mixed biscuits

The local yokel yodels

Eleven benevolent elephants

Red lorry, yellow lorry, red lorry, yellow lorry

Is this your sister's sixth zither, sir?

A big black bug bit a big black bear, made the big black bear bleed blood

Scissors sizzle, thistles sizzle

We shall surely see the sun shine soon

A noisy noise annoys an oyster

Three free throws

Cheap ship trip

How much wood would a woodchuck chuck if a woodchuck could chuck wood?

Mrs Smith's Fish Sauce Shop

Black bug's blood

Fred fed Ted bread and Ted fed Fred bread

Six slick slim sick sycamore saplings

Irish wristwatch

Six slippery snails slid slowly seaward

Friendly Frank flips fine flapjacks

Selfish shellfish

Peter Piper picked a peck of pickled peppers
Did Peter Piper pick a peck of pickled peppers?
If Peter Piper picked a peck of pickled peppers,
Where's the peck of pickled peppers Peter Piper picked?

Oxymorons

Army Intelligence, Civil Servant, Easy Payments, Working Lunch, Corporate Hospitality, Amicable Divorce, Business Trip, Friendly Fire, Metal Woods, Executive Decision, Operator Service, Guest Host, Mercy Killing, Business Ethics, Microsoft Works, Virtual Reality, Jumbo Shrimp, Committee Decision, Same Difference, Free Trade, Student Teacher, Airline Food, Floppy Disk, Civil Disobedience, Working Holiday, Crash Landing, Educated Guess, Martial Law, Paid Volunteer

A WRITING GUIDE

Steer well clear of clichés; give them a wide berth.

Do not be redundant; do not use more words to express an idea or concept than you really need to use.

All verbs has to agree with subjects.

Always avoid annoying alliteration.

Be specific, more or less.

Parenthetical remarks (however pertinent) are (almost certainly) superfluous.

Complete sentences only, please.

The passive voice is to be avoided.

Foreign words and phrases are *de trop*.

Delete commas, that are, not necessary.

One should never generalize.

Eschew ampersands & abbreviations, etc.

Analogies in writing are like pyjamas on a cat.

Never use a big word where a diminutive expression would suffice.

Eliminate quotations. As Ralph Waldo Emerson said, 'I hate quotations.'

A mixed metaphor, even one that flies like a bird, should be given its marching orders.

Who needs rhetorical questions?

Exaggeration is a million times worse than understatement.

Proofread carefully to see if you any words out.

Foreign words and phrases are de trop

Botox treatment

Gloria Hunniford, Jennifer Ellison, Madonna, Sir
Cliff Richard, Patsy Kensit, Joan Rivers, Elizabeth
Hurley, Meg Mathews, Celine Dion, Kirstie Alley,
Tom Cruise, Jamie Lee Curtis, Julian Clary, Denise
Van Outen, Princess Michael of Kent

Facelifts

**Loni Anderson, Cher, Jane
Fonda, Dolly Parton, Joan
Rivers, Ivana Trump, Mary Tyler
Moore, Angela Lansbury, Fay
Weldon, Roseanne, Liberace,
Lucille Ball, Gary Cooper, Joan
Crawford, Julie Christie, Marlene
Dietrich, Rita Hayworth, Kirk
Douglas, Henry Fonda, Michael
Jackson, Dean Martin, Jacqueline
Kennedy, Mary Pickford, Elvis Presley,
Debbie Reynolds, Frank Sinatra,
Barbara Stanwyck, Dame Elizabeth
Taylor, Lana Turner, Cherri Gilham, Bea
Arthur, Phyllis Diller, Nicky Haslam, Debbie Harry,
Mary Archer, Barbra Streisand,
Sharon Osbourne**

HAD THEIR LIPS DONE

Madonna, Lynne Perrie, Suzanne Mizzi, Cher, Loni Anderson, Pamela Anderson, Melanie Griffith, Ivana Trump, Dame Elizabeth Taylor, Leslie Ash, Sharon Osbourne

NOSE JOBS

Peter O'Toole, Cilla Black, Edwina Currie, Caroline Aherne, Bonnie Langford, Tom Jones, Cher, Belinda Lang, Dale Winton, Marilyn Monroe, Fanny Brice, Barbara Eden, Rhonda Fleming, Annette Funicello, Eva Gabor, Zsa Zsa Gabor, Mitzi Gaynor, Lee Grant, Juliette Greco, Joan Hackett, Carole Landis, Rita Moreno, Stefanie Powers, Jill St John, Talia Shire, Dinah Shore, Sissy Spacek, Raquel Welch, Milton Berle, Vic Damone, Joel Grey, George Hamilton, Al Jolson, Dean Martin, Lynsey De Paul, Natalie Appleton, Melanie Blatt, Shaznay Lewis, Charlie O'Neil, Lisa Kudrow, Natasha Richardson, Jodie Marsh, Roseanne

LIPOSUCTION

Michael Ball (from his stomach)

Demi Moore (from her thighs, bottom and stomach)

Joan Rivers (from her thighs)

Anna Nicole Smith (from her stomach)

Sir Michael Caine (from his stomach)

Melanie Griffith (from her stomach and thighs)

Kenny Rogers (from his stomach)

Roseanne (from her stomach)

Don Johnson (from his chin and cheeks)

Dolly Parton (from her hips and waist)

Alexander McQueen (from his stomach)

Nicole Appleton (from her thighs and hips)

Mariah Carey (from her midsection)

Linsey Dawn McKenzie (from her thighs)

Geri Halliwell (from her stomach and thighs)

Jordan (from her thighs)

Jamie Lee Curtis (from underneath her eyes)

Pierced nipples

Tim Roth, Tommy Lee, Howard Donald, Jaye Davidson, Drew Carey, Gail Porter, Davina McCall, Faye Tozer, Meg Mathews, Lene Nystrom, Billy Connolly, Sarah Cawood, Steve Tyler, Liv Tyler, Paul Cattermole, Christina Aguilera, Britney Spears, Paloma Bailey, Janet Jackson, Evan Davis

Pierced tongues

Mel B, Keith Flint, Kathy Acker, Ross Hale, Zara Phillips, Sinéad O'Connor, Janet Jackson, Ashia Hansen

Pierced navels

Oona King, Sarah Michelle Gellar, Britney Spears, Ashia Hansen, Della Bovey, Stella Tennant, Denise Van Outen, Lisa Faulkner, Rachel Stevens, Tracy Shaw, Denise Welch, Naomi Radcliffe, Jo O'Meara, Jennifer Ellison, Paloma Bailey, Danniella Westbrook, Serena Williams, Harriet Scott, Zara Phillips, Princess Charlotte of Monaco, Jessie Wallace, Madonna, Janet Jackson, Rosie Millard, Andrea Catherwood, Keira Knightley

MNEMONICS AND AIDES-MEMOIRE

The kings and queens of England and the United Kingdom since 1066

Willie, Willie, Harry, Ste
Harry, Dick, John, Harry three
One two three Edward, Richard two
Henry, four, five, six then, who?
Edward four, five, Dick the Bad
Harry twain then Ned the lad
Mary, Bessie, James the vain
Charlie, Charlie, James again
William and Mary, Ann Gloria
Four Georges, William, then Victoria
Edward, George, then Ned the eighth
quickly goes and abdicateth
Leaving George, then Liz the second
And with Charlie next it's reckoned
That's the way our monarchs lie
Since Harold got it in the eye!

The order of planets in distance from the Sun

Mercury, Venus, Earth, Mars, Jupiter, Saturn, Uranus, Neptune, Pluto – My Very Easy Method: Just Set Up Nine Planets.

The order of colours in the rainbow

Red, Orange, Yellow, Green, Blue, Indigo, Violet – Richard Of York Gave Battle In Vain.

The order of geological time periods

Cambrian, Ordovician, Silurian, Devonian, Carboniferous, Permian, Triassic, Jurassic, Cretaceous, Paleocene, Eocene, Oligocene, Miocene, Pliocene, Pleistocene, Recent – Cows Often Sit Down Carefully. Perhaps Their Joints Creak? Persistent Early Oiling Might Prevent Painful Rheumatism.

The countries of Central America in geographical order
Belize, Guatemala, Honduras, Nicaragua, Costa Rica, Panama
– BeeGee's Hen! Se 'er pee?

The order of Mohs hardness scale, from 1 to 10
Talc, Gypsum, Calcite, Fluorite, Apatite, Orthoclase feldspar, Quartz, Topaz, Corundum, Diamond
– Toronto Girls Can Flirt, And Other Queer Things Can Do.

The order of sharps in music
FCGDAEB
– Father Charles Goes Down And Ends Battle.

The order of notes to which guitar strings should be tuned
EBGDAE
– Easter Bunnies Get Drunk At Easter.

The order of notes represented by the lines on the treble clef stave
EGBDF
– Every Good Boy Deserves Favour.

The order of taxonomy in biology
Kingdom, Phylum, Class, Order, Family, Genus, Species
– Kids Prefer Cheese Over Fried Green Spinach.

The four oceans
Indian, Arctic, Atlantic, Pacific
– I Am A Person.

The seven continents
Europe, Antarctica, Asia, Africa, Australia, North America, South America
– Eat AN ASpirin AFter AUgmenting Noah's Ship.

The Great Lakes
Huron, Ontario, Michigan, Erie, Superior
– HOMES.

For the Great Lakes in order of size
Superior, Huron, Michigan, Erie, Ontario
– Sam's Horse Must Eat Oats.

The Confederate States of America
South Carolina, Louisiana, Georgia, North
Carolina, Alabama, Arkansas, Virginia, Mississippi,
Florida, Tennessee and Texas
– Sultry Carol Languished Grumpily Near Carl,
Always Aware Virginal Men Frequently Take Time.

2001: A Space Oddity

Apes, Bones, Cosmic Device … Evolution! Floating Giant Hub.
Investigate Jupiter. Komputer Loopy. Man Nears Outsized Plinth.
Queer Readings. Starry Turbulence. Unexpected Very Weird
Xyschedelia Yielding Zen.

LUCKY CHARMS

Billy Crystal: a toothbrush he used to pretend was a microphone
when he was a child. He now carries it on stage whenever he
performs.

James Goldsmith: the late businessman always kept a stone frog in
his pocket.

Luciano Pavarotti: a bent nail, which he always wears in his top
pocket when he performs.

Damon Hill: has an Austrian lucky charm called a *Gamsbart*. It's a
tassle made of goat hair and was given to Hill by his trainer Erwine
Gollner.

Jo Brand: green toilet paper because: 'I did a brilliant gig once when
I had a piece of green toilet paper in my pocket as I had a cold. After
that I went through a phase of believing that green toilet paper was
my lucky charm.'

Vic Reeves: black onyx cufflinks.

Yves Saint Laurent: a jewel, a heart made of grey diamonds with
rubies. 'It's at home, in a secret place. I only take it out for
collections.'

Michael Schumacher: a ceramic amulet on a leather lace.

Cameron Diaz: a necklace given to her by a friend.

Heidi Klum: all her baby teeth, which she keeps in a little leather pouch.

Salute magpies

Mel C, Robert Howley, Sir Peter O'Sullevan, David Beckham, Amanda Holden, Adrian Maguire

Bite nails

Gordon Brown, Dustin Hoffman, Phil Collins, Johnny Mathis, Liza Minnelli, Steven Spielberg, Cate Blanchett, Britney Spears (after hypnosis failed, she painted her nails with a red-hot pepper polish that burnt her tongue), Mel B (toenails), Jon Lee (toenails – 'Urgh, but I do it!'), Scott Robinson (toenails), Will Young, Elijah Wood, Gina Bellman, Emilia Fox, Melanie Sykes, Greg Proops, Jamie Theakston, Bryan Ferry, Louis Theroux, Orlando Bloom (after giving up smoking)

Chainsmokers

Donatella Versace, Joaquin Phoenix, F.W. de Klerk, Gérard Depardieu, Tom Clancy, Robbie Williams, Rich Hall, Emily Watson (briefly, because of her role in *Angela's Ashes*), Kate Moss, Michel Platini, Seamus Mallon, Felix Dennis

Recovering alcoholics

Mel Gibson, Barry Humphries, Sir Anthony Hopkins, Eric Clapton, Jimmy Greaves, Dick Van Dyke, Buzz Aldrin, Patrick Swayze, Mike Yarwood, Tony Adams, John Daly, Jim Davidson, Anthony Booth, Brian Barnes, Keith Chegwin, Roseanne, Dennis Quaid, Drew Barrymore, Ken Kercheval, Dame Elizabeth Taylor, Ringo Starr, Sharon Gless, Sir Elton John, Gary Oldman, Robbie Williams, Anne Robinson

Had/have an alcoholic parent

Marlon Brando (both)

Jonathan Winters (father)

Suzanne Somers (father)

Lauren Hutton (mother)

Shane Richie (father)

Sir Alec Guinness (mother)

Sir Charles Chaplin (father)

Michael Barrymore (father)

Kenneth Clarke (mother)

Adam Ant (father)

Demi Moore (mother)

Richard Burton (father)

Meat Loaf (father)

Eminem (mother)

Sinéad O'Connor (mother)

Mo Mowlam (father)

Ronald Reagan (father)

Richard Farleigh (father)

Ben Affleck (father)

Nora Ephron (both)

Halle Berry (father)

Sir Norman Wisdom (father)

Rod Steiger (mother)

Rosemary Clooney (both)

Brian Wilson (mother)

Gérard Depardieu (father)

Nell Gwyn (mother)

Andie MacDowell (mother)

Samantha Mumba (father)

Tom Cruise (father)

Money

American Airlines saved $40,000 in 1987 by eliminating one olive from each salad served in first class.

More Monopoly money is printed in a year than real money throughout the world.

Lee Harvey Oswald's cadaver tag sold at an auction for $6,600 in 1992.

In 1979, Judy Garland's false eyelashes were sold at auction for $125.

During World War Two, W.C. Fields kept $50,000 in Germany 'in case the little bastard wins'.

Sigmund Freud bought his first sample of cocaine for $1.27 per gram.

Woodpecker scalps, porpoise teeth and giraffe tails have all been used as money.

There are two credit cards for every person in the US.

In Monopoly, the most money you can lose in one trip round the board (going to jail only once) is £26,040. The most money you can lose in one turn is £5,070. If, on the other hand, no one ever buys anything, players could eventually break the bank.

97 per cent of paper money in the US contains traces of cocaine.

After their Civil War, the US sued Great Britain for damages caused by ships the British had built for the Confederacy. The US asked for $1 billion, but settled for $25 million.

WENT BANKRUPT

Kevin Maxwell, Margot Kidder, Walt Disney, Alan Bond, Eddie Fisher, Grace Jones, Mark Twain, Mickey Rooney, MC Hammer, Peter Adamson, Eddie 'The Eagle' Edwards, Lionel Bart, Frank Lloyd Wright, Buster Bloodvessel, Mica Paris, Toni Braxton, John Bindon (twice), Jake Thackray, Daniel Defoe, Henry Kelly, Michael Barrymore (twice)

Remarkable People

Tommy Lee has a Starbucks in his house.

Marlon Brando's occupation on his passport was 'Shepherd'.

Demis Roussos was on a plane hijacked and taken to Beirut.

Julio Iglesias once had 5 gallons of water flown from Miami to LA so he could wash his hair.

Jacqueline Wilson had the magazine *Jackie* named after her.

Sir Anthony Hopkins used to be able to hypnotize people by pulling their earlobes.

David Lynch always leaves one shoelace untied.

Michael Jackson owns the rights to the South Carolina state anthem.

Jim Dale co-wrote the song 'Georgy Girl'.

Simon Le Bon has kept bees.

Christopher Trace, the first presenter of *Blue Peter*, was Charlton Heston's body double in *Ben-Hur*.

Debra Winger was the voice of ET.

Robbie Williams made a cameo appearance in 1995 in *EastEnders* making a telephone call from a payphone in the Queen Vic.

Liza Tarbuck was voted Kleenex Nose of the Year by *OK!* readers.

Dusty Springfield once successfully sued Bobby Davro for an imitation he did of her.

Woody Allen won't take a shower if the drain is in the middle.

Carol Vorderman was crowned Head of the Year 2000 by the National Hairdressers' Federation.

Alan Davies bought the *Big Brother* diary room chair for £30,000.

Queen Latifah wears the key for the motorcycle on which her brother suffered a fatal crash on a chain around her neck.

John Grisham shaves just once a week – before church on Sunday.

Jewel is a champion yodeller – and has been since her childhood (even though it is 'impossible' for children to yodel because their vocal cords aren't sufficiently developed).

Anna Kournikova hasn't cut her waist-length hair since she was seven.

Robert Downey Jr once spent a night in jail with Tommy Lee.

Cate Blanchett gave her husband plaster casts of her ears as a present.

Arm wrestling is one of Helena Bonham Carter's favourite pastimes.

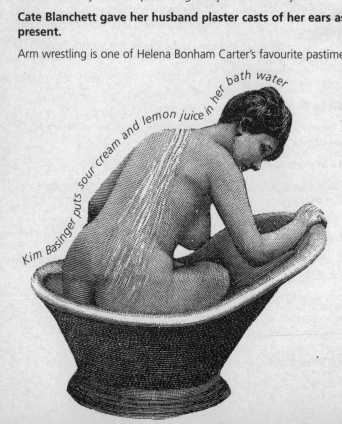

Kim Basinger puts sour cream and lemon juice in her bath water

Charlie Dimmock was Best Giggler 1999 – awarded by Butterkist. She had to take a bath in popcorn.

Renée Zellweger keeps a 'grateful journal', a collection of her favourite things, on her bedside table.

Cindy Crawford believes placentas should be buried under trees for good luck.

Bernard Manning did his National Service in the Military Police and one of his duties was guarding Albert Speer and Rudolf Hess in Spandau.

Sean (P Diddy) Combs wears a diamond-encrusted watch to protect against pollution from his mobile phone.

Ainsley Harriott was a Wimbledon ball boy.

Betty Boothroyd had a Belfast gay nightclub named after her.

As a teenager, Naomi Campbell used to hang around for an autograph outside Boy George's house.

Nicolas Cage was 28 before he first went abroad (to a screening in Cannes). He employs his own pizza chef and has a special pizza oven in his house.

During their marriage, Angelina Jolie and Billy Bob Thornton bought an electric chair for their dining room.

Billy Connolly topped a survey to find Britain's top fantasy cab companion (Kate Moss and Jordan were runners-up).

Gisele Bundchen owns over 200 belts.

James Woods is ambidextrous.

Missy Elliott spends four hours a day on her hair.

Diane Keaton's old college named a street after her in 2000.

Shaggy was a Royal Marine and served in the first Gulf war.

Harrison Ford has a species of spider named after him.

INVENTED OR DISCOVERED BY AMERICANS

Lightning rod (1752)

Bifocals (1760)

Cotton gin (1793)

Revolver (1835)

Telegraph (1837)

Vulcanization of rubber (1839)

Fibreglass (1839)

Ether as a human anaesthetic (1842)

Sewing machine (1846)

Safety pin (1849)

Bessemer converter (1851)

Cylinder lock (1851)

Elevator (1852)

Condensed milk (1853)

Oil well (1859)

Machine gun (1862)

Aluminium manufacture (1866)

Typewriter (1867)

Air brake (1868)

Vacuum cleaner (manual; 1869)

Barbed wire (1873)

Earmuffs (1873)

Denim jeans (1874)

Carpet sweeper (1876)

Telephone (1876)

Phonograph (1877)

Mechanical cash register (1879)

Saccharin (1879)

Light bulb (1880)

Electric fan (1882)

Fountain pen (1884)

Electric transformer (1885)

Coca-Cola (1886)

Hand-held camera (1888)

Automatic telephone exchange (1889)

Juke box (1889)

Zipper (1891)

AC electric generator (1892)

AC electric motor (1892)

Paper matchbook (1892)

Motion pictures (1893)

Escalator (1894)

Electric stove (1896)

Pepsi-Cola (1898)

Tractor (1900)

Safety razor (1901)

Gyrocompass (1905)

Electric washing machine (1906)

Vacuum cleaner (upright; 1907)

Electric toaster (1908)

Bakelite (1910)

Air conditioning (1911)

Aircraft autopilot (1912)

Moving assembly line (1913)

False eyelashes (1916)

Automatic rifle (1918)

Bulldozer (1923)

Cine camera (1923)

Frozen food (1924)

Liquid-fuelled rocket (1926)

Electric induction (1928)

Electric razor (1928)

Car radio (1929)

Scotch tape (1929)

Cyclotron (1931)

Defibrillator (1932)

FM radio (1933)

Nylon (1935)

Richter scale (1935)

Xerography (1938)

Single-rotor helicopter (1939)

Teflon (1943)

Electronic computer (1946)

Microwave oven (1947)

Transistor (1947)

Polaroid camera (1948)

Oral contraceptive (1951)

Polio vaccine (1952)

Video recorder (1952)

Measles vaccine (1953)

Nuclear submarine (1955)

Internal heart pacemaker (1957)

Superconductivity (1957)

Laser (1960)

Industrial robot (1962)

Pull-tab opener (1963)

Quasars (1963)

Electronic musical synthesizer (1965)

Quarks (1967)

Barcodes for retail use (1970)

CD (1972)

Electronic mail (1972)

Personal computer (1976)

Implantable defibrillator (1980)

Permanent artificial heart implant (1982)

PURE TRIVIA

Monaco's national orchestra is bigger than its army.

As a young and struggling artist, Pablo Picasso kept warm by burning his own paintings.

Rin Tin Tin is buried in Père-Lachaise cemetery in Paris.

Enid Blyton, writer of the Famous Five, had 59 stories published in 1959.

Pablo Picasso was abandoned by the midwife just after his birth because she thought he was stillborn. He was saved by an uncle.

Ludwig van Beethoven was once arrested for vagrancy.

The phrase 'the 3 Rs' ('reading, writing and arithmetic') was coined by Sir William Curtis, who was illiterate.

Dante died on the day he completed his masterpiece *The Divine Comedy*.

Actress Sarah Bernhardt played the part of Juliet (13 years old) when she was 70.

EMI stands for 'Electrical and Musical Instruments'.

1 kg of lemons contains more sugar than 1 kg of strawberries.

About 70 per cent of all living organisms in the world are bacteria.

Each episode of *Dr Kildare* had three suffering patients.

Soda water does not contain soda.

The yo-yo originated in the Philippines, where it was used as a weapon in hunting.

The board game Monopoly was originally rejected by Parker Brothers who claimed it had 52 fundamental errors.

The screwdriver was invented before the screw.

The screwdriver cocktail was invented by oilmen, who used the tool to stir the drink.

At the height of his addiction, the poet Samuel Taylor Coleridge drank about 2 litres of laudanum (tincture of opium) each week.

The metre was originally defined as one 10-millionth of the distance from the equator to the pole.

A fully loaded supertanker travelling at normal speed takes at least 20 minutes to stop.

North American Indians ate watercress to dissolve stones in the bladder.

In Russia, suppositories cut from fresh potatoes were used for relief from haemorrhoids.

Opium was used widely as a painkiller during the American Civil War. More than a hundred thousand soldiers became addicts.

The girls of the Tiwi tribe in the South Pacific are married at birth.

Ralph and Carolyn Cummins had 5 children between 1952 and 1966, all of whom were born on 20 February.

The Zambian authorities don't allow tourists to take pictures of Pygmies.

Alexander Graham Bell, inventor of the telephone, never phoned his wife or mother as both were deaf.

The warrior tribes of Ethiopia used to hang the testicles of those they killed in battle on the ends of their spears.

Eau de Cologne was originally marketed as a way of protecting yourself against the plague.

The Crystal Palace at the Great Exhibition of 1851 contained 92,900 square metres of glass.

South American gauchos put raw steak under their saddles before starting a day's riding to tenderize the meat.

There are 240 white dots in a Pacman arcade game.

Blackbird, chief of the Omaha Indians, was buried sitting on his favourite horse.

A group of geese on the ground is a gaggle; a group of geese in the air is a skein.

After Custer's last stand, Sioux leader Chief Sitting Bull became an entertainer and toured the country with Buffalo Bill's Wild West Show.

Genghis Khan's cavalry rode female horses so soldiers could drink their milk.

Aztec emperor Montezuma had a nephew, Cuitlahac, whose name meant 'plenty of excrement'.

Bananas contain about 75 per cent water.

Chewing gum while peeling onions will keep you from crying.

Chewing gum has rubber as an ingredient.

Coca-Cola was originally green.

Cuckoo clocks come from the Black Forest in Germany – not Switzerland.

An inch of snow falling evenly on one acre of ground is equivalent to about 2,715 gallons of water.

During the Middle Ages, people used spider webs to try to cure warts.

In 1967, the American Association of Typographers made a new punctuation mark that was a combination of the question mark and an exclamation point, and called it an interrobang. It was rarely used and hasn't been seen since.

Aeschylus, the founder of Classical Greek tragedy, is said to have died when an eagle passing overhead dropped a tortoise on his head.

Given sufficient amounts of chocolate, pigs can master video game skills.

BRIGHTON BUSES NAMED AFTER THEM

Norman Cook, Desmond Lynam, Sir Norman Wisdom, Lord Richard Attenborough, Dora Bryan, Chris Eubank, Adam Faith, Sally Gunnell, Derek Jameson, Annie Nightingale, Leo Sayer, Dusty Springfield, Lord Laurence Olivier, Max Miller, Dame Flora Robson, Sir Winston Churchill, Rudyard Kipling, Dame Anna Neagle

PHOTOGRAPHIC MEMORIES

Truman Capote, Carole Caplin, Sid Owen, Hu Jintao, Peter Buck, Neil Hamilton, Simon Wiesenthal, Robert Mitchum, Shaun Woodward, Anne Kirkbride, Gerard Depardieu, Bill Clinton, Bill Gates

HOTEL SUITES NAMED AFTER THEM

Sir Arthur C. Clarke (at the Hotel Club Oceanic, Sri Lanka)

Luciano Pavarotti (Pangkor Laut Island Resort, Malaysia)

Dame Barbara Cartland (Heritage Hotel at Helmsdale in Sutherland)

James Michener (Oriental Hotel in Thailand)

Dave Brubeck (The Hotel Viking, Newport, Rhode Island)

Samuel Clemens (aka Mark Twain: The Painted Lady Hotel, Elmira, New York)

Jenny Lind (Willard Intercontinental, Washington)

Sir Roger Moore (Grand Lido Sans Souci Resort, Ocho Rios, Jamaica)

Dame Agatha Christie (The Old Cataract Hotel, Aswan, Egypt)

Marlene Dietrich (The Hotel Lancaster, Paris)

Princess Michael of Kent (St George Lycabettus Hotel, Athens)

James Galway (Tara Hotel, London)

Michael Jordan (Atlantis Hotel, Bahamas)

Mata Hari (American Hotel, Amsterdam)

John Lennon (Queen Elizabeth Hotel, Montreal)

Liam Neeson (Fitzpatrick Hotel, Chicago)

Marilyn Monroe (The Legend Hotel, Kuala Lumpur)

Graham Greene (The Sofitel Metropole, Hanoi)

Lord Andrew Lloyd Webber (Hotel Gellert, Budapest, Hungary)

CELEBRITIES AND THE NUMBERS OF PAIRS OF TRAINERS THEY OWN

Goldie (1,600)

Mel C (over 200)

Justin Timberlake (450 – including every model of Air Jordans ever made)

Johnny Vegas (30)

Craig David (200)

Damon Dash (3,000)

NB Sean (P Diddy) Combs throws his away after wearing them for just one day

SPONSORED/ADOPTED AN ANIMAL AT LONDON ZOO

Paul Young (fruit bat)

George Cole (American alligator)

Letitia Dean (chimpanzee)

Fiona Fullerton (Asian elephant)

Andy Crane (crowned crane)

Robert Kilroy-Silk (black-and-white-ruffed lemur)

Cerys Matthews (Margery, à 21-year-old white-faced saki monkey)

Kym Marsh (hippo)

'SAW' GHOSTS

The Queen When they were children, the Queen and her sister, Princess Margaret, believed they saw the ghost of Queen Elizabeth I at Windsor Castle.

Daniel Day-Lewis thought he had seen the ghost of his father (the late Poet Laureate Cecil Day-Lewis) when he was acting in *Hamlet* in 1989. When the actor playing the ghost of Hamlet's father said, 'I am thy father's spirit,' Daniel Day-Lewis went off stage and wouldn't come back – convinced that he'd 'seen' his father.

Jim Davidson once lived with a girlfriend in the Old Kent Road in a flat that was said to be haunted by the ghost of a woman who'd been murdered there many years before. Jim was properly sceptical but was bothered when he couldn't find a rational explanation for all the strange noises that went on throughout the night. Eventually, after 'seeing' crucifixes moving around the room, Jim and his girlfriend moved out.

Sting awoke to 'find' a 'figure' dressed in Victorian clothes in his room. He thought it was his wife until he saw her in bed next to him. She also saw the apparition and they held each other tight, staring at it until it faded away, never to return.

Patti Boulaye In 1992, the singer was about to take on the lead role in the show *Carmen Jones* at the Old Vic, and was watching it from a private box when she felt a draught as though someone had opened the door to the box. When she turned round, no one was there. She mentioned it to someone who told her it was the ghost of the late manager of the theatre, Lilian Baylis.

Bob Hoskins Before finding fame, he was working as a porter in Covent Garden and was in a cellar when he 'saw' a nun. She held her hands out to him and spoke but he didn't understand what she said. Later he was told that Covent Garden had formerly been Convent Garden and had been owned by the Benedictines. The legend was that anyone who saw a nun's ghost would have a lucky life.

Cilla Black would be in bed at home when the ghost of a teenage girl would visit her regularly. The girl, who wore a Victorian nightdress, had a mournful expression on her face. It later turned out that the land on which Cilla's house was built had been farmland worked in the 19th century by a gardener who died, leaving a young daughter, who herself died at the age of 13.

June Brown saw something worse than a ghost, she saw a ghostly tunnel. She was walking with a friend along an abandoned single-track railway line when she saw a tunnel, which they started to walk down. Realizing that the tunnel had no end and feeling a little spooked, they turned and ran back. The next day, they went back to where they had entered the tunnel and found it had mysteriously vanished.

Miriam Karlin believes she is 'haunted' by her father's ghost whenever she has to make a speech in public. Her father was a barrister and she is convinced that he 'feeds' her her lines and makes her much more articulate than she would otherwise be.

Prince Charles Some years ago he and his valet Ken Stronach were going into the library at Sandringham when they felt inexplicably cold and became convinced that someone was standing behind them. When they looked round, no one was there. They ran out.

Paul Gascoigne believes he was attacked by a ghost while he was staying in a converted barn in Italy. The ghost, a man, was holding two foxes. It held him down until 'it sort of relaxed the pressure and I shoved my way up and out of the room and called everyone up. It happened and it wasn't a dream because I wasn't sleeping well enough to dream.'

Will Carling At Sedbergh School when he was 14, he saw a 'very dark figure wearing a cloak' standing at the other end of a long corridor. 'We stood there, facing each other, for about thirty seconds, and I can say, quite honestly, that I was pretty scared. Eventually, I couldn't face it any more and I just turned and ran downstairs.'

Noah Wyle's California ranch – bought from Bo Derek – was apparently haunted by the late John Derek. He said that John's ghost kept making 'strange noises' when he and his fiancée tried to sleep in the master bedroom, so they moved to a guest bedroom and had the main suite remodelled.

Will Young claims that he saw a ghost while staying in a converted monastery in the south of France.

Britney Spears says a ghost used to tweak her nipple ring and hide her belongings as she got ready to go out in the mornings.

Amanda Holden became so aware of a ghostly presence at London's Shaftesbury Theatre (where she was playing the title role in *Thoroughly Modern Millie*) that she required someone to walk round the theatre with her.

NB Ghosts appear in four of Shakespeare's plays: *Julius Caesar*, *Richard III*, *Hamlet* and *Macbeth*.

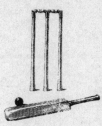

MADE IT TO 100 YEARS OLD

George Burns, Hal Roach, Rose Kennedy, Irving Berlin, Sir Thomas Sopwith, Emanuel Shinwell, Dorothy Dickson, Dame Freya Stark, Athene Seyler, Eubie Blake, Geoffrey Dearmer, The Queen Mother, Adolph Zukor, Bob Hope, Grandma Moses, Mother Jones, Princess Alice, Duchess of Gloucester, George Abbott, Estelle Winwood, Leni Riefenstahl, Gwen Ffrancon-Davies, Hartley Shawcross, Strom Thurmond, Sir Robert Mayer, Alf Landon, Dame Ninette De Valois

FEATURED ON STAMPS

Michael Jackson (Tanzania)

Sir Elton John (Grenada and Australia)

Sir Mick Jagger (St Vincent)

Whitney Houston (Tanzania)

Cher (Grenada)

Jerry Seinfeld (US)

Elle Macpherson (Australia)

Ian Botham (St Vincent)

Arnold Schwarzenegger (Mali)

Clive Lloyd (Guyana)

Dolly Parton (Grenada)

Viv Richards (Antigua)

Frank Sinatra (St Vincent)

Jimmy Connors (Lesotho)

Carl Lewis (Niger)

Eddie Murphy (Tanzania)

Muhammad Ali (Liberia)

Baroness Thatcher (Kenya)

Nick Faldo (St Vincent)

Stevie Wonder (Tanzania)

Gladys Knight (Tanzania)

Bruce Springsteen (Grenada)

Barbra Streisand (St Vincent)

George Michael (St Vincent)

Robert De Niro (Gambia)

Boris Becker (Central African Republic)

Prince (St Vincent)

Tina Turner (Tanzania)

Björn Borg (Ivory Coast)

Paul Newman (The Maldives)

Elliott Gould (Gambia)

Gary Lineker (Gambia)

Pele (Brazil)

John McEnroe (Sierra Leone)

Martina Navratilova (Ivory Coast)

Kirk Douglas (Mali)

MADE PARACHUTE JUMPS

Jim Davidson, Phillip Schofield, Tom Baker, Ian Ogilvy, Matthew Kelly, Jeremy Beadle, Suzanne Dando, Sarah Kennedy, Tony Blackburn, Prince Charles, David Davis, Janet Ellis, Lorraine Chase, Alex Best, Alan Davies, Christian Califano, Matt LeBlanc, Billy Connolly, Jon Finch, David Hasselhoff

CAN COMMUNICATE IN SIGN LANGUAGE

Jane Fonda, Holly Hunter, William Hurt, Richard Griffiths, Hugh Grant, Sinéad O'Connor, Richard Dreyfuss, Louise Fletcher

LEARNED TO SWIM AS ADULTS

Frank Skinner, Dame Norma Major, Dame Shirley Bassey, Sir Paul McCartney, Tina Turner, Pablo Picasso, Sir Peter O'Sullevan, Donna D'Errico, Robin Williams, Sir David Frost, Adam Faith

PROFICIENT MAGICIANS

Prince Charles, Christo Van Rensburg, Muhammad Ali, General Norman Schwarzkopf, Michael Jackson, Arsenio Hall

Wrote children's books

Susannah York (*The Last Unicorn*)

Ian Fleming (*Chitty Chitty Bang Bang*)

David Byrne (*Stay Up Late*)

Roger McGough (*The Magic Fountain*)

Dame Elizabeth Taylor (*Nibbles And Me*)

Prince Charles (*The Old Man of Lochnagar*)

Terry Jones (*Lady Cottington's Pressed Fairy Book*)

Colonel Muammar Gaddafi (*The Village, The Village, The Earth, The Earth ... And The Suicide of The Spaceman*)

Lenny Henry (*Charlie And The Big Chill*)

Nanette Newman (*Spider The Horrible Cat*)

Jamie Lee Curtis (*Where Do Balloons Go?*)

Madonna (*The English Roses*)

Bill Cosby (*Friends Of A Feather*)

John Lithgow (*Marsupial Sue*)

Will Smith (*Just The Two Of Us*)

LeAnn Rimes (*Jag*)

Kylie Mynogue (*The Showgirl Princess*)

Ian Ogilvy (*Measle and the Wrathmonk*)

Sir Paul McCartney (*High In The Clouds: An Urban Furry Tail*)

Billy Crystal (*I Already Know I Love You*)

Maria Shriver (*What's Happening To Grandpa*)

Jerry Seinfeld (*Halloween*)

Ricky Gervais (*Flanimals*)

Harry Hill (*Tim The Tiny Horse*)

INVENTORS

Jamie Lee Curtis ('baby wipe diaper')

Hedy Lamarr (a machine that helped the Americans target U-boats)

Julie Newmar (bottom-shaping tights and a bosom-firming bra)

Steve McQueen (low-slung bucket seat for racing cars)

Neil Young (portable exercise device)

Harry Connick Jr (computer program that allows musicians to follow the score on a screen)

Benjamin Franklin (the rocking chair)

HAD THEIR PAINTINGS EXHIBITED

Tony Curtis, David Hemmings, Joni Mitchell, Desmond Morris, Prince Charles, Anthony Quinn, Bryan Ferry, Ronnie Wood, Sylvester Stallone, Miles Davis, Sir Noel Coward, Adolf Hitler, Sir Paul McCartney, Rolf Harris, Jeff Bridges, David Bowie, Rod Stewart, Jennifer Aniston (at the Metropolitan Museum of Art in New York), Marilyn Manson, Dennis Hopper, Steve Kanaly, Artie Shaw, Elke Sommer, Red Skelton, Herve Villechaize, Donna Summer, e.e. cummings, Nelson Mandela

GENUINE THINGS WRITTEN BY DRIVERS ON INSURANCE FORMS

'I didn't think the speed limit applied after midnight.'

'I knew the dog was possessive about the car but I would not have asked her to drive it if I had thought there was any risk.'

'I consider that neither car was to blame, but if either one was to blame, it would be the other one.'

'I knocked over a man. He admitted it was his fault as he had been run over before.'

'I remember nothing after passing the Crown Hotel until I came to and saw PC Brown.'

'Coming home I drove into the wrong house and collided with a tree I don't have.'

'I collided with a stationary truck coming the other way.'

'In my attempt to kill a fly, I drove into a telephone pole.'

'The other car collided with mine without giving warning of its intentions.'

'I had been shopping for plants all day and was on my way home. As I reached an intersection, a hedge sprang up, obscuring my vision, and I did not see the other car.'

'I had been driving for forty years when I fell asleep at the wheel and had an accident.'

'I was on my way to the doctor with rear end trouble when my universal joint gave way causing me to have an accident.'

'My car was legally parked as it backed into the other vehicle.'

'As I approached the intersection a sign suddenly appeared in a place where no sign had ever appeared before, making me unable to avoid the accident.'

'I told the police I was not injured, but upon removing my hair, I found that I had a fractured skull.'

'I was sure the old fellow would never make it to the other side of the road when I struck him.'

'I saw a slow-moving, sad-faced old gentleman as he bounced off the roof of my car.'

'The indirect cause of the accident was a little guy in a small car with a big mouth.'

'I was thrown from my car as it left the road, and was later found in a ditch by some stray cows.'

'A pedestrian hit me and went under my car.'

'I thought my window was down, but I found out it was up when I put my head through it.'

'To avoid hitting the bumper of the car in front, I struck the pedestrian.'

'The guy was all over the road. I had to swerve a number of times before I hit him.'

'An invisible car came out of nowhere, struck my car and vanished.'

ALLEGEDLY GENUINE RESPONSES GIVEN BY MOTHERS TO THE CHILD SUPPORT AGENCY IN THE SECTION ASKING FOR FATHERS' DETAILS

'Regarding the identity of the father of my twins, child A was fathered by [name given]. I am unsure as to the identity of the father of child B, but I believe that he was conceived on the same night.'

'I am unsure as to the identity of the father of my child as I was being sick out of a window when taken unexpectedly from behind. I can provide you with a list of names of men that I think were at the party if this helps.'

'I do not know the name of the father of my little girl. She was conceived at a party at [address given] where I had unprotected sex with a man I met that night. I do remember that the sex was so good that I fainted. If you do manage to track down the father can you send me his phone number? Thanks.'

'I don't know the identity of the father of my daughter. He drives a BMW that now has a hole made by my stiletto in one of the door panels. Perhaps you can contact BMW service stations in this area and see if he's had it replaced?'

'I have never had sex with a man. I am awaiting a letter from the Pope confirming that my son's conception was immaculate and that he is Christ risen again.'

'I cannot tell you the name of child A's dad as he informs me that to do so would blow his cover and that would have cataclysmic implications for the British economy. I am torn between doing right by you and right by the country. Please advise.'

'I do not know who the father of my child was as all squaddies look the same to me. I can confirm that he was a Royal Green Jacket.'

'[name given] is the father of child A. If you do catch up with him can you ask him what he did with my AC/DC CDs.'

'From the dates it seems that my daughter was conceived at EuroDisney. Maybe it really is the Magic Kingdom.'

'So much about that night is a blur. The only thing that I remember for sure is Delia Smith did a programme about eggs earlier in the evening. If I'd have stayed in and watched more TV rather than going to the party at [address given], mine might have remained unfertilized.'

'I am unsure as to the identity of the father of my baby. After all, when you eat a can of beans you can't be sure which one made you fart.'

RELATIVE VALUES

Whoopi Goldberg's first grandchild was born on her 35th birthday

Hilary Swank is Rob Lowe's sister-in-law

Zubin Mehta's first ex-wife is married to his brother

Norman Cook's father was responsible for introducing the bottle bank to Britain

Richard Blackwood's father used to be married to Naomi Campbell's mother

Alicia Silverstone filed for emancipation from her parents at the age of 15 so that she could work as an adult

Natalie Portman has never revealed her true surname as she wants to protect her family's privacy

Carol Vorderman's great-grandfather had two butterflies named after him

Jane Seymour used to be Nigel Planer's sister-in-law

Elizabeth Hurley's grandfather – a Mr Tit – used to be Tara Palmer-Tomkinson's milkman

Jeremy Clarkson's father-in-law won the VC

Peter Kay's school metalwork teacher was Steve Coogan's father

Kathleen Turner and Donna Karan are sisters-in-law

USED THEIR MOTHER'S MAIDEN NAME

Ryan Giggs (instead of Wilson)

Shirley MacLaine (Beaty)

Marilyn Monroe (Baker)

Lauren Bacall (Perske)

Shelley Winters (actually, her mother's maiden name was Winter)

Catherine Deneuve (Dorleac)

Ed Stewart (Mainwaring)

Kevin Spacey (Fowler)

Beck Hansen (Campbell)

Chris De Burgh (Davidson)

Elvis Costello (MacManus)

Marti Pellow (McLachlan)

Ivor Novello (Davies)

Patsy Palmer (Harris)

Sir Ian Holm (Cuthbert)

Klaus Maria Brandauer (Steng)

Jonathan Rhys Meyers (O'Keefe – his mother's maiden name was Meyers and he added the Rhys)

Dr Seuss (Geisel)

Olivia Hussey (Osura)

Joan Jeft (Larkin)

MEN WHO CAN USE ROMAN NUMERAL III AFTER THEIR NAMES

Loudon Wainwright, Ted Turner, Davis Love, Ted Danson, Alec Baldwin, Cliff Robertson, Luke Perry, Bill Gates, Eminem (Marshall Mathers III), Sam Shepard (born Samuel Shepard Rogers III)

PEOPLE WHO ADOPTED CHILDREN

Ellen Burstyn, Tom Hanks, Angelina Jolie, Ilie Nastase, President Ronald Reagan, Lionel Richie, Marlon Brando, Bob Monkhouse, David Bellamy, Lord David Steel, Burt Reynolds & Loni Anderson, Linda Ronstadt, Sheena Easton, Steven Spielberg & Kate Capshaw, Burt Bacharach & Carole Bayer Sager, Jill Ireland & Charles Bronson, Ted Danson, Graham Chapman, Graham Gouldman, Magic Johnson, Prue Leith, Dora Bryan, Muhammad Ali, David Niven, Una Stubbs, Henry Fonda, Rosie O'Donnell, Isabella Rossellini, Robin Givens, Ella Fitzgerald, Kate Jackson, Kevin Lloyd, John Denver, Joan Crawford, George Burns, Patti LaBelle, Walt Disney, James Cagney, Bob Hope, Jerry Lewis, Paul Newman & Joanne Woodward, Bette Davis, Bernard Matthews, George Orwell, Josephine Baker, Imelda Marcos, Harpo Marx, Hugh Jackman, Scott Bakula

PEOPLE WITH FAMOUS STEP-PARENTS

Adam Hart-Davis – Dame Peggy Ashcroft

Sally Field – Jock Mahoney

David Cassidy – Shirley Jones

Paloma Picasso – Jonas Salk

Mark Nicholas – Brian Widlake

Nicolette Sheridan – Telly Savalas

Christian Bale – Gloria Steinem

Cherie Blair – Pat Phoenix

Carlene Carter – Johnny Cash

Liv Tyler – Todd Rundgren

Bijou Phillips – Michelle Phillips

NB Gore Vidal shared a stepfather with Jacqueline Kennedy (his mother, Nina, married Jackie's stepfather, Hugh Auchincloss)

BABYSITTERS

Little Eva babysat for Carole King's children – which is how she came to sing Carole King's hit 'The Locomotion'

Lindsay Wagner babysat for Glen Campbell's children

Billy Crystal had Billie Holiday as a babysitter

Edward Norton had Betsy True as a babysitter

Vicki Michelle's au pair as a child was Elke Sommer

Daniel Radcliffe had *Gangster Number One* director Paul McGuigan as a babysitter

CAR ACRONYMS

Audi
Accelerates Under Demonic
Influence
Always Unsafe Designs
Implemented

BMW
Born Moderately Wealthy
Break My Windows
Bought My Wife

Buick
Big Ugly Indestructible Car Killer

Chevrolet
Car Has Extensive Valve Rattle On
Long Extended Trips
Cheap, Hardly Efficient, Virtually
Runs On Luck Every Time

Chevy
Cheapest Heap Ever Visioned Yet

Dodge
Dangerous On Days Gears Engage

Fiat
Failed Italian Automotive
Technology
Failed In All Tests

Ford
Fix Or Repair Daily
Fails On Rainy Days
Fast Only Rolling Downhill

Honda
Had One – Never Did Again

Hyundai
Hope You Understand Nothing's
Driveable And Inexpensive

Mazda
Most Always Zipping Dangerously
Along

Mercedes
Many Expensive Repairs Can
Eventually Discourage Extra Sales

Nissan
Needs Immediate Salvage So
Abandon Now

Oldsmobile
Overpriced, Leisurely Driven Sedan
Made Of Buick's Irregular Leftover
Equipment

Pontiac
Poor Old Nut Thinks It's A Cadillac

Porsche
Proof Only Rich Suckers Can Have
Everything

Rolls-Royce
Regarded Only as Luxury Life Style.
Runs Over Your Current Expenses

Saab
Sad Attempt At Beauty
Send Another Automobile Back

Subaru
Screwed Up Beyond All Repair
Usually

Toyota
Too Often Yanks Overprice This
Auto

Volvo
Very Odd Looking Vehicular Object

HARLEY-DAVIDSON OWNERS

Arnold Schwarzenegger, Whitney Houston, Burt Reynolds, Eric Clapton, Sylvester Stallone, Billy Idol, Jon Bon Jovi, Wynonna, Nicky Clarke, Liam Neeson, Ian Wright, George Clooney, Bruce Willis, Damon Hill, Eddie Irvine, Chris Eubank, David Copperfield, Ronan Keating, Paul Young, Kurt Russell, Colin Farrell, Neil Fox, Steve McQueen, Jim Bowen, Errol Flynn, Elvis Presley, T.E. Lawrence, Bill Haley, George Sanders, Clark Gable, Howard Hughes, Viscount Linley, Midge Ure

SURVIVED A HELICOPTER CRASH

Christy O'Connor Jnr, Christie Brinkley, Sarah Greene, Mike Smith, Kirk Douglas, Joe Longthorne, Alessandro Nannini, Adam Faith, Leni Riefenstahl (at the age of 97), Simon Schama

ASTRONOMY

Buzz Aldrin's mother's maiden name was Moon.

The Sun is 93 million miles from Earth, which is 270 times closer than the next nearest star.

When the Americans sent a man into space, they spent a million dollars developing a pen that could write upside down in conditions of zero gravity. The Russians used a pencil.

It would take about 2,000 years to walk to the Sun.

Since the Moon has no atmosphere, footprints left there by astronauts will remain visible for at least 10 million years.

All the planets in our solar system could be placed inside the planet Jupiter.

All the moons of the solar system are named after Greek and Roman mythology, except the moons of Uranus, which are named after Shakespearean characters.

If you take one pound of cobwebs and spread them out in one straight line, it will go twice around the Earth.

Neutron stars are so condensed that a fragment the size of a sugar cube would weigh as much as all the people on Earth put together.

A lightning bolt generates temperatures five times hotter than those found at the Sun's surface.

**A car travelling at 100mph would take
more than 29 million years to reach the nearest star –
but you could reach the Sun by car in a little over 106 years.**

If you were standing on Mercury, the Sun would appear 2.5 times larger than it appears on Earth.

It takes 8.5 minutes for light to get from the Sun to the Earth.

The Milky Way galaxy contains 5 billion stars larger than our Sun.

The Earth weighs approximately 6,588,000,000,000,000,000 tons.

10 tons of space dust fall on the Earth every day.

Every year the Sun loses 360 million tons.

The pressure at the Earth's inner core is 3 million times the Earth's atmospheric pressure.

Over one thousand planets the size of the Earth could fit inside the Sun.

The average modern home computer is more powerful than all of NASA's computers at the time of the Apollo moon landings put together.

In 1963, baseball pitcher Gaylord Perry remarked, 'They'll put a man on the moon before I hit a home run.' On 20 July 1969, a few hours after Neil Armstrong set foot on the moon, Gaylord Perry hit his first – and only – home run.

NB: The Mount of Jupiter and the Girdle of Venus are found on the palm of your hand.

Uranus is visible to the naked eye

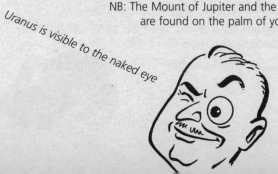

NUMBER 142,857

142,857 is a cyclic number: when multiplied by a number up to 6, it will produce a number containing the same digits in the same order – albeit starting in a different place.

$$1 \times 142{,}857 = 142{,}857$$
$$2 \times 142{,}857 = 285{,}714$$
$$3 \times 142{,}857 = 428{,}571$$
$$4 \times 142{,}857 = 571{,}428$$
$$5 \times 142{,}857 = 714{,}285$$
$$6 \times 142{,}857 = 857{,}142$$

Look what happens when you multiply 142,857 by 7: it equals 999,999.

When 1 is divided by 7 it comes to 0.142857,142857,142857.

If you multiply 142,857 by 8, you get 1,142,856. If you take off the first digit (1) and add it to the last six digits, see what happens: 1 + 142,856 = 142,857.

Similarly, if you multiply 142,857 by – say – 17, you get 2,428,569. Now take off the first digit (2) and add it to the last six digits and see what happens: 2 + 428,569 = 428,571 – which is, of course, the original number in stage three of its cycle.

You can do this with every number except multiples of 7 (although these also produce interesting results).

If you take the number 142,857 and split it into two – 142 and 857 – and then add those two numbers, you get 999.

MORE NUMBERS

Japanese researchers have calculated pi to 1.2411 trillion places. If you need to remember pi, just count the letters in each word of the sentence: 'May I have a large container of coffee?' If you get the coffee and are polite say: 'Thank you,' and get two more decimal places: 3.141592653 …

The 772nd to 777th digits of pi are 999999.

For the ancient Greeks any number more than 10,000 was a 'myriad'.

In the carol 'Twelve Days of Christmas', the total number of gifts that 'my true love gave to me' is 364.

When 21,978 is multiplied by 4, the result is 87,912 – which is 21,978 reversed.

Any number, squared, is equal to one more than the numbers on either side of it multiplied together – 5x5=25 and 4x6=24; 6x6=36 and 5x7=35 etc.

The Roman numerals for 1666 are MDCLXVI (1000+500+100+50+10+5+1) – the only year featuring all the Roman numerals from the highest to the lowest.

One penny doubled every day becomes over £5 million in just 30 days.

37 x 3 = 111

37 x 6 = 222

37 x 9 = 333

37 x 12 = 444

37 x 15 = 555

37 x 18 = 666

37 x 21 = 777

If you add up the numbers 1–100 consecutively (1+2+3+4+5 etc.) the total is 5,050.

1961 was the most recent year that could be written both upside down and right side up and appear the same. The next year this will be possible will be 6009.

The smallest number with three letters is 1

… with four letters is 4

… with five letters is 3

… with six letters is 11

… with seven letters is 15

… with eight letters is 13

… with nine letters is 17

… with 10 letters is 24

The word INTERCHANGEABILITY contains the numbers THREE, EIGHT, NINE, TEN, THIRTEEN, THIRTY, THIRTY-NINE, EIGHTY, EIGHTY-NINE, NINETY and NINETY-EIGHT.

In English, the only number that has the same number of letters as its name is FOUR. Here are some other languages and the only numbers that contain precisely the same number of letters:

Basque BEDERATZI (9)

Catalan U (1)

Czech TRI (3)

Danish and Norwegian TO (2), TRE (3), FIRE (4)

Dutch VIER (4)

Esperanto DU (2), TRI (3), KVAR (4)

Finnish VIISI (5)

German VIER (4)

Italian TRE (3)

Pilipino APAT (4)

Polish PIATY (5)

Portuguese and Spanish CINCO (5)

Romanian CINCI (5)

Serbo-Croatian TRI (3)

Swedish TRE (3), FYRA (4)

Turkish DÖRT (4)

One thousand contains the letter A, but none of the words from one to nine hundred ninety-nine has an A.

TWO OF A KIND

OWNS A STUD FARM

Charlie Watts

Susan George

DIED IN AN APARTMENT OWNED BY HARRY NILSSON

Mama Cass Elliot

Keith Moon

SON OF DEAF PARENTS

Lon Chaney

Richard Griffiths

WROTE A BALLET

David Bellamy (*Heritage*)

Sir Patrick Moore (*Lyra's Dream*)

EYES OF DIFFERENT COLOURS

Jane Seymour (one green and one brown)

David Bowie (one green and one blue)

MARRIED A WOMAN CALLED KELLY PRESTON (NOT THE SAME WOMAN)

Lou Diamond Phillips

John Travolta

EX-*BLIND DATE* CONTESTANT

Jenni Falconer

Amanda Holden

MODELLED FOR TEEN PHOTO-ROMANCE STORIES

Hugh Grant

George Michael

HAD A SONG WRITTEN ABOUT HIM BY STING

Rod Stewart ('Peanuts')

Quentin Crisp ('An Englishman In New York')

HOLDER OF HGV LICENCE

Rowan Atkinson

Chris Eubank

ENDOWED A UNIVERSITY PROFESSORSHIP

Barbra Streisand (in Intimacy and Sexuality)

Sir Cameron Mackintosh (in Musical Theatre)

EX-BULLFIGHTER

Frederick Forsyth

Gabriel Byrne

THE QUEEN

The Queen was the first (future monarch) to be born in a private house – 17 Bruton Street, London W1 – which is now the site of a bank. She was delivered by caesarean section on a Wednesday.

When she was born she was third in line to the throne (her father and her uncle David, later King Edward VIII, were ahead of her).

She learned to curtsey perfectly before the age of two and made her last curtsey in 1952, to her father's body in St George's Chapel, Windsor.

She's 5 feet 4 inches and weighs about 8 stones.

She and Prince Philip were related before they married. They're third cousins (through their descent from Queen Victoria) and second cousins once removed (through King Christian IX of Denmark).

The Queen has only once signed an autograph for a member of the public. In 1945, Sergeant Pat Hayes asked for her autograph and was given it.

Private Eye's nickname for her is 'Brenda'; her childhood nickname was 'Lilibet' which was the way she mispronounced her own name and is now the name by which her closest relatives know her; her grandmother, Queen Mary, called her 'the bambino'.

At the precise moment in 1952 when she acceded to the throne, she was wearing a shirt, a cardigan and a pair of slacks.

She's superstitious: she throws salt over her left shoulder if she accidentally spills any, she won't have 13 people at the dinner table and she's been known to touch wood before her horses run.

Whenever she travels abroad she always takes with her barley water, a specially formulated egg and lemon shampoo and her feather pillow.

As Queen, she can or could: drive without taking a driving test;

disobey the laws of the land because they are, of course, *her* laws; refuse to give evidence in court as the courts are *her* courts (she also can't be sued); declare war on another country (the armed forces are under her command); disband the army and sell all the Navy's ships; send letters without putting stamps on (her letters carry the Royal cipher); give as many honours – including peerages and knighthoods – as she likes; declare a State of Emergency (which she once did – on 31 May 1955 because of the railway strike); turn any parish in the country into a university; pardon any (or all) of the prisoners in *her* jails; dismiss the government, and get rid of the Civil Service.

The Queen's retinue includes: Keeper of the Queen's Swans, Mistress of the Robes, The Queen's Raven Master, The Clerk of the Closet, Lady of The Bedchamber, Woman of the Bedchamber, Hereditary Grand Falconer, Royal Bargemaster, The Queen's Racing Pigeon Manager and Grand Almoner.

The Queen loves: military march music, popular classical works and musicals, champagne, corgis, watching TV (favourite programmes include *Dad's Army*, *Brideshead Revisited* and *The Good Life*), horse racing, crossword puzzles, impersonations (she's also a gifted impressionist herself) and charades.

The Queen hates: dictating letters, garlic, cats, tennis, pomposity, the cold, smoking and any mention of King Edward VIII whose abdication pushed her father on to the throne, the stress of which (or so the Queen Mother always believed) caused his early death.

TITLES HELD BY PRINCE PHILIP

Privy Councillor, Knight of the Thistle, Admiral of the Royal Yacht Squadron, Grand Master of the Guild of Air Pilots and Air Navigators, Field-Marshal, Marshal of the RAF, Admiral of the Fleet, Knight of the Garter, Chancellor of the University of Cambridge.

KING EDWARD VIII

Edward had more names than any other king in history. He was baptized with the names Edward Albert Christian George Andrew Patrick David – a total of seven.

When he was a little boy, the nurse who looked after him (and his brothers) was determined to set his parents against him. She used to pinch him before he was sent in to see his parents so he'd walk in crying and be sent away in disgrace.

Whatever talents he had, billiards wasn't one of them. Once when playing with his father at Sandringham, he miscued and ripped the felt. His father banned him from the table for a year.

It wasn't only his father who was strict with him. Once he was eating with his grandfather, King Edward VII, and, on trying to talk to him, was told to wait for permission. When this permission was finally  granted, he said: 'It's too late now, Grandpa. There was a caterpillar on your lettuce but you've eaten it.'

Wallis wasn't the first married woman he fell for – in fact, all his lovers were married. When he set his sights on Freda Dudley Ward, he sent round a note – addressed to Mrs Dudley Ward – requesting an invitation to tea. To his shock, he found himself alone at tea with an elderly woman: Freda's mother-in-law, Mrs Dudley Ward!

On 1 January 1936, Sir Winston Churchill, commenting on the growing crisis caused by the relationship of Edward and Mrs Simpson, said, 'He falls instantly in and out of love. His present attachment will follow the course of all the others.' In fact, the relationship lasted until the duke's death in 1972 (at the age of 77 from throat cancer).

Looking back over his brief reign, Edward reckoned that all he'd done was introduce the King's Flight and end the rule that Beefeaters had to have beards.

He was an admirer of Adolf Hitler and Nazism. The reason he was sent off to the Bahamas during World War Two was because the establishment was bothered that he might be a focus for conciliation with the Germans in the event of an invasion. He once said to Diana Mosley (wife of British fascist leader Oswald), 'Every drop of blood in my veins is German.'

Edward liked to indulge in Americanisms such as 'hot-diggerty dog', 'makin' whoopee' and 'okey-dokey'.

As a result of Edward's abdication, the year 1936 saw three different kings on the throne: his father, George V, himself and his brother George VI. There are two other years when this has happened: 1066 (Edward The Confessor, Harold and William The Conqueror) and 1483 (Edward IV, Edward V and Richard III).

As Prince of Wales, he was a great fashion leader. At Oxford University, he wore plus-fours and made turned-up trousers fashionable. He introduced the bowler hat to America. He also invented the Windsor tie knot, which, along with his affected Cockney accent, annoyed his father, George V.

He had a tendency to monophobia, the morbid fear of being alone.

The legendary actress, Marlene Dietrich, took it into her head that she could persuade the King to give up Mrs Simpson and, to that end, she tried phoning him on many occasions, but he refused to take her calls. Eventually, she tried to see him in person but she was refused entry and decided to give up her quest.

King George V had no illusions about his children. He once said, 'I pray to God that my eldest son (Edward) will never marry and have children and that nothing will come between Bertie (George VI) and Lilibet (Elizabeth II) and the Throne.'

When he was Governor of the Bahamas, he used to make black people use the back door.

When the writer Harold Nicolson said to H.G. Wells that Edward had 'charm', Wells contradicted him: 'Glamour.'

Although he was King, he was never actually crowned. He abdicated in December 1936; his coronation had been arranged for the following May.

When he came to sign the instrument of abdication, he found there was 'no damned ink in the pot'.

Although his duchess spent money like a sailor on shore leave, the duke was much more frugal. For example, he always saved his half-smoked cigars from the evening before.

The duke and duchess had a code for when they wanted to leave uninteresting parties: one of them would refer to the 'bore hunt'.

THE WAY WE LIVE

90 per cent of women who walk into a department store immediately turn to the right. No one knows why.

Tuesday is the most productive day of the working week.

908,000 US one-dollar bills weigh exactly one ton.

The average woman uses about 6 pounds of lipstick during her lifetime.

It is estimated that at any one time 0.7 per cent of the world's population is intoxicated.

There has never been a sex-change operation performed in Ireland.

90 per cent of movies released in the United States are porn films.

Couples who marry in January, February or March have the highest divorce rate.

75 per cent of Japanese women own vibrators. The global average is 47 per cent.

The Christmas holidays are the busiest time in plastic surgeons' offices.

80 per cent of women wash their hands after leaving a public toilet; only 55 per cent of men do.

No, no – this way, Martha.

In Turkey the colour of mourning is violet. In most Muslim countries and in China it is white.

In China, the bride wears red.

40 per cent of people who come to a party in your home have a look in your medicine cabinet.

One in every eight boss–secretary romances ends in marriage.

25 per cent of all businesses in the US are franchises.

People who work at night tend to weigh more than people who work during the day.

On an average work day, a typist's fingers travel 12.6 miles.

One out of five pieces of the world's garbage is generated in the United States.

6 per cent of American men propose marriage by phone.

On average, Americans stand

There's an average of 178 sesame seeds on a Big Mac bun.

About 75 per cent of the people in the US live on 2 per cent of the land.

In the vast majority of the world's languages, the word for 'mother' begins with the letter 'm'.

Mexico City has more taxis than any other city in the world.

85 per cent of international phone calls are conducted in English.

The largest toy distributor in the world is McDonald's.

The average person drinks 70,000 cups of coffee in a lifetime.

After a three-week holiday, your IQ can drop by as much as 20 per cent.

In the course of a lifetime, the average person spends about two years on the phone.

14 inches apart when they converse.

The typical driver will honk their car horn 15,250 times during their lifetime.

The average British adult will eat 35,000 biscuits in their lifetime.

Every year 8,000 people injure themselves while using a toothpick.

In the USA 9 milligrams of rat droppings are allowed in a kilogram of wheat.

Every year the average person eats 428 bugs by mistake.

The average Briton is 38 years old.

One in every four Americans has appeared on television.

17,000 individual Smarties are eaten every minute in the UK.

Peanuts are one of the ingredients of dynamite.

If a statue in the park of a person on a horse has both front legs in the air, the person died in battle; if the horse has one front leg in the air, the person died as a result of wounds received in battle; if the horse has all four legs on the ground, the person died of natural causes.

30 per cent of all the non-biodegradable rubbish buried in American landfills is disposable nappies.

The stall closest to the door in a public toilet is the cleanest, because it is the least used.

People spend two weeks of their life kissing.

People spend more than five years of their lives dreaming.

A typist's left hand does 56 per cent of the work.

The average driver will be locked out of their car nine times during their lifetime.

When asked for a colour, three out of five people say red.

YOGA PRACTITIONERS

Geri Halliwell, Ali MacGraw, Gillian Anderson, Jerry Hall, Sting, Trudie Styler, Woody Harrelson, Goldie Hawn, Madonna, Gwyneth Paltrow, Raquel Welch, Brooke Shields, Michael Jackson, Patricia Arquette, Al Pacino, Flea, Courtney Love, Jemima Khan, Jodie Foster, Cindy Crawford, Ricky Martin, Dani Behr, Helen Hunt, Catrina Skepper, Zeinab Badawi, Jerry Seinfeld, Mel C, Kristin Davis, Tobey Maguire, Justin Timberlake, Sadie Frost, Reese Witherspoon, Rachel Weisz, Heather Graham, Darcey Bussell, Demi Moore, James Spader, Leah Bracknell, Linda Barker, Penny Smith

EYES CORRECTED BY LASER SURGERY

Sir Richard Branson, Simon Le Bon, Courteney Cox, Cilla Black, Tiger Woods, Brad Pitt, Julianne Moore, Lee Westwood, Sir Clive Woodward, Sharron Davies, Dennis Waterman, Padraig Harrington, Myleene Klass, Nicole Kidman, Adam Sandler, Sally Jessy Raphael, Ewen McGregor, Peter Jackson, Jessica Simpson, Jonathan Edwards, Princess Michael of Kent

USED HRT (HORMONE REPLACEMENT THERAPY)

Kate O'Mara, Marjorie Proops, Teresa Gorman, The Duchess of Kent, Joan Collins, Fay Weldon, Angela Thorne, Germaine Greer, Lizzie Webb, Jill Gascoine, Stephanie Beacham, Dr Miriam Stoppard, Isla Blair, Judy Finnigan, Anne Robinson

HAD A VASECTOMY

Dean Martin, Richard Madeley, Faron Young, Paul Ross, Billy Eckstine, Abbie Hoffman, Michael Parkinson, Howard Hughes, George Melly, Neil Kinnock, Adrian Edmondson

HAD A LIVER TRANSPLANT

George Best, Larry Hagman, Jack Bruce, David Crosby, Jim Baxter, Rory Gallagher, Brian Clough

HAD A KIDNEY TRANSPLANT

Lucy Davis (from her mother), Gary Coleman (two)

FLAT FEET

Stan Collymore, Linda Lusardi, Roger Black, Zoë Ball, Edwina Currie, Dame Alicia Markova, Newt Gingrich, Prince Charles, Cyndi Lauper, Stephen King, Robin Smith, Terence Stamp

HARD OF HEARING

George Melly, David Hockney, Eric Sykes, Lester Piggott, Bill Clinton, Norman Mailer, King Juan Carlos, Rob Lowe (deaf in his right ear), Luciano Pavarotti, Dominick Dunne, Sir John Mills, Stephanie Beacham, Sir George Martin, Brian Wilson (deaf in one ear and so has never heard his songs in stereo), Lucinda Lambton (deaf in her right ear), Halle Berry (lost 80 per cent hearing in her left ear after ex-lover beat her), Rodney Marsh (deaf in his left ear), Richard Thomas, Kate Adie, Des O'Connor (deaf in one ear)

NB Thomas Edison was completely deaf in his left ear and had limited hearing in his right ear

SURVIVED A STROKE

Dickie Davies, Raymond Blanc, Bill Maynard, Kirk Douglas, Sir John Harvey-Jones, Barbara Windsor, Boris Yeltsin, Keith Floyd, Sharon Stone

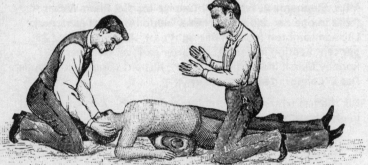

HAD KIDNEY STONES

Michael Heseltine, Edward Stourton, Sir Gary Sobers, Anne Diamond, Sir Ranulph Fiennes, Bob Dole, Letitia Dean, Montserrat Caballe, Henry Kelly, Michael Crawford, Lord Richard Attenborough, Steve Cram

HAD APPENDIX REMOVED

Dave Stewart (unnecessarily so – it was just wind), Dian Fossey (as a precaution before going into the jungle), Mel Gibson, Sir Steven Redgrave, Pope John Paul II, Isla Blair, Mika Hakkinen, Patsy Palmer, Sue Barker, Ann Widdecombe, Robert Powell, Steven Norris, Jeremy Beadle, Fidel Castro, Lisa Snowdon, Meg Mathews, Jenna Bush, Minnie Driver, Kelsey Grammer, Tim Allen, Glenda Jackson, Gavin Hastings, Vicky Entwistle, Jo O'Meara, Prince Charles, Kevin Costner, Gyles Brandreth, Dame Vera Lynn, Julia Volkova (of Tatu), Kate Beckinsale, Jonny Wilkinson, Lindsay Lohan

HAD TONSILS REMOVED AS AN ADULT

David Coulthard, Ringo Starr, Bryan Ferry, Don Maclean (twice – as a child and as an adult when they'd grown back), Kelly Holmes, Kyran Bracken, Judy Simpson, Paul Way, Roger Cook, Drew Barrymore, Ben Okri, Rudolf Nureyev, Claire Richards, Graham Taylor, Billie Piper, Tina O'Brien, Scarlett Johansson

HEART MURMUR

Judy Finnigan, Arnold Schwarzenegger, Bridget Fonda, Retief Goosen, Rachel Hunter, Evander Holyfield, Dame Elizabeth Taylor, Tony Blair, Barbara Windsor, Keith Duffy, Sir Alex Ferguson

HAS A HEART PACEMAKER

Sir Elton John, Dick Cheney, Sir Patrick Moore, James Major, Gareth Hale, Sir Alex Ferguson, Sir Roger Moore, George Cole

HAD EPILEPTIC FITS

Julius Caesar, Alexander The Great, Cameron Sharp, François Pienaar, Lord Byron, Michael Miles, Vincent van Gogh, Julia Somerville, Edward Lear, Derek Bentley, Peter The Great, Max Clifford, Billy Idol, Neil Young, Ward Bond, Ian Curtis, Margaux Hemingway, Florence Griffith Joyner

SURVIVED MENINGITIS

Victoria Beckham, Jerry Lewis, Lee Sharpe, Queen Beatrix of the Netherlands, Steve Elkington, Peter Francisco, Dr Phil Hammond, Nick Conway, Maria Shriver, John Morris, Bruce Grobelaar, Johnny Rotten (Lydon), Ben Peyton, Kirsty Young

HAS SUFFERED FROM ASTHMA

Nick Hancock, Adam Woodyatt, Tony Robinson, Edwina Currie, Liz McColgan, Lee Hurst, Dewi Morris, Gerald Scarfe, Rodney Bewes, Ian Wright, Jason Donovan, Steven Seagal, Alan Freeman, Peter Sissons (had an asthma attack while reading the news), Wynonna, Stephen Fry, Joe Jackson (used to be put into oxygen tents in hospital), Kathleen Quinlan, Shirley Manson, Karen Pickering, Nikki Sanderson, Austin Healey, Paul Scholes

SUFFERED FROM ANOREXIA

Sinitta, Marina Ogilvy, Lena Zavaroni, Karen Carpenter, Patsy Palmer, Tracy Shaw, Patricia Cornwell, Kate Beckinsale, Davina McCall, Jenny Éclair, Rory Bremner

TINNITUS SUFFERERS

Russell Grant, Pete Townshend, Barbra Streisand, Julia McKenzie, Alan Bleasdale

SUFFERED FROM BULIMIA

Diana, Princess of Wales, Zina Garrison, Lysette
Anthony, Uri Geller, Jane Fonda, Emma Thompson,
Sir Elton John, Geri Halliwell, Kym Marsh, Linda
Thorson, Adam Rickitt, Carre Otis, Lucy Pargeter, Russell
Brand, Michelle Dewberry, Kirsty Young (for a few
months as a teenager)

PARKINSON'S DISEASE

**Ray Kennedy, Michael J. Fox, Sir Michael Redgrave,
Mao-Tse Tung, Sir John Betjeman, Muhammad Ali, Johnny
Cash, Janet Reno, Deborah Kerr, Billy Graham**

SUFFERED FROM MANIC DEPRESSION

Axl Rose, Spike Milligan, Nicola
Pagett, Sir James Goldsmith,
Vincent van Gogh, Ted
Turner, Vivien Leigh,
Jeremy Brett, Freddie
Starr, Jess Yates, Robert
Schumann, Abbie
Hoffman, Patricia
Cornwell, Margot Kidder,
Mario Lanza, Capucine,
Dorothy Dandridge, Patty
Duke

SUFFERED FROM CHILDHOOD POLIO

Alan Alda, Ian Dury, Lord Snowdon, Kerry Packer, Sir Walter Scott, Joni Mitchell, Sir Julian Critchley, Neil Young, Itzhak Perlman, Steve Harley, Joe Coral, Sir Harold Hobson, Wilma Rudolph, Ruskin Spear, Dinah Shore, Francis Coppola

DIABETICS

Gary Mabbutt, Bill Maynard, Bernard Manning, Lisa Harrow, Michael Barry, Mary Tyler Moore, Halle Berry, Wasim Akram, Sir Steven Redgrave, Mick Fleetwood, Sharon Stone, B.B. King, George Lucas, Meat Loaf, Brian Cox, Elaine Strich

SURVIVED A HEART ATTACK

Edward Woodward, Sue Townsend, Martin Sheen, Michael Heseltine, Omar Sharif, Eddy Grant, Jerry Lee Lewis, Eddie Large, Paul O'Grady, Nigel Lythgoe, Ian Lavender, Diego Maradona

SUFFERS FROM ARTHRITIS

John Cleese, The Queen, Claire King, Tommy Smith, José Maria Olazabal, Dame Elizabeth Taylor, Prince Philip, Simon Geoghegan, Dermot Reeve, Jack Nicklaus, Lord Nigel Lawson, Malcolm Allison, Chris Broad, Joe Royle, Dame Julia Neuberger, Jo Durie, Barry Gibb, Kathleen Turner

Survived a nervous breakdown

Emily Lloyd, David Helfgott, Honor Blackman, Bob Hoskins, Leslie Phillips, The Duchess of Kent, Yitzhak Rabin, Leslie Caron, Brian Wilson, Daniel Day-Lewis, Brian Blessed, Yves St Laurent, Kylie Minogue, Lee Evans, Roseanne, Tuesday Weld, Sarah Lancashire, Mariah Carey, Beyoncé Knowles, Kate Beckinsale, Norman Cook

Lost a finger

Jerry Garcia, Boris Yeltsin, James Doohan, Dr Alex Comfort, Telly Savalas, Daryl Hannah (wears a prosthetic fingertip), Admiral Isoroku Yamamoto (who planned attack on Pearl Harbor), Matt Perry (lost middle finger in kindergarten accident), Gary Burghoff (Radar from M*A*S*H – left hand always hidden by clipboard), Dave Allen (missing tip of one finger), Terry Nutkins (fingertip bitten off by an otter), Dustin Hoffman (lost the tip of his finger when a seat collapsed while filming *Neverland* in 2003)

BLIND

Stevie Wonder, David Blunkett, John Milton, Ray Charles, Louis Braille, Claude Monet, Helen Keller, Jose Feliciano, James Thurber, Joseph Pulitzer, Peggy Mount, George Shearing, Sue Townsend

LOST AN EYE

Gordon Banks, Sir Rex Harrison, Herbert Morrison, Joe Davis, James Thurber, Colin Milburn, John Ford, Moshe Dayan, Peter Falk, John Milton, Sammy Davis Jr, Sandy Duncan, Alan Jay Lerner, Raoul Walsh, Ry Cooder

NB Gordon Brown and Amanda Barrie are both blind in one eye

Have used Viagra

Jim Carrey, Jerry Springer, Bob Dole, Hugh Hefner, Julio Iglesias, Ryan O'Neal, Johnnie Walker, Vidal Sassoon, Ben Affleck (once – 'all it did was make me sweat and feel dizzy. I felt no sexual effects whatsoever'), Kim Cattrall, Jack Nicholson, Ozzy Osbourne

Pregnancy cravings

Catherine Zeta-Jones – beetroot (first child), Branston Pickle and curry (second child)

Lowri Turner – red meat

Fiona Phillips – cream and then mints

Mel B – peanut butter, cheesecake, ice cream and chips

Gloria Estefan – sweetened condensed milk

Victoria Beckham – gherkins

Kate Winslet – fizzy cola sweets, blackcurrant juice and tomatoes

Madonna – butternut squash

Zoë Ball – lettuce and fruit

Marie Osmond – grapefruit sorbet topped with sardines

Davina McCall – tabasco sauce and Coca-Cola (first child); radishes and Coca-Cola (second child)

Cate Blanchett – sardines

Natasha Hamilton – sweet puddings and fried breakfasts

Jade Goody – pickled onion Monster Munch dipped in hummus

Brooke Shields – extremely strong coffee and nutmeg

Ms Dynamite – strawberry flavour Ben and Jerry's ice cream

Ulrika Jonsson – digestive biscuits (third child)

Melinda Messenger – cucumber

NATURE

Millions of trees are accidentally planted by squirrels that bury nuts and then forget where they left them.

The smallest trees in the world are Greenland dwarf willows.

It snowed in the Sahara desert on 18 February 1979.

The canopy of a rainforest is so thick that only 1 per cent of sunlight reaches the ground.

An ordinary raindrop falls at about 7 miles per hour.

Lightning strikes the Earth about 200 times a second.

Heavy rain pours down at the rate of about 20 miles per hour.

The Siberian larch accounts for more than 20 per cent of the world's trees.

The giant water lily grows almost a foot a day.

Some bamboo plants grow 3 feet a day.

Oak trees do not produce acorns until they are at least 50 years old.

A cucumber is 96 per cent water.

There is cyanide in apple pips.

A notch in a tree will remain the same distance from the ground as the tree grows.

If you put a raisin in a glass of champagne, it will keep floating to the top and sinking to the bottom.

Almonds are part of the peach family.

There are more stars in the universe than grains of sand on all the beaches in the world.

There are 10 million bacteria in a litre of milk; that's equivalent to the population of Greece.

Cranberries are one of just three major fruits native to North America. Blueberries and Concord grapes are the other two.

A ripe cranberry will bounce.

Wheat is the world's most widely cultivated plant; grown on every continent except Antarctica.

All snow crystals are hexagonal.

The water we drink is 3 billion years old.

The average iceberg weighs 20 million tons.

You can figure out which way is south if you are near a tree stump. The growth rings are wider on the south side.

It is estimated that a plastic container can resist decomposition for as long as 50,000 years.

The most abundant metal in the Earth's crust is aluminium. The Chinese were using aluminium to make things as early as AD300. Western civilization didn't rediscover it until 1827.

The angle of the branches from the trunk of a tree is constant from one member to another of the same species.

The cashew is a member of the poison ivy family.

Strawberries are a member of the rose family.

Most orchids are bisexual.

SCIENCE

If you slowly pour a handful of salt into a totally full glass of water it will not overflow. In fact, the water level will go down.

Hot water freezes quicker than cold water.

Magnesium was used in early flash photography because it burns with a brilliant light.

A scientific satellite needs only 250 watts of power to operate.

The letter J does not appear on the periodic table of the elements.

Minus 40 degrees Celsius is exactly the same temperature as minus 40 degrees Fahrenheit.

Radio waves travel so much faster than sound waves that a broadcast voice can be heard sooner 18,000 km away than in the back of the room in which it originated.

Waves break when their height reaches more than 7/10ths of the depth of the water.

X-ray technology has shown that there are three different versions of the *Mona Lisa* under the one that's visible.

Because of the rotation of the earth, an object can be thrown farther

In an atom, the electron weighs 1/2000th the weight of the proton.

At the deepest point of the ocean (11.034 km), an iron ball would take more than an hour to sink to the ocean floor.

When scientists at Australia's Parkes Observatory began picking up radio waves, they thought they had proof of alien life. However, it transpired that the emissions came from a microwave oven in the building.

Only 13.5 per cent of scientists are women.

Sterling silver contains 7.5 per cent copper.

Hydrogen gas is the least dense substance.

Ocean waves can travel as fast as a jet plane.

Aspirin was the first drug offered as a water-soluble tablet, in 1900.

Mercury is the only metal that is liquid at room temperature.

In a scientific study, children were told to imagine that they were wearing heavy mittens. The temperature of their fingertips went up.

1/25th of the energy put out by a light bulb is light. The rest is heat.

No matter how high or low it flies, an aeroplane's shadow is always the same size.

if it is thrown west.

GUEST APPEARANCES IN TV PROGRAMMES

ABSOLUTELY FABULOUS

Germaine Greer, Richard E. Grant, Marianne Faithfull, John Wells, Jo Brand, Zandra Rhodes, Britt Ekland, Eleanor Bron, Marcella Detroit, Nicky Clarke, Christian Lacroix, Bruce Oldfield, Dora Bryan, Richard Madeley, Judy Finnigan, Stephen Gately, Anita Pallenberg, Dave Gorman, Dale Winton, Whoopi Goldberg, Debbie Harry, Fern Britton, Kristin Scott Thomas, Mariella Frostrup, Minnie Driver, Emma Bunton, Sir Elton John

BLACKADDER

Angus Deayton, Jim Broadbent, Rik Mayall, Miriam Margolyes, Tom Baker, Robbie Coltrane, Chris Barrie, Nigel Planer, Adrian Edmondson, Geoffrey Palmer

CHEERS

Glynis Johns, Dick Cavett, Sherilyn Fenn, Senator Gary Hart, Lisa Kudrow, Arsenio Hall, Bobby Hatfield, Mike Dukakis, Celeste Holm, Harry Connick Jr, Harvey Fierstein, Senator John Kerry, Johnny Carson

FILTHY RICH & CATFLAP

Midge Ure, Lynda Bellingham, David Baddiel, Stephen Fry, The Nolan Sisters, Barbara Windsor, Mel Smith, Hugh Laurie

GOODNIGHT SWEETHEART

John Motson, Timothy West, Bonnie Langford

M*A*S*H

Leslie Nielsen, Ron Howard, Loudon Wainwright III, Brian Dennehy

MEN BEHAVING BADLY

Hugo Speer, Ulrika Jonsson

RED DWARF

Koo Stark, Tony Slattery, Glynis Barber, Arthur Smith, Nicholas Ball, Jane Horrocks, Anita Dobson, Brian Cox, Geraldine McEwan

THE VICAR OF DIBLEY

Alistair McGowan, Dervla Kirwan, Stephen Tompkinson, Terry Wogan, Darcey Bussell, Richard Griffiths, Martyn Lewis

YES, MINISTER/YES, PRIME MINISTER

Bob McKenzie, Robert Dougall, Sue Lawley, Eleanor Bron, Graeme Garden, John Fortune, John Wells, Bill Bailey, John Bird

GUESTED IN *STAR TREK*

Joan Collins, Stephanie Beacham, Whoopi Goldberg, Teri Garr, Linda Thorson, Kelsey Grammer, Professor Stephen Hawking, Steven Berkoff, Mick Fleetwood, David Soul, Iggy Pop, King Abdullah of Jordan (had a cameo non-speaking role)

PRESENTED *TOP OF THE POPS*

Angus Deayton, The Spice Girls, Julia Carling, Chris Eubank, Dannii Minogue, Vic Reeves and Bob Mortimer, Frankie Dettori, Jarvis Cocker, Leo Sayer, Russ Abbot, Jack Osbourne, Davy Jones, Sir Elton John, Roger Daltrey, Sir Cliff Richard, Kevin Keegan, Lenny Henry, Mr Blobby, Meat Loaf, Jack Dee, Julian Clary, Malcolm McLaren, Steve Punt and Hugh Dennis, Kylie Minogue, Michelle Gayle, Lily Savage, Neneh Cherry, Damon Albarn, Gary Glitter, Keith Allen, Phill Jupitus, Whigfield, Dale Winton, Jo Brand, Mark Lamarr, Robbie Williams, Suggs, Louise, Ronan Keating, Stephen Gately, Björk, Lulu, Lee Evans, Ian Wright, Peter Andre, Nigel Kennedy, Ian Broudie, Rhona Cameron, Phil Daniels, Noddy Holder, Denise Van Outen

GREAT MISQUOTATIONS

'I never said I want to be alone, I only said I want to be left alone.'
(Greta Garbo)

'Alas, poor Yorick, I knew him well.'

'Alas poor Yorick! I knew him, Horatio.' (Hamlet in *Hamlet* by William Shakespeare)

'A little knowledge is a dangerous thing.'

'A little learning is a dangerous thing.' (Alexander Pope)

'Spare the rod, spoil the child.'

'He who spares the rod hates his son, but he who loves him is careful to discipline him.' (Bible, Proverbs 13:24)

'Money is the root of all evil.'

'For the love of money is the root of all evil.' (Bible, Timothy 6:10)

'Abandon hope, all ye who enter here.'

'Abandon all hope, you who enter.' (*The Divine Comedy* by Dante)

'Water, water everywhere, and not a drop to drink.'

'Water, water everywhere, nor any drop to drink.' (*Rime of the Ancient Mariner* by Samuel T. Coleridge)

'Hell hath no fury like a woman scorned.'

'Heaven has no rage, like love to hatred turned, Nor hell a fury, like a woman scorned.' (*The Mourning Bride* by William Congreve)

'Music has charms to soothe a savage beast.'

'Music has charms to soothe a savage breast.' (*The Mourning Bride* by William Congreve)

'Come up and see me sometime.'

'Why don't you come up sometime, and see me?' (Mae West to Cary Grant in *She Done Him Wrong*)

'Pride goes before a fall.'

'Pride goeth before destruction and an haughty spirit before a fall.' (Bible, Proverbs 16:18)

'My lips are sealed.'

'My lips are not yet unsealed.' (Stanley Baldwin)

'Nice guys finish last.'

'Nice Guys Finish Seventh.' (Brooklyn Dodgers manager Leo Durocher speaking in the days when the National League had seven teams so seventh was, in fact, last)

'Elementary, my dear Watson.'

'Elementary.' (Sherlock Holmes to Dr Watson in Sir Arthur Conan Doyle's stories)

'Hubble bubble, toil and trouble.'

'Double double, toil and trouble.' (The witches in *Macbeth* by William Shakespeare)

'Methinks the lady doth protest too much.'

'The lady does protest too much, methinks.' (Gertrude in *Hamlet* by William Shakespeare)

'To gild the lily.'

'To gild refined gold, to paint the lily.' (The Earl of Salisbury in *King John* by William Shakespeare)

'Me Tarzan, you Jane.'

Tarzan and Jane pointed at themselves and each said their own name in *Tarzan The Ape Man*

'He who hesitates is lost.'

'The woman that deliberates is lost.' (*Cato* by Joseph Addison)

'Et tu, Brutus?'

'Et tu, Brute?' (*Julius Caesar*. In the unlikely event that he said those words, Brutus would have taken the vocative)

'When in Rome do as the Romans do.'

'If you are at Rome, live after the Roman fashion; if you are elsewhere, live as they do there.' (St Ambrose)

'I disapprove of what you say but I will defend to the death your right to say it.'

'Think for yourselves and let others enjoy the privilege to do so too.' (Voltaire)

'Don't look a gift horse in the mouth.'

'Never inspect the teeth of a gift horse.' (original proverb)

'Discretion is the better part of valour.'

'The better part of valour is discretion.' (Falstaff in *King Henry IV, Part I* by William Shakespeare)

'There's method in his madness.'

'Though this be madness, yet there is method in't.' (Polonius in *Hamlet* by William Shakespeare)

'In the future, everybody will be famous for 15 minutes.'

'In the future, there won't be any more stars. TV will be so accessible that everybody will be a star for 15 minutes.' (Andy Warhol)

PEOPLE AND THE FILMS THEY DIRECTED

Norman Mailer – *Tough Guys Don't Dance* (1987)

Frank Sinatra – *None But The Brave* (1965)

Joan Rivers – *Rabbit Test* (1978)

Anthony Quinn – *The Buccaneer* (1958)

Rossano Brazzi – *The Christmas That Almost Wasn't* (1966)

James Clavell – *To Sir, With Love* (1967)

Arnold Schwarzenegger – *Christmas In Connecticut* (1992)

Michael Crichton – *Westworld* (1973)

Albert Finney – *Charlie Bubbles* (1968)

Patrick McGoohan – *Catch My Soul* (1973)

Timothy Leary – *Cheech And Chong's Nice Dream* (1981)

Sir Tom Stoppard – *Rosencrantz & Guildenstern Are Dead* (1990)

Michael Nesmith – *Doctor Duck's Super Secret All-Purpose Sauce* (1985)

Ringo Starr – *Born To Boogie* (1972)

Howard Hughes – *Hell's Angels* (1930)

Larry Hagman – *Son of Blob* (1972)

Richard Burton – *Dr Faustus* (1967)

PEOPLE AND THE FILMS THEY APPEARED IN

**Martin Amis
– *A High Wind In Jamaica***

Saul Bellow – *Zelig*

**Salman Rushdie
– *Bridget Jones's Diary***

Andrea Corr – *Evita*

**Anna Kournikova
– *Me, Myself And Irene***

Naomi Campbell – *Girl 6*

Simon Cowell – *Scary Movie 3*

Sergio Garcia – *Stuck On You*

**Bruce Springsteen
– *High Fidelity***

Gary Lineker
– *Bend It Like Beckham*

Dani Behr – *Rancid Aluminium*

Sophie Dahl
– *A Revenger's Tragedy*

Jackie Collins – *All At Sea*

Craig Stadler – *Tin Cup*

**Herb Alpert
– *The Ten Commandments***

Earl Spencer – *Another Country*

**Magic Johnson
– *Grand Canyon***

Ernest Hemingway – *The Old Man And The Sea*

**Justin Timberlake
– *Model Behavior***

Germaine Greer
– *Universal Soldier*

**John McEnroe
– *Anger Management***

Christopher Isherwood
– *Rich And Famous*

**Pablo Picasso
– *Life Begins Tomorrow***

Michael Parkinson
– *Love Actually*

**Leon Trotsky
– *My Official Wife***

Björk
– *Dancer In The Dark*

**Mark Twain
– *A Curious Dream***

Graham Greene – *Day for Night*

**Sir David Frost
– *The VIPs***

Elle MacPherson – *Sirens*

Jean Shrimpton – *Privilege*

Sir Henry Cooper
– *Royal Flash*

Yoko Ono – *Satan's Bed*

Kirsty Young – *Trauma*

WALT DISNEY

Born on 5 December 1901, Walt(er) Elias Disney first started drawing cartoons professionally in exchange for free haircuts.

When he was 16, Disney tried to enlist in the US Army but was refused admission because of his age. So he tried the Canadian Army – with the same result. Eventually, he went to France as a Red Cross ambulance driver.

While waiting to become an ambulance driver, he worked as a postal clerk in Chicago. When he returned from France, he worked as a postal clerk in Kansas City.

Disney started the Laugh-O-Gram Corporation, a vehicle for his animated fairy tales, in Kansas City in 1921 with $15,000 from investors. He went bankrupt two years later when his backers pulled out as a result of problems with New York distributors.

 **In 1923, he went to Hollywood to go into partnership with his brother Roy, taking all his worldly possessions: one jacket, one pair of trousers, one shirt, two sets of underwear and a few drawing materials.**

For four years, Disney and his wife, the actress Lillian Bounds, lived in poverty until he had a (relative) success with *Oswald The Lucky Rabbit.*

The same year, Disney took inspiration from the mice that used to play in his studio and created Mickey Mouse. He originally called him 'Mortimer', but his wife thought 'Mickey' sounded better. Disney himself supplied the voice for Mickey in the 1928 hit talkie *Steamboat Willie*. Disney once said of his creation: 'I love Mickey more than any woman I've ever known.'

Disney's 1940 film *Pinocchio* is regarded as a classic, but Paulo Lorenzini, the nephew of the original author of *Pinocchio*, Carlo

Lorenzini, wanted the Italian government to sue Disney for making Pinocchio too American. He failed to persuade the authorities to launch a lawsuit.

When Disney set out to make his film of *Peter Pan*, he became stuck when it came to how Tinker Bell should be depicted. In the end, he decided to model her on the ideal American woman: Marilyn Monroe.

By the time of his death on 15 December 1966 at the age of 65, Disney had won more Oscars (32) than anyone else in history.

THINGS ROBERT DE NIRO HAS DONE TO 'FIND' HIS CHARACTERS

The Godfather Part 2 (1974) It was for this role, as the young Vito Corleone, that De Niro won his first Oscar. To get into character and play the part with conviction, De Niro learned to speak Sicilian Italian.

Taxi Driver (1976) For this role, De Niro was obliged to lose weight – some two and a half stones. He also worked as a taxi-driver. Once he picked up a fare who, recognizing him, said, 'You're the actor, aren't you? Guess it's hard to find steady work.'

New York, New York (1977) Most actors when required to portray musicians settle for a rough approximation of pretending to play their instruments. Not De Niro. Cast as a saxophonist, he learned to play the saxophone. His playing was still dubbed over by a professional but his finger-placement earned him praise from the experts.

The Deer Hunter (1978) In this film, De Niro played a steelworker, so he went to live in a steelworking community for a few weeks before starting to film. He also performed his own stunts – including one where he has to jump from a helicopter into the river.

Raging Bull (1980) For his Oscar-winning role as boxer Jake La Motta, De Niro learned how to box – training with La Motta for six months and breaking the caps on the ex-boxer's teeth. La Motta later said that if De Niro tired of acting he could earn a living as a boxer. For the film's scenes where his character becomes fat, De Niro gained 60 pounds, which he later shed.

True Confessions (1981) One of De Niro's less memorable movies. He played a priest who gets caught up in a murder case involving his policeman brother. Once again, De Niro learnt a language for a role – this time, Latin.

The Untouchables (1987) For his brief but brilliant portrayal of Al Capone, De Niro put on weight and inserted plugs into his nose to make him look and sound more like the infamous gangster. He also wore silk underwear bought from the firm that had supplied Capone.

Midnight Run (1988) In this comedy-thriller, De Niro played a bounty hunter. To prepare for the role, he went out on the road with a real bounty hunter to see how the job is done. He also learned how to pick a lock for one scene and managed to do it so well that the scene had to be dropped for fear that children would learn the technique from it.

Cape Fear (1991) The actor trained for eight months to get his body fat down to just 3 per cent for his role as Max Cady.

A Bronx Tale (1993) This was De Niro's first film as a director and he was determined that it would be absolutely accurate. He was also playing a part himself – as a bus driver. He trained and then took the New York bus drivers' exam, passing second time round.

ACCOMPLISHED ROLLER-BLADERS

Tom Cruise, Lady Helen Taylor, Janet Jackson, Dustin Hoffman, Warren Beatty, Tiggy Legge-Bourke, Peter Gabriel, Emilio Estevez, Nicole Kidman, Annabel Croft, Robbie Williams, Phillip Schofield, Cher, Viscount Linley, Daryl Hannah, Bruce Willis, Madonna, Sarah Michelle Gellar, Charisma Carpenter, Lisa Scott-Lee

KEEN ANGLERS

Dame Diana Rigg, Chris Tarrant, Jack Charlton, Jeremy Paxman, Steve Guppy, Sean Wilson, Nick Faldo, Robert Redford, Nicholas Soames, Prince Charles, Michael Atherton, Paul Gascoigne, Barry Hearn, Michael Chang, Fiona Armstrong, Geoff Capes, Michael Barrymore, Robson Green, Paul Young, Kate Groombridge, Tiger Woods, Eric Clapton, Pierce Brosnan, Liam Neeson, Timothy Dalton, Dermot O'Leary, Brad Pitt, Carl Hiaasen, Charlie Sheen, Darren Clarke, Matthew Modine, Michael Keaton, Peter O'Toole, Roger Federer, Sam Neill

KEEN DIVERS

Nick Ross, Nicholas Lyndhurst, Loyd Grossman, John Simpson, Richard E. Grant, David Jason, Jeff Probyn, Chris De Burgh, John Prescott, Sid Owen, Gillian Anderson, Mariella Frostrup, Esther McVey, Catrina Skepper, Nick Carter, Patrick Duffy, Jason Statham (was a professional), Kathleen Quinlan

ADEPT AT NEEDLEPOINT

Elizabeth Hurley, Dillie Keane, Katie Boyle, Nanette Newman, Dame Joan Sutherland, Elizabeth Jane Howard, Wendy Richard, Sian Phillips, Lea Salonga, Judy Parfitt, Sam West, Loretta Swit

KEEN CHESS PLAYERS

Madonna, Guy Ritchie, Sting, Bono, Jude Law, Ewan McGregor, Arnold Schwarzenegger, Jennifer Lopez, Stephen Fry, Jonathan Edwards, Loyd Grossman, Roger Lloyd Pack, Greta Scacchi, James Galway, Sir Patrick Moore, Martin Amis, Joe Bugner, Michael Jayston, Dane Bowers, Boris Becker, Al Pacino, Dennis Quaid, Lennox Lewis, Steve Davis, Keith Allen

KEEN SKIERS

Ruthie Henshall, Michel Roux, Jane Asher, Jeremy Irons, Melanie Griffith, Angus Deayton, Sandi Toksvig, Patsy Kensit, Sarah, Duchess of York, Michael Brandon, Mike Oldfield, Sir Richard Branson, Elaine Paige, Prince Charles, David Gower, Sir Roger Moore, Kim Wilde, Don Johnson, Nick Ross, Jeremy Paxman, Jason Donovan, Patsy Palmer, Nicky Clarke, Tamzin Outhwaite, Jurgen Prochnow

Keen waterskiers

Nicky Clarke, Esther McVey, Prince William, Sophie, Countess of Wessex, Minnie Driver, Ruthie Henshall, Richard Dunwoody, David Emanuel, Ian Woosnam, Susan Hampshire, Mark Pitman

Karate black belts

John Fashanu, Sharon Stone, Chris Silverwood, Nigel Mansell, Taki, Phil Spector, Jean Jacques Burnel, Chuck Norris, Glen Murphy, Jennifer James, Guy Ritchie, Dane Bowers, Danny Grewcock, John Saxon, Justin Langer

NB: Emma Bunton's mother is a karate instructor and has taught her daughter to a high standard

Real-tennis players

David Gower, Sally Jones, David Troughton, Martina Navratilova, Prince Edward, Gabriela Sabatini, Alan Alda

Fencers

Marcel Marceau, Neil Diamond, Anita Harris, Bryan Mosley, Sir Rocco Forte, Gene Wilder, J.P. Donleavy, David Acfield, Mick Fleetwood, Bruce Dickinson, Ioan Gruffudd, Antonio Banderas, Sylvester Stallone, Robson Green, Sir Christopher Bland (also fenced in the Olympics), Catherine Zeta-Jones, Elijah Wood, Keira Knightly, Madonna, Uma Thurman, Goran Visnjie, James McAvoy

ADEPT AT JUDO

Laetitia Casta (Brown belt)

Tony Slattery (Black belt)

Honor Blackman (Brown belt)

Tony Bullimore (Black belt)

David Lee Roth (Black belt)

Kelly Holmes (Blue belt)

Manuel Noriega (Black belt)

Nigel Mansell (Black belt)

Vladimir Putin (Black belt)

Dawn Airey (Black belt)

James Cagney (Black belt)

KEEN HORSERIDERS

Charisma Carpenter, Kate Moss, Shane Filan, Kylie Minogue, Frazer Hines, Liza Goddard, Keith Chegwin, Jimmy Hill, Cybill Shepherd, Jane Seymour, Janet Jackson, Angela Rippon, Tracy Edwards, Prue Leith, Alan Coren, Lynn Redgrave, Alan Titchmarsh, Joe Brown, Michael Kitchen, Sir Chay Blyth, Patsy Kensit, Tracey Ullman, Lucy Speed, David Emanuel, Michael Brandon, Jeremy Irons, Sue Carpenter

POLO PLAYERS

Kenny Jones, Prince Charles, Kerry Packer, Trevor Eve, William Devane, Stacy Keach, Stefanie Powers, Rory Bremner, Jodie Kidd, Prince William, Ginger Baker, Prince Harry

GOOD AT DIY

Nick Faldo, Harrison Ford (a former carpenter),
Courteney Cox, Brad Pitt, Jennifer Lopez, David
Beckham, Jeremy Irons, Colin Montgomerie, Liza
Tarbuck, David Jason, Bill Wyman, Craig Phillips,
Daniel Day-Lewis, Dennis Waterman, Nick
Knowles, Sandra Bullock, Tim Allen, Adrian Mills

POKER PLAYERS

Brad Pitt, Steve Davis, Jimmy White, David Mamet, Bill Gates, Martin Amis, Matt Damon, Stephen Hendry, Keith Allen, Raj Persaud, Patrick Marber, Ben Affleck, David Schwimmer

KEEN KNITTERS

Julia Roberts, Cameron Diaz, Russell Crowe,
Uma Thurman, Winona Ryder, Goldie Hawn,
Naomi Campbell, Julianne Moore, David
Duchovny, Kate Beckinsale, Bridget Fonda, Sandra Bullock,
Anjelica Huston, Kate Moss, Eva Herzigova, Ulrika Jonsson, Craig
Charles, David Arquette, Geri Halliwell, Madonna, Iman, Hilary
Swank, Daryl Hannah, Sarah Jessica Parker

CARTOONISTS / CARICATURISTS

**David Beckham, Moby, Patricia Cornwell, Will
Self, George Clooney, Gary Cooper (political
cartoonist)**

RELIGION

Psalm 117 (O praise the LORD, all ye nations: praise him, all ye people. For his merciful kindness is great toward us: and the truth of the LORD endureth for ever. Praise ye the LORD) is the shortest chapter in the Bible: it is also the centre chapter in the Bible. However, the middle two *verses* of the Bible are in Psalm 118.

49 different kinds of food are mentioned in the Bible.

The religion of the Todas people of southern India forbids them to cross any kind of bridge.

On 1 July 2003, the First Baptist Church in Forest, Ohio was struck by lightning just as the visiting evangelist was telling the congregation that 'God's voice often sounds like thunder'.

Some saints in the Middle Ages were dirty because they thought it would bring them closer to God.

During the First Crusade, a band of religious hysterics marched behind a goose they believed was filled with the Holy Spirit.

Belief in the existence of vacuums used to be punishable by death under church law.

Playing music containing augmented 4th chords was avoided because it was thought to invoke the Devil.

There's a temple in Sri Lanka dedicated to a tooth of the Buddha.

In 1654, Bishop Ussher of Ireland, having analysed all the 'begats' in Genesis, concluded that planet Earth had been created at 9 a.m. on 26 October 4004BC, a Thursday.

St John was the only one of the 12 apostles to die a natural death.

Most of the villains in the Bible have red hair.

David is the most common name in the Bible. Jesus is second.

Pope Paul IV was so outraged when he saw the naked bodies on the ceiling of the Sistine Chapel that he ordered Michelangelo to paint garments on them.

The term 'devil's advocate' comes from the Roman Catholic Church. When considering whether someone should be created a saint, a devil's advocate was appointed to give an alternative view.

The word Sunday is not in the Bible.

A GUIDE TO DIFFERENT RELIGIONS

Taoism: Shit happens.

Zen: What is the sound of shit happening?

Hinduism: This shit's happened before.

Buddhism: If shit happens, it isn't really shit.

Islam: If shit happens, it's the will of Allah.

Protestantism: Shit happens because we don't work hard enough.

Catholicism: Shit happens because we are bad.

Christian Fundamentalism: Shit happens because the Bible says so.

Jehovah's Witness: Knock, knock. 'Shit happens.'

Judaism: Why does shit always happen to us?

Agnosticism: We don't know shit.

Atheism: No shit.

Hare Krishna: Shit happens – rama rama ding ding.

Rastafarianism: Let's smoke this shit.

SCIENTOLOGISTS

Tom Cruise, Chick Corea, John Travolta, Priscilla Presley, Kirstie Alley, Isaac Hayes, Anne Archer, Kelly Preston, Mimi Rogers, Sharon Stone

PRACTISING BUDDHISTS

Uma Thurman, Stephanie Beacham, Keanu Reeves, Cindy Crawford, Susan Sarandon, Sandie Shaw, Woody Harrelson, Tina Turner, Courtney Love, Harrison Ford, Richard Gere, Koo Stark, Oliver Stone, Pamela Stephenson, Claudia Schiffer, Lulu, Annie Lennox, Jim Carrey, Björk, Orlando Bloom

ROMAN CATHOLICS

Christina Aguilera, Farrah Fawcett, Eddie Van Halen, Nick Nolte, Rosie O'Donnell, Regis Philbin, Celine Dion, Rupert Everett, Ben Affleck, Jean-Claude Van Damme, Antonio Banderas, Martin Scorsese, Nicolas Cage, Camille Paglia, Brigitte Bardot, Sylvester Stallone, Pierce Brosnan, Pele, Lara Flynn Boyle, Sir Paul McCartney, Catherine Deneuve, Faye Dunaway, Mel Gibson, Martin Sheen, Liam Neeson, Madonna, Cyndi Lauper, Arnold Schwarzenegger, Brooke Shields, Sean Penn, Bianca Jagger, Al Pacino, Robert De Niro, John McEnroe, Anne Bancroft, Bill Murray, Luciano Pavarotti, Sophia Loren, Alanis Morissette, Natalie Imbruglia, Heather Graham, Tommy Hilfiger, Claudia Schiffer,

Gabriel Byrne, Danny DeVito, Jim Carrey, Martin Short, Joe Pesci, Catherine Zeta-Jones, Jennifer Lopez, Salma Hayek, John Cusack, Haley Joel Osment, Matt Dillon, Rachel Hunter, Kelsey Grammer, Lucy Lawless, Chris O'Donnell, Gwen Stefani, Alyssa Milano, Noel & Liam Gallagher, Patsy Kensit, Brendan Fraser, Juliette Binoche, Ray Liotta, Mira Sorvino, Elvis Costello, Mary Tyler Moore, Mia Farrow, Alan Alda, Meg Ryan, Melissa Joan Hart, Tom Clancy, Dan Aykroyd, Aidan Quinn, Jack Nicholson, Denise Richards, J.D. Salinger, Charlotte Church, Minnie Driver, Joey Fatone, Lea Salonga, Jon Bon Jovi, Pete Postlethwaite, Judy Davis, Victoria Principal, Mandy Moore, Anne Robinson, Michael Crawford, Christy Turlington, Gloria Estefan, Axl Rose, Tracy Shaw, Ann Widdecombe, Cherie Blair, Julian Clary, Jodie Foster, Ray Liotta, Anna Nicole Smith, Diego Maradona, Belinda Carlisle, Gary Lineker, Cilla Black, Jimmy Tarbuck, Jimmy Saville, Pat Cash, Goran Ivanisevic, Franz Beckenbauer, Elijah Wood, Bruce Springsteen, Delia Smith, Chris De Burgh, Whoopi Goldberg, Johnny Vaughan

JEWS

Alicia Silverstone, Gwyneth Paltrow, David Copperfield, William Shatner, Randy Newman, Yasmine Bleeth, Ben Stiller, Jerry Seinfeld, Harrison Ford, Natalie Portman, Sarah Jessica Parker, Joel Stransky, Gary Kasparov, Calvin Klein, Debra Winger, Geraldo Rivera, David Blaine, Rodney

Dangerfield, Artie Shaw, Dame Elizabeth Taylor (convert), Harvey Keitel, Leonard Nimoy, Tony Curtis, Gene Simmons, Barry Manilow, Hank Azaria, Barbra Streisand, Neil Diamond, Manfred Mann, Leonard Cohen, Adam Sandler, Sacha Baron Cohen, Vidal Sassoon, Herb Alpert, Lauren Bacall, Dyan Cannon, Peter Green, Cyd Charisse, Gloria Steinem, Jerry Springer, Marcel Marceau, Carly Simon, Roman Polanski, Phil Spector, Mel Torme, Jody Scheckter, Larry King, Howard Stern, Felicity Kendal (convert), Neil Sedaka, Norman Mailer, James Caan, Lou Reed, Paul Simon, Art Garfunkel, Bette Midler, Billy Crystal, Billy Joel, Geraldo Rivera, Henry Winkler, Goldie Hawn, Rachel Stevens, Winona Ryder, Carole King, Bob Dylan, Noah Wyle, Burt Bacharach, Helen Reddy, Ruth Prawer Jhabvala, Dame Alicia Markova, Barbara Walters

JEHOVAH'S WITNESSES

Hank B. Marvin, Venus & Serena Williams, The Jacksons (although Michael joined the Nation of Islam in December 2003), Prince, Dwight Eisenhower (raised as one), Roy Harper, Mickey Spillane, Viv Nicholson

LUTHERANS

Loni Anderson, Beau Bridges, Jeff Bridges, David Hasselhoff, William Hurt, William H. Macy, Ann-Margret, David Soul, Sally Struthers, Liv Ullman, Bruce Willis, Gary Larson, Theodore Geisel (aka Dr Seuss), Elke Sommer, Dana Carvey, Johann Sebastian Bach, John Woo, General Norman Schwarzkopf, Edwin Meese, William Rehnquist, Kris Kristofferson, Lyle Lovett, John Mellencamp, Dag Hammarskjöld, Soren Kierkegaard, Dr Albert Schweitzer, Dietrich Bonhoeffer, Martin Niemoeller, Lou Gehrig, Andy North, Duffy Waldorf, Garrison Keillor

MORMONS

Rick Schroeder, Matthew Modine, Robert Walker, The Osmonds, Gladys Knight, Randy Bachman

QUAKERS

Dame Judi Dench, Sheila Hancock, Paul Eddington, Joel Cadbury, Margaret Drabble, Richard Nixon, James Michener, Anna Wing, A.S. Byatt, Herbert Hoover, David Lean, Cheryl Tiegs, Bradley Whitford

BAPTISTS

Britney Spears, John Bunyan, Warren G. Harding, Harry S. Truman, Bill Clinton, Clarence Thomas, Newt Gingrich, Al Gore, Martin Luther King,

Jesse Jackson, Payne Stewart, Glen Campbell, Donna Summer, Jessica Simpson, Otis Redding, Aretha Franklin, John Grisham, Chuck Norris, Billy Graham

CONVERTED TO ISLAM

Michael Jackson, Muhammad Ali, Jemima Khan, Mike Tyson, Malcolm X, Gérard Depardieu (although he later converted back to Christianity), Art Blakey, Cat Stevens, Chris Eubank

CHRISTIAN SCIENTISTS

John Simpson, Joyce Grenfell, Ginger Rogers, Jim Henson, Dame Gwen Ffrangcon-Davies, H.R. Haldeman, Sir Harold Hobson, Dame Edith Evans, Doris Day, Carol Channing, Lady Nancy Astor, Robert Duvall, Joan Crawford, Val Kilmer

NB The parents of Sir V.S. Pritchett, Dame Elizabeth Taylor, Peter Barkworth, Jean Harlow, Ellen DeGeneres and Dudley Moore were all Christian Scientists

BORN-AGAIN CHRISTIANS

Mandy Smith, David Suchet, Jason Robinson, Charlene Tilton, Alvin Stardust, Glenn Hoddle, Andre Agassi, Marcus Gayle, Rosemary Conley, Cyrille Regis, Tommy Cannon, Bobby Ball, Samantha Fox, Tiffany, Gina G, Cuba Gooding Jr, Jane Russell

INTO KABBALAH

Madonna, Guy Ritchie, Demi Moore, Sir Elton John, Sir Mick Jagger, Jeff Goldblum, Naomi Campbell, Dame Elizabeth Taylor, Barbra Streisand, Courtney Love

LAY PREACHERS

Sir David Frost, David Blunkett, George Foreman, Dr Brian Mawhinney, Peter Pollock, Jimmy Armfield, Alan Beith, Paul Daniels, Frank Williams (the vicar in *Dad's Army*), Sir James Anderton, Nigel Benn

CHILDREN OF LAY PREACHERS

Frank Bruno, David Bellamy, Baroness Thatcher, Brian Moore, John Poulson, Jonah Lomu, Alistair Cooke, James Baldwin, Paula Jones, Herol Graham, Mark Thomas

CONSIDERED BECOMING PRIESTS

Joseph Stalin, David Alton, Christopher Marlowe, Ben Vereen, Morten Harket, Alan Bennett, Charles Darwin, Kenny Everett, Mike McShane, Bob Guccione, Bernhard Langer, Gabriel Byrne, Nigel Pivaro, Roberto Benigni, Tom Cruise (aged 14, he enrolled in a seminary but dropped out after a year), John Woo, Johnny Vegas (trained to be a priest but quit after getting drunk on the clerics' sherry), Stephen Tompkinson, Pete Postlethwaite, declan Donnelly

CONSIDERED BECOMING RABBIS

Gene Simmons, Ian Mikardo, Leonard Bernstein

NB Jackie Mason was a rabbi

MIGHT HAVE BECOME NUNS

Heather Graham (her parents had ambitions for her to become one)

Kristin Scott Thomas (at 16, she enrolled in a convent school with a view to becoming a nun)

Cher ('There was a time when I nearly became a nun myself, but it didn't last long')

Zoë Wanamaker ('Despite being born Jewish …')

Francesca Annis (wanted to be a nun)

AGNOSTICS

Brian Sewell, Martin Amis, Uma Thurman, Michael Palin, Ken Livingstone, Nicky Campbell, Esther Rantzen, David Bowie, Professor Stephen Hawking, Carrie Fisher, James Taylor, Sean Penn, Larry King, Roman Polanski, Matt Groening, Al Stewart

ATHEISTS

Dr David Starkey, Sir John Mortimer, Paul McKenna, Raymond Briggs, Dave Allen, Billy Bragg, Dame Mary Peters, Robin Cook, Bill Gates, Claire Rayner, Woody Allen, Sir Richard Branson, Arthur C. Clarke, Amanda Donohoe, Patrick Duffy, Larry Flynt, Dario Fo, Jodie Foster, Debbie Harry, Margot Kidder, Clive Barker, Alex Cox, David Cronenberg, Brian Eno, John Fowles, Kinky Friedman, Janeane Garofalo, Roy Hattersley, Björk, John Carpenter, Fidel Castro, Harvey Fierstein, Angelina Jolie, Neil Jordan, Neil Kinnock, John Malkovich, Barry Manilow, Warren Mitchell, Desmond Morris, Camille Paglia, Steven Soderbergh, Gore Vidal, James Watson, Nick Mason, Sir Ian McKellen, Terry Pratchett, Howard Stern, Michael Stipe, Tom Lehrer, Mike Leigh, Alexander McQueen, Arthur Miller, Randy Newman, Jack Nicholson, Gary Numan, James Randi, Christopher Reeve, Griff Rhys Jones, Captain Sensible, Donald Sutherland, Julia Sweeney

FLAGS

The state flag of Alaska was designed by a 13-year-old boy.

Egypt, Dominica, Mexico, Fiji, Zambia and Kiribati all have birds on their flags.

Texas is the only US state allowed to fly its state flag at the same height as the US flag.

The Dominican Republic has the only national flag with a bible on it.

Cyprus has its outline on its flag.

Nepal is the only country without a rectangular flag.

Libya has the only flag that's one colour (green) with nothing else on it.

LENNON AND MCCARTNEY SONGS NEVER RELEASED BY THE BEATLES (APART FROM ON THE ANTHOLOGIES)

'Bad To Me' (Billy J. Kramer and the Dakotas)

'Nobody I Know' (Peter and Gordon)

'Like Dreamers Do' (The Applejacks)

'Tip Of My Tongue' (Tommy Quickly)

'Step Inside Love' (Cilla Black)

'That Means A Lot' (P.J. Proby)

'A World Without Love' (Peter and Gordon)

'I'm In Love' (The Fourmost)

'One And One Is Two' (The Strangers with Mike Shannon)

'It's For You' (Cilla Black)

'Hello Little Girl' (The Fourmost)

'I'll Keep You Satisfied' (Billy J. Kramer and the Dakotas)

COVERS OF BEATLES SONGS

'Got To Get You Into My Life' (Joe Pesci)

'Something' (Telly Savalas)

'Lucy In The Sky With Diamonds' (William Shatner)

'I Am The Walrus' (Jim Carrey)

'Love Me Do' (The Brady Bunch)

'A Hard Day's Night' (Peter Sellers)

'Blackbird' (Kevin Spacey)

'I Want You (She's So Heavy)' (Donald Pleasence)

'We Can Work It Out' (George Burns)

'Come Together' (Robin Williams)

'When I'm 64' (Jon Pertwee)

'All My Loving' (Alvin and the Chipmunks)

'Hey Jude' (Tottenham Hotspur FC)

'Yellow Submarine' (Milton Berle)

'Ob-La-Di Ob-La-Da' (Jack Wild)

'I Want To Hold Your Hand' (Metal Mickey)

'Maxwell Silver Hammer' (Jessica Mitford)

'Mean Mr Mustard' (Frankie Howerd)

'Can't Buy Me Love' (Pinky and Perky)

BEATLES SONGS AND THEIR WORKING TITLES

'Hello Goodbye' – Hello Hello

'A Day In The Life' – In The Life Of

'Yesterday' – Scrambled Eggs

'It's Only Love' – That's A Nice Hat

'Think For Yourself' – Won't Be There With You

'Flying' – Aerial Tour Instrumental

'Eleanor Rigby' – Miss Daisy Hawkins

'Thank You Girl' – Thank You Little Girl

'Love You To' – Granny Smith

'I Saw Her Standing There' – Seventeen

ACTS SIGNED TO APPLE RECORDS

Mary Hopkin, Badfinger, James Taylor, The Black Dyke Mills Band, Hot Chocolate, Ronnie Spector, Billy Preston, Jackie Lomax

SONGS ABOUT THE BEATLES

'All I Want For Christmas Is A Beatle' (Dora Bryan)
The most successful Beatles' tribute record in the UK – it reached No. 20 in 1963.

'We Love You Beatles' (The Carefrees)
The most successful Beatles' tribute song in the US – it reached No. 39 in 1964.

'My Girlfriend Wrote A Letter To The Beatles' (The Four Preps)
And guess what? They didn't write back.

'I Wanna Be A Beatle' (Gene Cornish and the Unbeatables)
Soon after recording this they changed their name to The Young Rascals (and had hits including 'Groovin'').

'Ringo I Love You' (Bonnie Jo Mason)
Bonnie Jo Mason was a pseudonym for Cher.

'A Beatle I Want To Be' (Sonny Curtis)
Sonny was one of Buddy Holly's Crickets – and the Fab Four had named themselves after The Crickets.

'I Hate The Beatles' (Allan Sherman)
Sherman was an American humorous singer whose only British hit was 'Hello Muddah, Hello Faddah'.

'Get Back Beatles' (Gerard Kenny)
Kenny later wrote the song 'New York New York' (not the Sinatra one but the one that goes 'New York New York, so good they named it twice') and also the music for the theme song for *Minder*.

'I'm Better Than The Beatles'
(Brad Berwick and the Bugs) History would suggest otherwise …

'The Beatles' Barber' (Scott Douglas)
About a man who has been put out of work because
the Fabs never have their mop tops cut. Or something.

'Ringo For President'
(Rolf Harris) American presidents have to be American –
which might explain why the song bombed.

Artists who had bigger hits with Lennon and McCartney songs than the Beatles did

Billy J. Kramer and the Dakotas: 'Do You Want To Know A Secret?'

The Overlanders: 'Michelle'

Joe Cocker: 'With A Little Help From My Friends'

Marmalade: 'Ob-La-Di Ob-La-Da'

Earth Wind And Fire: 'Got To Get You Into My Life'

Steve Harley and Cockney Rebel: 'Here
Comes The Sun'

Emmylou Harris: 'Here There And Everywhere'

Kenny Ball and his Jazzmen: 'When I'm 64'

Billy Bragg: 'She's Leaving Home'

Singers who refer to themselves by name in songs

'The Universal' (The Small Faces – Steve Marriott on
vocals 1968)

'I Feel For You' (Chaka Khan 1984)

'Blue Motel Room' (Joni Mitchell 1976)

'My Name Is Prince' (Prince 1992)

'Sweet Baby James' (James Taylor 1970)

'Strong Persuader' (Robert Cray 1986)

'Creeque Alley' (The Mamas and the Papas – Mama Cass Elliot on vocals 1967)

'The Mind of Love' (k.d. lang 1992)

'Float On' (The Floaters – all of them individually 1977)

'Wannabe' (The Spice Girls – all of them individually 1996)

'Brooklyn Roads' (Neil Diamond 1976)

DUETS

Madeline Kahn & Frankie Laine on 'Blazing Saddles' in 1973

Catherine Zeta-Jones & David Essex on 'True Love Ways' 1994

Rock Hudson & Rod McKuen on 'Love Of The Common Celebrities' 1970

Peter Sellers & Sophia Loren on 'Goodness Gracious Me' 1959

Don Johnson & Barbra Streisand on 'Till I Loved You' (Love Theme From Goya) 1988

Beavis and Butt-Head & Cher on 'I Got You Babe' 1994

Bruce Willis & The Pointer Sisters on 'Respect Yourself' 1987

Ewan McGregor & Nicole Kidman on 'Come What May' 2001

Michael J. Fox & Joan Jett on 'Light of Day' 1986

Victoria Principal & Andy Gibb on 'All I Have To Do Is Dream' 1981

Joan Collins & Bing Crosby on 'Let's Not Be Sensible' 1962

Alain Delon & Shirley Bassey on the album *Shirley Bassey & Alain Delon* 1984

PEOPLE IMMORTALIZED IN SONG TITLES

Smokey Robinson – 'When Smokey Sings' (ABC 1987)

Spencer Tracy – 'He Looks Like Spencer Tracy Now' (Deacon Blue 1988)

Grigori Rasputin – 'Rasputin' (Boney M 1978)

Buddy Holly – 'I Feel Like Buddy Holly' (Alvin Stardust 1984)

Otis Redding – 'Ode To Otis Redding' (Mark Johnson 1968)

Elvis Presley – 'Elvis Presley And America' (U2 1984)

Dolly Parton – 'Dolly Parton's Guitar' (Lee Hazlewood 1977)

Jackie Wilson – 'Jackie Wilson Said' (Van Morrison 1972)

Bo Diddley – 'The Story Of Bo Diddley' (The Animals 1964)

Hank Williams – 'The Night Hank Williams Came to Town' (Johnny Cash 1986)

Sir Michael Caine – 'Michael Caine' (Madness 1984)

Dickie Davies – 'Dickie Davies Eyes' (Half Man Half Biscuit 1986)

Benito Mussolini – 'Do The Mussolini' (Cabaret Voltaire 1978)

Robert De Niro – 'Robert De Niro's Waiting' (Bananarama 1984)

Bonnie Parker & Clyde Barrow – 'Ballad of Bonnie And Clyde' (Georgie Fame 1967)

James Callaghan – 'Jim Callaghan' (Mr John Dowie 1977)

Sean Penn – 'Sean Penn Blues' (Lloyd Cole and the Commotions 1987)

Christine Keeler – 'Christine Keeler' (The Glaxo Babies 1979)

Kaiser Wilhelm II – 'I Was Kaiser Bill's Batman' (Whistling Jack Smith 1967)

Aretha Franklin – 'Aretha, Sing One For Me' (George Jackson 1971)

Michael Jackson – 'Dear Michael' (Kim Fields 1984)

Lee Remick – 'Lee Remick' (The Go-Betweens 1978)

Bette Davis – 'Bette Davis Eyes' (Kim Carnes 1981)

John Wayne – 'John Wayne Is Big Leggy' (Haysi Fantayzee 1982)

Tom Baker – 'Tom Baker' (Human League 1980)

Linda Evans – 'Linda Evans' (The Walkabouts 1987)

Vincent van Gogh – 'Vincent' (Don McLean 1972)

Andy Warhol – 'Andy Warhol' (David Bowie 1971)

Graham Greene – 'Graham Greene' (John Cale 1973)

Jim Reeves – 'Tribute To Jim Reeves' (Larry Cunningham 1964)

Marvin Gaye – 'Marvin' (Edwin Starr 1984)

Nerys Hughes – 'I Hate Nerys Hughes' (Half Man Half Biscuit 1985)

PURE TRIVIA

It is physically impossible for pigs to look up into the sky.

The man who invented FM radio was Edwin Armstrong. The first men to use FM radio to communicate with Earth from the Moon's surface were Edwin 'Buzz' Aldrin and Neil Armstrong.

Iceland consumes more Coca-Cola per capita than any other nation.

Camel-hair brushes are made from squirrel hair.

Genghis Khan's original name was Temujin. He started out as a goatherd.

The Lazy Susan is named after Thomas Edison's daughter. He invented it to impress a gathering of industrialists and inventors.

Mickey Mouse's ears are always turned to the front, no matter which direction his nose is pointing.

Cows give more milk when they listen to music.

Mozart never went to school.

Jellyfish are 95 per cent water

Nanotechnology has produced a guitar no bigger than a blood cell. The guitar, 10 micrometres long, has strings which can be strummed.

7 per cent of the entire Irish barley crop goes into the making of Guinness.

To see a rainbow, you must have your back to the sun.

Rubber bands last longer when refrigerated.

South Africa used to have two official languages. Now it has eleven.

On 29 March 1848, Niagara Falls stopped flowing for 30 hours because of an ice jam blocking the Niagara river.

The national anthem of Greece is 158 verses long.

The original Guinness Brewery in Dublin has a 6,000-year lease.

Since 1896, the beginning of the modern Olympics, only Greece and Australia have participated in every games.

Thomas Edison, the inventor of the light bulb, was afraid of the dark.

The Albanian language, one of Europe's oldest, isn't derived from any other language.

Abraham Lincoln's Gettysburg Address was just 267 words long.

Men of the Walibri tribe of central Australia greet each other by shaking each other's penis instead of each other's hand.

Huge wine jugs were often used by the ancient Greeks as coffins.

Wade Morrison, the inventor of Dr Pepper, named the drink after Dr Charles Pepper who had given him his first job.

Bugs Bunny was originally called 'Happy Rabbit'.

Mao Tse-Tung never brushed his teeth but washed his mouth with tea instead.

The average four-year-old child asks over 400 questions a day.

The oldest living thing in the world is a creosote bush in south-western California, which is more than 11,000 years old.

The average ratio of yellow kernels to white kernels in a bag of popcorn is 9:1.

The expression 'second string', meaning replacement or back-up, comes from the Middle Ages. An archer always carried a second string in case the one on his bow broke.

Counting how many times a cricket chirps in 15 seconds and then adding 40 to that number will tell you roughly what the outside temperature is in Fahrenheit.

Studies indicate that weightlifters working out in blue gyms can handle heavier weights.

Pepper was sold in individual grains during Elizabethan times.

215 pairs of jeans can be made with one bale of cotton.

APPEARED IN POP VIDEOS

Denise Van Outen – 'Proper Crimbo' by Avid Merrion

Jennifer Lopez – 'That's The Way Love Goes' by Janet Jackson

Elijah Wood – 'Ridiculous Thought' by The Cranberries

Wesley Snipes – 'Bad' by Michael Jackson

Neil Kinnock – 'My Guy' by Tracey Ullman

Phill Jupitus – 'Happy Hour' by The Housemartins

Sir Ian McKellen – 'Heart' by The Pet Shop Boys

Naomi Campbell – 'I'll Tumble For Ya' by Culture Club

French and Saunders – 'That Ole Devil Called Love' by Alison Moyet

Chevy Chase – 'You Can Call Me Al' by Paul Simon

Tamzin Outhwaite – 'Even Better Than The Real Thing' by U2

Frances Tomelty – 'Sister Of Mercy' by The Thompson Twins

Mike Tyson – 'Bad Boy 4 Life' by Sean (P Diddy) Combs

Donald Sutherland – 'Cloudbusting' by Kate Bush

Robert Bathurst & Claudia Schiffer – 'Uptown Girl' by Westlife

Diana Dors – 'Prince Charming' by Adam and the Ants

Kirsten Dunst – 'I Knew I Loved You' by Savage Gardens

Joss Ackland – 'Always On My Mind' by The Pet Shop Boys

Carmen Electra – 'We Are All Made Of Stars' by Moby

Michelle Collins – 'Up The Junction' by Squeeze

Danny DeVito – 'When The Going Gets Tough' by Billy Ocean

Frankie Howerd – 'Don't Let Me Down' by The Farm

Michelle Pfeiffer – 'Gangsta's Paradise' by Coolio (she was also in the horn section for B.B. King's 'In The Midnight Hour')

Daryl Hannah – 'Feel' by Robbie Williams

George Clooney – 'She's Just Killin' Me' by ZZ Top

Angelina Jolie – 'Rock & Roll Dreams Come Through' by Meat Loaf

Matt Lucas – 'Country House' by Blur

Benicio Del Toro – 'La Isla Bonita' by Madonna

Jamie Bell – 'Wake Me Up When September Ends' by Green Day

A GUIDE TO ABBA

In the Bible, 'Abba', meaning 'father', is used to refer to God. In Sweden, Abba is the name of a fish-canning company.

Abba made their name by winning the 1974 Eurovision Song Contest with 'Waterloo', but they were originally going to do a song called 'Hasta Mañana', which featured a lead vocal by Agnetha. In they end, they chose 'Waterloo' because it was a group song.

Abba's former name was 'Festfolk'. It was under this name that the foursome of Björn, Benny, Agnetha and Anni-Frid made their debut in a Gothenberg restaurant in November 1970.

When Abba played the Royal Albert Hall in February 1977, they were the first Swedish artistes to perform there for over a hundred years.

'Fernando' is the biggest-selling single in Australian chart history – having spent 15 weeks at No. 1 there. It was also featured, along with other Abba songs, in the Australian film *Muriel's Wedding*.

Abba's only No. 1 single in the US is 'Dancing Queen', although they have had other Top 10 hits – starting with 'Waterloo', which was the first Eurovision Song Contest song to reach the US Top 10.

Benny owns a riding stables and has named some of his horses after guitars – e.g. 'Burns', 'Gretch' and 'Rickenbacker'.

Lasse Hallström (*Cider House Rules*, *Chocolat*) directed almost every one of Abba's music videos – as well as *Abba: The Movie*.

Abba's distinctive vocal-harmony sound was invented by their engineer Michael B Tretow, who, inspired by Phil Spector, found a way to alter the speed slightly between overdubs.

DRUMMERS

Rick Astley (Give Way – also drummed in a band with Gary Barlow)

Jim Davidson (various bands)

Madonna (The Breakfast Club)

Mark King (various holiday camp bands)

David Essex (The Everons)

Andrew Neil (various bands)

Joe Cocker (The Cavaliers)

Russ Abbot (The Black Abbots)

Richard Desmond (various bands)

Frank Zappa (The Black-outs)

Richard Hannon (The Troggs)

Greg Knight (Dime – and once drummed with The Four Seasons)

Jamie Oliver (Scarlet Division)

Billy Bob Thornton (Tres Hombres, a ZZ Top covers band)

John Altman (Resurrection – also plays guitar)

Mel Brooks (various bands)

Peter Gabriel (various bands)

Rageh Omaar (The Swindlers – at prep school)

Peter Sellers (in dance bands)

Courtney Cox

Bing Crosby (The Musicaladers)

APRIL FOOLS' DAY PRANKS

Probably the most famous British April Fools' Day prank was the Spaghetti Harvest on BBC TV's *Panorama* in 1957. Its presenter was the venerable Richard Dimbleby, definitely *not* a prankster, and millions of people were taken in when he told them about the spaghetti harvest and showed them the spaghetti 'growing' and being 'dried' in the sun.

In 1976, Patrick Moore told radio listeners that while Pluto passed behind Jupiter there would be a decrease in gravitational pull. He said that if people were to jump in the air they would feel as though they were floating. Several people rang up to say that they had enjoyed doing just that.

In 1994, Mars took out full-page advertisements in newspapers announcing their 'New Biggest Ever Mars Bar'. The 'Emperor'-sized Mars Bar was 32lb of 'thick chocolate, glucose and milk'. It was 'on sale' for only one day. April 1.

In 1977, the *Guardian* produced a supplement on the island of San Seriffe. Many readers were taken in by the authentic nature of the words and pictures. In fact, it was a fine spoof with plenty of clues – mostly relating to printing terms – for sharper minds.

In 1979, London's Capital Radio announced that because of all the constant changing between British Summertime and Greenwich Mean Time, we had gained an extra 48 hours, which would have to be lost by the cancellation of 5 April and 12 April. Readers phoned in wondering what would happen to birthdays, anniversaries and other such things.

Not to be outdone, in 1980, the BBC World Service told its listeners that Big Ben's clock-face would be replaced by a digital face. Since the World Service is treated with a lot of reverence, many people were taken in – only to be relieved by discovering the truth.

In 1992, a joker fitted a huge sign onto the roof of the stand at the Hollywood Park racetrack reading 'WELCOME TO CHICAGO'. This was visible to all passengers on flights coming into Los Angeles and caused no little consternation.

In 1983, the German car firm BMW ran a full-page advertisement for 'The first open-top car to keep out the rain even when it's stationary' (supposedly something to do with 'artificial airstreams'). Other years have produced gems such as 'A BMW you need never wash again', 'WARNING: are you driving a genuine BMW?' and, in 1993, a TV commercial introducing an 'anti-tracking device for secret lovers everywhere'.

In 1973, a Dr Ronald Clothier gave a serious-sounding lecture on Radio 3 about Dutch elm disease in which he 'revealed' that rats that had been exposed to the disease had developed a resistance to the human cold. It was eventually revealed that Dr Clothier was, in fact, Spike Milligan.

PEOPLE WHO DROPPED THEIR SURNAMES

Angelina Jolie (born Angelina Jolie Voight)

Richard E. Grant (Richard Grant Esterhuysen)

Richmal Crompton (Richmal Crompton Lamburn)

Bela Lugosi (Bela Lugosi Blasko)

John Leslie (John Leslie Stott)

Sam Shepard (Samuel Shepard Rogers III)

Tom Cruise (Thomas Cruise Mapother IV)

Roger Vadim (Roger Vadim Plemmiankov)

Fiona Apple (Fiona Apple Maggart)

Ray Charles (Ray Charles Robinson)

Bonnie Bedelia (Bonnie Bedelia Culkin)

Eddie Albert (Edward Albert Heimberger)

David Blaine (David Blaine White)

Joe Louis (Joseph Louis Barrow)

Derby firsts

The first Derby was held on 4 May 1780 and won by Diomed.

The first Earl of Derby to win the race was Edward Stanley, who won in 1787 with his horse, Sir Peter Teazle.

The first dead-heat was in 1828 and the two horses concerned raced again later that afternoon. (There was a second in 1884: the two jockeys met in the weighing room and decided to share the prize money.)

In 1895, The Derby became the first horse race to be filmed.

The Derby became the first horse race to be televised in 1932.

1949 saw the first Derby to be decided by a photo finish.

Starting stalls were used for the first time in the 1967 Derby.

The first winning horse to be owned by a reigning monarch was Minoru in 1909.

In 1801, Eleanor became the first filly to win both The Derby and, the following day, The Oaks.

In 1894, Earl Rosebery became the first prime minister to be the owner of a Derby winner.

Won oxbridge blues

Hugh Laurie (Rowing)

Lord Jeffrey Archer (Athletics & Gymnastics)

Kris Kristofferson (Boxing)

Howard Jacobson (Table Tennis). NB 'Minor' sports such as table tennis attract Half Blues rather than Full Blues

Frank Bough (Soccer)

Lord Colin Moynihan (Rowing & Boxing)

Lord Snowdon (Rowing)

Lord James Douglas-Hamilton (Boxing)

Ian Balding (Rugby Union)

Sir Adrian Cadbury (Rowing)

John Gosden (Athletics)

Wonderfully named (genuine) soccer fanzines

Linesman You're Rubbish (Aberystwyth Town)

***Only The Lonely* (Airdrie)**

Shots In The Dark (Aldershot)

***Up The Arse!* (Arsenal)**

The Ugly Duckling (Aylesbury United)

***Revenge of The Killer Penguin* (Bath City)**

Where's The Vaseline? (Billericay Town)

***4,000 Holes* (Blackburn Rovers)**

Our Flag's Been To Wembley (Braintree Town)

Beesotted (Brentford)

And Smith Must Score (Brighton & Hove Albion)

Addickted (Charlton Athletic)

Super Dario Land (Crewe Alexandra)

Mission Impossible (Darlington)

The Gibbering Clairvoyant (Dumbarton)

It's Half Past Four ... And We're 2–0 Down (Dundee)

One Team In Dundee (Dundee United)

Away From The Numbers (East Fife)

We'll Score Again! (Exeter City)

There's Only One F In Fulham (Fulham)

Brian Moore's Head Looks Uncannily Like The London Planetarium (Gillingham)

Sing When We're Fishing (Grimsby Town)

Crying Time Again (Hamilton Academicals)

Monkey Business (Hartlepool Town)

Still Mustn't Grumble (Hearts)

From Hull To Eternity (Hull City)

The Keeper Looks Like Elvis (Kidderminster Harriers)

To Elland Back (Leeds United)

Where's The Money Gone? (Leicester City)

Another Wasted Corner (Liverpool)

Mad As A Hatter (Luton Town)

Bert Trautmann's Helmet (Manchester City)

Dial M For Merthyr (Merthyr Tydfil)

No One Likes Us **(Millwall)**

Waiting For The Great Leap Forward (Motherwell)

Once Upon A Tyne **(Newcastle United)**

What A Load Of Cobblers (Northampton Town)

Frattonise **(Portsmouth)**

The Memoirs of Seth Bottomley (Port Vale)

Ooh, I Think It's My Groin! **(QPR)**

Exceedingly Good Pies (Rochdale)

Get A Grip, Ref! **(Scunthorpe United)**

The Ugly Inside (Southampton)

A View To A Kiln **(Stoke City)**

It's The Hope I Can't Stand! (Sunderland)

Nobody Will Ever Know **(Swansea City)**

Friday Night Fever (Tranmere Rovers)

Moving Swiftly On … **(Walsall)**

Flippin' Heck Ref, That Was A Foul Surely! (Waterlooville)

Winning Isn't Everything **(Welling United)**

The Sheeping Giant (Wrexham)

She Fell Over **(Yeovil Town)**

A GUIDE TO SNOOKER

The game was started in India in 1875 by Colonel Sir Neville Chamberlain (no, not that one) as a hybrid of pyramids, black pool and billiards. The game was brought over to England some ten years later.

The name 'snooker' came from the nickname given to cadets at the Royal Military Academy in Woolwich.

The well-known saying about skill at snooker being the sign of a misspent youth comes from Herbert Spencer, the Victorian social philosopher, who said to an opponent: 'A certain dexterity in games of skill argues a well-balanced mind, but such dexterity as you have shown is evidence, I fear, of a misspent youth.'

As every snooker fan knows, 147 is the magic number – it's the maximum break (15 reds each followed by the black and then all the colours). With free balls after a foul shot, 155 is technically the highest score possible, but the highest break ever recorded was 151 by Cliff Thorburn, who achieved his score with the benefit of a foul shot from his opponent.

The first officially ratified 147 break was made by Joe Davis in 1955. Davis is clearly the surname to have if you want to become a snooker champion: Joe, his brother Fred and Steve (no relation) have all managed it.

Snooker was at the height of its popularity in the 1980s when a survey was conducted which proved conclusively that Steve Davis was seen on TV more often than either the Queen or Margaret Thatcher.

'Whispering' Ted Lowe was the greatest of all snooker commentators but even he put his foot in it sometimes. Two of his best are: 'Fred Davis, the doyen of snooker, now 67 years of age and too old to get his leg over, prefers to use his left hand', and 'And for those of you watching this in black-and-white, the pink sits behind the yellow'.

GOALKEEPERS WHO SCORED GOALS

Brad Friedel (Blackburn Rovers v. Charlton Athletic 2004)

Peter Schmeichel (Aston Villa v. Everton 2001)

Steve Sherwood (Watford v. Coventry City 1984)

Steve Ogrizovic (Coventry City v. Sheffield Wednesday 1986)

Ray Cashley (Bristol City v. Hull City 1973)

Peter Shilton (Leicester City v. Southampton 1967)

Iain Hesford (Maidstone United v. Hereford United 1991)

Pat Jennings (Tottenham Hotspur v. Manchester United 1967)

Andy Goram (Hibernian v. Morton 1988)

Paul Robinson (Tottenham Hotspur v. Watford 2007)

RAN THE LONDON MARATHON

Gordon Ramsay, Babs Powell, Jasper Carrott, Dennis Canavan, Brenda Blethyn, Rhodri Morgan, Charlie Dimmock, Patrick Kielty, Jonathan Aitken, Sir Jimmy Savile, Susan Tully, Eric Morley, Peter Duncan, Stephanie Lawrence, Graham Taylor, John Conteh, Gavin Campbell, Alan Minter, Nigel Dempster, Simon Thomas, Steve Cram, Julia Carling, Steve Rider, Jeremy Bates, Jerome Flynn, Chris Chittell, Chris Kamara, Graham Gooch, Frank Bruno, Nick Gillingham, Niamh Cusack, Jason Flemyng, Jonny Lee Miller, John Gregory, Floella Benjamin, Alastair Campbell, Lucy Benjamin, Mark Hughes

FOOTBALL DIRECTORS

Jim Davidson: AFC Bournemouth 1981–1982

Delia Smith: Norwich City 1996–

Michael Grade: Charlton Athletic 1997–

Arthur English: Aldershot 1981–1990

Jasper Carrott: Birmingham City 1979–1982

Sir Elton John: Watford 1976–1990; 1991–

Tommy Cannon: Rochdale 1986–1987

Sir Richard Attenborough: Chelsea 1969–1982

Sir Norman Wisdom: Brighton & Hove Albion 1970–1978

Steve Davis: Leyton Orient 1997–

Fred Dinenage: Portsmouth 1995–

Sean Bean: Sheffield United 2002–

FORMER BOXERS

Bob Hope, Kris Kristofferson, Chris Isaak, Colin Moynihan, Eamonn Andrews, Terence Trent D'Arby, Berry Gordy, Sir Norman Wisdom, Billy Joel, Mark McManus, Liam Neeson, Chuck Berry, Michael Flatley, 50 Cent

DID THE CRESTA RUN

David Gower, Errol Flynn, Emma Freud, the Duke of Kent

A GUIDE TO GOLF

In the 13th century, the Dutch used to play a game known as 'Spel metten colve' ('Game played with a club'). This became just 'colve', then 'colf' and, eventually, 'golf'.

A golfer is defined as 'one who shouts "fore", takes five and writes down three', while a golfing beginner is 'one who moves heaven and earth to get a game and then moves heaven and earth while playing'.

Robin Williams reckoned: 'Golf is a game where white men can dress up as black pimps and get away with it.'

Sir Winston Churchill described golf as 'an ineffectual attempt to direct an uncontrollable sphere into an inaccessible hole with instruments ill-adapted to the purpose'.

The first recorded hole-in-one was by the great Tom Morris in 1868.

Bing Crosby died immediately after playing a round of golf.

When someone told Gary Player that he was 'lucky', the great golfer replied: 'That's funny, the more I practise, the luckier I get.'

Michael Green's definition of the 'coarse golfer': one who has to shout 'fore' when he putts.

Golf spelt backwards is 'flog'. Another thing to consider is that golf carts are better than caddies because golf carts can't count.

Nick Faldo and his caddie Fanny Sunneson were lining up a shot at the Scottish Open when the commentator said: 'Some weeks Nick likes to use Fanny, other weeks he prefers to do it by himself.'

More people die playing golf than any other sport – from heart attacks and lightning, etc.

A GUIDE TO WACKY RACES

THE ELEVEN RACERS WERE:

00: Dick Dastardly & Muttley (The Mean Machine)

01: The Slag Brothers (Boulder Mobile)

02: The Gruesome Twosome (Creepy Coupe)

03: Prof. Pat Pending (Convert-A-Car)

04: The Red Max (Crimson Haybailer)

05: Penelope Pitstop (Compact Pussycat)

06: Sarge & Pvt. Pinkley (Army Surplus Special)

07: The Ant Hill Mob (Bulletproof Bomb)

08: Luke & Blubber Bear (Arkansas Chugabug)

09: Peter Perfect (Turbo Terrific)

10: Rufus Ruffcut & Sawtooth (Buzzwagon)

THE FINAL RANKINGS WERE:

Boulder Mobile 28 points

Buzzwagon 25 points

Bulletproof Bomb 24 points

Compact Pussycat 21 points

Creepy Coupe 21 points

Crimson Haybailer 20 points

Arkansas Chugabug 18 points

Convert-A-Car 18 points

Turbo Terrific 18 points

Army Surplus Special 11 points

Dick Dastardly & Muttley 0 points

THINGS SAID BY GROUCHO MARX

'Quote me as saying I was misquoted.'

'I've had a perfectly wonderful evening. But this wasn't it.'

'I was married by a judge. I should have asked for a jury.'

'Now that I think of it, I wish I had been a hell-raiser when I was thirty years old. I tried it when I was fifty but I always got sleepy.'

'This would be a better world for children if parents had to eat the spinach.'

'I've been around so long I can remember Doris Day before she was a virgin.'

'From the moment I picked your book up until I laid it down I was convulsed with laughter. Someday I intend reading it.'

'Military justice is to justice what military music is to music.'

'A man's only as old as the woman he feels.'

'I must say that I find television very educational. The minute somebody turns it on, I go to the library and read a book.'

'Women should be obscene and not heard.'

'Time wounds all heels.'

'Behind every successful man is a woman, behind her is his wife.'

'Outside of a dog, a book is man's best friend. Inside of a dog, it's too dark to read.'

'Age is not a particularly interesting subject. Anyone can get old. All you have to do is live long enough.'

'I sent the club a wire stating, "Please accept my resignation. I don't care to belong to any club that will accept me as a member."'

'It isn't necessary to have relatives in Kansas City in order to be unhappy.'

'Money frees you from doing things you dislike. Since I dislike doing nearly everything, money is handy.'

'Go, and never darken my towels again.'

'Humour is reason gone mad.'

'I chased a girl for two years only to discover that her tastes were exactly like mine: We were both crazy about girls.'

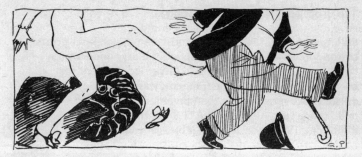

'Here's to our wives and girlfriends … may they never meet.'

'I remember the first time I had sex – I kept the receipt.'

'The secret of life is honesty and fair dealing. If you can fake that, you've got it made.'

'When I was young I was amazed at Plutarch's statement that the elder Cato began at the age of eighty to learn Greek. I am amazed no longer. Old age is ready to undertake tasks that youth shirked because they would take too long.'

'I didn't like the play, but then I saw it under adverse conditions – the curtain was up.'

'The husband who wants a happy marriage should learn to keep his mouth shut and his chequebook open.'

'Paying alimony is like feeding hay to a dead horse.'

'Well, art is art, isn't it? Still, on the other hand, water is water! And east is east and west is west and if you take cranberries and stew them like applesauce they taste much more like prunes than rhubarb does. Now, you tell me what you know.'

'I'm going to Iowa for an award. Then I'm appearing at Carnegie Hall, it's sold out. Then I'm sailing to France to be honoured by the French government. I'd give it all up for one erection.'

'Those are my principles. If you don't like them, I have others.'

THINGS INVENTED BY WOMEN

Bulletproof vest, fire escape, windscreen wiper, laser printer, cotton gin, sewing machine, alphabet block, underwater telescope, cotton sewing thread (awarded the very first US patent), brassiere, jockstrap, cordless phone, pulsar (discovered rather than invented), condensed milk, space suit, AIDS drugs AZT and protease inhibitors, TV dinner, Jell-O, Barbie, chocolate-chip cookie, circular saw, dishwasher, disposable nappy, electric hot water heater, ironing board, crash helmet, life raft, medical syringe, rolling pin, rotary engine, Scotchgard fabric protector.

THE ONLY PEOPLE TO HAVE RECEIVED HONORARY US CITIZENSHIP GRANTED BY ACT OF CONGRESS

Sir Winston Churchill (1963), Raoul Wallenberg (1981), William and Hannah Penn (1984), Mother Teresa (1996)

THE SIMPSONS

The characters of Homer, Marge, Lisa and Maggie were given the same first names as Simpsons creator Matt Groening's real-life father, mother and two sisters.

On *The Simpsons* monopoly board, TYRE YARD is the equivalent of Old Kent Road and BURNS MANOR is the equivalent of Mayfair.

In an episode of *The Simpsons*, Sideshow Bob's criminal number is 24601 – the same as Jean Valjean's prison number in *Les Misérables*.

'APPEARED' ON *THE SIMPSONS*

Danny DeVito (Herb Powell)

Jack Lemmon (Frank Ormand, the Pretzel Man)

Donald Sutherland (Hollis Hurlbut)

Joe Mantegna (Fat Tony)

Willem Dafoe (Commandant)

Tracey Ullman (Emily Winthrop)

Johnny Cash (Coyote)

Kirk Douglas (Chester J. Lampwick)

Rodney Dangerfield (Larry Burns)

Anne Bancroft (Dr Zweig)

Penny Marshall (Ms Botz)

Harvey Fierstein (Karl)

Glenn Close (Mother Simpson)

Gillian Anderson (Scully)

David Duchovny (Mulder)

Jackie Mason (Rabbi Krustofski)

Beverly D'Angelo (Lurleen Lumpkin)

Kelsey Grammer (Sideshow Bob)

Michelle Pfeiffer (Mindy Simmons)

Sam Neill (Molloy)

Kathleen Turner (Stacy Lovell)

Winona Ryder (Allison Taylor)

Meryl Streep (Jessica Lovejoy)

Patrick Stewart (Number One)

Susan Sarandon (The Ballet Teacher)

Mandy Patinkin (Hugh Parkfield)

Albert Brooks (Hank)

Jeff Goldblum (MacArthur Parker)

Dustin Hoffman (Mr Bergstrom)

Cloris Leachman (Mrs Glick)

Dame Elizabeth Taylor (Baby Maggie)

John Waters (John)

James Earl Jones (The Narrator)

Ed Asner (Editor of *The Springfield Shopper*)

John Goodman (Meathook)

Henry Winkler (Ramrod)

Tim Robbins (Jim Hope)

Lisa Kudrow (Alex Whitney)

Robert Englund (Freddy Krueger)

Isabella Rossellini (Astrid Weller)

Michael McKean (Jerry Rude)

Martin Sheen (Sergeant Seymour Skinner)

Helen Hunt (Renée)

Rod Steiger (Captain Tenille)

Steve Martin (Ray Patterson)

Drew Barrymore (Sophie)

Patrick McGoohan (Prisoner no. 6)

Michael Keaton (Jack)

Pierce Brosnan (Computer)

Ben Stiller (Garth Motherloving)

Reese Witherspoon (Greta Wolfcastle)

Eric Idle (Desmond)

Professor Frink Senior (Jerry Lewis)

PLAYED THEMSELVES ON
THE SIMPSONS

Buzz Aldrin, Paul Anka, Tony Bennett, Ernest Borgnine, Mel Brooks, James Brown, Johnny Carson, David Crosby, Dennis Franz, Joe Frazier, George Hamilton, Hugh Hefner, Bob Hope, Magic Johnson, Tom Jones, Tom Kite, Linda McCartney, Sir Paul McCartney, Bette Midler, Bob Newhart, Leonard Nimoy, Luke Perry, Linda Ronstadt, Mickey Rooney, Brooke Shields, Ringo Starr, Sting, Dame Elizabeth Taylor, James Taylor, Adam West, Barry White, James Woods, Professor Stephen Hawking, Britney Spears, Mel Gibson, Mark McGwire, Tom Arnold, Lucy Lawless, Dick Clark, Ron Howard, Penn & Teller, Butch Patrick, Gary Coleman, Bachman Turner Overdrive, Betty White, Ed McMahon, Regis Philbin, Kathie Lee Gifford, Jerry Springer, Alec Baldwin, Kim Basinger, The Moody Blues, Cyndi Lauper, Rupert Murdoch, Dolly Parton, Ed Begley Jr, Sir Elton John, Joe Namath, Jay Leno, U2, Elvis Costello, Sir Mick Jagger, Keith Richards, Lenny Kravitz, Tom Petty, Mark Hamill, Kid Rock, Willie Nelson, Pete Townshend, Roger Daltrey, Stephen King, Richard Gere, Elvis Costello, Little Richard, Tony Blair, J.K. Rowling, Sir Ian McKellen, Tom Clancy, Thomas Pynchon, Matt Groening, Nichelle Nichols, James Caan, 50 Cent, Gary busey, Robert Wagner, Jason Bateman, Dennis Rodman, William H Macy, Joe Frazier, Susan Sarandon, Rob Reiner, Melanie Griffith, Tom Wolfe, Gore Vidal

FLOWERS

The chrysanthemum is never grown in the Japanese city of Himeji because of a legend about a girl called O-Kiku ('Chrysanthemum Blossom') who drowned, leaving behind a troubled spirit that could be settled only if the people of Himeji didn't grow the flower of her name.

The tiger lily in Lewis Carroll's *Through The Looking-Glass* claims that flowers talk 'when there's anybody worth talking to' but that 'in most gardens they make the beds too soft, so that the flowers are always asleep'.

When a fan tried to present the great Italian conductor Toscanini with flowers at the end of a performance, he said, 'They are for prima donnas or corpses: I am neither.'

Dame Iris Murdoch on the subject of flowers: 'People from a planet without flowers would think we must be mad with joy the whole time to have such things about us.'

What William Wordsworth said about daffodils:
'I wandered lonely as a cloud
That floats on high o'er vales and hills,
When all at once I saw a crowd,
A host, of golden daffodils.'

WILD PLANT NAMES

Baldmoney, Bastard Balm, Bloody Crane's-Bill, Butcher's Broom, Creeping Jenny, Devil's Bit Scabious, Enchanter's Nightshade, Fairy Foxglove, Fat-Hen, Fool's Parsley, Good-King-Henry, Hairy Violet, Hemlock Water-Dropwort, Hogweed, Hound's Tongue, Jack-by-the-Hedge, Jacob's Ladder, Lady's Bedstraw, Lady's Tresses, Lamb's Ear, Leopard's Bane, Lords-and-Ladies, Love-in-a-Mist, Mind-Your-Own-Business, Purple Loosestrife, Red-Hot Poker, Scarlet Pimpernel, Shepherd's Purse, Solomon's Seal, Stinking Hellebore, Traveller's Joy, Twiggy Spurge, Venus's Looking Glass, Viper's Bugloss, Wavy Hair Grass

PEOPLE WHO HAD A FLOWER OR PLANT NAMED AFTER THEM

Madonna (gladiolus)

Dame Edna Everage (gladiolus)

Emma Bunton (bergamot)

Frank Bruno (carnation)

Carol Vorderman (fuchsia – named 'Countdown Carol')

Charlie Dimmock (fuchsia)

Alan Titchmarsh (dianthus, lupin and fuchsia)

Audrey Hepburn (fuchsia)

Elvis Presley (sempervivum)

Ricky Martin (orchid – Renaglottis Ricky Martin is yellow and crimson and produces lasting flowers all year)

Patricia Hodge (fuchsia)

Katie Melua (tulip)

Vegetarians

Jude Law, Leonardo DiCaprio, Danny DeVito, Charlie Watts, Belinda Carlisle, Dustin Hoffman, Christie Brinkley, Billy Idol, Kim Basinger, Damon Albarn, Seal, Billy Connolly, Gwyneth Paltrow, Ted Danson, Daryl Hannah, Richard Gere, Julie Christie, Candice Bergen, Rosanna Arquette, Brooke Shields, Paul Newman, Peter Gabriel, Boy George, Martina Navratilova, Sir Ian McKellen, LaToya Jackson, Prince, John Peel, Ringo Starr, Terence Stamp, Michael Jackson, Whitney Houston, Michael Bolton, Imelda Staunton, Morrissey, Chrissie Hynde, Lenny Kravitz, Ricki Lake, Vanessa Williams, Don McLean, Ozzy Osbourne, Sir Peter Hall, Yasmin Le Bon, Stevie Nicks, Sir Paul McCartney, Tony Blackburn, Victoria Wood, Gaby Roslin, Kate Bush, Elvis Costello, Bob Dylan, Yoko Ono, Twiggy, Jerry Seinfeld, Penelope Cruz, Tobey Maguire, Shania Twain (during her impoverished childhood, she made gins and snares to catch rabbits for the family to eat)

Lapsed vegetarians

Anthea Turner, Paul Weller, Jeanette Winterson, Liv Tyler, Drew Barrymore, Sting, Jessica Biel, Meat Loaf, The Dalai Lama

Pure trivia

An artist from Chicago named Dwight Kalb created a statue of Madonna made out of 180 pounds of ham.

About 10 million bacteria live in 1 gram of soil.

The record for finishing the Rubik's cube is 16.5 seconds.

Nintendo was established in 1889 and started out making playing cards.

Himalaya means 'home of snow'.

The range of a medieval longbow was 220 yards.

The steepest street in the world is Baldwin Street in Dunedin, New Zealand, with an incline of 38 per cent.

Watermelons, which are 92 per cent water, originated from the Kalahari Desert in Africa.

Goat meat contains up to 45 per cent less saturated fat than chicken meat.

The sound made by the Victoria Falls in Zimbabwe can be heard 40 miles away.

Pumpkins were once recommended for removing freckles.

Aoccdnrig to a rscheearhc at Cmabgride Uinevrtisy, it deson't mtater waht oerdr the ltteres in a wrod are – so lnog as the frist and lsat ltteer are in the crorect pclae. Tihs is bcuseae we dno't raed ervey lteter but the wrod as a wlohe.

Americans eat approximately 20 billion pickles every year.

In Belgium, there is a strawberry museum.

Sheep buried in snowdrifts can survive for up to two weeks.

Worldwide, grapes are grown more than any other fruit.

The mongoose was brought to Hawaii to kill rats but the project failed because rats are nocturnal while the mongoose hunts during the day.

Rhode Island is the smallest US state but it has the longest official name: Rhode Island and Providence Plantations.

If you were locked in a completely sealed room, you'd die of carbon dioxide poisoning before you'd die of oxygen deprivation.

There are 556 officially recognized Native American tribes.

The last time American green cards were actually green was 1964.

Harvard uses 'Yale' brand locks on its buildings.

The (American) football huddle originated in the 19th century at Gallaudet University, Washington DC, when the deaf football team found that opposing teams were reading their signed messages and intercepting plays.

Charles Lindbergh took just four

In the 1994 World Cup the entire Bulgarian team had surnames ending with the letters 'ov'.

Carnivorous animals will not eat another animal that has been hit by a lightning strike.

A mule is the offspring of a female horse and a male donkey but the offspring of a male horse and a female donkey is called a hinny.

Sir Isaac Newton was an ordained priest in the Church of England.

Dalmatian dogs are born pure white and only get their spots when they're a few days old.

Heroin is the brand name of morphine once marketed by Bayer.

The tango originated as a (practice) dance between two men.

Ben and Jerry's send their waste to local pig farmers to use as feed. Pigs love all the flavours except Mint Oreo.

sandwiches with him on his famous transatlantic flight.

Politics

'A government which robs Peter to pay Paul can always depend on the support of Paul.' (George Bernard Shaw)

'Politics is the art of looking for trouble, finding it everywhere, diagnosing it incorrectly and applying the wrong remedy.' (Groucho Marx)

'Politicians are the same all over. They promise to build a bridge even where there's no river.' (Nikita Khrushchev)

'A politician is an arse upon which everyone has sat except a man.' (e.e. cummings)

'Democracy must be something more than two wolves and a sheep voting on what to have for dinner.' (James Bovard)

'Giving money and power to government is like giving whiskey and car keys to teenage boys.' (P.J. O'Rourke)

'Just because you do not take an interest in politics doesn't mean politics won't take an interest in you.' (Pericles in 430BC)

'Suppose you were an idiot. And suppose you were a member of Congress. But I repeat myself.' (Mark Twain)

'I believe that all government is evil, and that trying to improve it is largely a waste of time.' (H.L. Mencken)

'The inherent vice of capitalism is the unequal sharing of the blessings. The inherent blessing of socialism is the equal sharing of misery.' (Sir Winston Churchill)

People who stood (unsuccessfully) for parliament

Sir Robin Day (Liberal)

Ted Dexter (Conservative)

Jonathan King (Royalist)

Pamela Stephenson (Blancmange Thrower)

David Bellamy (Referendum)

Vanessa Redgrave (Workers' Revolutionary)

Dennis Potter (Labour)

Cynthia Payne (Payne and Pleasure)

John Arlott (Liberal)

Lindi St Clair (Corrective)

A GUIDE TO DIFFERENT POLITICAL SYSTEMS

Communism: You have two cows. The government takes both and gives you a little sour milk.

Fascism: You have two cows. The government takes both, hires you to take care of them, and sells you the milk.

Bureaucracy: You have two cows. To register them, you fill in twenty-three forms in triplicate and don't have time to milk them.

Socialism: You have two cows. The government takes one of them and gives it to your neighbour.

Feudalism: You have two cows. Your lord takes some of the milk.

Democracy: You have two cows. A vote is held, and the cows win.

Environmentalism: You have two cows. The government bans you from milking or killing them.

Libertarianism: Go away. What I do with my cows is none of your business.

Capitalism: You have two cows. You sell one and buy a bull.

NB Surrealism: You have two porcupines. The government invites you to take cello lessons.

THINGS YOU DIDN'T KNOW ABOUT US PRESIDENTS

Before winning the 1860 US presidential election, Abraham Lincoln had lost eight elections for various offices.

Every US president with a beard has been Republican.

Abraham Lincoln's mother died when the family dairy cow ate poisonous mushrooms and Mrs Lincoln drank the milk.

Robert Todd Lincoln, son of Abraham Lincoln, was present at the assassinations of three US presidents: Lincoln, Garfield and McKinley.

There are more handwritten letters in existence by George Washington (1789–97) than there are by John F. Kennedy (1961–3).

In 1849, David Atchison became president of the United States for just one day (most of which he spent sleeping).

John Quincy Adams (1825–9) owned a pet alligator, which he kept in the east room of the White House. He swam in the Potomac River every morning – naked. His wife, Louisa Adams, was the first (and only) foreign-born First Lady of the US; she was born in London.

John F. Kennedy (1961–3) and Warren Harding (1920–3) were both survived by their fathers.

Lyndon Johnson's (1963–8) family all had the initials LBJ: Lyndon Baines Johnson, Lady Bird Johnson, Linda Bird Johnson and Lucy Baines Johnson. His dog was called Little Beagle Johnson.

Theodore Roosevelt's (1901–12) wife and mother died on the same day.

On New Year's Day 1907, Theodore Roosevelt shook hands with 8,150 people at the White House.

Since World War Two, every US president who has addressed the Canadian House of Commons in his first term of office has been re-elected to a second term. Eisenhower, Nixon, Reagan and Clinton all did so, while Kennedy, Johnson, Ford, Carter and Bush Snr didn't.

Franklin Pierce (1853–7) was the first president to have a Christmas tree in the White House.

When Franklin D. Roosevelt (1933–45) was five years old, he visited the White House and was told by the then president, Grover Cleveland (1885–9): 'My little man, I am making a strange wish for you: it is that you may never be president of the United States.' It is also worth noting that Roosevelt's mother dressed him exclusively in dresses until he was five.

Another president meeting a future president was in 1963 when Bill Clinton (1993–2001) shook hands with John F. Kennedy (1961–3) at a White House reception for members of Boys' Nation.

Richard Nixon's (1969–74) mother, who named her son after King Richard the Lionheart, originally wanted him to be a Quaker missionary.

William Henry Harrison (1841) was the first president to die in office.

Richard Nixon's mother wanted him to be a Quaker missionary

Martin Van Buren (1837–41) was the first president to be born a US citizen.

Gerald Ford (1974–7) was the only president never to have been elected as either president or vice-president.

Grover Cleveland (1885–9; 1893–7) was the only president elected to two non-consecutive terms.

Zachary Taylor (1849–50) moved around the country so much that he kept being unable to register to vote. He reached 62 before he voted.

John Tyler (1841–50) was the first president to marry in office.

James A. Garfield (1881) is the only man in US history to be simultaneously a congressman, a senator-elect and a president-elect.

Gerald Ford (1974–7) and Bill Clinton (1993–2001) were both adopted as children.

George Washington was the only president not to belong to a political party. He was also the only president to be elected unanimously. In the 1820 election, James Monroe (1817–25) would have got every electoral vote except that a New Hampshire delegate didn't want Washington to lose this distinction and so didn't vote for Monroe.

James Madison (1809–17) was the first president to wear long trousers; all the previous presidents had worn knee breeches.

NB Daniel Webster, a 19th-century US congressman, wanted to be president. He was offered the vice-presidency by William Henry Harrison, but turned it down. Then Harrison died in office. Again Webster was offered the vice-presidency, by Zachary Taylor, but turned it down. Taylor too died in office and Webster never did become president.

US PRESIDENTS WHO WON WITH LESS THAN HALF THE POPULAR VOTE

1824 John Quincy Adams (Democratic-Republican: 30.5%) beat Andrew Jackson (Democratic-Republican: 43.1%), Henry Clay (Democratic-Republican: 13.2%) and William H. Crawford (Democratic-Republican: 13.1%)

1844 James K. Polk (Democrat: 49.58%) beat Henry Clay (Whig 48.12%) and James G. Birney (Liberty: 2.3%)

1848 Zachary Taylor (Whig: 47.33%) beat Lewis Cass (Democrat: 42.54%) and Martin Van Buren (Free Soil: 10.13%)

1856 James Buchanan (Democrat: 45.32%) beat John C. Fremont (Republican: 33.13%) and Millard Fillmore (American: 21.55%)

1860 Abraham Lincoln (Republican: 39.83%) beat Stephen A. Douglas (Democrat: 29.46%), John C. Breckinridge (Southern Democrat: 18.1%) and John Bell (Constitutional Union: 12.61%)

1876 Rutherford B. Hayes (Republican: 48.03%) beat Samuel J. Tilden (Democrat: 51.06%)

1880 James A. Garfield (Republican 48.3%) beat Winfield S. Hancock (Democrat: 48.28%) and James B. Weaver (Greenback-Labor: 3.32%)

1884 Grover Cleveland (Democrat: 48.52%) beat James G. Blaine (Republican: 48.27%), Benjamin F. Butler Greenback (Labor/Anti-Monopoly: 1.74%) and John P. St. John (Prohibition: 1.47%)

1888 Benjamin Harrison (Republican: 47.86%) beat Grover Cleveland (Democrat: 48.66%), Clinton B. Fisk (Prohibition: 2.2%) and Anson J. Streeter (Union Labor: 1.29%)

1892 Grover Cleveland (Democrat: 46.08%) beat Benjamin Harrison (Republican: 42.99%), James B. Weaver (People's: 8.5%) and John Bidwell (Prohibition: 2.25%)

1912 Woodrow Wilson (Democrat: 41.85%) beat Theodore Roosevelt (Progressive: 27.39%), William H. Taft (Republican: 23.19%), Eugene V. Debs (Socialist: 5.99%) and Eugene W. Chafin (Prohibition: 1.38%)

1916 Woodrow Wilson (Democrat: 49.33%) beat Charles E. Hughes (Republican: 46.2%), A. L. Benson (Socialist: 3.19%) and J. Frank Hanly (Prohibition: 1.19%)

1948 Harry S. Truman (Democrat: 49.56%) beat Thomas E. Dewey (Republican: 45.07%), Strom Thurmond (States' Rights Democrat: 2.41%) and Henry Wallace (Progressive: 2.37%)

1960 John F. Kennedy (Democratic: 49.94%) beat Richard M. Nixon (Republican: 49.77%)

1968 Richard M. Nixon (Republican: 43.43%) beat Hubert H. Humphrey (Democrat: 42.73%) and George C. Wallace (American Independent: 13.54%)

1992 Bill Clinton (Democrat: 43.02%) beat George Bush (Republican: 37.46%) and H. Ross Perot (Independent: 18.91%)

1996 Bill Clinton (Democrat: 49.15%) beat Robert Dole (Republican: 40.86%), H. Ross Perot (Independent: 8.48%), Ralph Nader (Green: 0.63%) and Harry Browne (Libertarian: 0.5%)

2000 George W. Bush (Republican: 47.87%) beat Al Gore (Democrat: 48.38%) and Ralph Nader (Green: 2.74%)

NB Where the percentages total less than 100% it is because of unlisted minor party candidates who polled fewer than 1%.

PRIME MINISTERS WHO COMMITTED ADULTERY

The Duke of Grafton,
The Earl of Bute, David
Lloyd George, Lord Melbourne, Lord
John Russell, Lord Grey, George Canning, The Duke
of Devonshire, The Duke of Wellington, Lord Palmerston,
Benjamin Disraeli, Sir Robert Walpole, Ramsay MacDonald,
Herbert Asquith, John Major

THE HOUSE OF COMMONS

MPs can wave their order papers and shout 'hear hear' to signal approval of a speech but they're not allowed to clap.

Electronic voting equipment is not used: MPs must still walk through the 'Aye' and 'No' lobbies.

If an MP wants to empty the public galleries he only has to say, 'I spy strangers.'

When Black Rod comes to the House of Commons (for the state opening of Parliament), he is traditionally refused admission. This dates back to King Charles I and his attempts to curb the power of parliament.

MPs are not allowed to mention the House of Lords. Like superstitious actors referring to Macbeth as 'the Scottish play', they call the House of Lords 'the other place'.

There are yeomen dressed in Tudor uniform who ritually search the cellars of the House of Commons for gunpowder.

The Serjeant-at-Arms, whose office dates back to King Richard II, wears a cocked hat, cutaway coat, knee breeches, a lace ruffle, black stockings and silver buckled shoes.

MPs must not mention other MPs by name. Instead, they must refer to them by their constituencies (e.g. 'The member for ...').

The Speaker of the House of Commons is obliged to show extreme reluctance on taking office.

Mayors

Frank Carson – Balbriggan in Ireland

Clint Eastwood – Carmel, California

Sonny Bono – Palm Springs, California

Richard Whiteley – Wetwang, Yorkshire

Liz Dawn – given the title Lady Mayoress of Leeds – thanks to her fundraising for cancer sufferers in Yorkshire

Sir Anthony Hopkins – Pacific Palisades (suburb of Los Angeles), California

BEN & JERRY'S TOP TEN FLAVOURS

Cherry Garcia Ice Cream

Chocolate Chip Cookie Dough Ice Cream

Chocolate Fudge Brownie Ice Cream

New York Super Fudge Chunk Ice Cream

Chunky Monkey Ice Cream

Half Baked! Ice Cream

Phish Food Ice Cream

Cherry Garcia Frozen Yogurt

Peanut Butter Cup Ice Cream

Chocolate Fudge Brownie Frozen Yogurt

CHARLES DICKENS

Dickens's father was a navy pay clerk who was made redundant and ended up in debtors' prison. Young Charles worked in a blacking factory to help the family's finances.

Dickens used his father as the inspiration for Mr Micawber, the ever-optimistic character from *David Copperfield*. W.C. Fields played the part of Micawber in the Hollywood film version and, when told that Dickens hadn't written anything about Micawber juggling, replied, 'He probably forgot.'

Later, Dickens became a journalist – working first as a court reporter and eventually graduating to editor.

Dickens was prone to fainting fits. He gave dramatic readings of his books and sometimes worked himself up into such a state of excitement that he keeled over.

Dickens was an insomniac. He was also a little neurotic about his insomnia – always making sure that his bed pointed due north and that he was positioned in the absolute centre of it.

In his letters to his wife Kate, Dickens called her his 'dearest mouse' and his 'darling pig'.

Dickens fell 'deeply and intimately' in love with his wife's sister, Mary, when she came to live with them. Mary died at the age of 17 and Dickens wore her ring for the rest of his life. He asked to be buried next to her but was buried in Westminster Abbey instead.

After Mary, Dickens fell for another of his wife's sisters – Georgina – who came to live with them. When Dickens and his wife separated after 22 years of marriage (and ten children), Georgina stayed with him.

PEOPLE WHO HAD BOOKS DEDICATED TO THEM

Christopher Isherwood (*Myra Breckinridge* by Gore Vidal)

Brigid Brophy (*The Good Apprentice* by Iris Murdoch)

Robert Bolt (*Second Fiddle* by Mary Wesley)

Diana Mosley (*Vile Bodies* by Evelyn Waugh)

Philip Larkin (*Lucky Jim* by Kingsley Amis)

Kingsley Amis (*XX Poems* by Philip Larkin)

Robert Conquest (*Hearing Secret Harmonies* by Anthony Powell)

William Makepeace Thackeray (*Jane Eyre* by Charlotte Brontë)

Iris Murdoch (*The Sweets of Pimlico* by A.N. Wilson)

Ivy Compton-Burnett (*The Spoilt City* by Olivia Manning)

Elizabeth Barrett Browning (*The Raven* by Edgar Allen Poe)

Robert Runcie (*Travels With A Primate* by Terry Waite)

Denis Compton (*The Lord's Companion* by Benny Green)

John Smith (*A Place Called Freedom* by Ken Follett)

Earl Mountbatten (*A Hell of A War* by Douglas Fairbanks Jr)

George Washington (*Rights of Man* by Thomas Paine)

Dame Edna Everage (*Dame Edna Everage's Coffee Table Book* by Dame Edna Everage)

WRITE POETRY

Damon Albarn, Bob Hoskins, Eric Cantona, Jack Dee, Paul Gascoigne, Susan George, Ray Davies, Bobby Ball, Steven Berkoff, Nigel Planer, David Carradine, Patti D'Arbanville, Robert Downey Jr, Woody Harrelson, Traci Lords, Judd Nelson, Michael J. Pollard, Carl Reiner, Robbie Williams, Charisma Carpenter, Mark Lamarr (started off as a poet), Tara Palmer-Tomkinson, Pamela Anderson, Denzel Washington, Tionne Watkins, Brandy, Courtney Love & Russell Crowe (together), Christina Aguilera, Val Kilmer (for Michelle Pfeiffer), Kate Moss, Viggo Mortensen

LEAP YEARS

February 29 occurs once every four years because instead of precisely 365 days in a year there are approximately 365 and a quarter. That is, it takes the earth 365 1/4 days to go round the sun and complete an astronomical year. The extra day every four years allows the man-made calendar to catch up with the astronomical calendar.

Leap years occur in any year that is divisible by 4, except those divisible by 100, though the 100-rule doesn't apply to those divisible by 400. So although 1900 was divisible by 4 it wasn't a leap year, but 2000 was. Thought: if there are 52 weeks in the year and 7 days in a week, why aren't there 364 days in the year?

Leap years are so called because with 365-day years, a day of the month falling on Monday in one year will fall on a Tuesday in the next and on Wednesday in the third, but when the fourth year comes along with its extra day, it will 'leap' over the Thursday to fall instead on the Friday.

On a Leap Year's Day in 1956, a Mrs Christine McDonnell of Church Street, Dublin, gave birth to a set of twins. On the next Leap Year Day, in 1960, she gave birth to another set of twins.

On Leap Year's Day in 1984, Lisa Dluchik of Swindon was born. Her mother Suzanne was also born on Leap Year Day (1956). The odds against a mother and a daughter both being born on February 29 have been calculated as 2,000,000–1.

On Leap Year's Day in 1996, bachelors fled to Leicester's Stapleford Park Hotel for a men-only break to avoid marriage proposals.

Things that have happened on Leap Year's Day in history: in 1960, the Moroccan city of Agadir was devastated by an earthquake followed by a tidal wave which killed more than 12,000 people. In 1956, Pakistan became an Islamic republic. In 1960, Hugh Hefner opened his first Playboy Club (in Chicago). In 1984, John Francome rode the 1,000th winner of his career.

BORN ON LEAP YEAR DAYS

Gioacchino Rossini (1792)

Ranchhodji Desai (1896)

Jimmy Dorsey (1904)

Dinah Shore (1916)

Joss Ackland (1928)

Gretchen Christopher (1940)

Jono Coleman (1956)

Anthony Robbins (1960)

Hendrik Sundstrom (1964)

James Ogilvy (1964)

Steve Hart (1972)

CHAT-UP LINES

'You don't know me but I dreamt about you last night.'

'Did it hurt when you fell from heaven?'

'If I could rearrange the alphabet, I'd put U and I together.'

'Can I buy you a drink or do you just want the money?'

'Do you believe in love at first sight or shall I walk past you again?'

'How do you like your eggs? Fertilized?'

'Get your coat, love, you've pulled.'

'Is that a ladder in your tights or the stairway to heaven?'

'This body leaves in five minutes, be on it.'

'Your clothes would look great on my bedroom floor.'

'Can I have your picture so I can show Santa what I want for Christmas?'

'I may not be the best-looking bloke in the room but I'm the only one talking to you.'

'You're a thief: You've stolen my heart!'

'You remind me of someone I'd like to know.'

'Can I borrow your mobile? I told my parents I'd phone them when I met the girl of my dreams.'

'Is it me or do you always look this good?'

'I need a map because I'm lost in your eyes.'

'The word "beautiful" wouldn't be the same without U.'

MIGRAINE CURES

Pills without prescription: aspirin, paracetamol and ibuprofen – available either in generic form or as branded drugs.

Prescription drugs: sumatripan – manufactured under the brand name Imigran – which boosts the effect of the 5-HT chemical that helps transmit messages within the brain; the beta-blocker Propranolol; Ergotamine, which constricts dilated blood vessels in the head.

Regular exercise This will help *prevent migraines*. Also make sure blood pressure is under control, and don't smoke.

Diet Eat regular meals – every two hours if possible. Never miss breakfast. Eat a diet rich in carbohydrate. Avoid red wine, chocolate, cheese and citrus fruits.

Acupuncture In Denmark, doctors found that acupuncture was almost as effective as drugs against migraine but without any of the side effects.

Regular sleep Too little or, interestingly, too much sleep can cause migraines. This is why a lot of people suffer from migraines on a Sunday when they've had a long lie-in.

Special rose-tinted spectacles, initially developed for children. In tests, the average number of migraine attacks suffered by children aged 8 to 14 fell from 6.2 to 1.6 per month when they wore these glasses. According to the head of the retina department of Birmingham's Eye Hospital, 'The spectacles are just as effective in preventing migraine in grown-ups as they are in children.'

Mental well-being Hypertension, stress, suppressed anger, anxiety and depression are all causes/contributory factors of migraines. If your migraines are frequent, try to alleviate the states of mind that might be causing them.

Medigen A gadget that emits minute electromagnetic impulses, which increase the brain's alpha waves.

Work Controversially, there are neurologists who believe that *not* giving in to a migraine, if possible, will see it off. A study of doctors who had worked through their migraines indicated that 'work suppressed their migraine … although once they reached home they took to bed'.

Botox injections People who've been to a botox clinic have found their migraines have mysteriously disappeared. Now people have the treatment for this reason.

Unconsummated marriages

Mary, Queen of Scots & Prince Francis of France

Stanley Spencer & Patricia Preece

Sir J.M. Barrie & Mary Ansell

Ronnie Kray & Kate Howard

George Bernard Shaw & Charlotte Townsend

Eva Bartok & William Wordsworth

Burt Lancaster & June Ernst

Zsa Zsa Gabor & Burhan Belge

Marie Stopes & Reginald Ruggles Gate

Prince Arthur (King Henry VIII's older brother) & Catherine of Aragon

Jean Harlow & Paul Bern

John Ruskin & Euphemia Gray (he was shocked to discover on their wedding night that she had pubic hair; she eventually left him for the artist John Millais, with whom she had eight children)

Rudolph Valentino & Jean Acker

Rudolph Valentino & Natasha Rambova

King Henry VIII & Anne of Cleves

Peter Tchaikovsky & Antonina Milyukova

Catherine & Peter The Great

Andre Gide & Madeleine Rondeaux

Fanny Brice & Frank White

Judy Garland & Mark Herron

Giuseppe Garibaldi & Giuseppina Raimondi

Zsa Zsa Gabor & Count Felipe de Alba

Note also that it took Marie Antoinette & King Louis XVI seven years to consummate their marriage.

MARRIED THEIR CHILDHOOD SWEETHEARTS

Ardal O'Hanlon, Jamie Oliver, Terry Wogan, Dick Cheney, Andrea McLean, Robbie Fowler, Perry Como, Ray Winstone, John Higgins, Colin McRae, Seve Ballesteros, Justine Henin-Hardenne, George Segal, Robert Smith, Ron Howard, Jon Bon Jovi, Tom Jones, Bono, George Carey, ex-Archbishop of Canterbury, Michael Parkinson, Bruce Rioch, Stephen Hendry, Nick Berry, Sir Ranulph Fiennes, Stephen King, Jeff Daniels, David Ginola, Al Gore, Gareth Edwards, Kevin Keegan, Carol Channing, Padraig Harrington, Rachel Griffiths, Martin Keown, Russell Watson

MARRIED AND DIVORCED THEIR CHILDHOOD SWEETHEARTS

Glenn Hoddle, Les Dennis, Bradley Walsh, Eamonn Holmes, Nigel Benn, David Blunkett, Harrison Ford, Sally Field, Michael Bolton, Angela Rippon, Sam Torrance, Gerhard Schröder, Sean Bean, Eminem, Richard Burton, Alan Cumming, Judy Collins

WHO THEY CHOSE AS THEIR BEST MAN

GROOM	BEST MAN
Ronald Reagan	William Holden
Sir Paul McCartney	**Mike McGear (both times)**
Spike Milligan	Sir George Martin
Bryan Forbes	**Sir Roger Moore**
Jack Nicholson	Harry Dean Stanton
William Shatner	**Leonard Nimoy**
Vincente Minnelli	Ira Gershwin
Dougray Scott	**Ewan McGregor**
Patrick Stewart	Brent Spiner
David Gest	**Michael Jackson**
Larry Fortensky	Michael Jackson
David Beckham	**Gary Neville**
Julian Holloway	Sir Albert Finney
Ossie Clarke	**David Hockney**
Kevin Kennedy	Michael Le Vell
Rowan Atkinson	**Stephen Fry**
Peter Sellers	David Lodge
Nicholas Soames	**Prince Charles**
Mick Jagger	Lord Patrick Lichfield
Jake La Motta	**Sugar Ray Robinson**
Josef Goebbels	Adolf Hitler
Christopher Hitchens	**Martin Amis**
Martin Amis	Christopher Hitchens
Rory Bremner	**Graham Cowdrey**
Howard Jacobson	Lord Melvyn Bragg
Ant	**Dec**

ENGAGEMENTS THAT DIDN'T LEAD TO MARRIAGE

Michelle Pfeiffer & Fisher Stevens

Ronan Keating & Vernie Bennett

Martine McCutcheon & Gareth Cooke

Van Morrison & Michelle Rocca

Olivia Newton-John & Bruce Welch

Thomas Muster & Mariella Theiner

Dervla Kirwan & Robert Caldwell

Shane Richie & Dawn Rodger

Stan Collymore & Lotta Farley

Samantha Fox & Peter Foster

Tania Bryer & Count Gianfranco Cicogna

James Gilbey & Lady Alethea Savile

Phil Tufnell & Jane McEvoy

Shannen Doherty & Dean Factor

Bobby Davro & Zoë Nicholas

Axl Rose & Stephanie Seymour

Julie Goodyear & Jack Diamond

Adam Sandler & Margaret Ruden

Neil Morrissey & Elizabeth Carling

Laura Dern & Billy Bob Thornton

Martine McCutcheon & Jonathan Barnham

Eriq LaSalle & Angela Johnson

Sinitta & Simon Cowell

Robbie Williams & Nicole Appleton

Heath Ledger & Naomi Watts

Ben Affleck & Gwyneth Paltrow

Pamela Anderson & Kid Rock

Lenny Kravitz & Adriana Lima

Sophie Anderton & Simon Rubel

Fred Couples & Tawnya Dodd

Sinitta & Thomas Arklie

Nicholas Lyndhurst & Gail Parr

Carole Landis & Busby Berkeley

Sir David Frost & Karen Graham

Tessa Dahl & Angus Gibson

Emma Samms & Marvin Hamlisch

Malandra Burrows & Jonathan Armstead

Princess Stephanie of Monaco & Jean-Yves LeFur

Jenson Button & Louise Griffiths

Lance Armstrong & Sheryl Crow

Charlie Sheen & Kelly Preston (later married to John Travolta)

Jonathan Cake & Olivia Williams

Nicole Appleton & Darren Brodin

Dodi Fayed & Kelly Fisher

David Coulthard & Andrea Murray

Victoria Adams (now Beckham) & Mark Wood

Sharon Stone & Michael Benasra

Alan Cumming & Saffron Burrows

Yasmine Bleeth & Ricky Paull Goldin

Tamara Beckwith & Michael Stone (Sharon's brother)

Dido & Bob Page

Rose McGowan & Marilyn Manson

Sara Cox & Leeroy Thornhill

WOMEN WHO WERE VIRGINS ON THEIR WEDDING DAY

Shirley Temple, Katy Hill, Lisa Kudrow, Dame Elizabeth Taylor, Gwen Taylor, Priscilla Presley, Marthe Bibesco, Marjorie Proops, Gloria Hunniford, Ava Gardner, Loretta Lynn, Raquel Welch, Catherine The Great, Dorothy Dandridge, Vivien Leigh, Gloria Swanson, Mrs Patrick Campbell, Colette, Hedda Hopper, Mary Martin, Jessica Simpson

MEN WHO WERE VIRGINS ON THEIR WEDDING DAY

Donny Osmond, William Gladstone, Mark Twain, Paul Muni, Victor Hugo (did it nine times on his wedding night), Tiny Tim, Jonathan Edwards, Lord Laurence Olivier, Terry Wogan, Sir Alfred Hitchcock, George S. Kaufman, Dr Benjamin Spock, Ronan Keating

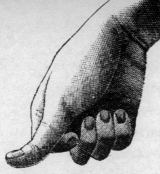

MARRIAGES THAT DIDN'T LAST

Eva Bartok & William Wordsworth (less than one day – after the wedding ceremony)

Giuseppe Garibàldi & Giuseppina Raimondi (less than one day)

Julie Goodyear & Tony Rudman (one day – he walked out on her during the wedding reception saying that he didn't like the idea of living in the spotlight)

Jean Arthur & Julian Anker (one day)

Katherine Mansfield & George Mansfield (one day)

Rudolph Valentino & Jean Acker (one day)

Adolf Hitler & Eva Braun (one day)

Robin Givens & Svetozar Marinkovic (one day)

Zsa Zsa Gabor & Felipe De Alba (one day)

Britney Spears & Jason Alexander (one day)

Fanny Brice & Frank White (three days)

Ethel Merman & Ernest Borgnine (four days)

John Heard & Margot Kidder (six days)

Dennis Hopper & Michelle Phillips (one week)

Cher & Gregg Allman (nine days)

Dennis Rodman & Carmen Electra (nine days)

Dennis Rodman & Annie Banks (twelve days)

Catherine Oxenberg & Robert Evans (twelve days)

Patty Duke & Michael Tell (two weeks)

Carole Landis & Irving Wheeler (three weeks)

Germaine Greer & Paul du Feu (three weeks)

Katharine Hepburn & Ludlow Ogden Smith (three weeks)

Shannen Doherty & Ashley Hamilton (three weeks)

Gloria Swanson & Wallace Beery (three weeks)

Roger Taylor & Dominique Beyrand (25 days)

John Milton & Mary Powell (one month)

Mike Oldfield & Diana Fuller (one month)

Jane Wyman & Eugene Wyman (one month)

Burt Lancaster & June Ernst (one month)

Greer Garson & Edward Snelson (five weeks)

George Brent & Constance Worth (five weeks)

Jean Peters & Stuart Cramer (five weeks)

Drew Barrymore & Jeremy Thomas (six weeks)

Derek Fowlds & Lesley Judd (two months)

Henry Fonda & Margaret Sullavan (two months)

Aaliyah & R. Kelly (three months – annulled because she was just 15)

Leslie Ash & Jonathan Weston (three months)

Nicolas Cage & Lisa Marie Presley (three months)

P.J. O'Rourke & Amy Lumet (three months)

Tracy Edwards & Simon Lawrence (three months)

Frank Lloyd Wright & Miriam Noel (three months)

Davina McCall & Andrew Leggett (three months)

Joanna Lumley & Jeremy Lloyd (four months)

Colin Farrell & Amelia Warner (four months)

Marco Pierre White & Lisa Butcher (four months)

Janet Jackson & James DeBarge (four months)

Renee Zellweger & Kenny Chesney (four months)

Charlie Sheen & Donna Peele (five months)

Carole Landis & Willie Hunts Jr (five months)

Sylvia Kristel & Alan Turner (five months)

Natasha Henstridge & Damian Chapa (five months)

Drew Barrymore & Tom Green (five months)

Fanny Cradock & Arthur Chapman (a few months)

Elton John & Renate Blauel (a few months)

Don Johnson & Melanie Griffith (the first marriage – a few months)

Arthur C. Clarke & Marilyn Mayfield (six months)

Patsy Palmer & Nick Love (six months)

Christie Brinkley & Ricky Taubman (seven months)

Axl Rose & Erin Everly (seven months)

Dennis Wilson & Karen Lamm (seven months the first time; two weeks the second time)

Jean Harlow & Hal Rosson (eight months)

Kelsey & Leanne Grammer (eight months)

Dodi Fayed & Suzanne Gregard (eight months)

Emma Samms & Bansi Nagji (eight months)

Judy Garland & David Rose (eight months)

Jennifer Lopez & Cris Judd (eight months)

Marilyn Monroe & Joe DiMaggio (nine months)

Sheena & Sandi Easton (nine months)

Suzanne Pleshette & Troy Donahue (nine months)

Jim Carrey & Lauren Holly (ten months)

Ellen Terry & George Watts (ten months)

Alyssa Milano & Cinjun Tate (ten months and 19 days)

Jim Davidson & Sue Walpole (eleven months)

Paul Simon & Carrie Fisher (eleven months)

Helen Hunt & Hank Azaria (eleven months)

Sarah Bernhardt & Aristides Damala (less than a year)

Whoopi Goldberg & Dave Claessen (less than a year)

Sheena Easton & Timothy Delarm (less than a year)

NAMED AS CO-RESPONDENTS IN DIVORCE CASES

Warren Beatty (in the divorce of Sir Peter Hall and Leslie Caron)

Anthea Turner (Grant and Della Bovey)

Mick Jagger (Marianne Faithfull and John Dunbar)

Anthony Booth (David Elliott and Stephanie Buckley)

George Weidenfeld (Cyril Connolly and Barbara Skelton)

Cyril Connolly (George Weidenfeld and Barbara Skelton)

> NB This was the order in which this remarkable true-life soap occurred.

Olivia Newton-John (Bruce and Ann Welch)

Jessie Matthews (Evelyn Laye and Sonnie Hale)

John Osborne (Dr Roger and Penelope Gilliatt)

Dorothy Squires (Roger Moore and Doorn van Steyn)

Georgie Fame (The Marquess and Marchioness of Londonderry)

Glenn Hoddle (Jeffrey and Vanessa Shean)

W. Somerset Maugham (Henry and Syrie Wellcome)

James Hewitt (David and Sally Faber)

Ross Kemp (Lucien Taylor and Helen Patrick)

SEXUAL OFFERS THAT WERE TURNED DOWN

Marianne Faithfull turned down Bob Dylan and Jimi Hendrix

Marlon Brando turned down Tallulah Bankhead and Anna Magnani

Carol White turned down James Caan

Veronica Lake turned down Errol Flynn

Olivia de Havilland turned down Errol Flynn and Leslie Howard

Marlene Dietrich turned down Ernest Hemingway and Adolf Hitler (after approaches to her were made by Goebbels and Von Ribbentrop on his behalf)

Britt Ekland turned down Ron Ely

Ava Gardner turned down Howard Hughes

Mary Pickford turned down Clark Gable

Greta Garbo turned down Aristotle Onassis

Evelyn Keyes turned down Harry Cohn

Katharine Hepburn turned down Douglas Fairbanks Jnr and John Barrymore

Jean Simmons turned down John F. Kennedy and Howard Hughes

Lord Laurence Olivier turned down Merle Oberon

Angela Baddeley turned down Lord Laurence Olivier

Lana Turner turned down Mickey Rooney

Joan Collins turned down Daryl F. Zanuck and Richard Burton

Liam Gallagher turned down Paula Yates (she once asked him to make love to her in a loo but he refused because, as he told friends, 'she's way too old')

Tallulah Bankhead turned down John Barrymore

Jean Harlow turned down Louis B Mayer

Clara Bow turned down Al Jolson

Zizi Jeanmaire turned down Howard Hughes (this was after he'd brought over the entire ballet company for a film – purely to seduce her)

Gina Lollobrigida turned down Howard Hughes

Janet Leigh turned down Howard Hughes

Vaslav Nijinsky turned down Isadora Duncan

Gertrude Stein turned down Ernest Hemingway

Ava Gardner turned down George C. Scott

Jaclyn Smith turned down Warren Beatty

Bette Davis turned down Joan Crawford (according to Hollywood legend – although their lifelong enmity is equally likely to be due to the fact that Davis had an affair with Franchot Tone while he was married to Crawford)

Marilyn Monroe turned down Joan Crawford

Anthony Perkins turned down Ingrid Bergman

Jacqueline Susann turned down Coco Chanel

Rita Hayworth turned down Harry Cohn

Bette Davis turned down Miriam Hopkins

Merle Oberon turned down Stewart Granger

Tyrone Power turned down Norma Shearer

Grace Kelly turned down Bing Crosby

Paul McCartney turned down Little Richard

Mrs Patrick Campbell turned down George Bernard Shaw

John Wayne turned down Marlene Dietrich

Barbara Windsor turned down Warren Beatty

CELEBRITIES WHO LOST THEIR VIRGINITY WITH ANOTHER CELEBRITY

Amanda Donohoe with Adam Ant

Anthony Newley with Diana Dors

Juliette Lewis with Brad Pitt

Mary Astor with John Barrymore Snr

Debbie Reynolds with Eddie Fisher

Ava Gardner with Mickey Rooney

Nastassja Kinski with Roman Polanski

Malcolm Maclaren with Vivienne Westwood

Julie Burchill with Tony Parsons

Brigitte Bardot with Roger Vadim

Cecil Beaton with Adele Astaire

Elliott Gould with Barbra Streisand

Brooke Shields with Dean Cain

Priscilla Beaulieu with Elvis Presley

Gloria Swanson with Wallace Beery

MEMBERS OF THE MILE-HIGH CLUB

Bill Clinton

Joe McGann

Georgina Hale

Frances Ruffelle

Mel B

Julia Roberts & Jason Patric

Alan Whicker ('my safari suit got quite crumpled')

Tori Spelling

Dennis Rodman (on Concorde)

Samantha Fox

Pamela Anderson Lee & Tommy Lee (in a toilet on a flight from LA to New York. She said: 'It was fantastic. When we came out everyone clapped and cheered')

John Travolta & Kelly Preston (on the private jet back to America from France where they were married)

John Cusack

Danniella Westbrook & Brian Harvey

Sir Richard Branson ('before Virgin Atlantic')

Jane fonda (with Ted Turner on his private jet)

The Maharaja of Baroda

Leonardo DiCaprio (hired an executive jet, served a girl strawberries and ice cream and then made love looking at the stars)

Kelsey Grammer (with his then wife)

Sid Owen

Saeed Jaffrey (with an American woman on a flight from London to Edinburgh)

Kylie Minogue (with Michael Hutchence – in first class, just a few seats away from the Australian PM)

Carmen Electra ('The craziest place I made love was in an aeroplane, in the bathroom. I thought it was hot, I loved it')

Sophie Anderton ('on a private plane with beds')

Note also that Björn Borg says he did so with first wife Mariana on a flight from Copenhagen to New York, but the stewardess looking after them said that Björn spent the time reading Mickey Mouse comics

Men who lost their virginity with prostitutes

Henry Fonda, David Niven (with a London girl nicknamed Nessie), Clifford Irving, Uri Geller (a Greek-Cypriot girl called Lola), Anton Chekhov, Chris De Burgh (a French girl), Simon Raven, Tony Mortimer, The Duke of Windsor, Napoleon Bonaparte, James Boswell, James Joyce, John F. Kennedy (the girl charged $3), Benito Mussolini, Stendhal, Leo Tolstoy, H.G. Wells, Groucho Marx, Mike Tyson, Sir Richard Branson, Ilie Nastase, Colin Farrell (taken by his father), Oliver Stone (taken by his father)

NB Ian Fleming's James Bond loses his virginity in Paris at the age of 16 with a prostitute called Martha Debrant.

AGE AT WHICH THEY LOST THEIR VIRGINITY

AGED 11

Casanova, Harold Robins

AGED 12

Shane Richie, Jimi Hendrix, Don Johnson, Paul McGann

AGED 13

Curt Smith, Peter Andre, Lennie Bennett,
Justin Hayward (with a girl of 20), Johnny Depp, James Caan, George
Michael (heterosexual sex), Gillian Anderson ('I feel very ashamed
looking back on it. It was only when I reached about 22 that I
realized that you could actually enjoy sex'), Mae West, Bob Geldof,
Jon Bon Jovi, Anton Chekhov

AGED 14

David Chokachi, David Niven, James Joyce,
Larry Adler, Derek Jameson, Dennis Waterman ('to an older woman'),
Clint Eastwood (with a 'friendly neighbour'), David Duchovny, James
Joyce, Cher, Nick Berry, Phil Collins (in an allotment), Bruce Willis ('I
was a 14-year-old bellboy at a Holiday Inn and it was the most
incredible experience of my life. This really gorgeous chick started
coming on to me, so we went down to the laundry room
together. She guided me through it and things got kind
of hot down there'), Kate Moss, Natalie Wood

AGED 15

John Barrymore (with his stepmother), Shelley Winters, Peter O'Toole, Art Buchwald, Bobby Davro, Burt Reynolds, Tina Turner, Jack London (with a girl who 'came with' a boat he bought), Uri Geller, Sophie Anderton (a week before her 16th birthday), Angela Griffin, Paul Ross, Sting, Tony Mortimer, Damon Albarn, Lisa Marie Presley (with a 24-year-old drug dealer), Sally Field, King Charles II (with his former wet nurse), Sir Michael Caine ('I was 15 and we did it in a park'), Stephen Fry (with a girl named Shelagh while listening to 'American Pie'), Sara Cox (to a boy called Scott in a field full of sheep), Jenny Éclair (the boy had done it to win a £15 bet), Charlie Sheen (with a prostitute - 'The problem was she wanted $400 se we used my dad's credit card'), Dustin Hoffman (with a girl who thought he was his older brother. 'She was a nymphomaniac called Barbara. She was 19 and I was 15½. My brother Ronnie threw a New Year's Eve party. It was over before it began but she thought she was making love to my brother and when she realized it was me, she screamed and ran out naked'), Björk, Madonna (in the back of a Cadillac with a guy called Russell), Jerry Hall (to a rodeo rider who kept his boots on), Jo Brand

AGED 16

Georgina Hale, Nell McAndrew, Benito Mussolini, Grigori Rasputin, Leo Tolstoy, Jean Harlow, Claire King (in the back of a Mini), Dorothy Squires, Samantha Janus, Carmen Electra ('It was in Cincinnati in the back seat of a car. It was not very glamorous and I don't remember it being such a great experience'), Mel C, Sir Richard Branson, Chris De Burgh, Richard Harris, Dean Gaffney, Teri Hatcher, Dani Behr, Raquel Welch, Shirley MacLaine, Ursula Andress, David Baddiel, Robert Burns, Sean Maguire, Shelley Duvall, Groucho Marx, Barbara Hutton, Jayne Mansfield, Mike Tyson, Darren Day (in a Tesco's car park), Brigitte Bardot (with Roger Vadim), Jordan

AGED 17

Ginger Rogers, Barry Newman, Alexander Dumas Snr, Steven Spielberg, Cyndi Lauper, Keith Chegwin, Erica Jong, Carrie Fisher, Dyan Cannon, Betty Boo, Mary Astor, Chris Evans, Samantha Fox, Bel Mooney, Alicia Silverstone, Bernard Manning, Donna D'Errico (in a car), Julie Burchill, Mark Lamarr, John Leslie (at a fancy dress party with a girl wearing a wedding dress with L-plates attached), Ronnie Biggs, Cathy Shipton, Liz Kershaw, Dr Ruth Westheimer, Shaw Taylor, John F. Kennedy, Neil Morrissey ('I didn't have a clue what I was doing'), Frank Skinner (to a prostitute in her 50s), Lee Evans (with the woman who became his wife), Geri Halliwell (to a boy called Toby, 'a sickly-looking ex-public schoolboy with a toffy accent'), Michelle Collins ('My virginity was something I'd hung on to but in the end I just thought, oh well, there it goes'), Joan Collins ('I was 17 and he was 33. It was just like my mother said - the pits'), Victoria Beckham, Tina Hobley (with her boyfriend after they'd been going out for exactly a year. 'But it was the first time for him too, so it was very disappointing. It was all over before we got started.')

AGED 18

Charles Baudelaire (on which occasion he contracted the venereal disease that would kill him 27 years later), Matt Goss, Baroness Issy Van Randwyck, Anthony Edwards, Brian Glover, Jancis Robinson, Patti Boulaye, Irma Kurtz, Zoë Ball, Victoria Principal, Emma Noble, Lisa Riley, Margi Clarke, Vivien Leigh, Tony Robinson (with the woman who became his wife), Susan Hayward, Walt Disney (on his birthday), Barbra Streisand, Brad Pitt, Harry Enfield, Zoe Ball, Peter Stringfellow, Jamie Lee Curtis, Napoleon Bonaparte, Brooke Shields (with Dean Cain), Daniella Westbrook, Sir Cliff Richard (with Carol Harris, the wife of Jet Harris of The Shadows), Lord Jeffrey Archer (in a wood), Gail Porter ('Let's just say it didn't last long and I wasn't the problem'), Leonardo DiCaprio, Anthea Turner ('to a 20-year-old student called Andy Simms. I felt incredibly happy afterwards. I thought: That's it, girl, now you've got it cracked.')

AGED 19

Lillian Hellman, Gerald Kingsland, Pattie Coldwell, 'Dr' Neil Fox, Alison Steadman, Carol Drinkwater, Marlon Brando (with an older Colombian woman), Leslie Thomas

AGED 20

Mary Wesley, Mira Sorvino, Victor Hugo, Gillian Taylforth ('At the vital moment he called me Brenda.'

AGED 21

Queen Victoria, Jonathan Ross

AGED 22

Libby Holman, Dudley Moore, Edvard Munch, Ioan Gruffudd, H. G. Wells, John Peel, Claire Sweeny, Chris Martin

AGED 23

Debbie Reynolds, Catherine the Great, Hugh Hefner, Esther Rantzen, D. H. Lawrence, Elliott Gould (with Barbra Streisand), Mariah Carey

AGED 24

John Cleese

AGED 25

Isadora Duncan

AGED 26

Bette Davis

AGED 27

Sir Alfred Hitchcock

AGED 29

Katy Hill (on her wedding night), William Gladstone, George Bernard Shaw

AGED 31

Lisa Kudrow ('I'm glad I waited till I was married. I decided my virginity was precious, an honour I was bestowing on a man.')

AGED 34

Mark Twain

AGED 39

Johann von Goethe

AGED 40

Marie Stopes

THINGS SAID ABOUT SEX

'I believe that sex is a beautiful thing between two people. Between five, it's fantastic ...' (Woody Allen)

'When women go wrong, men go right after them.' (Mae West)

'My father told me all about the birds and the bees. The liar – I went steady with a woodpecker till I was 21.' (Bob Hope)

'Sex is one of the nine reasons for reincarnation – the other eight are unimportant.' (Henry Miller)

'Conventional sexual intercourse is like squirting jam into a doughnut.' (Germaine Greer)

'Being a sex symbol is a heavy load to carry – especially when one is tired, hurt and bewildered.' (Marilyn Monroe)

'It's strange to become a sex symbol at 40. And even to be described as a kind of Warren Beatty. The truth is that, until I met my wife at 35, I only had two girlfriends.' (Colin Firth)

'I come from a strict Catholic upbringing and sex was a taboo subject. That makes you crave sex 10 times more for the rest of your life.' (Salma Hayek)

'It sounds strange for me to be saying this, but I've come around to the idea that sex really is for procreation.' (Eric Clapton)

'Sex is important, but by no means the only important thing in life.' (Mary Whitehouse)

'Sex is about as important as a cheese sandwich. But a cheese sandwich, if you ain't got one to put in your belly, is extremely important.' (Ian Dury)

'The only unnatural sexual behaviour is none at all.' (Sigmund Freud)

'I always thought coq au vin was love in a lorry.' (Victoria Wood)

'I honestly prefer chocolate to sex.' (Dale Winton)

'It's been so long since I made love, I can't remember who gets tied up.' (Joan Rivers)

'Sex appeal is 50 per cent what you've got and 50 per cent what people think you've got.' (Sophia Loren)

'If you were married to Marilyn Monroe – you'd cheat with some ugly girl.' (George Burns)

'Sex – the poor man's polo.' (Clifford Odets)

'My favourite sexual fantasy is smearing my naked body with chocolate and cream – then being left alone to lick it off.' (Jo Brand)

'It [sex] ruins friendships between men and women.' (Julia Roberts)

'Accursed from their birth they be/ Who seek to find monogamy./ Pursuing it from bed to bed/ I think they would be better dead.' (Dorothy Parker)

'I'm never through with a girl until I've had her three ways.' (John F. Kennedy)

'I know it does make people happy but to me it is just like having a cup of tea.' (Cynthia Payne)

'I believe that sex is the most beautiful, natural and wholesome thing that money can buy.' (Steve Martin)

'If I took all my clothes off I wouldn't be sexy any more. I'd just be naked. Sex appeal is about keeping something back.' (Jennifer Lopez)

'The greatest pleasure that one person can offer another is carnal pleasure.' (Coco Chanel)

'The number of available orgasms is fixed at birth and can be expended. A young man should make love very seldom or he will have nothing left for middle age.' (Ernest Hemingway)

'I've never considered myself addicted to anything, but if I was, sex was it.' (Clint Eastwood)

'What comes first in a relationship is lust, then more lust.' (Jacqueline Bisset)

'Sex is a bad thing because it rumples the clothes.' (Jacqueline Kennedy Onassis)

'A man with an erection is in no need of advice.' (Samuel Pepys)

'Sex has never interested me much. I don't understand how people can waste so much time over sex. Sex is for kids, for movies – it's a great bore.' (Sir Alfred Hitchcock)

'Sex is as important as food and drink.' (Britt Ekland)

'Some things are better than sex and some things are worse, but there's nothing exactly like it.' (W.C. Fields)

'The minute you start fiddling around outside the idea of monogamy, nothing satisfies any more.' (Richard Burton)

'You know, of course, that the Tasmanians, who never committed adultery, are now extinct.' (W. Somerset Maugham)

'It has to be admitted that we English have sex on the brain – which is a very unsatisfactory place to have it.' (Malcolm Muggeridge)

'All this fuss about sleeping together; for physical pleasure I'd sooner go to my dentist any day.' (Evelyn Waugh)

PURE TRIVIA

Velcro was invented by a Swiss man who noticed the way burrs attached themselves to clothing.

Physicist Murray Gell-Mann picked the name quarks from a line in James Joyce's *Ulysses*, 'Three quarks for Muster Mark!'

When a film is in production, the last shot of the day is known as 'the Martini shot'.

Goldfish can suffer motion sickness.

The distress term 'Mayday' comes from the French term 'm'aidez' meaning 'help me'.

In Disney's *Fantasia*, the Sorcerer's name is Yensid, which is Disney backwards.

A metal coat hanger is forty-four inches long when straightened.

Columbia University is the second largest landowner (after the Catholic Church) in New York City.

The most common name in Italy is Mario Rossi.

Roosters can't crow if their necks aren't fully extended.

Shirley Temple always had 56 curls in her hair.

The three largest landowners in England are the Queen, the Church of England and Trinity College, Cambridge.

Most American car horns beep in the key of F.

Native speakers of Japanese learn Spanish much more easily than they learn English.

Dirty Harry's badge number was 2211.

The US has never lost a war in which mules were used.

All gondolas in Venice have to be painted black unless they belong to a high official.

Rhinos are thought to have inspired the myth of the unicorn.

The sport with the highest ratio of officials to participants is tennis. A singles match should have 13: ten line umpires, one net official, one foot-fault official and a chair umpire.

The shortest intercontinental commercial flight is from Gibraltar (Europe) to Tangier (Africa). The distance is 34 miles and the flight takes 20 minutes.

The quartz crystal in a wristwatch vibrates 32,768 times a second.

The US has more bagpipe bands than Scotland.

There's no sand in sandpaper.

Mark Wahlberg has a third nipple (airbrushed out of the Calvin Klein underwear ad).

Elvis Presley never gave an encore.

Gone With the Wind was set in the US Civil War but didn't feature a single battle scene.

Flamingo tongues were a delicacy in ancient Rome.

Frosties' Tony the Tiger turns 50 in 2005.

The Jolly Green Giant turns 77 in 2005.

The YKK on a zip stands for Yoshida Kogyo Kabushibibaisha, the world's largest zip manufacturer.

Before 1800 there was no such thing as separate shoes for left and right feet.

Things said about lawyers

'The first thing we do, let's kill all the lawyers.' (William Shakespeare, *King Henry VI, Part Two*)

'Ninety-nine per cent of lawyers give the rest a bad name.' (Steven Wright)

'A town that can't support one lawyer can always support two.' (Lyndon B. Johnson)

'Woodpeckers and lawyers have long bills.' (Dr K.C. Allen)

'There is never a deed so foul that something couldn't be said for the guy. That's why there are lawyers.' (Melvin Belli)

'I don't think you can make a lawyer honest by an act of legislature. You've got to work on his conscience. And his lack of conscience is what makes him a lawyer.' (Will Rogers)

'The trouble with law is lawyers.' (Clarence Darrow)

'Lawyers, I suppose, were children once.' (Charles Lamb)

'To some lawyers all facts are created equal.' (Felix Frankfurter)

'Between grand theft and a legal fee, there only stands a law degree.' (Anon)

'People whose profession it is to disguise matters.' (Sir Thomas More)

'If law school is so hard to get through, how come there are so many lawyers?' (Calvin Trillin)

'If you laid all of the lawyers in the world, end to end, on the equator – it would be a good idea to leave them there.' (Anon)

'God works wonders now and then. Behold! A lawyer, an honest man.' (Benjamin Franklin)

'Two farmer were arguing over the ownership of a cow. While one farmer pulled the head, the other pulled the tail. The lawyer sat in the middle milking the cow.' (Hebrew proverb)

'The legal trade is nothing but a high-class racket.' (Professor Fred Rodell)

'A lawyer is a learned gentleman who rescues your estate from your enemies and keeps it for himself.' (Lord Brougham)

'It is the trade of lawyers to question everything, yield nothing, and to talk by the hour.' (Thomas Jefferson)

'He saw a lawyer killing a viper on a dunghill hard by his own stable/ And the Devil smiled, for it put him in mind of Cain and his brother Abel.' (Samuel T. Coleridge)

'Lawyers are the only persons in whom ignorance of the law is not punished.' (Jeremy Bentham)

'Old lawyers never die, they just lose their appeal.' (Anon)

'What happens when a lawyer takes Viagra? He gets taller.' (Anon)

'An incompetent attorney can delay a trial for months or years. A competent attorney can delay one even longer.' (Evelle J. Younger)

'Lawyers are like rhinoceroses: thick-skinned, short-sighted but always ready to charge.' (Anon)

'Everyone ought to take every opportunity to blast lawyers.' (Marlin Fitzwater)

'As we watched Judge Clarence Thomas's Supreme Court confirmation hearings, all of the commentators said the same thing: "One of these people in the room is lying." Do you believe that? You've got two lawyers and fourteen senators in the room, and only *one* of them is lying?' (Jay Leno)

'Lawyers spend a great deal of their time shoveling smoke.' (Oliver Wendell Holmes)

'Win your lawsuit, lose your money.' (Spanish proverb)

'If all the lawyers were hanged tomorrow, and their bones sold to a mahjong factory, we'd be freer and safer, and our taxes would be reduced by almost half.' (H. L. Mencken)

'A man may as well open an oyster without a knife as a lawyer's mouth without a fee.' (Barten Holyday)

'A lawyer is a man who helps you get what's coming to him.' (Laurence J. Peter)

'No poet ever interpreted nature as freely as a lawyer interprets truth.' (Jean Giraudoux)

'Those who use the law as shoemakers use leather; rubbing it, pressing it, and stretching it with their teeth, all to the end of making it fit their purposes.' (King Louis XII)

'If it weren't for lawyers, we wouldn't need them.' (Anon)

'How do you get along at the office? Do you trust each other? Or does each have a separate safe for his money?' (Groucho Marx to his lawyer)

'I think we may class the lawyer in the natural history of monsters.' (John Keats)

'He is no lawyer who cannot take two sides.' (Charles Lamb)

A GUIDE TO CHIPS

The chip was first made in France – hence the name 'French fries'.

In Britain the first mention of chips is to be found in an 1854 recipe book, *Shilling Cookery*, in which chef Alexis Soyer referred to a recipe with 'thin cut potatoes cooked in oil'.

In 1857, Charles Dickens referred to plates of 'potato sticks cooked in oil'.

Gram for gram, chips contain a quarter of the fat of doughnuts.

In Britain we eat over two million tonnes of chips every year – that's 37 kg for each person every year.

Chips are the biggest-selling frozen vegetable in the world.

There are 8,500 fish and chip shops in the UK. In the 1950s there were more than 30,000. Nevertheless, fish and chip shops are still the most popular take-away restaurants in the UK.

69 per cent of us put salt on our chips; 57 per cent vinegar; 24 per cent tomato ketchup; 8 per cent brown sauce; 5 per cent mayonnaise and 2 per cent gravy.

Only the British sprinkle their chips with vinegar. The French usually have a pinch of salt, the Belgians use mayonnaise, while the Americans use tomato ketchup.

At the largest frozen chip factory in Britain, 3.5 tonnes of potatoes are processed every hour.

In 1996, the Irish introduced edible bags for chips to cut down on litter. According to someone who ate one, the bags 'taste a bit like mashed potato'.

When Arsene Wenger became manager of Arsenal, one of the first things he did was to ban chips from his players' diets.

American *Vogue* ran into trouble when it published a recipe that recommended using horse lard to cook tastier French fries.

80 per cent of the population visit fish and chip shops at least once a year. 22 per cent go at least once a week.

In the 19th century fish- and chip-fryers were social outcasts because of the strong odour of frying, which remained on their clothes.

Chippies officially remained an offensive trade until 1940. If the fat was not changed every day, the shops smelt awful and were usually confined to the poorer districts of town. As their popularity grew, however, the equipment and premises became more sophisticated.

Chips are a good source of vitamin C and complex carbohydrates in the form of starch. They also provide protein, fibre, iron, and other vitamins.

Every year British fish and chip shops chop up 500,000 tons of potatoes for chips – that's one twelfth of all the potatoes eaten in Britain.

The Germans have invented a revolutionary oven that produces a greaseless chip.

CELEBRITIES AND CHIPS

According to her mother, Carol Vorderman and her siblings were fed chips every day.

The actress Cameron Diaz says she has a 'love affair with French fries', which plays havoc with her skin. 'I've always been a salty, greasy kind of girl,' she declares.

Nick Faldo shocked the American golfing establishment when he ordered chips for the 1997 Masters dinner. As defending champion, it was up to him to choose the menu for the Past Champions dinner in the Augusta National clubhouse. After his two previous victories, he chose steak and kidney pie and shepherd's pie, but in 1997 he selected British fish, chips and, of course, mushy peas.

In *Pulp Fiction*, John Travolta, as Vincent Vega, the heroin-addled hit man, tells Samuel L. Jackson, 'Did you know McDonald's serves French fries with mayonnaise in Amsterdam?'

HEIGHT INDEX

4 foot 11: Charlene Tilton, Nancy Walker, Lynsey De Paul, Lil' Kim

5 foot: Dawn French, Geraldine Chaplin, Sir Norman Wisdom, Jada Pinkett Smith, Lucy Benjamin

5 foot 1: Kylie Minogue, Danny DeVito, Ronnie Corbett, Petula Clark, Sheena Easton, Carrie Fisher, Debbie Reynolds, Stevie Nicks, Lucy Liu, Lulu

5 foot 2: Holly Hunter, Sally Field, Joan Rivers, Linda Ronstadt, Sissy Spacek, Gloria Estefan, Rachel Stevens, Joan Collins, Jane Horrocks, Dame Judi Dench, Emma Bunton, Geri Halliwell, Suzanne Shaw, Jodie Marsh, Reese Witherspoon

5 foot 3: Julia Sawalha, Mickey Rooney, Sarah Michelle Gellar, Bernie Ecclestone, Prince Naseem Hamed, Christina Aguilera, Kerry McFadden, Helena Bonham Carter, Kathy Bates

5 foot 4: Madonna, Michael J. Fox, Roman Polanski, Drew Barrymore, Britney Spears, The Queen, Anne Robinson (and half an inch), Melinda Messenger, Tina Turner, Scarlett Johansson

5 foot 5: Belinda Carlisle, Sachin Tendulkar, Mel B, Jennifer Aniston, Natasha Hamilton, Joe Pesci, Sanjeev Bhaskar

5 foot 6: Pauline Quirke, Martin Amis, Princess Anne, Jayne Middlemiss, Calista Flockhart, Victoria Beckham, Carol Vorderman, Elijah Wood

5 foot 7: Laura Bailey, Sir Mick Jagger, Laetitia Casta, Tom Cruise, Kate Winslet, Catherine Zeta-Jones, Mark Wahlberg, Keira Knightley

5 foot 8: Phil Collins, Anne Bancroft, Rita Coolidge, Lauren Hutton, Billy Joel, Ringo Starr, Robin Williams, Robert Redford, Mel Gibson, Ali Landry, Elizabeth Hurley, Tobey Maguire, Mackenzie Crook

5 foot 9: Claire Rayner, Vic Reeves, Lauren Bacall, Liam Gallagher, Prince Charles, Shannon Elizabeth, Cameron Diaz, Richard Whiteley, Abs Breen, Liz McLarnon, Nell McAndrew

5 foot 10: Naomi Campbell, Harry Enfield, Lily Tomlin, Fiona Bruce, Nicole Kidman, Natasha Henstridge, Paul Nicholls, Gwyneth Paltrow, Minnie Driver

5 foot 11: George Michael, Bea Arthur, Vanessa Redgrave, Brooke Shields, Sigourney Weaver, Adam Rickitt, Claudia Schiffer, Jerry Hall, Lucy Lawless, Sophie Dahl

6 foot: Eva Herzigova, Terry Wogan, Brad Pitt, Macy Gray, Prince Edward, Prince Andrew, Tony Blair, Leonardo DiCaprio, Matthew Perry, Allison Janney

6 foot 1: Janet Street-Porter, Pete Sampras, Venus Williams, Pierce Brosnan, Freddie Prinze Jr, Janet McTeer, Chris Isaak, Enrique Iglesias, Jodie Kidd

6 foot 2: Julie T. Wallace, Russ Abbot, Chris Evans, Richard Madeley, Lindsay Davenport, Steve Penk, Tiger Woods, George W. Bush, Thierry Henry, Timothy Dalton

6 foot 3: Michael Barrymore, Clint Eastwood, Muhammad Ali, Jon Voight, Jamie Theakston, Al Gore, Brendan Fraser

6 foot 4: Frank Bruno, Chevy Chase, Louis Gossett Jr, Ralph Nader, Tom Selleck, John Wayne, Ben Affleck, Billy Campbell, Goran Visnijc, Benicio Del Toro, Heath Ledger, Rupert Everett, John Kerry

6 foot 5: Mick Fleetwood, John Leslie, Tim Robbins, Howard Stern

6 foot 6: Dolph Lundgren, Tommy Tune, Hulk Hogan

6 foot 7: Terry Waite, John Cleese

6 foot 9: Michael Crichton

7 foot 2: Richard Kiel

BRAINS

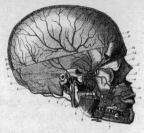

The brain is the second heaviest organ in the human body (after the liver and ahead of the lungs and the heart).

A brain weighs around 3 pounds. All but 10 ounces is water.

The brain uses more than 25 per cent of the oxygen required by the human body.

The brain uses less power than a 100-watt bulb.

Is eating fish good for the brain? Up to a point. The brain needs decosahexaenoic acid to develop and this is found in oily fish. P.G. Wodehouse's Jeeves attributed his brainpower to the eating of fish.

Albert Einstein's brain was preserved after his death. So was Lenin's.

Vincent van Gogh's brain was destroyed by the mercury he took to counteract syphilis.

MENSA PEOPLE

Sir Clive Sinclair, Sir Jimmy Savile, Geena Davis, Carol Vorderman, Leslie Charteris, Jamie Theakston, Carol Smillie, Jeremy Hanley, Sally Farmiloe, Adrian Moorhouse.

Jessica Simpson, John Thomson, Caroline Aherne, Bill Clinton and James Woods have all been measured at above Mensa entry level

THE BUFFALO THEORY

A herd of buffalo only moves as fast as the slowest buffalo. So when the herd is hunted, it is the weakest and slowest ones at the back that get killed first. This example of natural selection is beneficial for the herd because the regular culling of the weakest animals improves the overall and average health and speed of the whole group. Similarly, the human brain can only work at the speed of its slowest cells. Now, too much alcohol kills brain cells – but, importantly, the weakest and slowest cells first. Consequently, regular beer consumption, by eliminating them, is making your brain work faster and better.

So the moral of this theory is: drink more beer.

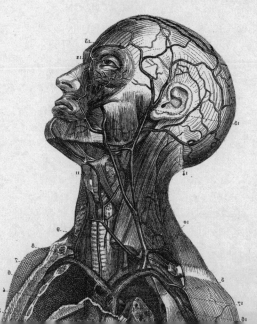

Unintentionally funny (genuine) newspaper headlines

HIGH SCHOOL DROPOUTS CUT IN HALF

COMPLAINTS ABOUT REFEREES GROWING UGLY

ASBESTOS SUIT PRESSED

PHYSICIST RECOMMENDS BIGGER BALLS TO SLOW DOWN MALE TENNIS PLAYERS

NEW STUDY OF OBESITY LOOKS FOR LARGER TEST GROUP

PUPILS TRAIN AS COUNSELLORS TO HELP UPSET CLASSMATES

TWO CONVICTS EVADE NOOSE: JURY HUNG

PANDA MATING FAILS – VETERINARIAN TAKES OVER

ORGAN FESTIVAL ENDS IN A SMASHING CLIMAX

DEALERS WILL HEAR CAR TALK AT NOON

TWO SISTERS REUNITE AFTER EIGHTEEN YEARS AT CHECKOUT COUNTER

POLICE DISCOVER CRACK IN AUSTRALIA

WAR DIMS HOPE FOR PEACE

BOY WANTS TO MOUNT AUTOGRAPHED GUITAR

BODY FOUND ON BOAT SEIZED BY BAILIFFS AND DUE TO BE AUCTIONED

MILK DRINKERS ARE TURNING TO POWDER

TYPHOON RIPS THROUGH CEMETERY; HUNDREDS DEAD

BABIES USED TO SNEAK DRUGS INTO PRISON

ARAFAT SWEARS IN CABINET

BANGKOK LAUNCHES ANTI-BUTT CAMPAIGN

NEW AUTOS TO HIT 5 MILLION

MARCH PLANNED FOR NEXT AUGUST

NEW HOUSING FOR ELDERLY NOT YET DEAD

TUNA BITING OFF WASHINGTON COAST

JUDGE ACTS TO REOPEN THEATER

WOMAN ATTACKED BY TRAIN STATION

CHOPPER SEARCH FOR MAN IN UNDERPANTS

BRITON GORED BY BULL IN INTENSIVE CARE

BULGE IN TROUSERS WAS ECSTASY

CARIBBEAN ISLANDS DRIFT TO LEFT

SOMETHING WENT WRONG IN JET CRASH, EXPERT SAYS

GOLFERS WARNED NOT TO LICK BALLS

DRUGS FINE FOR BUSINESSMAN

COPS QUIZ VICTIM IN FATAL SHOOTING

SEX SCANDAL VICAR SEEKS NEW POSITION

CIRCUMCISION NOW SEEN AS POINTLESS

DOWN UNDER LOVE FOR PRINCESS ANNE'S DAUGHTER

BLIND BISHOP APPOINTED TO SEE

MAN WITH ONE ARM AND LEG CHEATS ON OTHER HALF

GIANT TEA BAGS PROTEST

POLICE CHIEF'S PLEDGE TO MURDER WITNESSES

MOST SURGEONS FACE CUTS

12 ON THEIR WAY TO CRUISE AMONG DEAD IN PLANE CRASH

STIFF OPPOSITION EXPECTED TO CASKETLESS FUNERAL PLAN

INCLUDE YOUR CHILDREN WHEN BAKING COOKIES

DAD WANTS BABY LEFT IN AEROPLANE

MALE NATURIST MEMBERS RISE

CUTS COULD HURT ANIMALS

CHEF THROWS HIS HEART INTO HELPING FEED NEEDY

PUBLIC SWINGS IN FAVOUR OF THE PRINCE

HALF MILLION ITALIAN WOMEN SEEN ON PILL

IDAHO GROUP ORGANIZES TO HELP SERVICE WIDOWS

L.A. VOTERS APPROVE URBAN RENEWAL BY LANDSLIDE

LESOTHO WOMEN MAKE GREAT CARPETS

EU MUST UNITE ON DRUGS

MEN RECOMMEND MORE CLUBS FOR WIVES

GUNMAN SHOT BY 999 COPS

PROSTITUTES TO HOLD OPEN DAY

SUBSTITUTE TEACHERS SEEKING RESPECT

NIGHT SCHOOL TO HEAR PEST TALK

HOME SECRETARY TO ACT ON VIDEO NASTIES

DIET OF PREMATURE BABIES 'AFFECTS IQ'

SEX UP AND DOWN AFTER SEPTEMBER 11

LARGEST AMOUNT OF CANNABIS EVER SEIZED IN JOINT OPERATION

STRAW'S PLEDGE TO RAPE VICTIMS

MAD COW TALKS

THE SENILITY PRAYER

God, grant me the senility to forget the people I never liked anyway, the good fortune to run into the ones that I do, and the eyesight to tell the difference.

DUMB THINGS PEOPLE HAVE SAID

'Everything that can be invented has been invented.' (Charles H. Duell, Commissioner, US Office of Patents, 1899)

'This "telephone" has too many shortcomings to be seriously considered as a means of communication. The device is inherently of no value to us.' (Western Union internal memo, 1876)

'If we can just get young people to do as their fathers did, that is, wear condoms.' (Sir Richard Branson)

'My imagination refuses to see any sort of submarine doing anything but suffocating its crew.' (H.G. Wells)

'The abdomen, the chest, and the brain will forever be shut from the intrusion of the wise and humane surgeon.' (Sir John Ericksen, Queen Victoria's surgeon, 1873)

'Louis Pasteur's theory of germs is ridiculous fiction.' (Pierre Pachet, Professor of Physiology, 1872)

'No flying machine will ever fly from New York to Paris.' (Orville Wright)

'Drill for oil? You mean drill into the ground to try and find oil? You're crazy.' (Drillers responding to Edwin L. Drake in 1859)

'Airplanes are interesting toys but of no military value.' (Marshal Foch)

'Who the hell wants to hear actors talk?' (Harry Warner of Warner Brothers, 1927)

'The wireless music box has no imaginable commercial value. Who would pay for a message sent to nobody in particular?' (Anonymous businessman declining to invest in radio in the 1920s)

'So we went to Atari and said, "Hey, we've got this amazing thing, even built with some of your parts – what do you think about funding us? Or we'll give it to you. We just want to do it. Pay our salary, we'll come work for you." And they said, "No." So then we went to Hewlett-Packard, and they said, "Hey, we don't need you. You haven't got through college yet."' (Apple Computer co-founder Steve Jobs)

'I'm just glad it'll be Clark Gable who's falling on his face and not Gary Cooper.' (Gary Cooper turning down the role of Rhett Butler in *Gone With The Wind*)

'Heavier-than-air flying machines are impossible.' (Lord Kelvin, President of the Royal Society, talking in 1895)

'Stocks have reached what looks like a permanently high plateau.' (Irving Fisher, Professor of Economics at Yale just before the 1929 Wall Street Crash)

'The concept is interesting and well-formed, but in order to earn better than a C, the idea must be feasible.' (A Yale University professor's comment on Fred Smith's paper proposing an overnight delivery service. Smith later founded Federal Express.)

SUICIDE

Three times as many men commit suicide as women. But women attempt suicide two to three times more often than men.

The season for suicides is the spring; the winter months have the lowest number of suicides.

In 1926, a Budapest waiter committed suicide. He left his suicide note in the form of a crossword and the police had to get help from the public to solve it.

Vincent van Gogh committed suicide while painting *Wheat Field with Crows*.

COMMITTED SUICIDE

Bobby Bloom, Kurt Cobain, Michael Hutchence, Gig Young, Richard Manuel, Ian Curtis, Jerzy Kosinski, Pete Ham, Terry Kath, Ron 'Pigpen' McKernan, Donny Hathaway, Paul Williams, Cleopatra, Ronnie Scott, Ernest Hemingway, Margot Hemingway, Marc Antony, Screaming Lord Sutch, Del Shannon, Graham Bond, Brian Epstein, James Whale, John Kennedy Toole, Joseph Goebbels, Nick Drake, Brian Keith, Phil Ochs, Yukio Mishima, George Sanders,
Tony Hancock, Hannibal, Freddie Prinze, Terence Donovan, Ted Moult, Primo Levi, Adolf Hitler, David Bairstow, Stuart Adamson, Robert Clive, Rory Storm, Nero, Kid McCoy, Lord Castlereagh, Sylvia Plath, Arthur Koestler, Pontius Pilate, Capucine, Virginia Woolf, Carole Landis, Alan Turing, Charles Boyer, Dorothy Dandridge, Herve Villechaize, Faron Young, Pete Duel, The Singing Nun, George Reeves, Margaret Sullavan, Randy Turpin, Jean Seberg, Thelma Todd, Lupe Velez,

Spalding Gray, Andreas Baader, Lady Isobel Barnett, Buster Edwards, Justin Fashanu, Rainer Werner Fassbinder, Rudolf Diesel (Inventor of the Diesel engine), Hannibal, James Leo Herlihy, Rudolf Hess, Heinrich Himmler, Judas Iscariot, Arthur Koestler, Jerzy Kosinski, Jack London, Frankie Lymon, Jan Masaryk, Freddie Mills, David Rappaport, Rachel Roberts, Erwin Rommel, Dr Harold Shipman, Stephen Ward

PEOPLE WHOSE FATHERS COMMITTED SUICIDE

Ernest Hemingway, Tara Fitzgerald, Hal Ashby, Phil Spector (on his tombstone were the words 'To know him was to love him'), Ted Turner, Betty Hutton, Rick Stein, Wendy Richard, Slobodan Milosevic, Dawn French, Ben Hogan, Martina Navratilova, Steve Strange, Ruth Prawer Jhabvala, Sarah Brightman, Jane Asher, Alger Hiss, Marsha Hunt, Jean Cocteau

PEOPLE WHOSE MOTHERS COMMITTED SUICIDE

Dale Winton, Alan Ladd, Sid Vicious, Jane Fonda, Sir Nikolaus Pevsner, Antonia de Sancha, Christopher Hitchens, Mike Oldfield, Slobodan Milosevic, Dame Margaret Rutherford, Lena Zavaroni, René Magritte, Truman Capote, Mikhail Baryshnikov, Richard Todd, Spalding Gray, Jean-Bedel Bokassa, Amos Oz, Kurt Vonnegut, Peter Fonda

PEOPLE WHOSE SONS COMMITTED SUICIDE

Gregory Peck, Theodore Roosevelt, Paul Newman, Bing Crosby (two sons), Ian Fleming, Dan Dailey, Mary Tyler Moore, Bobby Womack, Hank Marvin, Thomas Mann, Charles Boyer, Richard Todd, Eugene O'Neill (two sons), Art Linkletter, Carroll O'Connor, Walter Winchell, Libby Purves

PEOPLE WHOSE DAUGHTERS COMMITTED SUICIDE

Margaret Sullavan, Karl Marx, Robert Frost, James Arness, Marlon Brando, John Barrymore, Timothy Leary

MEN WHOSE WIVES COMMITTED SUICIDE

Adolf Hitler (with him), Ted Hughes, Percy Bysshe Shelley, Timothy Leary, Jackson Browne, Henry Brooks Adams, Arthur Koestler (with him), Heinrich Mann, John Hiatt, Joseph Goebbels (with him), Joseph Stalin, Lord Melvyn Bragg, Henry Fonda

WOMEN WHOSE HUSBANDS COMMITTED SUICIDE

Courtney Love, Katharine Graham, Diana Dors (after her death), Joan Rivers, June Brown

SURVIVED SUICIDE ATTEMPTS

Drew Barrymore, Sir Elton John, Marianne Faithfull, Frank Sinatra, Tom Baker, Tuesday Weld, Danniella Westbrook, Billy Joel, Brenda Fricker, Sinéad O'Connor, Vanilla Ice, Gary Glitter, Mickey Rooney, Yannick Noah, Caroline Aherne, Jo O'Meara, Pamela Anderson, Mel B, Halle Berry, Jack Osbourne

ENOUGH TO END IT ALL?

In 1927, Edwin Wakeman of Manchester committed suicide leaving this note: 'I married a widow with a grown daughter. My father fell in love with my stepdaughter and married her – thus becoming my son-in-law. My stepdaughter became my stepmother because she was my father's wife. My wife gave birth to a son, who was, of course, my father's brother-in-law, and also my uncle, for he was the brother of my stepmother. My father's wife became the mother of a son, who was, of course, my brother, and also my grandchild, for he was the son of my stepdaughter. Accordingly, my wife was my grandmother, because she was my stepmother's mother. I was my wife's husband and grandchild at the same time. And, as the husband of a person's grandmother is his grandfather, I am my own grandfather.'

DIED ON STAGE (LITERALLY)

Tommy Cooper

Sid James

Leonard Rossiter

Marie Lloyd

Simon Barere (pianist)

Les Harvey (Stone The Crows musician – electrocuted by touching a live microphone with wet feet in 1972)

Richard Versalle (opera singer – after singing the line 'Too bad you can only live so long' in 1996)

Linda Wright (nightclub singer)

Leonard Warren (opera singer)

DIED VIRGINS

Immanuel Kant, Sir J.M. Barrie, Nikolai Gogol, Queen Elizabeth I, Sir Isaac Newton, Anton Bruckner, Alma Cogan, Hans Christian Andersen, Edith Sitwell

DIED INTESTATE

Jayne Mansfield, George Gershwin, Karl Marx, Rita Hayworth, Howard Hughes, Abraham Lincoln, Pablo Picasso, Duke Ellington, Lenny Bruce, Paolo Gucci, Pat Phoenix, Phil Lynott, Sylvia Plath, Keith Moon, Robert Johnson

BELIEVE IN REINCARNATION

Jesper Parnevik, Glenn Hoddle, Eric Cantona, Joan Collins, Louise Jameson, k.d. lang, Keanu Reeves, Conchita Martinez, Tori Amos, Shirley MacLaine, Gillian Anderson, Sarah Jessica Parker

Famous men's last words

'I'm still alive.' (Caligula, AD41)

'Tomorrow, I shall no longer be here.' (Nostradamus – possibly the only prophecy he got right, 1566)

'Friends, applaud, the comedy is over.' (Ludwig van Beethoven, 1827)

'Such is life.' (Ned Kelly, 1880)

'Who is it?' (Billy the Kid before being shot by Sheriff Pat Garrett, 1881)

'Go on, get out! Last words are for fools who haven't said enough.' (Karl Marx, 1883)

'I'm tired of fighting. I guess this is going to get me.' (Harry Houdini, 1926)

'Four o'clock. How strange. So that is the time. Strange. Enough.' (Sir Henry Morton Stanley, 1904)

'It is never too late for a glass of champagne.' (Anton Chekhov, 1904)

'Don't let it end like this. Tell them I said something.' (Pancho Villa, 1923)

'So little done, so much to do.' (Cecil Rhodes, 1902)

'If this is dying, I don't think much of it.' (Lytton Strachey, 1932)

'Never felt better.' (Douglas Fairbanks Sr, 1939)

'But, but, Mister Colonel …' (Benito Mussolini, 1945)

'Go away. I'm all right.' (H.G. Wells, 1946)

'Born in a hotel room and – God damn it – died in a hotel room.' (Eugene O'Neill, 1953)

'Dying is easy. Comedy is difficult.' (Edmund Gwenn, 1959)

'Oh God, here I go.' (Max Baer, 1959)

'Dying is a very dull affair. My advice to you is to have nothing whatever to do with it.' (W. Somerset Maugham, 1965)

'It hurts.' (Charles de Gaulle, 1970)

'Drink to me.' (Picasso, 1973)

'OK, I won't.' (Elvis Presley, after his girlfriend told him not to fall asleep in the bathroom, 1977)

'That was a great game of golf, fellas.' (Bing Crosby, 1977)

'I would like two lightly poached eggs.' (Roy Jenkins, 2003)

'Channel 5 is all s*, isn't it? Christ, the c**p they put on there. It's a waste of space.' (Adam Faith, 2003)**

NB When Albert Einstein died in 1955, his final words died with him – the nurse at his side didn't understand German.

FAMOUS WOMEN'S LAST WORDS

'Hold the cross high so I may see it through the flames!' (Joan of Arc, 1431)

'All my possessions for a moment of time.' (Queen Elizabeth I, 1603)

'Sir, I beg your pardon.' (Marie Antoinette, Queen of France, 1793, as she stepped on the executioner's foot)

'Nothing but death.' (Jane Austen, when asked if she wanted anything, 1817)

'Oh, I am not going to die, am I? He will not separate us, we have been so happy.' (Charlotte Brontë, 1855, to her husband of nine months)

'Beautiful.' (Elizabeth Barrett Browning, 1861, in answer to her husband's query as to how she was feeling)

'I must go in, the fog is rising.' (Emily Dickinson, 1886)

'Is it not meningitis?' (Louisa M. Alcott, 1888)

'It is unbelievable.' (Mata Hari, 1917)

'Farewell, my friends. I go to glory.' (Isadora Duncan, 1927)

'Get my swan costume ready.' (Anna Pavlova, 1931)

'KHAQQ calling Itasca. We must be on you, but cannot see you. Gas is running low.' (Amelia Earhart, 1937)

'What is the question?' (Gertrude Stein, 1946 after her partner, Alice B. Toklas, asked her, 'What is the answer?')

'Is everybody happy? I want everybody to be happy. I know I'm happy.' (Ethel Barrymore, 1959)

'Am I dying or is this my birthday?' (Lady Nancy Astor, 1964)

'Codeine … bourbon.' (Tallulah Bankhead, 1968)

'Damn it! Don't you dare ask God to help me.' (Joan Crawford, 1977, to her housekeeper who was praying for her)

'My God. What's happened?' (Diana, Princess of Wales, 1997)

DIED BEFORE THE AGE OF 40

King Louis XVII of France 10

King Edward V 12

Saint Agnes 13

Saint Pancras 14

Anne Frank 15

King Edward VI 16

Lady Jane Grey 16

Ritchie Valens 17

Tutankhamun 18

Joan of Arc 19

Catherine Howard 20

Nancy Spungen 20

Dorothy Stratten 20

Duncan Edwards 21

Eddie Cochran 21

Stu Sutcliffe 21

Sid Vicious 21

Lillian Board 22

Aaliyah 22

Billy The Kid 22

Pocahontas 22

Buddy Holly 22

Freddie Prinze 22

Bonnie Parker 23

River Phoenix 23

Duane Allman 24

Tammi Terrell 24

Lee Harvey Oswald 24

James Dean 24

Frankie Lymon 25

Clyde Barrow 25

Françoise Dorleac 25

John Keats 25

Baron Manfred von Richtofen 25

Gram Parsons 26

Otis Redding 26

Sharon Tate 26

Nick Drake 26

Kurt Cobain 27

Jimi Hendrix 27

Robert Johnson 27

Brian Jones 27

Janis Joplin 27

Ron 'Pigpen' McKernan 27

Jim Morrison 27

Bix Beiderbecke 28

Caligula 28

Brandon Lee 28

Catherine Parr 28

Ruth Ellis 28

J. P. Richardson (aka 'The Big Bopper') 28

Karen Silkwood 28

Marc Bolan 29

Fletcher Christian 29

Ronnie Van Zant 29

Hank Williams 29

Anne Brontë 29

Percy Bysshe Shelley 29

Jean Vigo 29

Emily Brontë 30

Jim Croce 30

Sylvia Plath 30

Jeff Buckley 30

Andreas Baader 30

Steve Biko 30

Brandon DeWilde 30

Andy Gibb 30

Lisa 'Left Eye' Lopes 30

Nero 30

Keith Moon 31

John Bonham 31

Sandy Denny 31

Pete Duel 31

Karen Quinlan 31

Minnie Riperton 31

John Kennedy Toole 31

Rudolph Valentino 31

Patsy Cline 31

Florence Ballard 32

John Dillinger 32

Queen Mary II 32

King Richard III 32

Charles Rolls 32

Jane Seymour 32

Robert Walker 32

Bruce Lee 32

Keith Relf 32

Karen Carpenter 32

Bill Hicks 32

Carole Lombard 33

Dick Turpin 33

Alexander The Great 33

John Belushi 33

Eva Braun 33

Eva Cassidy 33

Charlotte Coleman 33

Sam Cooke 33

Mama Cass Elliot 33

Unity Mitford 33

Sanjay Gandhi 33

Donny Hathaway 33

Eva Perón 33

King Richard II 33

Yuri Gagarin 34

Gerald Hoffnung 34

Jesse James 34

Ayrton Senna 34

Joe Orton 34

Jayne Mansfield 35

Charlie Parker 35

Stevie Ray Vaughan 35

Wolfgang Mozart 35

Jesse James 35

Anne Boleyn 35

Guy Fawkes 35

Roger Tonge 35

King Henry V 35

Phil Ochs 35

Peter Revson 35

Marilyn Monroe 36

Robespierre 36

George Custer 36

Rainer Werner Fassbinder 36

Bob Marley 36

Mike Bloomfield 36

Princess Diana 36

Bob 'The Bear' Hite 36

Marie-Antoinette 37

Jill Dando 37

Bobby Darin 37

Rosalind Franklin 37

Lou Gehrig 37

Michael Hutchence 37

George Mallory 37

Sal Mineo 37

Christina Onassis 37

Irving Thalberg 37

Vincent van Gogh 37

Georges Bizet 37

Alexander Pushkin 37

Robert Burns 37

Charlotte Brontë 38

Felix Mendelssohn 38

Joanne Campbell 38

Harry Chapin 38

Stephen Foster 38

George Gershwin 38

Amelia Earhart 38

Florence Griffith Joyner 38

John Kennedy Jr 38

Mario Lanza 38

Federico Lorca 38

Van McCoy 38

David Rappaport 38

Che Guevara 39

Frederic Chopin 39

Dylan Thomas 39

Dr Martin Luther King 39

Blaise Pascal 39

Dennis Wilson 39

Pier Angeli 39

Neil Bogart 39

Tim Hardin 39

Wild Bill Hickock 39

Jim Reeves 39

Sabu 39

Fats Waller 39

Dinah Washington 39

Malcolm X 39

Emiliano Zapata 39

Lynne Frederick 39

Grace Metalious 39

John Garfield 39

Anna Nicole Smith 39

DIED IN A PLANE CRASH

Roald Amundsen (1928)

Will Rogers (1935)

Carole Lombard (1942)

Leslie Howard (1943)

Charles Paddock (1943)

Antoine de Saint-Exupéry (1944)

Glenn Miller (1944)

Orde Wingate (1944)

Mike Todd (1958)

Duncan Edwards (1958)

Buddy Holly (1959)

J.P. Richardson ('The Big Bopper'; 1959)

Ritchie Valens (1959)

Dag Hammarskjöld (1961)

Patsy Cline (1963)

Jim Reeves (1964)

Herbert Marshall (1966)

Otis Redding (1967)

Yuri Gagarin (1968)

Rocky Marciano (1969)

Audie Murphy (1971)

Prince William of Gloucester (1972)

Jim Croce (1973)

Graham Hill (1975)

Ronnie Van Zant (1977)

Steve Gaines (1977)

Cassie Gaines (1977)

Sanjay Gandhi (1980)

Ricky Nelson (1985)

Larry Shue (1985)

General Muhammad Zia ul-Haq (1988)

Stevie Ray Vaughan (1990)

Senator John Tower (1991)

Bill Graham (1991)

Ron Brown (1996)

John Denver (1997)

Payne Stewart (1999)

John F. Kennedy Jr (1999)

DIED IN A ROAD ACCIDENT

T.E. Lawrence (1935)

Tom Mix (1940)

General George S. Patton (1945)

Margaret Mitchell (1949)

James Dean (1955)

Jackson Pollock (1956)

Prince Aly Khan (1960)

Eddie Cochran (1960)

Albert Camus (1960)

Ernie Kovacs (1962)

Jayne Mansfield (1967)

Françoise Dorleac (1967)

Duane Allman (1971)

Dickie Valentine (1971)

Brandon De Wilde (1972)

Marc Bolan (1977)

Harry Chapin (1981)

Grace Kelly (1982)

David Penhaligon (1986)

Cozy Powell (1988)

Falco (1988)

Pete DeFreitas (1989)

Diana, Princess of Wales (1997)

Dodi Fayed (1997)

Ian Bannen (1999)

Desmond Llewelyn (1999)

Aaliyah (2001)

Lisa 'Left Eye' Lopes (2002)

Helmut Newton (2004)

THE LAST LINE OF EVERY SHAKESPEARE PLAY

All's Well That Ends Well: 'Your gentle hands lend us, and take our hearts.' (King)

Antony And Cleopatra: 'Come, Dolabella, see/High order in this great solemnity.' (Octavius Caesar)

As You Like It: 'If I were a woman, I would kiss as many of you as had beards that pleased me, complexions that liked me and breaths that I defied not: and, I am sure, as many as have good beards, or good faces, or sweet breaths, will, for my kind offer, when I make curtsy, bid me farewell.' (Rosalind)

The Comedy of Errors: 'Nay, then, thus:/We came into the world like brother and brother;/And now let's go hand in hand, not one before another.' (Dromio of Ephesus)

Coriolanus: 'Though in this city he/Hath widow'd and unchilded many a one,/Which to this hour bewail the injury,/Yet he shall have a noble memory.—Assist.' (Aufidius)

Cymbeline: 'Never was a war did cease,/Ere bloody hands were wash'd, with such a peace.' (Cymbeline)

Hamlet: 'Take up the bodies: such a sight as this/Becomes the field, but here shows much amiss./Go, bid the soldiers shoot.' (Fortinbras)

Henry IV, Part One: 'Rebellion in this land shall lose his sway,/Meeting the check of such another day:/And since this business so fair is done,/Let us not leave till all our own be won.' (Henry IV)

Henry IV, Part Two: 'I will lay odds that, ere this year expire,/We bear our civil swords and native fire/As far as France: I heard a bird so sing,/Whose music, to my thinking, pleas'd the king./Come, will you hence?' (Lancaster – followed by an epilogue)

Henry V: 'Then shall I swear to Kate, and you to me;/And may

our oaths well kept and prosperous be!' (Henry V – followed by a chorus)

Henry VI, Part One: 'Margaret shall now be queen, and rule the king;/But I will rule both her, the king, and realm.' (Suffolk)

***Henry VI, Part Two*: 'Sound drums and trumpets, and to London all:/And more such days as these to us befall!' (Warwick)**

Henry VI, Part Three: 'Sound drums and trumpets! farewell sour annoy!/For here, I hope, begins our lasting joy.' (Edward IV)

***Henry VIII*: 'This day, no man think/Has business at his house; for all shall stay:/This little one shall make it holiday.' (Henry VIII – followed by an epilogue)**

Julius Caesar: 'So call the field to rest; and let's away,/To part the glories of this happy day.' (Octavius)

***King John*: 'Nought shall make us rue,/If England to itself do rest but true.' (Bastard)**

King Lear: 'The weight of this sad time we must obey;/Speak what we feel, not what we ought to say./The oldest hath borne most: we that are young/Shall never see so much, nor live so long.' (Albany)

***Love's Labours Lost*: 'The words of Mercury are harsh after the songs of Apollo. You that way: we this way.' (Armado)**

Macbeth: 'Of this dead butcher and his fiend-like queen,/Who, as 'tis thought, by self and violent hands/Took off her life; this, and what needful else/That calls upon us, by the grace of Grace,/We will perform in measure, time, and place:/So, thanks to all at once, and to each one,/Whom we invite to see us crown'd at Scone.' (Malcolm)

Measure For Measure: **'So, bring us to our palace; where we'll show/What's yet behind that's meet you all should know.' (Duke Vicentio)**

The Merry Wives of Windsor: 'Let it be so. Sir John,/To Master Brook you yet shall hold your word/For he, tonight, shall lie with Mistress Ford.' (Ford)

The Merchant of Venice: **'Well, while I live, I'll fear no other thing/So sore as keeping safe Nerissa's ring.' (Gratiano)**

A Midsummer Night's Dream: 'So, good night unto you all./Give me your hands, if we be friends,/And Robin shall restore amends.' (Puck)

Much Ado About Nothing: **'Think not on him till tomorrow:/I'll devise thee brave punishments for him./Strike up, pipers.' (Benedick)**

Othello: 'To you, lord governor,/Remains the censure of this hellish villain;/The time, the place, the torture: O, enforce it!/Myself will straight aboard; and to the state/This heavy act with heavy heart relate.' (Lodovico)

Pericles: **'So, on your patience evermore attending,/New joy wait on you! Here our play has ending.' (Gower)**

Richard II: 'Lords, I protest, my soul is full of woe,/That blood should sprinkle me to make me grow:/Come, mourn with me for that I do lament,/And put on sullen black incontinent:/I'll make a voyage to the Holy Land,/To wash this blood off from my guilty hand:/March sadly after; grace my mournings here;/In weeping after this untimely bier.' (Henry Bolingbroke)

Richard III: 'Now civil wounds are stopp'd, peace lives again:/That she may long live here, God say amen!' (Richmond)

Romeo And Juliet: 'A glooming peace this morning with it brings;/The sun, for sorrow, will not show his head:/Go hence, to have more talk of these sad things;/Some shall be pardon'd, and some punished:/For never was a story of more woe/Than this of Juliet and her Romeo.' (Prince)

The Taming of The Shrew: ''Tis a wonder, by your leave, she will be tamed so.' (Lucentio)

The Tempest: 'Now I want/Spirits to enforce, art to enchant,/And my ending is despair,/Unless I be relieved by prayer,/Which pierces so, that it assaults/Mercy itself, and frees all faults./As you from crimes would pardon'd be,/Let your indulgence set me free.' (Prospero)

Timon of Athens: 'Bring me into your city,/And I will use the olive with my sword,/Make war breed peace; make peace stint war; make each/Prescribe to other, as each other's leech./Let our drums strike.' (Alcibiades)

Titus Andronicus: 'See justice done on Aaron, that damn'd Moor,/By whom our heavy haps had their beginning:/Then, afterwards, to order well the state,/That like events may ne'er it ruinate.' (Lucius)

Troilus And Cressida: 'Brethren and sisters of the old-door trade,/Some two months hence my will shall here be made:/It should be now, but that my fear is this,/Some galled goose of Winchester would hiss:/Till then I'll sweat, and seek about for eases;/And at that time, bequeath you my diseases.' (Pandarus)

Twelfth Night: 'Cesario, come:/For so you shall be while you are a man;/But, when in other habits you are seen,/Orsino's mistress, and his fancy's queen.' (Duke – followed by Clown's song)

***Two Gentlemen of Verona*: 'Come, Proteus; 'tis your penance but to hear/The story of your loves discovered:/That done, our day of marriage shall be yours;/One feast, one house, one mutual happiness.' (Valentine)**

The Winter's Tale: 'Good Paulina,/Lead us from hence, where we may leisurely/Each one demand, and answer to his part/Perform'd in this wide gap of time, since first/We were dissever'd: hastily lead away!' (Leontes)

Finally ...

'All I've ever wanted was an honest week's pay for an honest day's work.' (Steve Martin)

'Early to rise and early to bed, makes a male healthy, wealthy and dead.' (James Thurber)

'I like long walks, especially when they are taken by people who annoy me.' (Fred Allen)

'I think a man can have two, maybe three affairs, while he is married, but three is maximum. After that, you're cheating.' (Yves Montand)

'You can kill, you can maim people, but to be boring is truly a sin. And God will punish you for that.' (Burt Reynolds)

'Gluttony is not a secret vice.' (Orson Welles)

'Wickedness is a myth invented by good people to account for the curious attractiveness of others.' (Oscar Wilde)

'Tip big and tip quietly. Fold the bills three times into small squares and pass them in a handshake.' (Frank Sinatra)

'Remember that as a teenager you are in the last stage of your life when you will be happy to hear that the phone is for you.' (Fran Lebowitz)

'My best feature's my smile. And smiles – pray heaven – don't get fat.' (Jack Nicholson)

'Life is a tragedy when seen in close-up but a comedy in long-shot.' (Charlie Chaplin)

'Happiness in life is good health and a bad memory.' (Ingrid Bergman)

'I do not believe that friends are necessarily the people you like best; they are merely the people who got there first.' (Sir Peter Ustinov)

'I did not become a vegetarian for my health. I did it for the health of the chickens.' (Isaac Bashevis Singer)

'At fifty everyone has the face he deserves.' (George Orwell)

'To his dog, every man is Napoleon, hence the constant popularity of dogs.' (Aldous Huxley)

'There are only two things a child will share willingly – communicable diseases and his mother's age.' (Benjamin Spock)

'You never really know a man until you have divorced him.' (Zsa Zsa Gabor)

'The worst part of having success is to try finding someone who is happy for you.' (Bette Midler)

'Whenever a friend succeeds, a little something in me dies.' (Gore Vidal)

'Punctuality is the virtue of the bored.' (Evelyn Waugh)

'That is the essence of science: ask an impertinent question, and you are on the way to a pertinent answer.' (Jacob Bronowski)

'When you sit with a nice girl for two hours, you think it's only a minute. But when you sit on a hot stove for a minute, you think it's two hours. That's relativity.' (Albert Einstein)

'I can take any amount of criticism, so long as it is unqualified praise.' (Noel Coward)

THE
OTHER
BOOK

FIRSTS

Orville Wright was involved in the **first** aircraft accident (his passenger was killed).

Thomas Jefferson grew the **first** tomatoes in the United States. He wanted to prove to Americans that they were not poisonous (which people believed them to be).

The **first** female guest host of *Saturday Night Live* was Candice Bergen.

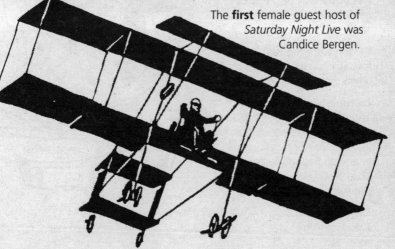

The **first** photograph of the moon was taken in 1839 (by Louis Daguerre).

The **first** electric Christmas lights were put together by a telephone switchboard installer. Candles were deemed to be too dangerous near a telephone switchboard so the installer took some lights from an old switchboard, connected them together, hooked them up to a battery and put them round a Christmas tree.

The **first** process of colour photography – using three colours – was patented (by William Morgan-Brown) in 1876.

Sunglasses **first** became popular in the 1920s when movie stars began wearing them to counteract the photographers' bright lights.

Pickled herrings were **first** eaten in the 14th century.

Jim Morrison of The Doors was the **first** rock star to be arrested on stage.

The world's **first** cash dispenser was opened by Reg Varney at Barclays Bank, Enfield, London in 1967.

Everton were the **first** British football club to introduce a stripe down the side of their shorts.

The **first** heart pacemaker (external) was fitted in 1952. The first *internal* pacemaker was fitted in 1958. The **first** successful heart operation had been carried out in 1896 by Louis Rehn in Frankfurt, Germany.

The duplicating machine was **first** patented by James Watt in 1780. The photocopier was invented in 1938 by Chester Carlson of New York.

Linoleum, the floor covering used in many kitchens, was **first** patented in 1863 by Frederick Walton of London.

The London Underground system was **first** used in 1863.

The typewriter was **first** patented by Henry Mill in 1714, but he never managed to market his invention.

The world's **first** scheduled passenger air service started in Florida in 1914.

The **first** toothbrush was invented in China in 1498.

The **first** supermarket in the world was in France.

In 1840 Henry Wadsworth Longfellow became the **first** American to have plumbing installed in his house.

Ties were **first** worn in Croatia (which is why they were called cravats, from *à la croate*).

The **first** British telephone directory was published by the London Telephone Company in 1880. It listed in excess of 250 names and numbers.

Lee Montague presented the **first** edition of *Jackanory* in 1964.

Sir Jimmy Savile presented the **first** edition of *Top Of The Pops* in 1964.

Jackie Rae presented the **first** edition of *The Golden Shot* in 1967.

The **first** word spoken by an ape in the movie *Planet of The Apes* was 'Smile'.

Sylvia Peters presented the **first** edition of *Come Dancing* in 1950.

Sir Alastair Burnet presented the **first** edition of *News At Ten* in 1967.

The **first** electric burglar alarm was installed in 1858 by one Edwin T. Holmes of Boston, Massachusetts. It is not recorded whether or not it worked.

Marilyn Monroe's **first** modelling agency had offices in the Ambassador Hotel – the same hotel in which Robert F. Kennedy was assassinated.

The **first** commercially successful escalator was patented in 1892 by Jesse Reno of New York.

Mark Knopfler wrote the **first** ever CD single ('Brothers In Arms').

The **first** ever organized Christmas Day swim in the freezing cold Serpentine in London's Hyde Park took place in 1864.

The **first** police force was established in Paris in 1667.

The **first** taxis with metered fares were operational in 1907.

The **first** British Christmas card showed people drinking and so the temperance societies tried to get it banned.

The **first** Harley Davidson motorcycle was built in 1903 and used a tomato can as a carburettor.

The **first** fax machine was patented in 1843, 33 years before Alexander Graham Bell demonstrated the telephone.

The **first** city in the world to have a population of over one million was London.

Construction workers' hard hats were **first** used in the building of the Hoover Dam in 1933.

The **first** episode of *Joanie Loves Chachi* was the highest-rated American programme in the history of Korean television. 'Chachi' is Korean for 'penis'.

Pitcairn Airlines was the **first** airline to provide sick bags (in 1922).

The **first** ever Royal Christmas broadcast was made by King George V on radio in 1932.

PEOPLE BORN ON SIGNIFICANT DAYS IN HISTORY

Fiona Phillips – the day the farthing coin ceased to be legal tender in the UK

Michael Imperioli – the day Colonel Jean-Bédel Bokassa took over the Central African Republic after a coup

Bridget Fonda – the day France and China announced their decision to establish diplomatic relations

Bonjour

Nicolas Cage – the day the Leyland Motor Company challenged the US blockade of Cuba by selling 450 buses to Cuba

Steven Soderbergh – the day George Wallace became Governor of Alabama

Aaliyah – the day the Shah of Iran fled the country

Dr Dre – the day The Gambia gained independence from the UK

Queen Latifah – the day Prince Sihanouk of Cambodia was deposed

Sarah Jessica Parker – the day Martin Luther King led civil rights activists on a march from Selma to Montgomery

Quentin Tarantino – the day Dr Beeching issued his report calling for huge cuts in Britain's rail network

Roger Black – the day the USSR launched Luna 10, which became the first spaceprobe to enter orbit around the moon

Uma Thurman – the day the US invaded Cambodia

Mike Myers – the day the Organization of African Unity was established

Heidi Klum – the day the Greek military junta overthrew the monarchy and proclaimed a republic

Alanis Morissette – the day there was an explosion at the Flixborough chemical plant

Anna Kournikova – the day Israel destroyed Iraq's nuclear reactor

Elizabeth Hurley – the day of the Battle of Dong Xoai in the Vietnam War

Joanne Harris – the day that President Johnson signed the Civil Rights Act into law

Lleyton Hewitt – the day that Jean Harris was convicted of murdering Dr Herman Tarnower, creator of the Scarsdale diet

Frank Finlay
– the day Gertrude
Ederle became the first
woman to swim the English Channel

Maria Von Trapp – the day the Cullinan Diamond was found

Hughie Green – the day Estonia was declared independent

John Grisham – the day Malenkov resigned in the USSR

Jean-Jacques Burnel – the day identity cards were abolished in Britain

Dame Kiri Te Kanawa – the day the US Air Force began daylight bombing raids on Berlin

Marti Pellow – the day an archbishop of Canterbury and a pope met for the first time in 400 years

Harold Robbins – the day British Summer Time began

Patsy Palmer – the day Thomas Cook was denationalized

Joe McGann – the day the first life peers were named

Christian Slater – the final day of Woodstock

Ken Norton – the day the atomic bomb was dropped on Nagasaki

José Feliciano – the day Vidkun Quisling was sentenced to death

Margaret Lockwood – the day the British army used tanks for the first time

Barnes Wallis – the day the gramophone was patented

Elie Wiesel – the day the discovery of penicillin was announced

Rick Parfitt – the day the first Morris Minor was produced

Dame Anita Roddick – the day the Battle of Alamein started

Spiro Agnew – the day the Kaiser abdicated

Peter Schmeichel – the day the Dartford Tunnel was opened

Calvin Klein – the day the Russians counterattacked at Stalingrad

Joe Walsh – the day Princess Elizabeth married Prince Philip

Jimi Hendrix – the day the French fleet was sunk at Toulon

Randy Newman – the day the Tehran Conference took place

Joanna Trollope – the day Tito formed a government in Yugoslavia

PEOPLE WHO WERE BORN/GREW UP IN POVERTY

Roman Abramovich, Michael Barrymore, Clara Bow, Kenneth Branagh, Robert Burns, Sir Michael Caine, Mariah Carey, Miguel de Cervantes, Coco Chanel, Ray Charles, Sir Arthur Conan Doyle, Billy Connolly, Joan Crawford, Kirk Douglas, Chris Eubank, Eusebio, Marty Feldman, Sir Tom Finney, Cary Grant, Alex Harvey, Susan Hayward, Jools Holland, Ken Hom, Harry Houdini, Jesse Jackson, Brian Kennedy, Nikita Khrushchev, Lennox Lewis, Sonny Liston, Harold Lloyd, Sophia Loren, John Lydon, Anna Magnani, Diego Maradona, Walter Matthau, Martine McCutcheon, Marilyn Monroe, Sir V.S. Naipaul, Makhaya Ntini, Dolly Parton, Pele, Sidney Poitier, Elvis Presley, Rene Russo, Gerhard Schröder, Maria Sharapova, Hilary Swank, Phil Taylor, Billy Bob Thornton, Mao Tse-tung, Shania Twain, Pancho Villa, Elisabeth Welch, Oprah Winfrey

PURE TRIVIA

Eskimos never gamble.

More than half the world's people have never made or received a telephone call.

The buzz generated by an electric razor in Britain is in the key of G. In America it is in the key of B flat.

Henry Ford never had a driving licence.

Popeye's friend Wimpy's full name is J. Wellington Wimpy.

Popeye's girlfriend Olive had a brother called Castor Oyl.

Tomato ketchup was once sold as a medicine.

Buenos Aires has more psychoanalysts per head than any other place in the world.

The original name of Pac-Man was going to be PUCK MAN, until executives saw the obvious potential for parody.

97 per cent of Canadians would not borrow a toothbrush if they forgot to pack their own.

The Snickers bar was named after a horse the Mars family owned.

Frank Baum got the name Oz in *The Wizard of Oz* from one of his alphabetized filing cabinets (O–Z).

Al Capone's older brother was a policeman in Nebraska.

There is enough lead in the average pencil to draw a line 35 miles long.

Humans have 46 chromosomes, peas have 14 and crayfish have 200.

***Dracula* is the most filmed story of all time. *Dr Jekyll and Mr Hyde* comes second and *Oliver Twist* third.**

Cabbage is 91 per cent water.

The straw was invented by Egyptian brewers to taste beer during brewing without disturbing the fermenting matter floating on the top.

Coca-Cola has a pH of 2.8.

65 per cent of Elvis impersonators are of Asian descent.

Donald Duck has a sister called Dumbella.

Oscars given out during World War Two were made of wood because metal was in short supply.

Siamese twins Chang and Eng Bunker once had a punch-up over alcohol.

George W. Bush was the 17th US state governor to become president.

Snow White's sister is called Rose Red.

Good Friday once fell on Boxing Day. (It was a horse named Good Friday and it fell in a race on 26 December 1899.)

PEOPLE AND THEIR FAVOURITE CHILDREN'S BOOK

Anthea Turner, Eamonn Holmes, Carol Smillie: *The Lion, The Witch And The Wardrobe*

Chris Evans: *Black Beauty*

Loyd Grossman: The Horatio Hornblower novels

Professor Stephen Hawking: *She*

Sir David Attenborough: *The Bird of Paradise*

Gary Oldman: *Gulliver's Travels*

Natalie Appleton: *Amelia Bedelia And The Surprise Shower*

Philippa Forrester: *The Talking Parcel*

Harold Pinter: *Ulysses*

V.I. Lenin: *Uncle Tom's Cabin*

Ian Rankin: *Fox in Socks*

Ed McBain: *The Cat In The Hat*

PLACES THAT HAVE BEEN CALLED THE VENICE OF THE NORTH

Hamburg

Stockholm

Amsterdam

Manchester

Bruges

Edinburgh

Amiens

St Petersburg

Birmingham

Giethoorn

Ottawa

PLACES THAT HAVE BEEN CALLED THE VENICE OF THE SOUTH

Fort Lauderdale

Mykonos

Zakynthos

Tarpon Springs

Sitangkai

Sète

PLACES THAT HAVE BEEN CALLED THE VENICE OF THE EAST

Bangkok

Udaipur

Alappuzha

Alleppey

Lijiang

Suzhou

Shan, Myanmar

Pii Mai

PLACES THAT HAVE BEEN CALLED THE VENICE OF THE WEST

Nantes

Galway

San Antonio, Texas

Seattle

ONLYS

John Laurie was the **only** member of the cast of *Dad's Army* to have served in the Home Guard.

The Ganges river in India has the **only** genuine freshwater sharks in the world.

Bill Clinton sent **only** two emails during his eight-year presidency. One was to John Glenn aboard the space shuttle, and the other was to test the email system.

Venus is the **only** planet that rotates clockwise.

Canada is the **only** country not to win a gold medal in the summer Olympic Games while hosting the event.

Madrid and Valletta are the **only** European capital cities that are not on a river.

The **only** living tissue in the human body that contains no blood vessels is the transparent cornea of the eye.

Salt is the **only** rock humans can eat.

Diane Keaton was the **only** cast member of the original production of *Hair* to refuse to take her clothes off.

Honey is the **only** food that doesn't spoil.

The Aleutian islands of Alaska are the **only** part of the United States invaded by the Japanese during World War Two.

The San Francisco cable cars are the **only** mobile national monuments in the US.

Texas is the **only** US state that permits residents to vote from space.

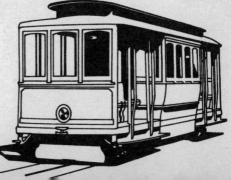

THE ONLY PEOPLE TO HAVE WON THE TONY AND THE OSCAR FOR THE SAME ROLE

José Ferrer for *Cyrano De Bergerac* (Tony: 1947/ Oscar: 1950)

Shirley Booth for *Come Back, Little Sheba* (1950/1953)

Yul Brynner for *The King And I* (1952/1956)

Rex Harrison for *My Fair Lady* (1957/1964)

Anne Bancroft for *The Miracle Worker* (1960/1962)

Paul Scofield for *A Man for All Seasons* (1962/1966)

Jack Albertson for *The Subject Was Roses* (1965/1968)

Joel Grey for *Cabaret* (1967/1973)

NB. Lila Kedrova did it the other way around. She won a 1964 Oscar for *Zorba the Greek*, and 20 years later won a Tony for the same role in *Zorba*.

THINGS INVENTED BY ITALIANS (AND NOT ALL OF THEM BY LEONARDO DA VINCI)

The parachute, the camera obscura, the piano, the pretzel, the radio, the espresso machine, spectacles, the mariner compass, the thermometer, the barometer, magnets, the telescope, the condom, scissors, the mechanical calculator, the pedometer, the wind vane, Fibonacci numbers, natural plastic, the ice cream cone

Everest firsts

First ascent: 29 May 1953 by Edmund Hillary and Tenzing Norgay.

First recorded deaths: 7 Sherpas in an avalanche in 1922.

First person to reach the summit twice: Nawang Gombu Sherpa on 20 May 1965.

First woman to reach the summit: Junko Tabei on 16 May 1975.

First ascent without bottled oxygen: Peter Habeler and Reinhold Messner on 8 May 1978.

First winter ascent: Krzysztof Wielicki on 17 February 1980.

First blind person to reach the summit: Erik Weihenmayer on 25 May 2001.

Cousins

Glenn Close & Brooke Shields

Cyrille Regis & John Regis

Imogen Stubbs & Alexander Armstrong

Brian Littrell & Kevin Richardson (both Backstreet Boys)

Andy Bell & Giant Haystacks

Alan Napier (Alfred in the *Batman* TV series) & Neville Chamberlain

Robert Aldrich & Nelson Rockefeller

Clive Allen & Paul Allen

Jack Cardiff & Kay Kendall

Russell Crowe & Martin Crowe

Olympia Dukakis & Michael Dukakis

Clive Dunn & Gretchen Franklin

Les Ferdinand & Rio Ferdinand

Joseph Fiennes & Sir Ranulph Fiennes

Ben Warriss & Jimmy Jewel

Tommy Lee Jones & Boxcar Willie

Mike Love & Brian Wilson

James Joyce & Adolphe Menjou

Michael Tilson Thomas & Paul Muni

Ramon Navarro & Dolores Del Rio

Bill Pertwee & Jon Pertwee

McLean Stevenson & Adlai Stevenson

Diane Ladd & Tennessee Williams

Marla Maples & Heather Locklear

Kate Robbins & Sir Paul McCartney

Dame Margaret Rutherford & Tony Benn

Gloria Vanderbilt & Beatrice Straight

Maryam D'Abo & Mike D'Abo

Sajd Mahmood & Amir Khan

PEOPLE WITH FAMOUS GODPARENTS

Crispian Mills (Hywel Bennett)

Anna Massey (John Ford)

Zak Starkey (Keith Moon)

Angelina Jolie (Maximilian Schell)

Skyler Shaye (Jon Voight)

Sheridan Morley (Alexander Wollcott)

Bryce Dallas Howard (Henry Winkler)

Patsy Kensit (Reggie Kray)

Juliet Mills (Vivien Leigh)

Bijou Phillips (Andy Warhol)

Phoebe Cates (Jacqueline Susann)

Henry Dent-Brocklehurst (Camilla, Duchess of Cornwall)

Joel Cadbury (Douglas Bader)

Scott Quinnell (Mervyn Davies)

Daniel Massey (Sir Noel Coward)

Chris Cowdrey (Peter May)

Kara Noble (Shelley Winters)

Sean Lennon (Sir Elton John)

Santa Palmer-Tomkinson
(Prince Charles)

Nicole Richie (Michael Jackson)

Amber Tamblyn (Dean Stockwell)

Jake Gyllenhaal (Jamie Lee Curtis)

PEOPLE WITH FAMOUS ANCESTORS

Issy Van Rendwick – William of Orange

Sir John Gielgud – Ellen Terry

Matthew Fleming – Ian Fleming

Queen Sofia of Spain – Queen Victoria

Joanna Trollope – Anthony Trollope

Jason Patric – Jackie Gleason (grandfather)

Pat Boone – Daniel Boone

Nelson Eddy – President Martin Van Buren

Sophie Dahl (Roald Dahl & Stanley Holloway – her grandfathers)

Holly Valance and Benny Hill are related: Benny was Holly's grandfather's cousin

Al Murray's great-great-great-great-grandfather was William Makepeace Thackeray

Christopher Plummer is the great-grandson of former Canadian Prime Minister Sir John Abbott

Jodie Kidd's great-grandfather was the first Lord Beaverbrook

Adam Hart-Davis's great-great-great-grandfather was King William IV

Wayne Rooney – Bob Fitzsimmons

John Kerry – King Henry III

Wayne Newton – Pocahontas

PEOPLE AND WHAT THEIR FATHERS DID FOR A LIVING

Sean Penn (Film director – but was out of work after being blacklisted as a Communist)

Amanda Burton (Headmaster)

Colin Farrell (Stockbroker)

Anna Kournikova (Wrestler)

Hugh Grant (Carpet salesman)

Ben Affleck (Social worker)

Damon Albarn (Art school lecturer)

Christian Bale (Airline pilot)

Ioan Gruffudd (Teacher)

Nicky Campbell (Map publisher)

Ryan Giggs (Rugby League professional)

Julia Ormond (Software designer)

Gareth Gates (Postman)

Sacha Baron Cohen (Menswear shop owner)

Jennifer Lopez (Computer specialist at Guardian Insurance in NYC)

Leonardo DiCaprio (Comic book dealer)

Teri Hatcher (Nuclear physicist)

Tom Cruise (Electrical engineer)

Peter Bowles (Chauffeur)

Francesca Annis (Banker)

John Cleese (Insurance salesman)

Vanessa Feltz (Knicker manufacturer)

Anthony Andrews (BBC musical arranger)

Freddie Starr (Carpenter)

Greta Scacchi (Artist)

Mike Read (Publican)

Lord Andrew Lloyd Webber (Organist)

Dame Elizabeth Taylor (Art dealer)

Neil Young (Journalist)

Bob Geldof (Commercial traveller)

Morrissey (Hospital porter)

Mark Knopfler (Architect)

Paul Daniels (Cinema projectionist)

Simon Le Bon (Foreign Office civil servant)

Rik Mayall (Teacher)

Will Smith (Refrigeration engineer)

Oliver Stone (Stockbroker)

Peter Stringfellow (Steelworker)

Michael Jackson (Crane driver)

Ruby Wax (Sausage-skin manufacturer)

Fiona Bruce (Managing director of Unilever)

Julia Somerville (Senior civil servant at GCHQ)

Gloria Estefan (Soldier in dictator Batista's bodyguard)

Keith Allen (Navy submariner)

J.K. Rowling (Engineer)

Delia Smith (Printer)

Jon Bon Jovi (Hairdresser)

Brendan Fraser (Tourism executive)

Leslie Nielsen (Royal Canadian Mountie)

Richard Briers (Bookmaker)

Dan Brown (Maths Professor)

Andrew Flintoff (Plumber)

PEOPLE WHOSE FATHERS WERE POLICEMEN

Siân Phillips, Adam Woodyatt, Paul Nicholls, Darren Day, Hywel Bennett, Ilie Nastase, Kevin Lloyd, Gordon Sherry, David May, Jacques Santer, Liz Robertson, Simon Gregson, Lord George Robertson, Fred MacAulay, Alice Faye, Pam Ferris, Christian Gross, Nicola Stephenson, Screaming Lord Sutch

PEOPLE WHOSE FATHERS WERE CLERGYMEN

John Motson, Virginia Wade, Lord David Steel, Pearl Bailey, Ingmar Bergman, Hugh Dennis, Erskine Caldwell, Alistair Cooke, George McGovern, Walter Mondale, Agnes Moorehead, Dean Rusk, Albert Schweitzer, Anna Richardson, Me-One, Jonathan Edwards, D'Angelo, David Tennant

PEOPLE WHOSE FATHERS WERE RABBIS

Lord Victor Mishcon, Mickey Duff, Josh Salzmann, Isaac Bashevis Singer, Michael Fabricant

PEOPLE WHOSE FATHERS WERE PROFESSIONAL FOOTBALLERS

Jason Weaver, Donald Houston, Robin Cousins, Gil Scott-Heron, Ian McShane, Colin Farrell, Steve Harley, Jimmy Nail, Les Dennis

PEOPLE WHOSE FATHERS WERE MPS

Baroness Sarah Hogg, Jeremy Thorpe, Baroness Ann Mallalieu (and her grandfather too)

PEOPLE WHOSE FATHERS WERE DOCTORS

Lisa Kudrow, Reese Witherspoon, Frances Edmonds,
Baroness Tessa Jowell, Sister Wendy Beckett, Sandra
Bernhard, John Dunlop, Mary Killen, Adnan Khashoggi,
Paul Bradley, Fred Zinnemann, M. Night Shyamalan

PEOPLE WHOSE FATHERS WERE BOXERS

Freddie Starr, Bruce Oldfield, Wayne Rooney, Rudy Giuliani, Jennifer
Capriati, Frank Sinatra, Steve Jones, Mikey Graham, Andre Agassi,
Paul Weller, Brian Glover, Craig Raine

BROUGHT UP BY A SINGLE PARENT

**Mick Hucknall, Barry Manilow,
Clive James, Susan Hampshire,
Billy Connolly, Fay Weldon,
Keanu Reeves, Drew
Barrymore, Dina Carroll,
Ulrika Jonsson,
Michael Crawford,
Jamie Bell,
Catherine Tate**

PEOPLE WITH TWIN BROTHERS/SISTERS

Scarlett Johansson (Hunter)

Gisele Bundchen (Patricia)

Plum Sykes (Lucy)

Ashton Kutcher (Michael)

Simon Cowell (Nicholas)

Janel Moloney (Carey)

Felipe Contepomi (Manuel)

Aaron Carter (Angel)

Steve Waugh (Mark)

Richard Hills (Michael)

Phil Neville (Tracey)

Jason Orange (Justin)

Finlay Calder (Jim)

Angela Eagle (Mark)

Shayne Ward (Emma)

Mario Andreth (Aldo)

Curtis Strange (Allen)

GIRLS WHO EMANCIPATED THEMSELVES FROM THEIR PARENTS

Bijou Phillips (at 14)

Alicia Silverstone (at 15. When she was a child, her overactive imagination led her to claim that her parents were aliens and that her mother, an airline stewardess, was Olivia Newton-John)

Michelle Williams (at 16)

Skyler Shaye (at 15)

Juliette Lewis (at 14)

PEOPLE WITH FAMOUS FATHERS

Helen Storey (David Storey)

Lucy Briers (Richard Briers)

Sophie Ward (Simon Ward)

Damon Hill (Graham Hill)

Abigail McKern (Leo McKern)

Jason Connery (Sean Connery)

Kiefer Sutherland (Donald Sutherland)

Julian Lennon (John Lennon)

Stella McCartney (Sir Paul McCartney)

Jacques Villeneuve (Gilles Villeneuve)

Kim Wilde (Marty Wilde)

Andrea Boardman (Stan Boardman)

Suzanne Charlton (Sir Bobby Charlton)

Kirsty MacColl (Ewan MacColl)

Julia Sawalha (Nadim Sawalha)

Linus Roache (William Roache)

Paula Yates (Hughie Green)

Liza Tarbuck (Jimmy Tarbuck)

Hannah Waterman (Dennis Waterman)

Jack Ryder (Jack Hues)

Bijou Phillips (John Phillips)

Kate Beckinsale (Richard Beckinsale)

WOMEN WHOSE FAMOUS MOTHERS HAVE A DIFFERENT SURNAME

Rudi Davies (Beryl Bainbridge)

Beatie Edney (Sylvia Syms)

Susannah Harker (Polly Adams)

Finty Williams (Dame Judi Dench)

Wynonna (Naomi Judd)

Keira Knightley (Sharman Macdonald)

PARENTS OF TWINS

Julia Roberts, Oliver Letwin, Dougray Scott, Geena Davis (at age 47), Dickie Davies, Madeleine Albright, Nigel Spackman, David Batty, Willie Thorne, Corbin Bernsen, David Coleman, Roy Boulting (himself a twin), Chris Cowdrey, Charles Moore, Ronald Searle, Desmond Wilcox, Fred Winter, Lou Diamond Phillips, Michael Aspel, Dr Hilary Jones, Jayne Irving, Lord Geoffrey Howe, Ed Asner, Henry Mancini, Rick Nelson, Meredith Baxter-Birney, Jim Brown, Andy Gibb (himself the brother of twins), Susan Hayward, Loretta Lynn, Otto Preminger, Nelson Rockefeller, Alice Beer, Graham Cowdrey, Rip Torn, Gabby Logan, Tilda Swinton, John Hannah, Sheila Ferguson, Holly Hunter (at age 47), Cheryl Tiegs (at age 52), Vic Reeves, John Terry, Marcia Gay Harden

GRANDPARENTS OF TWINS

Sir Alex Ferguson, Tammy Wynette, Tony Britton, Frances Shand-Kydd, George Bush, Arthur Scargill, Richard Stilgoe, Lady Antonia Fraser, Lord Michael Heseltine, Lord Colin Cowdrey

FAMOUS PEOPLE WHO WERE BORN 'ILLEGITIMATE'

T.E. Lawrence, William the Conqueror, Richard Wagner, Sophia Loren, Willy Brandt, Sir Alec Guinness, Sarah Bernhardt, Leonardo da Vinci, Demi Moore, Macaulay Culkin, Ella Fitzgerald, Oprah Winfrey, Ryan Giggs, Naomi Campbell, Coco Chanel, Dame Catherine Cookson, Sir Cyril Smith, Ruud Gullit, Samantha Janus, Fidel Castro, Franco Zeffirelli, The Duchess of Windsor, Tony O'Reilly, Marilyn Monroe, Eric Clapton, Bruce Oldfield, Gary Glitter, Billie Holiday, Mike Tyson, Saddam Hussein, Paul Cézanne, Jesse Jackson, Maria Montessori, August Strindberg, Juan Perón, Sadie Frost

PEOPLE WHO NEVER KNEW THEIR FATHERS

Kerry Katona, Kelly Holmes, David Blaine, Denise Lewis, Alan Milburn, Charlene Tilton, Gary Glitter, Gregor Fisher, Rodney Bickerstaffe, Shaun Scott, Prince Michael of Kent, Natalia Makarova, Lee Trevino, Rod Steiger, Marilyn Monroe, Gerhard Schröder, Peter Ackroyd, Fidel Edwards, Riddick Bowe, Sir Alec Guinness, Lee Harvey Oswald, Pat Barker, Lord Byron

PEOPLE WHO NEVER KNEW THEIR MOTHERS

Sir Laurence Olivier, Helen Suzman, Eric Sykes

PEOPLE WITH A GERMAN PARENT

Eric Bana (Mother)

Leonardo DiCaprio (Mother)

Dennis Franz (Father)

PEOPLE WITH A FRENCH PARENT

Joanne Harris (Mother)

John Hegley (Father – half-French)

Melanie Blatt (Mother)

Claire Tomalin (Father)

Davina McCall (Mother)

Alison Moyet (Father)

Brian Capron (Father)

Sir James Goldsmith (Mother)

Peter De Savary (Father)

Mary Pierce (Mother)

Kevin Maxwell (Mother)

Raymond 'Teasy-Weasy' Bessone (Mother)

Melissa Bell (Mother)

Irene Handl (Mother)

Francesca Annis (Mother – half-French)

Jane Lapotaire (Mother – half-French)

Jodie Foster (Mother)

Cardinal Basil Hume (Mother)

Claire Trevor (Father)

PEOPLE AND THE SUBJECTS THEY STUDIED AT UNIVERSITY

J.K. Rowling – French and Classics

Mira Sorvino – East Asian Studies

Robin Williams – Political Science

Martin Short – Social Work

Thandie Newton – Anthropology

Alistair McGowan – English

Cate Blanchett – Economics and Fine Arts

John Cleese – Law

Richard Blackwood – Business Studies

Glenn Close – Anthropology

Hugh Grant – English

Brian May – Physics

Sanjeev Bhaskar – Marketing

Lucy Liu – Asian Languages and Culture

Brooke Shields – French

Hugh Bonneville – Theology

Rory Bremner – French and German

Brad Pitt – Journalism

Rowan Atkinson – Electrical Engineering

Paul Simon – English

Chris Lowe – Architecture

Jonathan Ross – East European Modern History

Donald Fagen – English

Victoria Principal – Law

Harry Enfield – Politics

Cindy Crawford – Chemical Engineering (on a full scholarship)

Lisa Kudrow – Sociobiology (originally wanted to be a doctor like her father, a headache expert)

NUMBERS

Multiply 37,037 by any single number (1–9), then multiply that number by 3. Every digit in the answer will be the same as that first single number.

In the US, a centillion is the number 1 followed by 300 zeros. In Britain it has 600 zeros.

The number 17 is considered unlucky in Italy.

There are 318,979,564,000 possible combinations of the first four moves in chess.

One year contains 31,557,600 seconds.

'Eleven plus two' is an anagram of 'Twelve plus one'.

Any number squared is equal to 4 (2 squared) more than the product of the numbers two either side of it:
5 squared is 25 (3 x 7 is 21)
8 squared is 64 (6 x 10 is 60)

Any number squared is equal to 9 (3 squared) more than the product of the numbers three either side of it:
5 squared is 25 (2 x 8 is 16)
8 squared is 64 (5 x 11 is 55), and so on.

HISTORY

People didn't always say hello when they answered the phone. When the first regular phone service was established in 1878 in the US, people said 'Ahoy'.

Of the 266 men who have been Pope, 33 have died violently.

In 18th-century Britain, you could take out insurance against going to hell.

In 1915, William Wrigley Jr sent chewing gum to everyone in the phone book.

Olive oil was once used for washing the body in Mediterranean countries.

Bagpipes were invented in Iran, then brought to Scotland by the Romans.

Ahoy!

The world's youngest parents were eight and nine, and lived in China in 1910.

In England in the 17th century, married women had, on average, 13 children.

India was the richest country in the world until the time of British invasion in the early 17th century.

The passion fruit was named by Spanish missionaries to whom the plant suggested the nails and thorns of Christ's suffering (or Passion) at the crucifixion.

Charles Dickens earned as much for his lectures as he did for his twenty novels.

In medieval Japan, it was fashionable for women to have black teeth.

When the *Mayflower* was no longer needed, it was taken apart and rebuilt as a barn.

Russia's Peter the Great taxed men who wore a beard.

In the 19th century, in an attempt to debunk the myth that Friday was an unlucky day for mariners, the British Navy named a new ship HMS *Friday*, found a Captain Friday to command it, and sent it to sea on a Friday. Neither ship nor crew were heard of again.

Apollo 11 had 20 seconds of fuel left when it landed.

In 18th-century English gambling dens, there was an employee whose only job it was to swallow the dice in the event of a police raid.

The formal name for the Pony Express was the Central Overland California & Pike's Peak Express Company.

In 1930, Grace Robin, a model, demonstrated contact lenses for the first time.

The streets of ancient Mesopotamia were literally knee deep in rubbish, since there was no effective way of getting rid of it.

In ancient Egypt, noblewomen were given a few days to ripen after death in order not to provide temptation for the embalmers.

George Washington's false teeth were carved from hippopotamus ivory and cow's teeth and fixed together with metal springs.

In ancient Rome, a crooked nose was considered to indicate leadership potential.

The gold earrings many sailors wore were to pay for a decent burial on their death.

St Patrick, the patron saint of Ireland, was not Irish.

The world's oldest active parliamentary body is the Icelandic Althing, which met first before the year 1000.

The Chinese used fingerprints as a method of identification as far back as AD700.

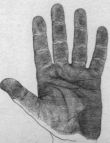

ALL THE UN SECRETARY-GENERALS SINCE ITS FORMATION

Trygve Lie (Norway) 1946–53

Dag Hammarskjöld (Sweden) 1953–61

U Thant (Burma) 1962–71

Kurt Waldheim (Austria) 1972–81

Javier Pérez de Cuéllar (Peru) 1982–91

Boutros Boutros-Ghali (Egypt) 1992–96

Kofi Annan (Ghana) 1997–2006

Ban Ki-moon (South Korea) 2007–

BIRDS ETC.

Pigeons can fly 600 miles in a day.

Flamingos get their colour from their food, tiny green algae which turn pink during digestion.

There are giant bats in Indonesia with a wingspan of nearly 1.8 metres (6 feet).

The common little brown bat of North America is, for its size, the world's longest-lived mammal. It can live to the age of 32.

Percentage of bird species that are monogamous: 90. Percentage of mammal species that are monogamous: 3.

Baby robins eat 4.25 metres (14 feet) of earthworms per day.

A duck has three eyelids.

Chickens, ducks and ostriches are eaten before they're born and after they're dead.

A robin's egg is blue, but if you put it in vinegar it turns yellow after 30 days.

Penguins have sex twice a year.

Big Ben lost five minutes one day when a flock of starlings perched on the minute hand.

Crows have the biggest brains of any bird, relative to body size.

Birds need gravity in order to swallow.

A parrot's beak can exert a force of 350 pounds per square inch as it snaps shut.

Many species of bird mate on the wing. They fly high and then mate on the descent.

Chickens that lay brown eggs have red ear lobes.

White cockatoos can be sexed by eye colour. The males have black irises and an invisible pupil; the females have a paler iris with a visible pupil.

The ostrich yolk is the largest single cell in the world.

To keep cool, ostriches urinate on their legs.

The Pallid Bat has immunity
to the poison of the scorpions upon which it feeds.

Some birds have eyes that weigh more than their brains.

Frog-eating bats find and identify edible frogs by listening to the mating calls. Frogs counter this by hiding and using short calls that are hard to locate.

Fishing bats use echolocation so well they can detect a hair's breadth of minnow fin above a pond surface.

Vampire bats adopt orphans and have been known to risk their lives to share food with less fortunate roost-mates.

BIRD NAMES

Jackass Penguin, Wandering Albatross, Red-faced Shag, Blue-footed Booby, Intermediate Egret, Short-toed Lark, Ovenbird, Solitary Sandpiper, Least Bittern, Adjutant Stork, Sacred Ibis, Horned Screamer, Smew, Killdeer, Turnstone, Beach Thick-knee, Laughing Gull, Fairy Tern, Masked Lovebird, Roadrunner, Screech Owl, Large Frogmouth, Chimney Swift, Train-bearing Hermit, Turquoise-browed Motmot, Toco Toucan, Barred Woodcreeper, Spotted Antbird, Cock-of-the-Rock, Ornate Umbrellabird, Vermilion Flycatcher, Reddish Plantcutter, Superb Lyrebird, Racquet-tailed Drongo, Crestless Gardener, Satin Bowerbird, Magnificent Riflebird, Spotted Creeper, Striped Jungle Babbler, Fairy Bluebird, Noisy Friarbird, Bananaquit, Painted Bunting, Social Weaver, Red-legged Honeycreeper, Junglefowl, Northern Shoveler, Wrinkled Hornbill, Blue-bearded Bee-eater, Dollarbird, Edible-nest Swiftlet, Buffy Fish Owl, Little Stint, Changeable Hawk Eagle, Straw-headed Bulbul, Spectacled Spiderhunter

PEOPLE WHO FAILED THE 11-PLUS

Sir Michael Gambon, Paul Merton, Delia Smith, David Essex ('on purpose because the secondary modern was a great sports school'), Zandra Rhodes, Alan Titchmarsh, Barbara Dickson, Susan Penhaligon, Bruce Robinson, Sue Townsend, Dame Anita Roddick, John Sullivan, Sir Bernard Ingham, Ken Livingstone, Brian Clough, Sir Alan Walters, Geoffrey Boycott, Ann Widdecombe (after getting whooping cough with complications), Magnus Mills, Elaine Paige, Sir Alan Sugar, Phil Redmond, Paula Hamilton, Colin Firth, Philip Gould, Martin McGuinness, Kay Mellor, John Prescott, Robert Lindsay, Trevor Baylis, Charles Dance, Chris Boardman, Robert Kilroy-Silk, Max Clifford, Carla Lane, Daniel Craig, Nigella Lawson (she refused to take a maths paper: 'I put my hand up, gave it back and said, "I'm sorry, I don't do this".')

GENUINE SIMILES TAKEN FROM GENUINE GCSE ENGLISH ESSAYS

The plan was simple, like my brother Phil. But unlike Phil, this plan just might work.

The little boat gently drifted across the pond exactly the way a bowling ball wouldn't.

His thoughts tumbled in his head, making and breaking alliances like underpants in a tumble dryer.

The young fighter had a hungry look, the kind you get from not eating for a while.

Her hair glistened in the rain like nose hair after a sneeze.

Her eyes were like two brown circles with big black dots in the centre.

Her vocabulary was as bad as, like, whatever.

He was as tall as a six-foot-three-inch tree.

Long separated by cruel fate, the star-crossed lovers raced across the grassy field towards each other like two freight trains, one having left York at 6.36 p.m. travelling at 55mph, the other from Peterborough at 4.19 p.m. at a speed of 35mph.

She had a deep, throaty, genuine laugh, like that sound a dog makes just before it throws up.

John and Mary had never met. They were like two hummingbirds who had also never met.

The thunder was ominous-sounding, much like the sound of a thin sheet of metal being shaken backstage during the storm scene in a play.

The red brick wall was the colour of a brick-red crayon.

The door had been forced, as forced as the dialogue during the interview portion of *Family Fortunes*.

Shots rang out, as shots are wont to do.

Her artistic sense was exquisitely refined, like someone who can tell butter from 'I Can't Believe It's Not Butter'.

The politician was gone but unnoticed, like the full stop after the Dr on a Dr Pepper can.

The knife was as sharp as the tone used by Glenda Jackson MP in her first several points of parliamentary procedure made to Robin Cook MP, Leader of the House of Commons, in the House Judiciary Committee hearings on the suspension of Keith Vaz MP.

The ballerina rose gracefully *en pointe* and extended one slender leg behind her, like a dog at a lamppost.

The revelation that his marriage of 30 years had disintegrated because of his wife's infidelity came as a rude shock, like a surcharge at a formerly surcharge-free cashpoint.

It was a working class tradition, like fathers chasing kids around with their power tools.

He was deeply in love. When she spoke, he thought he heard bells, as if she were a dustcart reversing.

She was as easy as the *Daily Star* crossword.

 She grew on him like she was a colony of E. coli and he was room-temperature British beef.

She walked into my office like a centipede with 98 missing legs.

Her voice had that tense, grating quality, like a first-generation thermal paper fax machine that needed a band tightened.

It hurt the way your tongue hurts after you accidentally staple it to the wall.

HEAD BOYS AT SCHOOL

Henry Olonga, Stephen Leahy, Terry Waite,
Liam Neeson, Lord John Taylor, Tim Pigott-
Smith, Chris Woodhead, Michael Grade,
Edward Stourton, Chris Barrie

HEAD GIRLS AT SCHOOL

**Clare Balding, Victoria Smurfit, Jennifer James, Chief
Constable Pauline Clare, Selina Scott, Glenys Kinnock,
Marcelle d'Argy Smith**

DEPUTY HEAD BOYS

Phil Neville, Jack Straw,
Dudley Moore, Euan Blair

DEPUTY HEAD GIRLS

**Santa Palmer-Tomkinson, Antonia Okonma,
Coleen McLoughlin (Wayne Rooney's
girlfriend)**

GENUINE THINGS WRITTEN BY SCHOOL STUDENTS IN HISTORY ESSAYS

In midevil times most people were alliterate.

The greatest writer of the Renaissance was William Shakespeare. He was born in the year 1564, supposedly on his birthday. He never made much money and is famous only because of his plays. He wrote tragedies, comedies and hysterectomies, all in Islamic pentameter. Romeo and Juliet are an example of a heroic couplet. Romeo's last wish was to be laid by Juliet.

The Bible is full of interesting caricatures. In the first book of the Bible, Guinessis, Adam and Eve were created from an apple tree. One of their children, Cain, asked, 'Am I my brother's son?'

A myth is a female moth

Johann Bach wrote a great many musical compositions and had a large number of children. In between he practised on an old spinster which he kept up in his attic. Bach died from 1750 to the present. Bach was the most famous composer in the world and so was Handel. Handel was half German, half Italian and half English. He was very large.

The Greeks were a highly sculptured people, and without them we wouldn't have history. The Greeks also had myths. A myth is a female moth.

The sun never set on the British Empire because the British Empire is in the East and the sun sets in the West. Queen Victoria was the longest queen. She sat on a thorn for 63 years. She was a moral woman who practised virtue. Her death was the final event which ended her reign.

The nineteenth century was a time of a great many thoughts and inventions. People stopped reproducing by hand and started reproducing by machine. The

invention of the steamboat caused a network of rivers to spring up. Cyrus McCormick invented the McCormick raper, which did the work of a hundred men. Louis Pasteur discovered a cure for rabbis. Charles Darwin was a naturalist who wrote the Organ of the Species. Madman Curie discovered radio. And Karl Marx became one of the Marx brothers.

The French Revolution was accomplished before it happened and catapulted into Napoleon. Napoleon wanted an heir to inherit his power, but since Josephine was a baroness, she couldn't have any children.

Beethoven wrote music even though he was deaf. He was so deaf he wrote loud music. He took long walks in the forest even when everyone was calling for him. Beethoven expired in 1827 and later died for this.

GENUINE ANSWERS GIVEN BY SCHOOL STUDENTS IN SCIENCE TESTS

H2O is hot water, and CO2 is cold water.

To collect fumes of sulphur, hold a deacon over a flame in a test tube.

Blood flows down one leg and up the other.

Water is composed of two gins, Oxygin and Hydrogin. Oxygin is pure gin. Hydrogin is gin and water.

A fossil is an extinct animal. The older it is, the more extinct it is.

The moon is a planet just like the earth, only it is even deader.

Three kinds of blood vessels are arteries, vanes and caterpillars.

Respiration is composed of two acts, first inspiration, then expectoration.

Artificial insemination is when the farmer does it to the cow instead of the bull.

Mushrooms always grow in damp places and so they look like umbrellas.

The skeleton is what is left after the insides have been taken out and the outsides have been taken off. The purpose of the skeleton is something to hitch meat to.

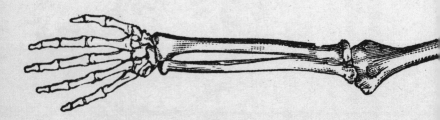

A supersaturated solution is one that holds more than it can hold.

Before giving a blood transfusion, find out if the blood is affirmative or negative.

A permanent set of teeth consists of eight canines, eight cuspids, two molars and eight cuspidors.

The tides are a fight between the earth and moon. All water tends towards the moon, because there is no water in the moon, and nature abhors a vacuum. I forget where the sun joins in this fight.

Many women believe that an alcoholic binge will have no ill effects on the unborn fetus, but that is a large misconception.

Germinate: To become a naturalized German.

Momentum: What you give a person when they are going away.

To remove dust from the eye, pull the eye down over the nose.

To prevent contraception, wear a condominium.

To keep milk from turning sour, keep it in the cow.

Redd Foxx was

PEOPLE WHO WERE EXPELLED FROM SCHOOL

Jeff Stryker (for 'standing up for a retard')

Chevy Chase (from Haverford College for taking a cow on to the third floor of a campus building)

Adam Clayton (from a boarding school)

Alain Delon (from many schools)

expelled on the first day for throwing a book at the teacher

Russell Brand (from Italia Conti because he was 'always in corridors with girls')

Brandon Lee (for misbehaving)

Shane MacGowan (from Westminster for using drugs)

Kris Marshall (from Wells Cathedral School for 'a multitude of sins')

Rudolph Valentino (from many schools)

Harvey Keitel (for repeated truancy)

John Lydon (from a Catholic comprehensive near Pentonville prison)

Monty Don (from primary school 'for putting nettles down girls' knickers and getting more black marks in one term than anyone else in their entire school career')

GENUINE NOTES SENT BY PARENTS TO SCHOOL TO EXPLAIN THEIR CHILDREN'S ABSENCE

My daughter wouldn't come to school on Monday because she was tired. She spent the weekend with some Marines.

Dear school: Please exkuse John for being absent on January 28, 29, 30, 31, 32 and 33.

I kept Billie home to do Christmas shopping because I didn't know what size she wears.

Lillie was absent from school yesterday as she had a gang over.

Please excuse Johnnie for being. It was his father's fault.

Please excuse Sara for being absent. She was sick and I had her shot.

Please excuse Joey on Friday; he had loose vowels.

PEOPLE WHO WERE FAT AS CHILDREN

Brian McFadden

Gary Turner

Kate Winslet (her childhood nickname was Blubber)

Meat Loaf (weighed more when he was ten than he does now)

John Malkovich (lost several stones in just a couple of months by only eating Jell-O)

Bob Monkhouse

Martyn Lewis

Kathy Burke

Sandy Lyle (his nickname was 'Podge')

Lucy Pargeter

Maxine Carr

Silent film star Roscoe 'Fatty' Arbuckle weighed 16 pounds at birth

PEOPLE WHO APPEARED IN ADVERTISEMENTS AS CHILDREN

Reese Witherspoon (appeared in a TV commercial when she was seven for a local Nashville florist)

Martine McCutcheon (Kool Aid and Pears Soap)

Lindsay Lohan (Pizza Hut, The Gap, Wendy's, Jell-O)

PEJORATIVE FRUITS

Fruit – an old-time homosexual

Gooseberry – a third party on a date

Plum – person prone to mistakes

Prune – an elderly person

Turnip – an idiot

Lemon – a naive person

Nut – psychopath

Grapes – haemorrhoids

Limey – US slang for the English

Fig – an inconsequential person

Catchphrases

'Hello, my darlings' (Charlie Drake)

'Just like that' (Tommy Cooper)

'Nick nick' (Jim Davidson)

'I thank *you*' (Arthur Askey – also 'Hello, playmates')

'I'm in charge' (Bruce Forsyth + many more including 'Nice to see you … ')

'It's the way you tell 'em' (Frank Carson)

'May your God go with you' (Dave Allen)

'Not a lot' (Paul Daniels)

'Awight?' (Michael Barrymore)

'Chase me' (Duncan Norvelle)

'Can you 'ear me, mother?' (Sandy Powell)

'You lucky people' (Tommy Trinder)

'Well, please yourselves' (Frankie Howerd)

'Aye, aye, that's your lot' (Jimmy Wheeler)

'Wotcher, cocks' (Leon Cortez)

'Can we talk?' (Joan Rivers)

'What a performance' (Sid Field)

'I'm the only gay in the village' (Matt Lucas as Dafydd in *Little Britain*)

'Lovely jubbly' (David Jason as Del Boy in *Only Fools And Horses*)

'Yeah, but no, but yeah but' (Matt Lucas as Vicky Pollard in *Little Britain*)

'Suits you, sir' (*The Fast Show*)

'Shut that door' (Larry Grayson)

'I don't believe it!' (Richard Wilson as Victor Meldrew in *One Foot In The Grave*)

'I have a cunning plan … ' (Tony Robinson as Baldrick in *Blackadder*)

'Well, here's another fine mess you've got me into' (Oliver Hardy to Stan Laurel)

'I'm a laydee' (David Walliams as Emily Howard in *Little Britain*)

'Stupid boy' (Arthur Lowe as Captain Mainwaring in *Dad's Army*)

'I'm free!' (John Inman as Mr Humphreys in *Are You Being Served?*)

'Back of the net' (Steve Coogan as Alan Partridge)

'Ooh, Betty!' (Michael Crawford as Frank Spencer in *Some Mothers Do Ave 'Em*)

'Is it coz I is black?' (Sacha Baron Cohen as Ali G)

'Yeah baby!' (Mike Myers as Austin Powers)

'You wouldn't let it lie!' (Vic Reeves)

PEOPLE WHO DID VSO

Michael Brunson, Jeremy Corbyn, Anton Lesser, David Essex (as an ambassador), Lord Bradford, Brian Hanrahan, Jon Snow, Robert Lacey, Robin Denselow

ACHIEVEMENTS AFTER THE AGE OF 80

At the age of 80, George Burns won an Oscar for his role in *The Sunshine Boys*. He died at the age of 100, having retired from live performing only three years before.

At the age of 82, Sir Winston Churchill published part one of his four-part *History Of The English Speaking Peoples*.

At the age of 84, William Gladstone was Prime Minister of Britain.

At the age of 84, W. Somerset Maugham published a collection of essays entitled *Points Of View*.

At the age of 85, Mae West starred in the film *Sextet*.

At the age of 87, Francis Rous was awarded the 1966 Nobel Prize for Medicine.

At the age of 87, Sir John Gielgud starred in the film *Prospero's Books*.

At the age of 88, Michelangelo was still sculpting.

At the age of 91, Eamon de Valera was President of Ireland.

At the age of 95, the American pianist Artur Rubinstein gave a public concert.

At the age of 95, Sir John Mills appeared in the film *Bright Young Things*.

PEOPLE WHO PUBLISHED THEIR DIARIES

Evelyn Waugh, Tony Benn, Sir Antony Sher, Sir Roger Moore, Piers Morgan, Andy Warhol, Richard Crossman, Will Carling, Barbara Castle, Sir Peter Hall, Vaslav Nijinsky, Robert Kilroy-Silk, Jeffrey Archer, Alan Clark, Claudio Ranieri, Brian Eno, Che Guevara, Samuel Pepys, Ian Hunter, Sir Alec Guinness, Anaïs Nin

ANIMALS ETC.

Sheep will not drink from running water.

Cows can smell odours six miles away.

A lion's muzzle is unique – no two lions have the same pattern of whiskers.

A Holstein's spots are unique – no two cows have the same pattern of spots.

Deer can't eat hay.

Montana mountain goats can butt heads so hard that their hooves fall off.

Cats can hear ultrasound.

The New Mexican whiptail lizard reproduces asexually, laying eggs that are clones of the mother. A courtship ritual is required between two female lizards in order to encourage the release of the eggs.

Giant pandas can eat 38 kilograms (83 pounds) of bamboo a day.

The underside of a horse's hoof is called a frog. The frog peels off several times a year with new growth.

You can tell a turtle's gender by the noise it makes: males grunt, females hiss.

The ferret was domesticated 500 years before the cat. The female ferret is a 'jill'.

Reindeer like bananas.

A rat would rather have a boiled sweet than some cheese.

Squirrels can't see red.

The tuatara lizard of New Zealand has three eyes – two that are positioned normally and an extra one on top of its head.

The woolly mammoth had tusks almost 5 metres (16 feet) long.

The sitatunga antelope is amphibious. Its water-adapted hooves are awkward on dry land.

A laboratory mouse runs 5 miles per night on its treadmill.

The world's smallest dog – the Teacup Chihuahua – weighs less than a pound when fully grown.

A bear has 42 teeth.

The Black Bear has a blue tongue.

Hamsters like crickets as food.

Polar bears cover their black noses with their paws for better camouflage.

Squirrels can climb faster than they can run.

A group of twelve or more cows is called a flink.

A blind chameleon still changes colour to match his environment.

Male monkeys go bald in much

A pig sleeps on its right side.

400 quarter-pound hamburgers can be made out of one cow.

Armadillos have four babies at a time and they are always all of the same sex.

A cow gives nearly 200,000 glasses of milk in her lifetime.

A zebra is white with black stripes.

The longest snake is the Royal Python, which can grow to 10.6 metres long (35 feet).

When opossums are playing possum, they are not 'playing' – they pass out from sheer terror.

If you are chased by a crocodile, run in a serpentine fashion – a crocodile isn't good at making sharp turns.

A monkey was once tried and convicted for smoking a cigarette in Indiana.

Crocodiles never outgrow the pool in which they live. If you put a baby croc in an aquarium, it would be small for the rest of its life.

the same way that men do.

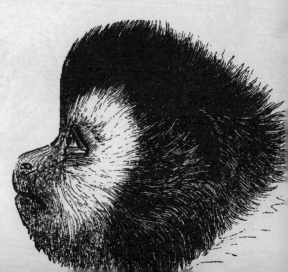

The kinkajou, which belongs to the same family as the raccoon, has a prehensile tail that is twice the length of its body. At night it wraps itself up in its tail to sleep.

The antlers of a male moose are more than 2 metres (about 7 feet) across. A moose's antlers are made up of the fastest-growing cells in the animal kingdom.

An adult hippo can bite a 3.6-metre (12-foot) adult male crocodile in half, and can open its mouth wide enough to fit a 1.2-metre (4-foot) child inside. A hippo can also outrun a man.

The world's smallest mammal (where skull size is the defining factor) is the bumblebee bat of Thailand.

A camel's backbone is as straight as a horse's.

Rabbits and parrots can both see behind themselves without turning their head.

Alligators cannot move backwards.

A squirrel cannot contract or carry the rabies virus.

Camels chew in a figure-of-eight pattern.

A kangaroo can only jump when its tail is touching the ground.

At full speed, a cheetah takes 8-metre (26-foot) strides.

The honey badger in Africa can withstand bee stings that would kill another animal.

80 per cent of the noise a hippo makes is done underwater.

A cat uses its whiskers to determine if a space is big enough to squeeze through.

Koalas don't drink water, but get fluids from the eucalyptus leaves they eat. In fact, 'koala' is believed to mean 'no drink' in an Aboriginal language. Koalas have no natural predators.

There are only three types of snakes on the island of Tasmania and all three are deadly poisonous.

ANIMAL HYBRIDS

Mule: cross between a male donkey and a female horse

Hinny: cross between a male horse and a female donkey

Zeedonk: cross between a zebra and a donkey

Wolfdog: cross between a wolf and a dog

Liger: cross between a male lion and a female tiger

Cama: cross between a camel and a llama

Tigon: cross between a male tiger and a female lion

Wolphin: cross between a whale and a dolphin (only one in existence)

PEOPLE AND THEIR PETS

PERSON	PET	NAME
Reese Witherspoon	Dog: Bulldog	Frank Sinatra
Pamela Anderson	**Dog: Golden Retriever**	**Star**
Liv Tyler	Dog	Neil
Hilary Duff	**Dog: Fox Terrier/ Chihuahua**	**Little Dog**
Mariah Carey	Dogs: Shihtzus	Bing and Bong
	Jack Russell	Jack
	Yorkshire Terrier	Ginger
Paul O'Grady	**Dogs: Shihtzu Cross/Shihtzu**	**Buster and Louis**
Johnny Vaughan	Dog: British Bulldog	Harvey
Jenny Seagrove	**Dog: Springer Spaniel**	**Kizzy**
Amanda Holden	Dogs: West Highland Terriers	Nobbie and Fudge
Linda Barker	**Dog: Dachshund**	**Tiger Lilly**
Antony Worrall Thompson	Dogs: Russian Black Terrier	Jessica
	Golden Retriever	Trevor

Adrien Brody	**Dog: Chihuahua**	**Ceelo**
Vanilla Ice	Wallaroo: a kangaroo/wallaby cross	Bucky
	Goat	Pancho
Michael Stipe	**Dog: Terrier**	**Helix**
Wayne Rooney	Dog: Chow-Chow	Fizz
Natascha McElhone	**Cat**	**Soup**
Kate Bosworth	Cats	Louise and Dusty

CELEBRITIES WHO GOT DOGS FROM BATTERSEA DOGS' HOME

Simon Callow (Basil the singing dog)

Geri Halliwell (Shihtzu)

Sean Hughes

Sir Elton John (tan and white Collie cross)

Jason Connery

Samantha Robson

Kevin Spacey

Ringo Starr

Katie Boyle

Lionel Blair

George Hamilton (Staffordshire bull terrier)

Jack Davenport

A GUIDE TO RABBITS

Rabbits are the fifth most popular pet in Britain (after goldfish, tropical fish, cats and dogs).

Rabbits are sociable creatures often found living in large groups in underground burrows or warrens. A colony of 407 rabbits was once found with a warren that had 2,080 exits.

The most popular names for British (pet) rabbits are – in order – Thumper, Flopsy and Charlie.

Most rabbits are cottontails.

A rabbit's eyes are capable of seeing in every direction, making it possible to watch predators in the air and on the ground.

Rabbits twitch their noses constantly because they depend on their sense of smell to warn them of danger.

The Ryukyu rabbit and Mexico's volcano rabbit are among the rarest mammals in the world.

The highest a rabbit has ever jumped is 46 centimetres (18 inches).

The only film Joan Rivers ever directed was entitled *Rabbit Test* (1978).

A farmer introduced 24 wild rabbits into Australia in 1859. There are now an estimated 300 million rabbits there.

Famous rabbits include: Brer Rabbit, The White Rabbit (in *Alice's Adventures in Wonderland*), Hazel, Fiver, Bigwig etc. (in *Watership Down*), Peter Rabbit, Benjamin Bunny, Bucky O'Hare, Rabbit (in A.A. Milne's Winnie the Pooh stories), Peter Cottontail, Bugs Bunny, Harvey (James Stewart's imaginary best friend in the 1950 film *Harvey*), Lola (in the film *Space Jam*), the Monster of Caer Bannog (in the film *Monty Python and the Holy Grail*), Oswald the Lucky Rabbit, Roger Rabbit, Thumper (in the film *Bambi*), Babs Bunny (in Steven Spielberg's *Tiny Toon Adventures*), Bean Bunny (in *The Muppets*), Benny Rabbit (in *Sesame Street*), the Easter Bunny.

Before fame

Lemmy used to be a roadie for Jimi Hendrix.

Tracey Ullman used to be a member of the Second Generation dance group.

Sir Elton John once auditioned for the group King Crimson.

Joseph Fiennes used to be a theatre usher and once told off Helen Mirren for not sitting down without realizing that she was one of the actresses.

Nicole Kidman and Naomi Watts both attended North Sydney Girls' High School.

Stephen Sondheim once tried out as a contestant on *The $64,000 Question* (answering questions on John Ford films).

Paul Bettany used to busk on Westminster Bridge.

Errol Flynn used to work on a farm where he had to castrate sheep by biting off their testicles.

Michael Crawford took his stage name off a biscuit tin.

Stockard Channing received a substantial inheritance at the age of 15 after the death of her shipping magnate father.

Hugh Grant appeared as a contestant in the TV quiz *Top of The Form*.

Colin Farrell auditioned for Boyzone but didn't get in.

As a young woman, Lorraine Bracco was once asked to pose nude for Salvador Dalí but she refused.

Danny Kaye was sacked from his job in an insurance company after accidentally paying a claimant $40,000 instead of $4,000.

PEOPLE AND WHAT THEY DID BEFORE BECOMING FAMOUS

Delia Smith – Receptionist

Angelina Jolie – Embalmer

Jennifer Saunders – Cook in a fire station

Sonia – Collected eggs from battery chickens

Damien Hirst – Roadie for Barry Manilow

Afroman – Worked in a chicken factory

Jason Biggs – Subway sandwich maker

Ricky Gervais – Pizza delivery boy

Richard Bacon – McDonald's

Mackenzie Crook – Worked at Pizza Hut, in a chicken factory and in hospitals

Shaznay Lewis – Gardener, postman and shop assistant in Top Man

Jim Davidson – Forklift-truck driver

Rolf Harris – Postman

Alexei Sayle – Illustrator

Shane MacGowan – Worked in a record shop

Christie Brinkley – Painter

Charlie Watts – Designer in advertising

Gabriel Byrne – Plumber's assistant, apprentice chef, archaeologist, teacher

Anthony Andrews – Farm labourer

Paul Newman – Encyclopaedia salesman

John Leslie – DJ at Top Shop in Edinburgh

Edna O'Brien – Trainee pharmacist

Jon Bon Jovi – Served in Burger King

Kim Wilde – Hospital cleaner

Bernard Manning – Cigarette factory worker

Carol Smillie – Shoe shop assistant, model

Gail Porter – Shoe shop assistant; VT operator

Freddie Starr – Bricklayer

Giorgio Armani – Window dresser

Paul Young – Apprentice toolmaker at Vauxhall

Gary Kemp – Prices clerk for the *Financial Times*

Jimmy Somerville – Baker

Danny DeVito – Janitor

Helen Lederer – Social worker

Reg Presley – Bricklayer

Joan Armatrading – Accounts assistant

Richard Ashcroft – Lifeguard

FORMER LIBRARIANS

Mao Tse-tung, Sir Ludovic Kennedy, Casanova, Laurie Taylor, Anthea Turner, Philip Larkin, August Strindberg, John Braine, David Hockney, J. Edgar Hoover, Pope Pius XI, Jane Gardam, Laura Bush, Howard W. Koch, Boris Pasternak, Lynne Truss

FORMER AIR STEWARDESSES

Janice Long, Melinda Messenger, Trisha Goddard, Alex Best

EX-PONTIN'S BLUECOATS

Shane Richie, Lee Mack, Brian Conley, Vicky Entwistle, Helen Chamberlain, Shaun Williamson, Bradley Walsh, Amanda Redington, Paul Usher

FORMER PLAYBOY BUNNIES

Debbie Harry, Lauren Hutton, Fiona Richmond, Gloria Steinem (on an undercover assignment)

FORMER MINERS

Paul Shane, Sir Jimmy Savile, Dennis Skinner, Charles Bronson, Anthony Shaffer and Peter Shaffer, Fred Trueman, Jeffrey Bernard, Jocky Wilson, Harold Larwood, Ray Reardon

TRAINED AS ENGINEERS

Lord John Birt, Will Hay, Rowan Atkinson, Walter Huston, Ringo Starr, Yasser Arafat, Carol Vorderman, Kate Bellingham, Nicholas Parsons, Naim Attallah, The Bachelors, Tom Conway

FORMER DANCERS

Madonna, Jennifer Lopez, Keira Knightley, Ken Russell, Clare Francis, Toyah Willcox, Christopher Beeny, Victoria Principal, Brigitte Bardot, Suzanne Vega, Baroness Betty Boothroyd, Tina Barrett

FORMER JOURNALISTS

Frederick Forsyth, Chrissie Hynde, Evelyn Waugh, Ali MacGraw, Jilly Cooper, Mark Knopfler, Neil Tennant, Steve Harley, Patrick Stewart

FORMER EDITORS

Michael Foot: *Evening Standard*

Nina Myskow: *Jackie*

John Freeman: *New Statesman*

Libby Purves: *Tatler*

Sally Beauman: *Queen*

Anthony Holden: *Sunday Today*

Sir Richard Branson: *Student*

Sir Julian Critchley: *Town*

Sir Alastair Burnet: *The Daily Express*

Kate Thornton: *Smash Hits*

Andrew Marr: *The Independent*

Janet Street-Porter: *The Independent on Sunday*

PEOPLE WHO LIVED ON A KIBBUTZ

Isla Fisher, Annie Leibovitz, Paul Kaye (aka Dennis Pennis), Jonathan Pearce, Bob Hoskins, Kit Hesketh-Harvey, Tony Hawks, Maeve Binchy, Anna Ford, Samantha Spiro, Sally Becker, Ruby Wax, Mike Leigh, Lynne Reid Banks (for nine years), Mary Tamm, Uri Geller, Dr Ruth Westheimer, Simon Le Bon, Sandra Bernhard, Jerry Seinfeld

FORMER FLATMATES

Gary Webster and Phil Middlemiss

Martin Tyler and Bob Willis

Paul Whitehouse and Harry Enfield

Taki and Peter Lawford

John Prescott and Dennis Skinner

Martin Offiah and Shaun Edwards

David Lynch and Peter Wolf

Lynda Bellingham and Julia Sawalha

Ioan Gruffudd and Matthew Rhys

Ant and Dec (then they bought houses two doors down from each other in Chiswick)

Brian McFadden and Ben Ofoedu

Rik Mayall and Rowland Rivron

Nastassja Kinski and Demi Moore

Jon Snow and Maya Angelou

Johnny Rotten and Sid Vicious

Patricia Hodge and Cheryl Campbell

MEN WHO WERE IN THE MERCHANT NAVY

Bob Mills, John Prescott, Bill Treacher, Dickie Davies, Peter
Stringfellow, Gareth Hunt, Christopher Ellison, Rutger Hauer, Bob
Hoskins, Jack Kerouac, Bernie Winters, Alan Weeks, Vivian
Stanshall, Allen Ginsberg, Roger Scott, Ken Russell, Tommy Steele,
Desmond Wilcox

PEOPLE WHO USED TO WORK IN SHOPS

Gaby Roslin (Selfridges, John Lewis and Harrods)

Katy Hill (The Body Shop and John Menzies)

Gary Numan (W.H. Smith)

Russ Abbot (Hepworths)

Mick Fleetwood (Liberty)

Betty Boo (Marks & Spencer)

Glenda Jackson (Boots)

Wendy Richard (Fortnum & Mason)

George Michael (BHS)

Annie Lennox (Mothercare)

Ted Rogers (W.H. Smith)

Bobby Davro (Bentalls)

Edwina Currie (Woolworths)

Jayne Middlemiss (Currys)

Lisa Scott-Lee (River Island: 'I used to spend hours making sure the hangers were spaced two fingers away from each other. It's quite therapeutic.')

Duncan James (Woolworths)

Charles Dance (Burton's – as a window-dresser)

Andrew Flintoff (Woolworths)

People who used to be waiters/waitresses

Annie Lennox, Rickie Lee Jones, Jacqueline Bisset, Dame Diana Rigg, Ellen Barkin, Paula Abdul, Alec Baldwin, Antonio Banderas, Jennifer Aniston, Ellen DeGeneres, Graham Norton, Angela Bassett (a singing waitress), Mariah Carey, Dustin Hoffman, Julianna Margulies, Edward Norton, Barbra Streisand, Russell Crowe, Kristin Davis, Julianne Moore, Robin Wright Penn, Emily Watson, Allison Janney, Julia Ormond, Monty Don, Renée Zellweger (in a topless bar – although she refused to take off her bra), Daniel Craig, Philip Seymour Hoffman (and was fired), Paul O'Grady (in a brothel in Manila), Kelly Clarkson, Geena Davis, Sienna Guillory, Tara Fitzgerald, Claire Goose, Ashley Judd, Roseanne, Lisa Snowdon, Meryl Streep, Davina McCall (at the Moulin Rouge in Paris), Rebecca Broussard

People who qualified as lawyers

Baroness Margaret Thatcher, Clive Anderson, Osvaldo Ardiles, Mahatma Gandhi, Sir Robin Day, Sir John Mortimer, Hoagy Carmichael, Tony Blair, Fidel Castro, Rossano Brazzi, Jerry Springer, Erle Stanley Gardner, Otto Preminger, Geraldo Rivera, Bob Mortimer

NB Bing Crosby, David Gower, Estelle Parsons and Cole Porter all studied law at university without getting their degrees.

PEOPLE WHO WORKED IN ADVERTISING

Ridley Scott (as a director – e.g. on Hovis)

Fay Weldon (as a copywriter – e.g. 'Go To Work On An Egg')

Salman Rushdie (as a copywriter – e.g. 'Cream Cakes – Naughty But Nice')

Murray Walker (as an account director. For most of his commentating career, Murray's day job was in advertising. He worked on the 'Mars A Day' campaign.)

James Herbert (as a copywriter)

Sir Alec Guinness (as a copywriter working on campaigns for Rose's Lime Juice, razors and radio valves)

Sir David Puttnam (as an account director)

Irma Kurtz (as a copywriter)

Len Deighton (as a copywriter)

Spike Lee (as a copywriter)

Martin Amis (as a copywriter)

Charlie Watts (as a designer)

Tim Allen (as a creative director)

Sela Ward (as an art director)

Hugh Grant (as an advertising account executive)

BIZARRE PLACE NAMES

Agenda (Wisconsin, USA)

Asbestos (Canada)

Banana (Australia)

Belcher (Louisiana, USA)

Bird-in-Hand (Pennsylvania, USA)

Blubberhouses (Yorkshire)

Boom (Belgium)

Boring (Oregon, USA)

Chicken (Alaska, USA)

Chunky (Mississippi, USA)

Ding Dong (Texas, USA)

Drain (Oregon, USA)

Eye (Suffolk)

Hell (Norway)

How (Wisconsin, USA)

Howlong (Australia)

Humpty Doo (Australia)

Lower Slaughter (Gloucestershire)

Loyal (Oklahoma, USA)

Luck (Wisconsin, USA)

Mars (Pennsylvania, USA)

Matching Tye (Essex)

Medicine Hat (Canada)

Moron (Mongolia)

Nasty (Hertfordshire)

Natters (Austria)

Normal (Illinois, USA)

Parachute (Colorado, USA)

Peculiar (Missouri, USA)

Pity Me (County Durham)

Pussy (France)

Puzzletown (Pennsylvania, USA)

Rottenegg (Austria)

Rough and Ready (California, USA)

Secretary (Maryland, USA)

Silly (Belgium)

Simmering (Austria)

Siren (Wisconsin, USA)

Smackover (Arkansas, USA)

Snapfinger (Georgia, USA)

Spit Junction (Australia)

Surprise (Arizona, USA)

Tiddleywink (Wiltshire)

Tightwad (Missouri, USA)

Toast (North Carolina, USA)

Truth or Consequences (New Mexico, USA)

Useless Loop (Australia)

Vulcan (Canada)

Wham (Yorkshire)

Zig Zag (Australia)

PEOPLE

Dick Van Dyke is ambidextrous.

Walt Disney's autograph bears no resemblance to the famous Disney logo.

Kirstie Alley bans anyone wearing perfume in her house (because of its destructive effect on the ozone layer).

Woody Allen eats out every day of the year.

Frank Sinatra was voted 'Worst Autograph Giver' by *Autograph Collector* magazine.

Noah Wyle is a Civil War buff.

Eddie Murphy crosses himself before he enters lifts.

Matt Groening incorporated his initials into the drawing of Homer: there's an M in his hair and his ear is the letter G.

Ben Affleck's reformed alcoholic father, Tim, became Robert Downey Jr's drug counsellor.

Richie Benaud is the president of French cricket.

Lucy Liu practises the martial art of Kali-Eskrima-Silat (knife and stick fighting).

Robert Duvall has a passion for the tango and practises every day.

Maurice Chevalier had a clause in his contract with Paramount Pictures that if he ever lost his French accent, they could terminate the contract.

Sheryl Crow's front two teeth are fake – her own were knocked out when she tripped on stage.

Nick Hancock owns Sir Stanley Matthews's 1953 FA Cup Winner's medal.

Thomas Jefferson introduced ice cream to the US.

Jennifer Lopez takes along her own sheets when she stays at a hotel.

Vincent van Gogh cut off his left ear. His 'Self-portrait with Bandaged Ear' shows the right one bandaged because he painted the mirror image.

Arnold Schoenberg suffered from triskaidecaphobia, the fear of the number 13. He died 13 minutes from midnight on Friday the 13th.

Sir Isaac Newton was just 23 years old when he discovered the law of universal gravitation.

Jordan is keen on sewing.

PEOPLE WHO WENT ON THE ORIGINAL CND MARCHES

Jeremy Beadle, Vanessa Redgrave, Humphrey Lyttelton, Rod Stewart, George Melly, Doris Lessing, Bryan Pringle, Arnold Wesker, Lindsay Anderson, Robert Bolt, Peter Vaughan, John Braine, John Arden, Michael Foot, Sheila Delaney, Dame Anita Roddick

MEMBERS OF THE DENNIS THE MENACE FAN CLUB

Joan Armatrading, Lenny Henry, Paul Gascoigne, Timmy Mallett, Suzanne Dando, Ian Woosnam, Mark Hamill, Mike Read

VEGANS

Fiona Apple, Kate Moss, Lindsay Wagner, Daryl Hannah, Martin Shaw, Yazz, Benjamin Zephaniah, Sophie Ward, Wendy Turner, Casey Affleck, Linda Blair, Julia Stiles, Tobey Maguire, Noah Wyle, Danni Minogue, William Shatner, Alicia Silverstone, Woody Harrelson, Joaquin Phoenix, Moby, Bryan Adams, Carl Lewis, Uri Geller, k. d. lang, Sinéad O'Conner, Heather Small

CELEBRITIES WHO BOUGHT OTHER CELEBRITIES' HOUSES

Dame Elizabeth Taylor lives in a house once owned by Frank Sinatra.

Jim Davidson's home near Dorking in Surrey was Oliver Reed's.

Gangsta rapper 50 Cent bought Mike Tyson's 17-acre estate in Farmington, Connecticut.

Brittany Murphy bought Britney Spears's Hollywood Hills house.

Doris Duke bought Rudolph Valentino's house.

Dorothy Squires bought Lillie Langtry's house.

David Blaine lives in a Gothic-style manor house in the Hollywood Hills that used to belong to Harry Houdini.

Madonna and Guy Ritchie own Ashcombe House, Wiltshire – where Sir Cecil Beaton lived from 1930 to 1945.

Gwyneth Paltrow and Chris Martin bought Kate Winslet's north London home in Belsize Park.

Shane Warne bought a house in Southampton that used to belong to Matt Le Tissier.

Mackenzie Crook bought Peter Sellers's old house in Muswell Hill.

Eddie Murphy bought the house in Benedict Canyon Drive that was once owned by Cher.

Sir Paul McCartney bought Courtney Love's old house in Los Angeles

Roman Abramovich bought the Hampshire estate of Kerry Packer

David Suchet bought Ronnie Barker's house in Pinner, Middlesex

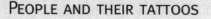

PEOPLE AND THEIR TATTOOS

Kelis: a giant orchid on her backside

Wayne Rooney: his girlfriend Coleen's name tattooed on his shoulder

Ewan McGregor: heart-and-dagger on his right shoulder

Rachel Hunter: bee logo for her production company, Bee Knees, on her lower back

Elijah Wood: elfish symbol on his hip

Patsy Kensit: 'Liam' with shamrock on ankle

George Shultz: tiger on bottom

Lord Patrick Lichfield: seahorse on arm

Princess Stephanie of Monaco: dragon on hip

Pamela Anderson: Tommy Lee's name on wedding finger

Johnny Depp: 'Winona Forever' on arm (changed to 'Wino Forever' when he and Winona Ryder split up)

Rachel Williams: arrow on bottom

Dean Holdsworth: 'Let He Without Sin Cast The First Stone' on arm

Brian Harvey: 'Eastside' on arm

Joan Baez: flower on back

Sharron Davies: elephant on bottom

Brian Conley: No Entry sign on bottom

Kelly McGillis: red rose on ankle

Suzi Quatro: star on wrist

Brigitte Nielsen: heart on bottom

Christy Turlington: heart on ankle

Liam Gallagher: 'Patsy' on arm

Whoopi Goldberg: Woodstock on breast

Alyssa Milano: the initials 'SRW' of her ex-fiancé on her right ankle

Natasha Henstridge: intertwined male and female symbols on her coccyx; bearded lion with crown – her star sign is Leo – on her bottom

Jo O'Meara: a Chinese emblem on the bottom of her spine, a butterfly on her bum, a dolphin on her belly, a flower on her ankle and a crescent moon on her foot

Mel B.: M for 'Max' on her buttock

Rose McGowan (woman on her right shoulder)

Jennifer Aniston (small heart on stomach)

PEOPLE WHO LIVE/LIVED ON HOUSEBOATS

Frederick Forsyth, Nigel Planer, Imogen Stubbs, Lemmy, Sir Richard Branson, Lord David Owen, Elizabeth Emanuel, David Suchet, Dr Conor Cruise O'Brien, Lawrence Dallaglio, Alexander Armstrong, Susan Penhaligon, Leo Sayer, Mike Barson, Glynn Edwards, David Gilmour, Damien Hirst

PEOPLE WHO MADE RICHARD BLACKWELL'S ANNUAL 'WORST-DRESSED WOMEN' LISTS

Paris Hilton (2003): 'How are you gonna keep 'em down on the farm after they've seen Paree? Grab the blinders, here comes Paris. From cyber disgrace to red carpet chills – she's the vapid Venus of Beverly Hills!'

Melanie Griffith (2003): 'Melanie defines "fatal fashion folly". A botox'd cockatoo in a painting by Dalí!'

Martha Stewart (1999): 'Dresses like the centerfold for the Farmer's Almanac. She's a 3-D girl: dull, dowdy and devastatingly dreary. Definitely not "a good thing".'

Kelly Osbourne (2002): 'A fright-wigged baby doll stuck in a goth prom gown.'

Elizabeth Hurley (2000): 'Her barely-there fashion bombs have hit a sour note – buy a coat.'

Anne Robinson (2001): 'Harry Potter in Drag ... a Hogwarts horror. Anne Robinson, you are fashion's Weakest Link!'

Sarah, Duchess of York (1996): 'The bare-toed terror of London town. She looks like an unemployed barmaid in search of a crown.' Also made the list in 1988 when she was accused of looking 'like a horse that came in last'. Blackwell went on to say 'she looks terrible, like she should be making beds on the second floor of a motel'.

Geena Davis (1992): 'Big Bird in heels.'

Yoko Ono (1972): 'Oh no Yoko.'

Roseanne (1989): 'Bowling alley reject.'

David Bowie (1973): 'A cross between Joan Crawford and Marlene Dietrich doing a glitter revival of New Faces.'

Faye Dunaway (1991): 'The Depressing Diva of Designer Dreck.'

Bette Midler (1978): 'She didn't go to a rummage sale, she wore it.'

Barbra Streisand (1990): 'What can I say? Yentl's gone mental.' 1983: 'A boy version of Medusa.'

Jane Seymour (1991): 'A paisley peepshow on parade.'

Debbie Harry (1979): 'Ten cents a dance with a nickel change.'

Madonna (1992): 'The Bare-bottomed Bore of Babylon.' 1988: 'Helpless, hopeless and horrendous.'

Dennis Rodman (1996): 'The "Fashion Menace" may be the Bad Boy of basketball, but in fishnet and feathers he's a unisex wreck.'

Ashlee Simpson & Jessica Simpson (2004): 'From gaudy to grim to downright frenetic... these two prove that bad taste is positively genetic.'

PEOPLE WHO OWN(ED)/ CO-OWN(ED) RESTAURANTS

Jean-Paul Belmondo: Stressa (Paris)

Alice Cooper: Cooperstown (Phoenix)

Jennifer Lopez: Madre's (Pasadena)

William Devane: Devane's (Palm Springs)

Wayne Gretzky: Wayne Gretzky's (Toronto)

Morton Harket: Figaro (Oslo)

Timothy Hutton: P.J. Clarke's (New York City)

Sir Elton John: Le Dome (Hollywood)

Ashton Kutcher: Dolce (Los Angeles)

Moby: TeaNY (New York City)

Ricky Martin: Casa Salsa (Miami Beach)

Rob Schneider: Eleven (San Francisco)

Tom Selleck: The Black Orchid (Honolulu)

Sylvester Stallone, Bruce Willis and Arnold Schwarzenegger: the Planet Hollywood chain

Chris Kelly: Midsummer House (Cambridge)

Mariel Hemingway: Sam's Restaurant (Dallas)

Sir Michael Caine: Langan's Brasserie (London)

Mikhail Baryshnikov: Columbus (New York City)

Robert De Niro, Bill Murray, Lou Diamond Phillips and Christopher Walken: TriBeCa (New York City)

Bill Wyman: Sticky Fingers (London)

Patrick Swayze: Mulholland Drive Café (Los Angeles)

Delia Smith: The City Brasserie (Norwich)

Dan Aykroyd: House of Blues restaurant/music club chain

Whoopi Goldberg, Joe Pesci, Steven Seagal: Eclipse (Hollywood)

Steven Spielberg and Jeffrey Katzenberg: Dive! (Las Vegas)

Cameron Diaz: Bamboo (Miami)

Britney Spears: Nyla (New York City)

PEOPLE WHO ARE SUPERSTITIOUS

Kylie Minogue, Paul Dickov, Norman Cook
(Fatboy Slim), Engelbert Humperdinck, Sir Elton
John, Fabien Barthez, Jenni Falconer, Jelena
Dokic, Michael Atherton, Henrietta Knight,
Martin Bell, Huw Edwards, Mariah Carey, Diana
Quick, Jilly Cooper, Michael Aspel, Tony
McCoy, Goran Ivanisevic

PEOPLE WHO WERE
ORDAINED DRUIDS

**William Blake, William Roache,
Sir Winston Churchill, John Lennon**

PEOPLE AND WHAT THEY COLLECT

Patrick Stewart – *Beavis and Butthead* merchandise

George Michael (as a boy) – lizards and insects

Andre Agassi – Barry Manilow records

Clint Eastwood – jazz records

Helena Christensen – perfume bottles

 Angelina Jolie – knives

Quentin Tarantino – old board games based on TV shows

Pink – stuffed frogs

Tara Palmer-Tomkinson – 'Do Not Disturb' signs from hotels around the world

Kevin Spacey – antique ashtrays

Jessica Biel – vintage glasses without lenses

Dan Aykroyd – police badges

Beau Bridges – Native American percussion instruments

George W. Bush – autographed baseballs

J.C. Chasez – Hard Rock Café menus

Bill Clinton – saxophones (real ones and miniatures)

Stephen Dorff – vintage cameras

Patrick Duffy – antique toys and children's books

Joey Fatone – Superman memorabilia

Larry Hagman – canes and flags

Mike Myers – model soldiers

Freddie Prinze – comic books

Noah Wyle – baseball cards

Philippa Forrester – first edition children's books

Jodie Foster – black & white photos

Sarah Michelle Gellar – rare books

Anna Kournikova – dolls from the countries she visits

Joan Rivers – Fabergé eggs

Roseanne – pigs

Trude Mostue – animals' testicles

Rachel Stevens – books of matches

Meat Loaf – stuffed toys

Norman Cook (Fatboy Slim) – smiley ephemera

Peter Jackson – World War One models of aeroplanes

Rachel Stevens – books of matches

Rose McGowan – Marlene Dietrich memorabilia

Demi Moore – Dolls

Donna Summer – silver pillboxes

Ivana Trump – women's compacts

SPORTING STARS WHO APPEARED IN FILMS

Sugar Ray Robinson – *Candy* (1968)

Muhammad Ali – *The Greatest* (1977)

Bobby Moore – *Escape To Victory* (1981)

Craig Stadler – *Tin Cup* (1996)

Ilie Nastase – *Players* (1979)

Magic Johnson – *Grand Canyon* (1991)

Pele – *Hot Shot* (1987)

Michael Johnson – *Space Jam* (1996)

Sir Henry Cooper – *Royal Flash* (1975)

Vijay Amritraj – *Octopussy* (1983)

Ken Norton – *Mandingo* (1975)

Sir Len Hutton – *The Final Test* (1953)

Fictional Characters and their First Names

Dr (John) Watson (*Sherlock Holmes*)

(Rupert) Rigsby (*Rising Damp*)

Mr (Quincy) Magoo

Inspector (Jules) Maigret

Inspector (Endeavour) Morse

Captain (George) Mainwaring (*Dad's Army*)

(Wilfred) Ivanhoe

(Hugh) Bulldog Drummond

(James) Shelley (*Shelley*)

Little Lord (Cedric) Fauntleroy

Gilligan of Gilligan's Island had a first name that was only used once, on the never-aired pilot show: Willy

NB Columbo's first name *isn't* Philip, despite claims that it is. His first name was never mentioned in the series.

Daft Labels

On a packet of Sainsbury's peanuts: 'Warning: Contains nuts.'

On a hairdryer: 'Do not use while sleeping.'

On a bar of Dial soap: 'Directions: Use like regular soap.'

On Marks & Spencer bread pudding: 'Product will be hot after heating.'

On Tesco's tiramisu dessert (printed on bottom of box): 'Do not turn upside down.'

On packaging for a Rowenta iron: 'Do not iron clothes on body.'

On Boots children's cough medicine: 'Do not drive a car or operate machinery after taking this medication.'

On Nytol Sleep Aid: 'Warning: May cause drowsiness.'

On a set of Christmas lights: 'For indoor or outdoor use only.'

On a Japanese food processor: 'Not to be used for the other use.'

On a child's Superman costume: 'Wearing of this garment does not enable you to fly.'

On a Swedish chainsaw: 'Do not attempt to stop chain with your hands.'

On a bottle of Palmolive dishwashing liquid: 'Do not use on food.'

MEMORABILIA SOLD AT CHRISTIE'S

Dorothy's ruby slippers from *The Wizard of Oz*: $666,000 (2000)

Paul Gascoigne's shirt from the 1990 World Cup semi-final against West Germany: £28,680 (2004)

Pele's shirt from the 1958 World Cup Final: £70,505 (2004)

Marilyn Monroe's eternity ring (given to her by Joe DiMaggio after their 1954 wedding): $772,500 (1999)

Eric Clapton's 1956 Fender Stratocaster (as used on *Layla*): $497,500 (1999)

George Harrison's 1964 Gibson SG Standard guitar: $567,000 (2004)

John Lennon's handwritten lyrics to the Beatles' song *Nowhere Man*: $455,500 (2003)

An autographed life-size picture of Marlene Dietrich used in the famous crowd scene in Peter Blake's design for the Beatles *Sergeant Pepper's Lonely Hearts Club Band* album cover: £86,250 (2003)

Britney Spears's school book report: $1,000 (2004)

The Rosebud sledge from *Citizen Kane*: $233,500 (1996)

James Bond's Aston Martin DB5: £157,750 (2001)

John Travolta's white suit from *Saturday Night Fever*: $145,500 (1995)

The Maltese Falcon icon from the 1941 film of the same name: $398,500 (1994)

Clark Gable's personal script for *Gone With The Wind*: $244,500 (1996)

Marilyn Monroe's dress when she sang *Happy Birthday* to President John F. Kennedy at Madison Square Garden, New York, in 1962: $1,267,500 (1999)

Elvis Presley's 1942 Martin D-18 acoustic guitar: £99,000 (1993)

Bob Dylan's acoustic guitar from the 1960s: $20,000 (2004)

Animation cell from Disney's 1934 *Orphan's Benefit*: $286,000 (1989)

A poster for *The Mummy* (1932): £80,750 (2001)

CELEBRITY ACHIEVEMENTS

Geoff Hoon and Mo Mowlam both achieved Gold in the Duke of Edinburgh's Award Scheme.

Carol Barnes and Dave Dee both became magistrates.

Gordon Brown won a *Daily Express* competition for a vision of Britain in the year 2000 when he was 21.

Sarah Michelle Gellar has a brown belt in tae kwon do.

Dame Helen Mirren was named Naturist of the Year 2004.

Of all his many talents, Leonardo da Vinci was proudest of his ability to bend iron with his bare hands.

Daryl Hannah invented a board game called Love It Or Hate It.

Paul Whitehouse won the Baby Smile of the Rhondda Valley award in 1963.

Robson Green has a category-four licence for doing professional fireworks displays.

Sir Michael Gambon and Eric Bana both became successful actors without receiving any formal acting training. The same was true for Art Carney and Beryl Reid.

David Walliams swam the English Channel.

PEOPLE WHO ARE FLUENT IN FOREIGN LANGUAGES

Clive James (Japanese)

Prince Philip (German)

Gary Lineker (Spanish)

Tim Roth (French and German)

Sir John Harvey-Jones (Russian)

Shirley Maclaine (Japanese)

Susannah York (French)

Lord Denis Healey (Italian)

Philip Madoc (German and Italian)

Kylie Minogue (French)

Gloria Estefan (Spanish and French)

Sandra Bullock (German)

David Soul (German and Spanish)

Salma Hayek (Arabic)

Renée Zellweger (German)

George W. Bush (Spanish)

Bill Clinton (German)

Stewart Copeland (Arabic)

Al Gore (Spanish)

William Shatner (French)

Montel Williams (Russian)

Melanie Blatt (French)

Fiona Bruce (French and Italian)

Kim Cattrall (German)

Geraldine Chaplin (Spanish)

Chelsea Clinton (German)

Jennifer Connelly (Italian and French)

Rebecca De Mornay (German and French)

Julie Dreyfus (Japanese)

Angie Everhart (French)

Molly Ringwald (French)

Sigourney Weaver (French and German)

J.K. Rowling (French)

Jennie Bond (French)

Ashley Judd (French)

Alex Kingston (German)

Donna Summer (German)

Jodie Foster (French)

Christy Turlington (Spanish)

Ted Koppel (Russian, German and French)

PARLEZ VOUS ENGLISH?

Christopher Lee (German)

Lyle Lovett (German)

Dolph Lundgren (German, French and Japanese)

Bill Paxton (German)

Famke Janssen (German and French)

Brigitte Nielsen (Italian and German)

Rosamund Pike (German and French)

Sophie Raworth (French and German)

Greta Scacchi (German)

Nastassja Kinski (French, Italian and Russian)

Greg Kinnear (Greek)

Sir Eddie George (Russian)

Prince Michael of Kent (Russian)

Michael Frayn (Russian)

Madeleine Albright (Russian)

Geoffrey Robinson (Russian)

DO YOU SPEAK FRANCAIS ?

People who have flown helicopters

Neil Fox, Ian Botham, Sarah, Duchess of York, Prince Andrew, Adam
Faith, Mark Thatcher, Kenny Jones, Noel Edmonds, Prince Charles,
Barry Sheene, David Essex, Harrison Ford, Patricia Cornwell (bought a
custom-painted Bell passenger helicopter, which she can legally fly
alone though she prefers to hire a co-pilot)

Awarded the Freedom of the City of ...

Sir Sean Connery (Edinburgh)

Sting (Newcastle)

Brigitte Bardot (Paris)

Jimmy Carter (Swansea)

Sarah, Duchess of York (York)

Nelson Mandela (Glasgow)

Jayne Torvill (Nottingham)

Christopher Dean (Nottingham)

Lord James Callaghan (Sheffield)

Lord Robert Runcie (Canterbury)

Sir David Attenborough (Leicester)

Lord Richard Attenborough (Leicester)

Jack Charlton (Dublin)

Sir Simon Rattle (Birmingham)

Norman Wisdom (Tirana)

Brian Clough (Nottingham)

Kenny Dalglish (Glasgow)

Mikhail Gorbachev (Aberdeen)

Helen Sharman (Sheffield)

Sir Paul McCartney (Liverpool)

Lisa Clayton (Birmingham)

Bill Clinton (Dublin)

Baroness Margaret Thatcher (Westminster)

John Tusa (London)

Pope John Paul II (Dublin)

Prince Charles (Swansea)

Stephen Roche (Dublin)

Gary Lineker (Leicester)

Sir Alex Ferguson (Manchester)

Kate Adie (Sunderland)

Dame Kelly Holmes (Tunbridge Wells)

AWARDED THE FREEDOM OF THE CITY OF LONDON

Billy Walker, Angela Rippon, Ernie Wise, Martyn Lewis, Sir Cliff Richard, Clare Francis, Lionel Bart, Terry Venables, Prunella Scales, Mike Oldfield, Clarissa Dickson Wright, Jimmy Tarbuck, Nelson Mandela, Sir Norman Wisdom, John Tusa, Prince Philip

PEOPLE WHO HAD AIRPORTS NAMED AFTER THEM

John Wayne (Santa Ana)

John F. Kennedy (New York)

Charles de Gaulle (Paris)

David Ben-Gurion (Tel Aviv)

Leonardo da Vinci (Rome)

Chiang Kai Shek (Taipei)

Pierre Trudeau (Montreal)

Jan Smuts (Johannesburg)

Pope John Paul II (Krakow)

Antoine de Saint-Exupéry (Lyon)

Marco Polo (Venice)

Jomo Kenyatta (Nairobi)

Pablo Picasso (Malaga)

Konrad Adenauer (Cologne)

John Lennon (Liverpool)

Chuck Yeager (Charleston)

George Bush (Houston)

Louis Armstrong (New Orleans)

Will Rogers (Oklahoma City)

Wolfgang Mozart (Salzburg)

George Best (Belfast)

Norman Manley (Kingston)

Indira Gandhi (New Delhi)

Charles Lindbergh (San Diego)

John Foster Dulles (Washington DC)

PEOPLE WHO HAD THEATRES NAMED AFTER THEM

Bob Hope (Eltham)

Sir John Gielgud (London)

Dame Peggy Ashcroft (Croydon)

Neil Simon (New York)

Sir Michael Redgrave (Farnham)

Sir Laurence Olivier (London)

Kenneth More (Ilford)

Dame Sybil Thorndike (Leatherhead)

Tony O'Reilly (Pittsburgh)

Dame Flora Robson (Newark)

Ivor Novello (London)

Sir Noel Coward (London)

People honoured with ticker-tape parades in New York City

David Lloyd George (5.10.1923)

Bobby Jones (2.7.1926 and 2.7.1930)

Charles Lindbergh (13.6.1927)

Ramsay MacDonald (4.10.1929)

Amelia Earhart (20.6.1932)

Howard Hughes (15.7.1938)

General Dwight Eisenhower (10.6.1945)

General Charles de Gaulle (27.8.1945 and 26.4.1960)

Winston Churchill (14.3.1946)

Eamon de Valera (9.3.1948)

Jawaharlal Nehru (17.10.1949)

Liaquat Ali Khan (8.5.1950)

Robert Menzies (4.8.1950)

General Douglas MacArthur (20.4.1951)

David Ben-Gurion (9.5.1951)

Ben Hogan (21.7.1953)

Emperor Haile Selassie (1.6.1954 and 4.10.1963)

Althea Gibson (11.7.1957)

Queen Elizabeth II (21.10.1957)

Willy Brandt (10.2.1959)

John F. Kennedy (19.10.1960)

John Glenn (1.3.1962)

Pope John Paul II (3.10.1979)

Nelson Mandela (20.6.1990)

PEOPLE AWARDED HONORARY UNIVERSITY DOCTORATES

Jack Higgins (Leeds Metropolitan)

Gary Player (St Andrews)

Michael Heseltine (Liverpool)

Virginia Wade (Sussex)

Richard Wilson (Glasgow)

Jack Rowell (Bath)

Denise Robertson (Sunderland)

John Cleese (St Andrews)

Tony Blair (Northumbria)

Sir Freddie Laker (City)

Sir David Puttnam (Leicester)

Dame Cleo Laine (Open)

Sir Edward Heath (Oxford)

Johnny Ball (Sheffield Hallam)

Michael Holroyd (East Anglia)

Michael Foot (Nottingham)

Sir Peter Ustinov (Durham)

Dame Janet Baker (Bradford)

Sir Trevor Huddleston (Warwick)

Sue Lawley (Wolverhampton)

Pat Jennings (Ulster)

Richard Baker (Strathclyde)

Jack Charlton (Northumbria)

Neil Kinnock (Cardiff)

Lord Denis Healey (Bradford)

John Tusa (London)

Sir Jimmy Savile (Leeds)

Sandy Gall (Aberdeen)

Nigel Mansell (Birmingham)

Lord Brian Rix (Dundee)

Betty Boothroyd (Cambridge)

Sir Trevor McDonald (Plymouth)

Dame Iris Murdoch (Cambridge)

Sir John Gielgud (London)

Virginia Bottomley (Portsmouth)

Sir Roger Bannister (Sheffield)

Sir John Mortimer (Nottingham)

Baroness Barbara Castle (Manchester)

Placido Domingo (Georgetown)

Nigel Kennedy (Bath)

Sir Ludovic Kennedy (Strathclyde)

Terry Waite (Durham)

Margaret Drabble (East Anglia)

Sir John Harvey-Jones (Exeter)

Sue Lawley (Bristol University)

Lord Richard Attenborough (Sussex University)

Sir Patrick Moore (Birmingham)

Cilla Black (Fellowship, John Moores University)

Esther Rantzen (South Bank University)

Sir Bobby Robson (Civil Law, Newcastle)

Pierce Brosnan (Dublin Institute of Technology)

Eddie Jordan (Dublin Institute of Technology)

PEOPLE APPOINTED UNIVERSITY CHANCELLORS

Prince Philip – Edinburgh

The Duchess of York – Salford

Baroness Betty Boothroyd – Open

Bill Bryson – Durham

Jon Snow – Oxford Brookes

Prince Charles – Cardiff

Chris Patten – Oxford

Sir David Puttnam – Sunderland

Lord MacLaurin – Hertfordshire

Baroness Margaret Thatcher – Buckingham

Lord Peter Palumbo – Portsmouth

Lord Brian Rix – East London

Lord Jack Ashley – Staffordshire

Lord Richard Attenborough – Sussex

Sir Trevor McDonald – South Bank

Lord Melvyn Bragg – Leeds

Patrick Stewart – Huddersfield

ALL THE RECTORS OF THE UNIVERSITY OF ST ANDREWS SINCE 1967

As voted for by the students.

Sir Learie Constantine (1967–70)

John Cleese (1970–73)

Alan Coren (1973–76)

Frank Muir (1976–79)

Tim Brooke-Taylor (1979–82)

Katharine Whitehorn (1982–85)

Stanley Adams (1985–88)

Nicholas Parsons (1988–91)

Nicky Campbell (1991–93)

Donald Findlay (1993–99)

Andrew Neil (1999–2002)

Sir Clement Freud (2002–2005)

Simon Pepper (2005–)

PEOPLE WHO LAUNCHED PRODUCTS

Fran Cotton and Steve Smith – sportswear (Cotton Traders)

Muhammad Ali – sportswear

Hilary Duff – canine clothing called Little Dog Duff

Sean P. Diddy Combs – Sean John, a 'tightly edited collection' of clothing

MC Hammer – a clothing range called the J. Slick Collection.

Catherine Zeta-Jones – babywear

Vinnie Jones – a clothing range called Vinnie

John Malkovich – a clothing range called Mrs Mudd

Madonna – a clothing range, the English Roses Collection

Bono – Edun ('nude' spelled backwards): socially conscious apparel

PEOPLE WHO LAUNCHED PERFUMES

Celine Dion – Belong

Stella McCartney – Stella

Paloma Picasso – Paloma Picasso

Sir Cliff Richard – Miss You Nights

Britney Spears – Curious

Paris Hilton – Paris Hilton

Jennifer Lopez – Miami Glow

David Beckham – David Beckham (and Instinct)

Antonio Banderos – Spirit

Sarah Jessica Parker – Lovely

Jade Goody – Shh

Andre Agassi – Aramis Life

How values in a game of Monopoly compare to real life

'DRUNK IN CHARGE' FINE £20 Someone found drunk in charge of a vehicle could expect a fine in the region of £500 – as well as a year's disqualification.

PAY HOSPITAL £100 At a private hospital, a basic operation such as having tonsils removed costs about £2,000.

WIN A CROSSWORD COMPETITION – COLLECT £100 Which is precisely how much *Saga* magazine, for example, gives away in its monthly crossword competition.

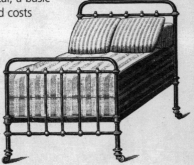

SPEEDING FINE £15 The price of a fixed speeding ticket is now £60 + 3 penalty points.

DOCTOR'S FEE £50 A Harley Street doctor will typically charge £120 for an initial consultation.

MAYFAIR In Monopoly, a house costs £200. A four-bedroom house in Mayfair would today cost a minimum of £4,000,000.

MAKE GENERAL REPAIRS ON ALL OF YOUR HOUSES. FOR EACH HOUSE PAY £25; FOR EACH HOTEL PAY £100 To make general repairs on a house – and assuming three men working for a week – would cost about £1,400; to make general repairs on a hotel – and assuming twelve men working for four weeks – would cost about £20,000.

YOU HAVE WON SECOND PRIZE IN A BEAUTY CONTEST, COLLECT £10 The runner-up in a typical small-town beauty contest could expect to win £250.

PAY SCHOOL FEES OF £150 Parents of a child boarding at a public school can expect to pay an average of £15,000 p.a.

FREE PARKING What, in Central London?

GENUINE THINGS WRITTEN TO TAX AND WELFARE AUTHORITIES

'Please send me a claim form as I have had a baby. I had one before, but it got dirty and I burned it.'

'Please correct this assessment. I have not worked for the past three months as I have broken my leg. Hoping you will do the same.'

'Re your request for P45 for new employee. You already have it and he isn't leaving here but coming, so we haven't got it.'

'I have not been living with my husband for several years, and have much pleasure in enclosing his last will and testament.'

'I cannot get sick pay. I have six children, can you tell me why?'

'I want money as quick as I can get it. I have been in bed with the doctor for two weeks and this doesn't seem to do me any good. If things don't improve I will be forced to send for another doctor.'

'My husband is in HM forces. I have no children. Trusting it will have your attention.'

'I am forwarding my marriage certificate and six children. I have seven but one died and was baptized on half sheet of paper.'

'I am writing to the Welfare Department to say that my baby was born two years old. When do I get my money?'

'Unless I get my money soon, I will be forced to lead an immortal life.'

'In accordance with your instructions, I have given birth to twins in the enclosed envelope.'

'Mrs Jones has not had any clothes for a year and has been visited regularly by the clergy.'

'I am very annoyed that you have branded my son illiterate, as this is a lie. I was married to his father a week before he was born.'

'I don't know why you should be interested in the length of my residence in Quebec, but I have nothing to hide. It is 31 feet 8 inches long and there's an attached garage.'

'Please send me an official letter advising that I can't claim the costs of taking my wife to conventions. I don't want her along but I need an excuse.'

'Thank you for explaining my income tax liability. You have done it so clearly that I almost understand it.'

THE BOOKER PRIZE

Two People Who Have Won The Booker Prize Twice: J.M. Coetzee for *Disgrace* in 1999, having won for *Life and Times of Michael K* in 1983, and Peter Carey for *True History of The Kelly Gang* in 2001, having won for *Oscar And Lucinda* in 1988.

Booker Prize Judge Who Became A Winner: A.S. Byatt is the only Booker Prize judge (1974) to subsequently become a winner (for *Possession* in 1990).

Judge Who Was On The Panel Which Shortlisted Her Husband: Elizabeth Jane Howard in 1974 (Kingsley Amis's *Ending Up* was shortlisted but didn't win).

Judges Who Resigned: Malcolm Muggeridge in 1971 (too much sex in the novels he had to read); Nicholas Mosley in 1991 (he couldn't get the book he wanted on to the shortlist).

First First Novel To Win: *The Bone People* (Keri Hulme).

Most Shortlisted Novelist: Dame Iris Murdoch (six times – winning once with *The Sea, The Sea* in 1978).

Novelists Who Have Been Shortlisted Without Ever Winning: Muriel Spark, Martin Amis, William Trevor, Doris Lessing, Beryl Bainbridge, Fay Weldon, Anthony Burgess.

When John Berger won (in 1972 for *G*), he attacked Booker McConnell, the sponsors, and declared that he was giving half the money to the Black Panthers.

In 1983, Selina Scott asked Fay Weldon, the chairman of the judges, on television whether she'd actually read all the books.

ELIGIBLE BOOKS THAT WEREN'T EVEN NOMINATED

Birdsong (Sebastian Faulks)

***Captain Corelli's Mandolin* (Louis de Bernières)**

The Curious Incident of The Dog In The Night-time (Mark Haddon)

***A Perfect Spy* (John Le Carré)**

Perfume (Patrick Süskind)

***Trainspotting* (Irvine Welsh)**

White Teeth (Zadie Smith)

***Monsignor Quixote* (Graham Greene)**

Girl With A Pearl Earring (Tracy Chevalier)

PEOPLE WHO HAVE SERVED AS BOOKER PRIZE JUDGES

Joanna Lumley

David Baddiel

Kenneth Baker

Mariella Frostrup

Gerald Kaufman

Nigella Lawson

Sir Trevor McDonald

WRITERS WHO HAD A MANUSCRIPT LOST OR STOLEN

Louis de Bernières (the first 50 pages of *A Partisan's Daughter*)

Ernest Hemingway

Malcolm Lowry

Thomas Wolfe (*Mannerhouse* – rewrote it entirely)

T.E. Lawrence (*Seven Pillars of Wisdom* – rewrote it in full after losing it while changing trains at Reading station in 1919)

John Steinbeck (*Of Mice And Men* – the first draft was eaten by his dog)

Jilly Cooper (*Riders*, her first big blockbuster book – she lost the first draft)

PEOPLE WHO WROTE JUST ONE NOVEL

Anna Sewell: *Black Beauty*

Margaret Mitchell: *Gone With The Wind*

Harper Lee: *To Kill A Mockingbird*

Emily Brontë: *Wuthering Heights*

Kenneth Grahame: *The Wind In The Willows*

PEOPLE (MORE FAMOUS FOR OTHER THINGS) WHO WROTE NOVELS

Robert Shaw (*The Sun Doctor*)

Anthony Sher (*Middlepost*)

Sarah Bernhardt (*In The Clouds*)

George Kennedy (*Murder On Location*)

Jean Harlow (*Today Is Tonight*)

Joan Collins (*Prime Time*)

Leslie Caron (*Vengeance*)

Mae West (*The Constant Sinner*)

Naomi Campbell (*Swan*)

Benito Mussolini (*The Cardinal's Mistress*)

Julie Andrews (*The Last of The Really Great Whangdoodles*)

Martina Navratilova (*Total Zone*)

Jilly Johnson (*Double Exposure*)

Sir Winston Churchill (*Savrola*)

Carly Simon (*Amy The Dancing Bear*)

Tony Curtis (*Kid Andrew Cody And Julie Sparrow*)

Whoopi Goldberg (*Alice*)

Jane Seymour (*This One And That One*)

Ethan Hawke (*The Hottest State*)

Johnny Cash (*Man In White*)

Jordan (*Crystal*)

CHOCOLATE BARS, ETC, AND WHEN THEY MADE THEIR DEBUTS

Fry's Chocolate Cream – 1866

Hershey Bars – 1900

Toblerone – 1900

Cadbury's Dairy Milk – 1905

Cadbury's Bournville – 1910

Mars Bar – 1923

Crunchie – 1929

Terry's All Gold – 1932

Rowntree's Black Magic – 1933

Kit-Kat – 1935 (although for the first two years of its existence it was known as 'Chocolate Crisp')

Aero – 1935

Quality Street – 1936

Dairy Box – 1936

Rolo – 1937

Milky Bar – 1937

Smarties – 1937

Cadbury's Roses – 1938

Bounty – 1951

Galaxy – 1958

Picnic – 1958

After Eight – 1962

Toffee Crisp – 1963

Twix – 1967

Yorkie – 1976

THINGS THAT BEGAN IN THE 1960s

Jiffy bags, aluminium kitchen foil, discotheques, flavoured potato crisps, plastic carrier-bags, trainers, hatchbacks, self-service petrol stations, tights (in the UK), fruit-flavoured yoghurts, football hooliganism, After Eight mints, pocket calculators, *Coronation Street*, fibre-tip pens, Weight Watchers, colour TV, MOT tests, longlife milk, *The Sun*, electric toothbrushes, the *QE2*, legal male homosexuality, the contraceptive pill, *Private Eye*, safety belts, abortion clinics, *Jackie* magazine, the Trimphone, Brut 33, Pedigree Chum, ASDA, Green Shield stamps, the mini skirt, James Bond films, pirate radio, the Booker Prize, Yellow Pages, Gold Blend coffee, Ibuprofen, Radio 1, *Top of the Pops*, the Homepride flour graders in their bowler hats, Peanuts, *Call My Bluff*, Shelter, *Songs of Praise*, BBC2, Mothercare, Habitat, Twister, Mr Kipling, Pringles, Fairy Liquid, clingfilm, the Jacuzzi, bar codes

THINGS THAT BEGAN IN THE 1970s

Bell bottoms, lava lamps, Argos catalogue, *The Antiques Road Show*, the CD, Grange Hill, *Scoobie Doo*, Mr Sheen, Pot Noodle, soft contact lenses, punk music, *Only Fools and Horses*, floppy disks, the VCR, Post-It Notes, liposuction, word processors, gay lib, North Sea oil, decimal currency, VAT, hotpants, (legal) commercial radio, three-day week, genetic engineering, cricket world cup, test-tube babies, palimony, *Fawlty Towers*, *Not The Nine O'Clock News*

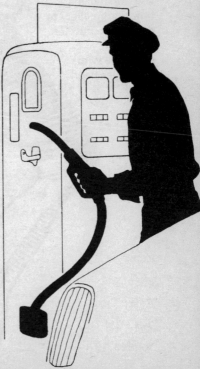

THE WAY WE LIVE

The average person spends two weeks over their lifetime waiting for the traffic lights to change.

One in ten people live on an island.

Married men change their underwear twice as often as single men.

Every year one ton of cement is poured for every man, woman and child in the world.

If you are struck by lightning once, you are 100,000 times more likely to get struck another time than someone who has never been struck.

It is said that small particles of faecal matter can become airborne during toilet flushing, and dentists recommend keeping your toothbrush 2 metres away from the toilet to avoid contamination. If your bathroom isn't big enough, put the lid down before flushing.

62 per cent of email is spam.

After hours working at a computer display, look at a blank piece of white paper. It will probably appear pink.

There is no such thing as naturally blue food – even blueberries are purple.

Astronauts have to be under 6 feet in height.

There's a systematic lull in conversation every seven minutes.

Paranormal experts say we reach the peak of our ability to see ghosts at the age of seven.

Laughing lowers levels of stress hormones and strengthens the immune system.

Women burn fat more slowly than men.

There are more mobile phones than people in Britain.

Only a third of the people who can twitch their ears can twitch them one at a time.

During menstruation, the sensitivity of a woman's middle finger is reduced.

71 per cent of office workers stopped on the street for a survey agreed to give up their computer passwords in exchange for a chocolate bar.

Amusement park attendance goes up after a fatal accident. It seems that people want to take the same ride that killed someone.

64 per cent of people can roll their tongue.

Most toilets flush in E flat.

During a lifetime, the average person drinks 8,000 gallons of water and uses 68,250 gallons of water to brush their teeth.

Car drivers tend to go faster when other cars are around. It doesn't matter where the other cars are – whether in front, behind or alongside.

Most digital alarm clocks ring in the key of B flat.

In the average lifetime, a person will walk the equivalent of 5 times round the equator.

Newborn babies are given to the wrong mother 12 times a day in maternity wards across the world.

Wearing headphones for an hour increases the bacteria in your ear 700 times.

A computer user blinks on average seven times a minute.

If you gave each human on earth an equal portion of dry land, including the uninhabitable areas, everyone would get roughly 100 square feet (30.4 square metres).

The average person flexes the joints in their fingers 24 million times in a lifetime.

Fingerprints provide traction for the fingers.

We forget 80 per cent of what we learn every day.

50 per cent of lingerie purchases are returned to the shop.

The average smell weighs 760 nanograms.

At 200 miles (322 km) per hour, airbags explode.

There are 4.3 births and 1.7 deaths in the world every second.

If we had the same mortality rate now as in 1900, more than half the people in the world today would be dead.

If Britain's gas mains were laid end to end, they would go round the world a dozen times.

If all the carpets sold in a year in Britain were laid end to end, they would go all the way to the moon and halfway back again.

If all the credit cards used in Britain today were laid end to end, they would stretch from London to Istanbul.

If all the Easter eggs sold in Britain in one year were laid end to end, they'd go from London to Australia and halfway back again.

The QWERTY typewriter was designed so that the left hand typed the most common letters – it was a means of slowing down typists and keeping the typewriters from jamming.

HONEY

The honeybee is the only insect that produces food eaten by humans.

Historically honey was used to treat cuts and burns.

The Romans used honey instead of gold to pay their taxes.

Honey was part of Cleopatra's daily beauty ritual.

Beehives were sometimes used in ancient warfare, lobbed at the enemy as a kind of bomb.

It takes the nectar from two million flowers to make one pound (450g) of honey. One bee would therefore have to fly around 90,000 miles – three times around the globe – to make a pound of honey.

A bee visits 50 to 100 flowers during a collection trip, and makes altogether about a twelfth of a teaspoon of honey during its life.

The buzz of a honeybee comes from its wings, which beat more than 11,000 times a minute.

Worker bees are all female.

An explorer who found a 2000-year-old jar of honey in an Egyptian tomb said it tasted delicious.

Bees use the shortest route possible to reach the flower of their choice, hence the expression 'making a beeline for …'.

Politicans who changed parties

Winston Churchill (Conservative-Liberal-Conservative)

Alan Howarth (Conservative-Labour)

Reg Prentice (Labour-Conservative)

Sir Oswald Mosley (Conservative-Labour-Fascist)

Dr David Owen (Labour-SDP)

Shirley Williams (Labour-SDP)

Roy Jenkins (Labour-SDP)

Bill Rodgers (Labour-SDP)

Christopher Mayhew (Labour-Liberal)

Emma Nicholson (Conservative-Liberal)

Sir Cyril Smith (Labour-Liberal)

Enoch Powell (Conservative-Ulster Unionist)

Robert Jackson (Conservative-Labour)

Shaun Woodward (Conservative-Labour)

Peter Hain (Liberal-Labour – although he never represented the Liberals in Parliament)

Quentin Davies (Conservative-Labour)

Former MPs

John Buchan, Hilaire Belloc, Andrew Marvell, Samuel Pepys, Daniel Defoe, Sir Thomas More, Richard Brinsley Sheridan, A.P. Herbert, Edward Gibbon, Jeffrey Archer

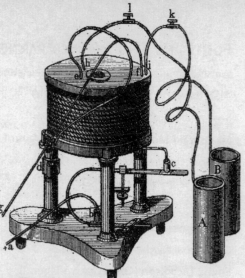

SCIENCE

Copper exposed to arsenic turns black.

The cracks in breaking glass move at speeds up to 3,000 miles (4,827 km) per hour.

A whip 'cracks' because its tip moves faster than the speed of sound.

Water freezes faster if it starts from a warm temperature than a cool one.

René Descartes came up with the theory of coordinate geometry by watching a fly walk across a ceiling.

Sound travels 15 times faster through steel than through air.

Methane gas can often be seen bubbling up in ponds. It is produced by decomposing plants and animals in the mud at the bottom.

An ounce of gold can be beaten into a thin film covering 100 square feet.

Lightning strikes our planet about 6,000 times a minute.

It is harder to reach the speed of sound at sea level than at altitude.

The silvery metal gallium is liquid at 29.8°C (85.6°F), which means it would melt in your hand. Cesium is another metal that would melt in your hand, but it would also react violently with your skin and possibly catch fire. The third metal that is liquid at more or less room temperature is mercury.

If you went unprotected into space, you would explode before you suffocated.

The holes in fly swatters are there to reduce air resistance. For the same reason, you should open your fingers when trying to kill mosquitoes by hand (it works).

Every megabyte sent over the internet needs two lumps of coal to power it.

A car travelling at 80 km/h needs half of its fuel just to overcome wind resistance.

A combustion engine wastes 75 per cent of the chemical energy contained in petrol.

The liquid inside young coconuts can be used as a substitute for blood plasma.

MUSIC

Johnny Depp played guitar on *Fade In-Out* by Oasis and appeared in the video for Tom Petty's *Into The Wide Great Open*.

John Cage composed 'Imaginary Landscape No.4', which was scored for twelve radios tuned at random.

Steve Davis once promoted a rock concert (for the French jazz-rock group Magma).

Actor Jon Voight's brother, Chip Taylor, wrote the song *Wild Thing*.

Myleene Klass, the singer and pianist, insured her hands for £1 million.

Karen Carpenter's doorbell chimed the first six notes of *We've Only Just Begun*.

Rolf Harris played didgeridoo on *The Dreaming* by Kate Bush.

Songs that don't feature their titles in the lyrics

'Killer' (Adamski)

'Martha's Harbour' (All About Eve)

'Pure Shores' (All Saints)

'A Life Less Ordinary' (Ash)

'A Day In The Life' (The Beatles)

'Ballad of John And Yoko' (The Beatles)

'For You Blue' (The Beatles)

'Tomorrow Never Knows' (The Beatles)

'Ambulance' (Blur)

'Space Oddity' (David Bowie)

'For What It's Worth' (Buffalo Springfield)

'Superstar' (The Carpenters)

'Why I Can't Stand One-Night Stands' (Catatonia)

'Tubthumping' (Chumbawumba)

'Death of a Ladies' Man' (Leonard Cohen)

'The Scientist' (Coldplay)

'Badge' (Cream)

'Suite: Judy Blue Eyes' (Crosby, Stills and Nash)

'7 Days' (Craig David)

'Annie's Song' (John Denver)

'It Takes a Lot to Laugh, It Takes a Train to Cry' (Bob Dylan)

'Positively 4th Street' (Bob Dylan)

'Subterranean Homesick Blues' (Bob Dylan)

'The Circus' (Erasure)

'Guilty Conscience' (Eminem)

'Kinky Afro' (Happy Mondays)

'Earth Song' (Michael Jackson)

'Jilted John' (Jilted John)

'The Riddle' (Nik Kershaw)

'Black Dog' (Led Zeppelin)

'The Battle of Evermore' (Led Zeppelin)

'#9 Dream' (John Lennon)

'Act of Contrition' (Madonna)

'Creeque Alley' (The Mamas and The Papas)

'Porcelain' (Moby)

'Alternate Title' (The Monkees – the original title, which they were obliged to drop, was 'Randy Scouse Git', which also didn't feature in the lyrics)

'Suedehead' (Morrissey)

'Hate This and I'll Love You' (Muse)

'Blue Monday' (New Order)

'Smells Like Teen Spirit' (Nirvana)

'Complex' (Gary Numan)

'Shakermaker' (Oasis)

'The Riverboat Song' (Ocean Colour Scene)

'Brain Damage' (Pink Floyd)

'American Trilogy' (Elvis Presley)

'Disco 2000' (Pulp)

'Bohemian Rhapsody' (Queen – although it did contain the title of the song that knocked it off the top of the British charts – Abba's 'Mamma Mia')

'Talk Show Host' (Radiohead)

'Endless Cycle' (Lou Reed)

'The Sidewinder Sleeps Tonight' (R.E.M.)

'The Millennium Prayer' (Cliff Richard)

'Unchained Melody' (The Righteous Brothers)

'Sympathy for the Devil' (The Rolling Stones)

'Pyjamarama' (Roxy Music)

'The Immigrant Song' (Neil Sedaka)

'For Emily, Whenever I May Find Her' (Simon and Garfunkel)

'Pretzel Logic' (Steely Dan)

'The Caves of Altamira' (Steely Dan)

'Father and Son' (Cat Stevens)

'Richard III' (Supergrass)

'The Logical Song' (Supertramp)

'The Unforgettable Fire' (U2)

'Tom's Diner' (Suzanne Vega)

'Excerpt From A Teenage Opera' (Keith West)

'Ball Park Incident' (Wizzard)

'After The Gold Rush' (Neil Young)

People who used to be in pop groups

Fiona Bruce was the singer with Chez Nous.

Richard Hannon, the racehorse trainer, used to be a drummer with The Troggs.

Keith Chegwin was the lead singer in Kenny (which had a Number 3 hit in 1975 with 'The Bump').

Su Pollard was the singer with the pop group Midnight News.

Dani Behr started her career as one third of the group Faith, Hope and Charity.

Bruce Willis was in the band Loose Goose.

Martine McCutcheon was the lead singer of a three-girl group called Milan.

Emma Freud was a backing singer for Mike Oldfield.

Michael Howard played in a skiffle band.

Ken Stott sang with the group Keyhole.

Nigel Short, the chess champion and world title contender, played in a rock band called The Urge.

Asil Nadir played in a rock group called The Asils.

Neil Kinnock played guitar in a skiffle group called The Rebels.

Vince Earl (Ron Dixon in *Brookside*) played the tea-chest bass in a skiffle group called The Teenage Rebels.

Will Self was lead singer in a band called Will Self and the Abusers.

Woody Harrelson is lead singer in the band Manly Moondog and the Three Kool Hats.

Denise Van Outen was in a girl band called Those Two Girls.

River Phoenix was the vocalist in Aleka's Attic.

INSTRUMENTS AND THE PEOPLE WHO PLAY THEM

Bass guitar (Gary Sinise)

Guitar (Paul Bettany)

Piano and cello (Rosamund Pike)

Violin (David James)

French horn and trumpet (Samuel L. Jackson)

Guitar (Minnie Driver)

Harmonica (Dan Aykroyd)

Banjo (Steve Martin)

Trombone (Fiona Phillips)

Bagpipes (Alastair Campbell)

Bagpipes (Ken Stott)

Tuba (Hannah Waterman)

Piano (Jeff Goldblum)

Guitar (Kate Hudson)

Bass Guitar (Vic Reeves)

Violin (Meryl Streep)

Guitar (Ricky Gervais)

BANDS WHO CAME UP WITH UNIMAGINATIVE SONG TITLES

Doop (Doop, 1994)

Immaculate Fools (Immaculate Fools, 1985)

Jilted John (Jilted John, 1978)

Living in a Box (Living in a Box, 1987)

Love and Money (Love and Money, 1987)

Natural Life (Natural Life, 1992)

The Singing Dogs (The Singing Dogs, 1955)

Small Ads (Small Ads, 1981)

Talk Talk (Talk Talk, 1982)

Tricky Disco (Tricky Disco, 1990)

THE BEATLES BY NUMBER

Note that some numbers appear in more than one song.

1/2 'Yesterday'

1 'Day Tripper'

2 'Two of Us'

3 'Come Together'

4 'You Never Give Me Your Money'

5 'She's Leaving Home'

6 'All Together Now'

7 'And Your Bird Can Sing'

8 'Eight Days A Week'

9 'Revolution 9'

10 'Being For The Benefit of Mr Kite'

12 'Cry Baby Cry'

15 'She Came In Through The Bathroom Window'

17 'I Saw Her Standing There'

19 'Taxman'

20 'Sergeant Pepper's Lonely Hearts Club Band'

31 'Maxwell's Silver Hammer'

50 'Maxwell's Silver Hammer'

64 'When I'm 64'

909 'One After 909'

1,000 'Paperback Writer' or 'The Fool On The Hill'

4,000 'A Day In The Life'

1,000,000 'Across The Universe'

1 2 3 4 can I have a little more

AROUND THE WORLD IN BEATLES SONGS

Amsterdam 'The Ballad of John And Yoko'

Bishopsgate 'Being For The Benefit of Mr Kite'

Blackburn, Lancashire 'A Day In The Life'

California 'Get Back'

Dakota 'Rocky Raccoon'

France 'The Ballad of John And Yoko'

Georgia 'Back In The USSR'

Gibraltar 'The Ballad of John And Yoko'

Holland 'The Ballad of John And Yoko'

Isle of Wight 'When I'm 64'

Lime Street 'Maggie Mae'

Liverpool 'Maggie Mae'

London 'The Ballad of John And Yoko'

LA 'Los Angeles' 'Blue Jay Way'

Miami Beach 'Back In The USSR'

Moscow 'Back In The USSR'

Paris 'The Ballad of John And Yoko'

Penny Lane 'Penny Lane'

Southampton 'The Ballad of John And Yoko'

Spain 'The Ballad of John And Yoko'

Tucson, Arizona 'Get Back'

Ukraine 'Back In The USSR'

Vienna 'The Ballad of John And Yoko'

THE BEATLES IN NEWSPAPERS

Daily Mail 'Paperback Writer'

The News of The World
'Polythene Pam'

**The Sun 'Here Comes The Sun'
– with apologies**

JUST SOME OF THE BEATLES TRIBUTE BANDS

The Bootleg Beatles

Cavern

All You Need Is Love

Apple

The Backbeat Beatles

The Brazilian Beetles

Come Together

The Eggmen

The Fake Beatles

The Upbeat Beatles

The Fab Beatles

The Beatels

Revolver

Backbeat

Day Tripper

Day Trippers

The Fab Walrus

Help!

The Imagine

The Moptops

Rain

The Fab Four

The Beatleg

Apple Pies

Shout!

Strawberry Fields

Yesterday

ALL THE ACTS THAT HAD THREE — OR MORE — BRITISH NUMBER-ONE HITS IN THE SAME YEAR

Frankie Laine (1953: I Believe, Hey Joe!, Answer Me)

Elvis Presley (1961: Are You Lonesome Tonight?, Wooden Heart, Surrender, Little Sister/His Latest Flame)

Elvis Presley (1962: Rock-A-Hula Baby/Can't Help Falling In Love, Good Luck Charm, She's Not You, Return To Sender)

The Beatles (1963: From Me To You, She Loves You, I Want To Hold Your Hand)

Gerry and The Pacemakers (1963: How Do You Do It, I Like It, You'll Never Walk Alone)

The Beatles (1964: Can't Buy Me Love, A Hard Day's Night, I Feel Fine)

The Rolling Stones (1965: The Last Time, (I Can't Get No) Satisfaction, Get Off Of My Cloud)

The Beatles (1965: Ticket To Ride, Help!, Day Tripper/We Can Work It Out)

Slade (1973: Cum On Feel The Noize, Skweeze Me Pleeze Me, Merry Xmas Everybody)

Abba (1976: Mamma Mia, Fernando, Dancing Queen)

Blondie (1980: Atomic, Call Me, The Tide Is High)

Frankie Goes To Hollywood (1984: Relax, Two Tribes, The Power of Love)

Jason Donovan (1989: Especially For You, Too Many Broken Hearts, Sealed With A Kiss)

Take That (1993: Pray, Relight My Fire, Babe)

The Spice Girls (1996: Wannabe, Say You'll Be There, 2 Become 1)

The Spice Girls (1997: Mama/Who Do You Think You Are, Spice Up Your Life, Too Much)

All Saints (1998: Never Ever, Under The Bridge/Lady Marmalade, Bootie Call)

B*Witched (1998: C'Est La Vie, Rollercoaster, To You I Belong)

Westlife (1999: Swear It Again, If I Let You Go, Flying Without Wings, I Have A Dream/Seasons In The Sun)

Westlife (2000: Fool Again, Against All Odds, My Love)

Elvis Presley (2005: Jailhouse Rock, One Night, It's Now Or Never)

NB Will Young and Gareth Gates each had two solo number ones in 2002 and a joint number one – which means they don't qualify for this list

CLASSIC SINGLES THAT DIDN'T MAKE THE BRITISH TOP 20

'Someone Saved My Life Tonight' (Elton John)

'We've Only Just Begun' (The Carpenters)

'Stop Your Sobbing' (The Pretenders)

'Last Train To Clarksville' (The Monkees)

'I Don't Believe In Miracles' (Colin Blunstone)

'Wouldn't It Be Nice' (The Beach Boys)

'Rikki Don't Lose That Number' (Steely Dan)

'Angel of The Morning' (P.P. Arnold)

'Year of The Cat' (Al Stewart)

'What A Fool Believes' (The Doobie Brothers)

CELEBRITIES AND THE SINGLES THEY RELEASED

Patrick Swayze: 'Raisin' Heaven And Hell Tonight'

David Copperfield: 'Summer Days'

Farrah Fawcett: 'You'

Dame Elizabeth Taylor: 'Wings In The Sky'

Stefan Dennis: 'Don't It Make You Feel Good'

Tom Watt: 'Subterranean Homesick Blues'

Clint Eastwood: 'I Talk To The Trees'

Leonard Nimoy: 'Proud Mary'

Terry Wogan: 'Floral Dance'

Ingrid Bergman: 'This Old Man'

David McCallum: 'Louie Louie'

Lon Chaney Jnr: 'Monster Holiday'

Diego Maradona: 'La Mano De Dios' – 'The Hand of God'

Russell Crowe: 'I Want To Be Like Marlon Brando'

Billy Crystal: 'The Christmas Song'

Meryl Streep: 'Amazing Grace'

Peter Fonda: 'Catch The Wind'

Linda Evans: 'Don't You Need'

Britt Ekland: 'Do It To Me'

Sir Anthony Hopkins: 'A Distant Star'

Oliver Reed: 'Lonely For A Girl'

Rebecca De Mornay: 'Oh Jimmy'

Gene Wilder: 'Pure Imagination'

Raquel Welch: 'This Girl's Back In Town'

Burt Reynolds: 'I Like Having You Around'

Robert Mitchum: 'Ballad of Thunder Road'

Princess Stephanie of Monaco: 'Live Your Life'

Richard Chamberlain: 'Love Me Tender'

William Shatner: 'Mr Tambourine Man

Kate Winslet: 'What If?'

SINGING DRUMMERS

Phil Collins, Kevin Godley, Don Henley, Dave Clark, Levon Helm, Ringo Starr, Stewart Copeland, Jim Capaldi, Karen Carpenter, Micky Dolenz

THE FIRST VIDEOS EVER SHOWN ON MTV (1981)

'Video Killed The Radio Star' (Buggles)

'You Better Run' (Pat Benatar)

'She Won't Dance With Me' (Rod Stewart)

'You Better You Bet' (The Who)

'Little Susie's On The Up' (PhD)

'We Don't Talk Anymore' (Cliff Richard)

'Brass In Pocket' (The Pretenders)

'Time Heals' (Todd Rundgren)

'Take It On The Run' (REO Speedwagon)

'Rockin' The Paradise' (Styx)

THE FIRST VIDEOS EVER SHOWN ON MTV EUROPE (1987)

'Money For Nothing' (Dire Straits)

'Fake' (Alexander O'Neal)

'U Got The Look' (Prince)

'It's A Sin' (The Pet Shop Boys)

'I Wanna Dance With Somebody (Who Loves Me)' (Whitney Houston)

'I Want Your Sex' (George Michael)

'Who's That Girl' (Madonna)

'I Really Didn't Mean It' (Luther Vandross)

'Misfit' (Curiosity Killed The Cat)

'Your Love Keeps Lifting Me Higher And Higher' (Jackie Wilson)

PEOPLE WHO HAD SONGS WRITTEN FOR THEM

Woody Harrelson – 'Woody' (Hootie and The Blowfish)

Gwyneth Paltrow – 'Moses' (Chris Martin)

Angie Bowie – 'Angie' (The Rolling Stones)

Nancy Sinatra – 'Nancy With The Laughing Face' (Frank Sinatra)

Carole King – 'Oh Carol' (Neil Sedaka)

Frances Tomelty – 'Every Breath You Take' (The Police)

Patti D'Arbanville – 'Lady D'Arbanville' (Cat Stevens)

Rosanna Arquette – 'Rosanna' (Toto)

Paula Yates – 'No-one Compares To You' (Michael Hutchence)

Paul McGrath – 'I Believe In God' (Nigel Kennedy)

Diana, Princess of Wales – 'Candle In The Wind 1997' (Elton John)

Magic Johnson – 'Positive' (Michael Franti)

David Geffen – 'A Free Man In Paris' (Joni Mitchell)

Eric Clapton – 'My Favourite Mistake' (Sheryl Crow)

Robert F. Kennedy – 'Long Time Gone' (David Crosby)

Syd Barrett – 'Shine On You Crazy Diamond' (Roger Waters)

Duke Ellington – 'Sir Duke' (Stevie Wonder)

Kari-Anne Jagger (wife of Chris Jagger) – 'Carrie Anne' (The Hollies)

Jodie Foster – 'Other Ways of Speaking' (Russell Crowe)

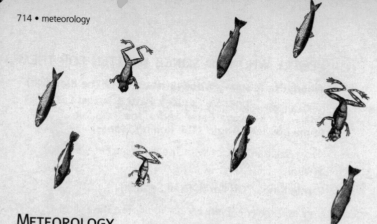

METEOROLOGY

It would take 7 billion particles of fog to fill a teaspoon. A cubic mile of fog is made up of less than a gallon of water.

No rain has ever been recorded in the Atacama desert in Chile.

The sunlight that strikes the earth at any given moment (in total) weighs as much as a large ocean liner.

500 million litres of rain can fall during a thunderstorm.

A snowflake can take up to an hour to land.

12 per cent of the earth's land surface is permanently covered by ice and snow.

The South Pole has no sun for 182 days each year.

On 17 July 1841, a shower of hail and rain in Derby was accompanied by a fall of hundreds of small fish and frogs – some of them still alive.

Small clouds that look like they have broken off from bigger clouds are called scuds.

A full moon always rises at sunset.

A full moon is nine times brighter than a half moon.

On 14 August 1979, a rainbow over North Wales lasted for three hours.

PEOPLE WHO GOT THEIR BREAK ON *NEW FACES*

Jim Davidson, Lenny Henry, Victoria Wood, Marti Caine, Michael Barrymore, Roger De Courcey, Patti Boulaye, Les Dennis, Malandra Burrows, Peter Andre, Joe Pasquale

PEOPLE WHO GOT THEIR BREAK ON *OPPORTUNITY KNOCKS*

Les Dawson, Tom O'Connor, Mary Hopkin, Engelbert Humperdinck, Bobby Crush, Bonnie Langford, Freddie Starr, Little & Large, Peters & Lee, Lena Zavaroni, Frank Carson, Pam Ayres, Max Boyce, Freddie Davies

PEOPLE WHO APPEARED IN SOAP OPERAS

Derek Nimmo – *Neighbours*

Jenny Hanley – *Emmerdale*

Clive James – *Neighbours*

Peter Purves – *EastEnders*

Angela Thorne – *Emmerdale*

David Jason – *Crossroads*

Diane Keen – *Crossroads*

Cat Deeley – *Hollyoaks*

Christian Slater – *Ryan's Hope*

Ricky Martin – *General Hospital*; started as a singing bartender and then got a regular role

Russell Crowe – *Neighbours*

Val Kilmer – *Knot's Landing*

Brad Pitt – *Dallas*

Jude Law – *Families*

Holly Valance – *Neighbours*

Demi Moore – *General Hospital*

Kevin Kline – *Search For Tomorrow*

Alec Baldwin – *The Doctors*

Tommy Lee Jones – *One Life To Live*

Morgan Freeman – *Another World*

Kevin Bacon – *Guiding Light*

Meg Ryan – *As The World Turns*

Christopher Walken – *Guiding Light*

Marisa Tomei – *As The World Turns*

Sigourney Weaver – *Somerset*

Ray Liotta – *Another World*

Susan Sarandon – *Search For Tomorrow*

David Walliams – *EastEnders*

Michael Palin – *Home And Away*

Dame Judi Dench – *The Archers*

PEOPLE WHO APPEARED IN *CORONATION STREET*

Richard Beckinsale (P.C. Willcocks)

Michael Ball (Malcolm Nuttall)

Prunella Scales (Eileen Hughes)

Davy Jones (Colin Lomax)

Martin Shaw (Robert Croft)

Dame Beryl Bainbridge (Ken Barlow's girlfriend)

Noddy Holder (Stan Potter)

Michael Elphick (Douglas Wormold)

Mel B. (Bettabuys worker)

Joanna Lumley (Elaine Perkins)

Peter Noone (Stanley Fairclough)

Gorden Kaye (Bernard Butler)

Sir Ben Kingsley (Ron Jenkins)

Max Wall (Harry Payne)

Bill Maynard (Mickey Malone)

Gilly Coman (Sugar La Marr)

Paul Shane (Frank Draper)

Kenneth Cope (Jed Stone)

Tony Anholt (David Law)

Kathy Staff (Vera Hopkins)

Leonard Sachs (Sir Julius Berlin)

Paula Wilcox (Janice Langton)

Mollie Sugden (Nellie Harvey)

Ian McKellen (Mel Hutchwright)

Peter Kay (Eric Garside)

Sir Norman Wisdom (Ernie Crabbe)

PEOPLE WHO APPEARED IN *GRANGE HILL*

Susan Tully (Suzanne Ross 1981–84)

Letitia Dean (Lucinda 1978)

Sean Maguire (Tegs Ratcliffe 1988–91)

Todd Carty (Peter 'Tucker' Jenkins 1978–82)

Alex Kingston (Jill Harcourt 1980)

Michelle Gayle (Fiona Wilson 1988–89)

Patsy Palmer (bit parts for three years)

John Alford (Robbie Wright 1985–90)

Naomi Campbell (Uncredited pupil 1978)

PEOPLE WHO MADE GUEST APPEARANCES IN *THE BILL*

Rik Mayall, Paul O'Grady, Brian Glover, Ray Winstone, Craig Charles, Leslie Phillips, Letitia Dean, Anita Dobson, Leslie Ash, Alex Kingston, Emma Bunton, Michelle Collins, Linda Robson, Robert Carlyle, Martin Kemp, Denise Van Outen, Leslie Grantham, Emmanuel Petit, Linda Lusardi, Tamzin Outhwaite

PEOPLE WHO MADE GUEST APPEARANCES IN *THE AVENGERS*

John Cleese, Donald Sutherland, Warren Mitchell, John Thaw, Charlotte Rampling, Ronnie Barker, Christopher Lee, Ron Moody, Joss Ackland, Peter Cushing, Arthur Lowe, Roy Kinnear, Gordon Jackson, Peter Wyngarde, Jon Pertwee, Yootha Joyce, Penelope Keith, Peter Bowles

PEOPLE WHO MADE GUEST APPEARANCES IN *CASUALTY*

Kate Winslet, Alfred Molina, Sadie Frost, Jonny Lee Miller, Julian Fellowes, Minnie Driver, Kathy Burke, Lionel Jeffries, Pete Postlethwaite, Amanda Redman, Christopher Eccleston, Sophie Okonedo, Nick Moran, Dorothy Tutin, Julia Sawalha

PEOPLE WHO MADE GUEST APPEARANCES IN *THE ADVENTURES OF ROBIN HOOD*

Peter Asher, Hubert Gregg, Richard O'Sullivan, Leo McKern, Leslie Phillips, Thora Hird, Nicholas Parsons, Jane Asher, Ian Bannen, John Schlesinger, Bernard Bresslaw, Patrick Troughton, Wilfrid Brambell, Harry H. Corbett, Nigel Davenport, Andrew Faulds, Lionel Jeffries, Geoffrey Bayldon, Ronald Allen, Billie Whitelaw, Gordon Jackson, Desmond Llewelyn, Michael Gough

PEOPLE WHO WERE ON *THIS IS YOUR LIFE* BEFORE THE AGE OF 30

Twiggy (aged 20)

Bonnie Langford (21)

Stephen Hendry (21)

Robin Cousins (22)

John Conteh (23)

George Best (25)

Ian Botham (25)

Kevin Keegan (27)

Elaine Paige (27)

Jim Davidson (29)

PEOPLE WHO WERE ON *THIS IS YOUR LIFE* TWICE

Lord Andrew Lloyd Webber, Frankie Vaughan, Richard Briers, Sir Jimmy Savile, Honor Blackman, Dame Shirley Bassey, Edward Woodward, Sir Harry Secombe, Dame Barbara Cartland, Dame Vera Lynn, Sir Peter Ustinov, George Best

PEOPLE WHO REFUSED TO GO ON *THIS IS YOUR LIFE*

Danny Blanchflower, Richard Gordon, Noel Gallagher

PEOPLE WHO WORKED ON
SPITTING IMAGE

Voices: Chris Barrie, Rory Bremner, Steve Coogan, Hugh Dennis, Adrian Edmondson, Harry Enfield, Alistair McGowan, Jan Ravens, John Sessions, Pamela Stephenson, John Thomson

Writers: Richard Curtis, Jack Docherty, Ben Elton, Ian Hislop, John O'Farrell, Steve Punt

PEOPLE WHO MADE GUEST APPEARANCES ON US TV SHOWS

Sir Richard Branson – *Baywatch*

Sir Paul McCartney – *Baywatch*

Leonard Cohen – *Miami Vice*

Ray Charles – *Moonlighting*

Norman Beaton – *The Cosby Show*

Peter Noone – *My Two Dads*

Phil Collins – *Miami Vice*

Frank Sinatra – *Magnum, P.I.*

Dionne Warwick – *The Rockford Files*

Carly Simon – *thirtysomething*

Boy George – *The A-Team*

Davy Jones – *My Two Dads*

Ewan McGregor – *ER*

GANFYD

At the back of *This Book* and *That Book*, I asked readers to come up with ideas. One reader who did was Dr Peter Davies, who sent me some examples of extraordinary requests for doctors' notes – under the heading Get A Note From Your Doctor (GANFYD) – collected from the website www.doctors.net.uk.

LETTER REQUESTED ...

To confirm that 'I'm too breathless to cut the grass'.

To confirm that a patient has an artificial limb.

To confirm that a patient's daughter is female, because the passport office had issued a passport with no stated sex on it.

To confirm that a 16-year-old girl does not have chicken pox.

To state that the doctor knows of no reason why a student should not massage members of the public.

To give to a school so that the father isn't sent to jail for the child's non-attendance.

To 'say that my daughter can appear in the school play'.

To 'say that my old-fashioned mobile phone is causing me tension headaches'.

To 'say that chewing gum at the checkout helps me breathe'.

To confirm that a patient gets backache – so he can get a more comfortable BMW from his firm.

To confirm that a potential employee 'is fit to handle cheese'.

To confirm that a patient is fit to drive, even though she'd just received an 18-month driving ban.

To confirm that a patient has latex allergy – 'so I couldn't possibly be guilty of kerb crawling as with this I would not want to wear a condom'.

To say that a patient's acne is so bad she cannot go to the gym (and so can get a refund).

To say that a patient's new coat caused them a rash (so that the shop would give a refund).

IT'S NOT ONLY THE PATIENTS:

A holiday insurance company asked whether a GP would have said a patient was fit to travel had the GP seen him before he left.

A school required a doctor's note before allowing a child with a leg in plaster of Paris to be excused swimming lessons.

An American state asks doctors to certify condemned prisoners as fit to be executed.

At a hospital: 'That's a new problem so before we can do anything you'll need to get a note from your doctor.'

At a dentist's: 'Due to pressure on the system get a note from the doctor if you need to see the dentist.'

A local bank rang the doctor's surgery to ask for a note confirming that the customer 'is who she says she is'.

'Periodically it is necessary to obtain proof that pensioners are being paid correctly and we would be grateful if you could complete this form to confirm that [X] is still alive ...'

you'll need a note from your doctor

PEOPLE WHO CHOSE 'MY WAY' ON *DESERT ISLAND DISCS*

Jimmy Tarbuck, Sir David Frost, Geoffrey Boycott, Russell Harty, Lord Norman Tebbit, David Broome, Jimmy Jewel, Gareth Edwards, Barry John, Johnny Speight, Alan Minter, Stewart Granger, Sir Stanley Kalms

PEOPLE WHO CHOSE PROUST'S *A LA RECHERCHE DU TEMPS PERDU* AS THEIR BOOK ON *DESERT ISLAND DISCS*

Tony Blair, Mary Archer, Sir Stephen Spender, Michael Portillo, Cyril Connolly, Michael White

PEOPLE WHO DECLINED TO GO ON *DESERT ISLAND DISCS*

Sir Laurence Olivier, George Bernard Shaw, Sir Albert Finney, Prince Charles, Leo Sayer (after the BBC couldn't find his favourite records)

EXTRAORDINARY LUXURIES CHOSEN ON *DESERT ISLAND DISCS*

Haemorrhoid cream – Jimmy McGovern

New York's Chrysler building – Terry Pratchett

Model of the Tower of London – Denis Norden

A suicide pill – Stephen Fry

The *Mona Lisa* – Arthur Scargill

Silk underwear – Dame Helen Mirren

A stick of marijuana – Norman Mailer

A car to clean – Rowan Atkinson

A replica of Broadcasting House – Sir Harry Secombe

Madge Allsop – Dame Edna Everage (the only time a 'person' has been allowed as a luxury on the show)

Electrical device to heat shaving foam – Billy Connolly

Big bag of plaster to make heads of friends – Virginia Ironside

A Barclaycard – Spike Milligan

The laws of the land (so he could break them) – Benjamin Zephaniah

A hot bath with extra tap for cold champagne – Jane Asher

The front seat of a Porsche – Iain Banks

Notting Hill Pizza Express – Richard Curtis

Space invaders – Clive James

A car to listen to music in – Sir Michael Gambon

A life-sized papier maché model of Margaret Thatcher and a baseball bat – John Cleese

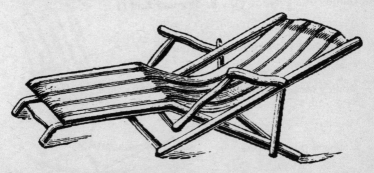

Having *The Sporting Life* delivered daily – Des O'Connor

An inflatable rubber woman – Oliver Reed

An inflatable woman and a puncture repair kit – Michael Crawford

A deckchair – Eric Morecambe

A deckchair ticket-machine – Ernie Wise

Nelson's Column – Lionel Bart

Nothing (he's had enough luxury to last a lifetime) – Colin Montgomerie

All-purpose prosthetic arm – Julian Clary

PEOPLE WHO CHOSE THEIR OWN SONGS ON *DESERT ISLAND DISCS*

Cilla Black ('Anyone Who Had A Heart')

Hylda Baker ('Give Us A Kiss')

Tony Bennett ('Smile')

Gary Glitter ('Rock And Roll I Gave You The Best Years Of My Life')

Dame Edna Everage ('My Bridesmaid And I')

Alan Price ('House of The Rising Sun')

Mel Brooks ('Springtime For Hitler')

Clive Dunn ('Grandad')

Dudley Moore ('Little Miss Britten')

FISH ETC.

During low tides, fiddler crabs darken in colour and emerge from their burrows; during high tides they turn pale and retreat. Kept in a laboratory far away from the ocean, they still keep time with the tide, changing colour as it ebbs and flows.

Dolphins don't breathe autonomically; breathing for them is a conscious act.

Jellyfish sometimes evaporate.

The Weddell seal can travel underwater for seven miles without surfacing for air.

A male sea lion can go for three months without eating.

In the Caribbean there are oysters that can climb trees.

The lantern fish has a glowing spot on its head that would be bright enough to read by.

A starfish can move in any direction without having to turn since it has no front or back.

Only one in a thousand creatures born in the sea reaches maturity.

Next to man, the porpoise is the most intelligent creature on earth.

Shrimps swim backwards.

A barnacle has the largest penis of any creature relative to its size.

The embryos of tiger sharks fight each other in the womb and only survivors get born.

Octopuses have gardens (as Ringo knew).

An octopus's eye has a rectangular pupil.

Tuna swim at a steady rate of 9 miles (14 km) per hour until they die – they never stop moving.

The mudskipper is a fish that can walk on land.

A blue whale's heart beats nine times a minute.

The blue whale, the largest creature on earth, weighs approximately as much as 224,000 copies of *Moby Dick*.

A lobster can lay 150,000 eggs at one time.

Texas horned toads can fire blood out of the corners of their eyes.

A sea squirt found in the seas near Japan has occasion at a certain point in its life to digest its own brain. When it reaches maturity, it attaches itself to a rock, and with no further need to move, dispenses with its brain by consuming it.

If you are served a crayfish with a straight tail, you shouldn't eat it. It was dead before it was cooked.

A baby grey whale drinks enough milk to fill more than 2,000 baby bottles a day.

A killer whale torpedoes a shark from underneath, bursting the shark by entering its stomach.

Pairs of People Born on the Same Day

Robert Palmer & Dennis Taylor (19.1.1949)

Heather Small & Sophie, Countess of Wessex (20.1.1965)

Vic Reeves & Nastassja Kinski (24.1.1959)

Andrew Ridgeley & Jose Mourinho (26.1.1963)

Roberta Flack & Peter Purves (10.2.1939)

Christina Ricci & Sarah Lancaster (12.2.1980)

Gene Pitney & Julia McKenzie (17.2.1941)

Andrew Strauss & Chris Martin (2.3.1977)

Eddy Grant & Elaine Paige (5.3.1948)

Rachel Weisz & Matthew Vaughn (7.3.1971)

Terry Holmes & Osama Bin Laden (10.3.1957)

Joe Bugner & William H. Macy (13.3.1950)

Gail Porter & Natascha McElhone (23.3.1971)

Eric Clapton & Johnnie Walker (30.3.1945)

Celine Dion & Donna D'Errico (30.3.1968)

Sarah Michelle Gellar & Freddie Ljungberg (14.4.1977)

Claire Sweeney & Jennifer Garner (17.4.1972)

Penelope Cruz & Vernon Kay (28.4.1974)

Benjamin Spock & Bing Crosby (2.5.1903)

Olga Korbut & Debra Winger & Hazel O'Connor (16.5.1955)

Caroline Charles & Nobby Stiles (18.5.1942)

Malcolm X & Pol Pot (19.5.1925)

Leo Sayer & Ian McEwan (21.5.1948)

Hergé & Sir Laurence Olivier (22.5.1907)

Gladys Knight & Faith Brown (28.5.1944)

Heidi Klum & Saffron Burrows (1.6.1973)

Michael J. Fox & Aaron Sorkin (9.6.1961)

Barry Hearn & Nick Drake (19.6.1948)

Jane Russell & Judy Holliday & Jean Kent (21.6.1921)

Marc Almond & Tom Hanks (9.7.1956)

Gough Whitlam & Reg Varney (11.7.1916)

Blake Edwards & Jason Robards (26.7.1922)

Gillian Anderson & Eric Bana (9.8.1968)

Adrian Lester & Darren Clarke (14.8.1968)

Martin Freeman & David Arquette (8.9.1971)

David Copperfield & Mickey Rourke (16.9.1956)

Lance Armstrong & Jada Pinkett Smith (18.9.1971)

Bruce Springsteen & Floella Benjamin (23.9.1949)

Mika Hakkinen & Naomi Watts (28.9.1968)

Rula Lenska & Marc Bolan (30.9.1947)

John Entwistle & Peter Tosh (9.10.1944)

Nicholas Parsons & Murray Walker (10.10.1923)

Ann Jones & Evel Knievel (17.10.1938)

Susan Tully & Monica Ali (20.10.1967)

Larry Mullen Jr & Peter Jackson (31.10.1961)

Griff Rhys Jones & Tony Parsons (6.11.1953)

Lucy Liu & David Batty (2.12.1968)

Jeff Bridges & Pamela Stephenson (4.12.1949)

Janet Street-Porter & Polly Toynbee (27.12.1946)

POTATOES

Potatoes were first eaten more than six thousand years ago by natives (later Incas) living in the Andes mountains of Peru.

The Incas measured time by how long it took for potatoes to cook.

Their descendants, the Quechua Indians, have more than a thousand different names for potatoes.

Sir Walter Raleigh introduced potatoes to Europe in the late 16th century and grew them at his Irish estate near Cork.

Religious leaders denounced the potato because it wasn't mentioned in the Bible.

Potatoes are the world's fourth food staple – after wheat, corn and rice.

Every year enough potatoes are grown worldwide to cover a four-lane motorway circling the world six times.

Potatoes are grown worldwide in over 125 countries (even in space – in 1995).

China is the world's largest producer.

King Louis XVI of France wore potato blossoms in his buttonhole while Marie Antoinette wore them in her hair.

The word 'spud' comes from the name for a narrow flat spade that was used for digging potatoes.

We each eat an average of 110 kilograms (240 pounds) of potatoes every year – not quite as much as the Germans consume.

The potato is about 80 per cent water and 20 per cent solids and is related to the tomato and tobacco.

Mr Potato Head was the first toy to be advertised on American television.

Some superstitious people say you should carry a potato in your pocket to ease toothache.

The botanical name for the common potato is Solanum tuberosum.

If you unscrew a light bulb and the bulb breaks, cut a potato in half and push the potato in the socket and turn. It should remove the remainder of the bulb.

Storing potatoes with apples stops them from sprouting.

In 1778 Prussia and Austria fought the Potato War in which each side tried to starve the other by consuming their potato crop.

Until the late 18th century, the French believed that potatoes caused leprosy.

During the Alaskan Klondike gold rush of the 1890s, potatoes were so valued for their vitamin C content that miners traded gold for them.

BODIES

Patrick Swayze has broken his left knee five times.

Will Carling can't cross his legs because they're too muscular.

Ashton Kutcher has two webbed toes on his left foot.

Shania Twain has used cow-udder balm as a moisturizer.

Joe Pesci, Christopher Walken, Kiefer Sutherland, Barbara Kellerman, Dan Aykroyd and Kate Bosworth each have eyes of different colours as did Aristotle and Alexander the Great.

PEOPLE AND WHAT THEY ARE ALLERGIC TO

Warren Beatty – oysters

Lindsay Lohan – blueberries

David Duchovny – metal (on his body)

Carol Channing – bleach

Rosie O'Donnell – cats and horses

Ian Kelsey – wood

Simon Mayo – sunlight

Gary Webster – animals

Philippa Forrester – bread

Drew Barrymore – bee stings and perfume

Charles Kennedy – dogs, grass and make-up

Ross Kemp – wasps

Darius Danesh – mushrooms

Kathy Burke – white wine

Anne Diamond – wine and beer

Tricia Penrose – dust

David Cassidy – garlic

Lleyton Hewitt – grass, horses and cats

Gail Porter – oil

Cleo Rocos – shellfish

Kyle MacLachlan – wool

Ioan Gruffudd – cats

Chris Bisson – sawdust

Nadia Sawalha – yeast

Alice Beer – wheat

Julia Sawalha – caffeine

Belinda Carlisle – wheat

Rene Russo – sesame

Gareth Gates – oranges, coffee and cheese

Gillian Anderson – cat hair

Alistair McGowan – wig glue

Brad Pitt – dogs

HAY FEVER SUFFERERS

Philippa Forrester, Tyra Banks, Jeremy Clarkson, Tiger Woods, Michelle Wie, Michael Fish, Simon Mayo, Chris Evans, Suzanne Charlton, John Major, Steffi Graf, Nigel Mansell, Bruce Oldfield, Paul Young, Sergio Garcia, Jesper Parnevik, Jimmy Hill, Michelle Wie

PEOPLE WHO SURVIVED TUBERCULOSIS

Nelson Mandela, Paul Eddington, Saffron Burrows, Stewart Granger, Sir Leonard Cheshire, Bill McLaren, Engelbert Humperdinck, Richard Harris, Alan Sillitoe, Sir Gordon Richards, Ray Galton, Alan Simpson (indeed, it was while convalescing from TB that Galton and Simpson met – and then went on to write *Hancock* and *Steptoe and Son*), Tom Jones, Archbishop Desmond Tutu, Vic Reeves

INSOMNIACS

Mia Farrow, Sir Magdi Yacoub, Una Stubbs, Damon Albarn, Dame Eileen Atkins, Dulcie Gray, Sarah Kennedy, Sir Winston Churchill, Jeremy Clarkson, Derek Jameson, Michael Aspel, Phil Edmonds, Alexander Dumas, Alexander Pope, Sebastian Faulks, Jenni Falconer, J 5ive, Colin Farrell, Justin Timberlake, Richard Burton, Ernest Hemingway, Groucho Marx, Audie Murphy

SLEEPWALKERS

Ann Widdecombe (during her late teens at school)

Antony Worrall Thompson (along Brighton seafront as a boy)

GOUT SUFFERERS

Greg Dyke, Jonathan King, Ronnie Biggs, Terry Wogan, Fran Cotton, Tony Robinson, Sam Torrance, Antonio Carluccio, Sam Mendes, Carl Wilson, Nicholas Coleridge, Joseph Conrad, Julius Caesar, John Milton, Dr Samuel Johnson

PEOPLE WHO SUFFERED FROM GALLSTONES

Dawn French, Aristotle Onassis, Alexandra Bastedo, Larry Hagman, Linda Robson, Rosemary Conley, Pam Ferris, Benazir Bhutto, Claire Rayner, Pope John Paul II, Harold Macmillan, Yasser Arafat

PEOPLE WHO HAVE HAD A HEART MURMUR

Tony Blair, Barbara Windsor, Keith Duffy, Sir Alex Ferguson, Judy Finnigan, Arnold Schwarzenegger, Bridget Fonda, Gareth Hale, Retief Goosen, Rachel Hunter, Evander Holyfield, Dame Elizabeth Taylor

PEOPLE WHO SUFFERED FROM OBSESSIVE COMPULSIVE DISORDER

Emily Lloyd, Michelle Pfeiffer, Billy Bob Thornton, Winona Ryder, David Beckham, Woody Allen, Jane Horrocks, Harrison Ford, Paul Gascoigne, Charles Dickens, Leonardo DiCaprio

NB Art Carney's father suffered from OCD

PEOPLE WHO HAVE SUFFERED FROM ECZEMA

Liz Earle, Liam Gallagher, Trudie Goodwin, Brett Anderson, Michaela Strachan, Neil Hamilton, Claire Sweeney

PEOPLE WITH BEAUTY SPOTS

Madonna, Robert De Niro, Cheryl Ladd, Sir Roger Moore, Cindy Crawford, Lisa Stansfield, Sherilyn Fenn, Lynsey De Paul, Chesney Hawkes, Marilyn Monroe

PEOPLE WHO HAVE USED HYPNOSIS

Lisa Kudrow (for stopping smoking)

Melanie Griffith (for stopping smoking)

Britney Spears (for stopping biting her nails)

Jennifer Aniston (for stopping smoking)

Pat Benatar (for relaxing her vocal cords)

Courteney Cox (for stopping smoking)

Tori Spelling (for her fear of flying)

Christy Turlington (for stopping smoking)

Salma Hayek (for fear of snakes)

Catherine Deneuve (for stopping smoking)

PEOPLE WHO ARE COLOUR-BLIND

William Hague, Paul Newman, Rod Stewart, Jack Nicklaus, Nicky Piper, Peter Bowles, Peter Ebdon, Sir Donald Sinden, Mark Williams, Bill Beaumont, George Michael

PEOPLE WHO HAVE SUFFERED FROM SERIOUS DEPRESSION

Billy Joel, Jill Gascoine, Charlotte Rampling, Judy Finnigan, Sir Elton John, Claire Rayner, Axl Rose, Paul Gascoigne, Sheryl Crow, Kenneth Branagh, Patsy Kensit, Sarah Lancashire, Bill Paxton, Marie Osmond, Kerry Katona, Lenny Henry, Trisha Goddard, Frances Barber, Paul O'Grady, Monty Don

PEOPLE WHO USED TO CUT THEMSELVES

Johnny Depp used to cut himself (the small knife-marks on his arms marked certain rites of passage)

Christina Ricci used to stub out burning cigarettes on her body and gouge herself with bottle tops. Interestingly, Ricci and Depp co-starred in *Sleepy Hollow*

Princess Diana used to cut herself with a penknife

Shirley Manson, as a teenager, used to slash her legs with a razor

PEOPLE WHO WORE BRACES ON THEIR TEETH AS ADULTS

Jill St John, Jack Klugman, Diana Ross, Carol Burnett, Cher, Tom Cruise

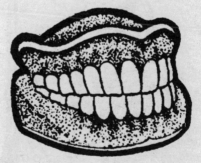

PEOPLE WHO HAD THEIR SPLEENS REMOVED

Keanu Reeves, Bob Hawke, Burt Reynolds, Geoffrey Boycott

PEOPLE WHO HAD A LUNG REMOVED

Tupac Shakur, Malcolm Allison, Auberon Waugh, Hughie Green, Vaclav Havel, Doug Mountjoy, Link Wray, Stewart Granger, King George VI, Robert Maxwell, Viscount Bernard Montgomery

INSECTS ETC.

Anteaters would rather eat termites.

The world's smallest winged insect is the Tanzanian parasitic wasp, which is smaller than a housefly's eye.

A large swarm of locusts can eat 80,000 tons of corn in a day.

A spider dismantling its web is a sure sign of a storm on the way.

It is said that 80 per cent of the creatures on earth have six legs.

The cockroach is the fastest thing on six legs: it can cover a metre a second.

Blood-sucking hookworms inhabit 700 million people worldwide.

Crickets 'hear' through their knees.

Maggots were once used to treat a bone infection called osteomyelitis.

There are 1 million ants for every person in the world.

The Madagascan hissing cockroach gives birth to live young (rather than laying eggs) – it is one of very few insects to do this.

The Venus flytrap takes less than half a second to slam shut on an insect.

Tarantulas extend and withdraw their legs by controlling the amount of blood pumped into them.

If you put a drop of alcohol on a scorpion, it will go mad and sting itself to death.

Dragonflies can fly at 30 miles per hour, but live for only 24 hours.

A species of earthworm in Australia can grow to 3 metres (about 10 feet) long.

Many hairy caterpillars carry a toxin that can be painful to humans if touched.

On waking, ants stretch and appear to yawn in a very human manner.

From hatching to pupation, a caterpillar increases its body size 30,000 times.

Only full-grown male crickets can chirp.

The largest insect on earth is the South American acteon beetle (*Megasoma acteon*), which measures 9cm by 5cm, and is 4cm thick.

The largest insects that ever lived were giant dragonflies with wingspans of 91cm.

The heaviest insect is the goliath beetle, weighing in at 100 grams.

The neck of the male long-necked weevil is twice as long as its body.

The colour of a head louse can depend on the colour of its human host's hair.

The sound made by bees, mosquitoes and other buzzing insects comes from their rapidly moving wings.

Monarch butterflies regularly migrate beween southern Canada and central Mexico, a distance of 2,500 miles. They weigh 0.5 gram, travel at 20 miles per hour and reach altitudes of 3,000 metres.

A scorpion could withstand 200 times more nuclear radiation than a human could.

Cockroaches like to eat the glue on the back of stamps.

The fastest Lepidoptera are the sphinx moths. They have been recorded at speeds of 60 kilometres (37 miles) per hour.

Mosquito repellents don't repel mosquitoes but rather prevent the mosquitoes from knowing you are there by blocking their sensors.

Termites will eat your house twice as fast if you play them loud music.

The silkworm, *Bombix mori*, is the only truly domesticated insect. The adult moths are so tame they can barely fly and must be fed by hand. About 10 pounds of mulberry leaves are needed for silkworms to manufacture 1 pound of cocoons, from which can be spun 100 miles of silk thread.

The millipede has approximately 750 legs.

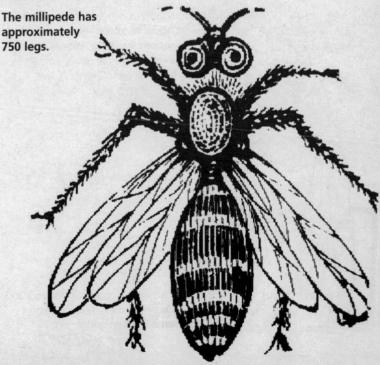

KEEN PAINTERS

Michelle Pfeiffer, Josh Hartnett, Heath Ledger, Marilyn Manson, Pierce Brosnan, Christopher Walken, Arnold Schwarzenegger, Donna Summer, Sir Sean Connery, Dame Beryl Bainbridge, Prince Charles, David Bowie, Eric Cantona, David Bailey, Robbie Coltrane, Will Carling, Cherie Lunghi, Björk, Holly Johnson, Lauren Hill, Sting, Sir Elton John, Peter Gabriel, Sir Cliff Richard, Brian May, Debbie Harry, Jarvis Cocker, Bob Dylan, Graham Coxon, Lulu, Bob Geldof, John Lithgow, Jane Seymour, Jeff Bridges, Viggo Mortensen, Dennis Hopper

KEEN POKER PLAYERS

Tobey Maguire, Jennifer Aniston, James Woods, Leonardo DiCaprio, Mark Williams, Eric Bristow, Phil Taylor, Stephen Fry, Ricky Gervais, Joan Collins, Guy Ritchie, Vinnie Jones, Salman Rushdie, Michael Owen, Caprice, Claire Goose, Jason Flemyng, Mike Tindall, Samuel West, Zara Phillips

Railway enthusiasts

Peter Snow, Chris Donald, Jim Bowen, Keith Floyd, Timothy West, Phil Collins, Michael Palin, Pete Waterman, Jools Holland, Rod Stewart (collects Hornby train sets), Patrick Stewart

Keen scrabble players

Jo Brand, Norman Cook (Fatboy Slim), Delia Smith, Jeremy Clarkson, Jonathan Ross, Nicky Haslam, Eno, Ginger Baker, Laura Davies, Guy Ritchie, Ant, Dec, Damon Albarn, Chris Martin, Alistair McGowan, Sean Hughes, Moby

Keen photographers

Lord Denis Healey, John Suchet, David Suchet, Steven Berkoff, Viggo Mortensen, Michael Bond, Prince Harry, Prince Andrew, Sir Ranulph Fiennes, Karl Lagerfeld, Helena Christensen, Morten Harket, Ben Kay, Bryan Adams, Jamie Theakston, Jeff Bridges, Mary-Kate Olsen, Michael Ancram, Penny Lancaster

Keen ornithologists

Bill Oddie, Norman Lamont, Prince Andrew, Judith Chalmers, Jack Cunningham, Nigel Planer, Magnus Magnusson, Daryl Hall, Bernard Cribbins, Neil Buchanan, Robin Oakley, Kenneth Clarke, Jarvis Cocker, Vic Reeves, Keith Flint

Keen gardeners

Penelope Keith, Sir Michael Caine, Anna Ford, Prunella Scales, Jimmy Greaves, Siân Phillips, Ken Livingstone, Roger Lloyd Pack, Elizabeth Hurley, Lord Michael Heseltine, Edward Fox, Nigel Havers, Sam Neill, Robert Kilroy-Silk, Richard Briers, Trevor Phillips, Hannah Gordon, Susannah York, Lynn Redgrave, Matthew Modine, Jenny Seagrove, Liza Tarbuck

Keen bridge players

Omar Sharif, Alan Coren, Raymond Illingworth, David Nobbs, Maeve Binchy, Joel Cadbury, Nick Ross, Gordon Honeycombe, James Mates, Bruce Critchley, Arnold Palmer, Ian Hislop, Sue Lawley, Angus Deayton, Clive Anderson, Damon Albarn, Honor Fraser, Martina Navratilova, Mike Gatting, Stephen Fry, Sting

Hobbies include sleeping

Terry Jones, Jon Bon Jovi, Jeremy Paxman, Phil Tufnell, Dame Beryl Bainbridge, Jane Corbin, Roy Hudd, Lord St John of Fawsley, Sir Jonathan Miller, Mel Giedroyc, Tim Vincent

KEEN CYCLISTS

Madonna, Jon Snow, Brad Pitt, Alexei Sayle, Jeremy Paxman, Boris Johnson, Eva Mendes, Jason Lewis, Matthew Marsden, Mena Suvari, Olivia Williams, Paul Usher, Robin Williams, Woody Harrelson

KEEN DIVERS

Anthony Head, Brian May, Brooke Shields, David Hasselhoff, Duncan James, Elijah Wood, Goran Visnjic, Heidi Klum, John Hannah, Josh Brolin, Julianna Margulies, Juliette Binoche, Martin Clunes, Michael Palin, Sir Mick Jagger, Natalie Imbruglia, Natasha Bedingfield, Neil Morrissey, Nick Carter, Pierce Brosnan, Prince Harry, Prince William, Ron Howard, Salma Hayek, Sandra Bullock, Tom Hanks, Val Kilmer

AROUND THE WORLD

In Italy, the entire town of Capena, just north of Rome, lights up cigarettes each year at the Festival of St Anthony. This tradition is centuries old, and even young children take part (though there are now moves to stop the smoking or at least revert to smoking rosemary, the traditional substance).

A difference of almost three inches in height separates the average North Korean seven-year-old from the average South Korean seven-year-old – the South Korean child is the taller.

It is the custom in Morocco for a bride to keep her eyes closed throughout the marriage ceremony.

The province of Alberta in Canada has been completely free of rats since 1905.

The letter 'O' in Irish surnames means 'grandson of'.

There are more Barbie dolls in Italy than Canadians in Canada.

There are more than 15,000 different varieties of rice.

The Amayra guides of Bolivia are said to be able to keep pace with a trotting horse for a distance of 100 kilometres.

In China, the entire population of over a billion shares only about 200 family names.

The Philippine flag is displayed with its blue field at the top in times of peace and the red field at the top in times of war.

The largest employer in the world is the Indian railway system, which employs over a million people.

Where the stones are of equal size, a flawless emerald is worth more than a flawless diamond.

In the Hebrides, what defines an island is the ability of the land to support at least one sheep.

At any one time, 0.7 per cent of the world's population is estimated to be drunk.

In Lima, Peru, there is a large brass statue of Winnie the Pooh – even though it's Paddington Bear who came from Peru.

Aircraft are not allowed to fly over the Taj Mahal.

The harmonica is the world's most popular musical instrument.

It used to be against the law in Swiss cities to slam the car door.

About 5,000 languages are spoken on earth.

After oil, coffee is the most traded commodity in the world.

More than a hundred cars can drive side by side on the Monumental Axis in Brazil, the world's widest road.

Panama hats come from Ecuador.

Soldiers from every country salute with their right hand.

Bulgarians eat more yogurt than anyone else.

The Tibetan mountain people use yak's milk as a form of currency.

Churches in Malta show two different (wrong) times in order to confuse the devil.

ECCENTRIC EVENTS FROM AROUND THE WORLD

The World Wife Carrying Championships (Finland)

World Screaming Championships (Poland)

World Mosquito Killing Championship (Finland)

Stilton Cheese Rolling Competition (Stilton, Cambridgeshire)

World Nettle Eating Championships (Marshwood, Dorset)

Air Guitar World Championships (Finland)

World Walking The Plank Championships (Isle of Sheppey, Kent)

World Bog Snorkelling Championships (Llanwrtyd Wells, Wales)

World Gurning Championships (Egremont, Cumbria)

The Munich Festival Beer Drinking Challenge (Germany)

Polar Bear Jump Off (Alaska, USA)

World Pea Throwing Competition (Lewes, East Sussex)

Trie-sur-Baïse Pig Screaming Championship (France)

Odalengo Truffle Hunting Competition (Italy)

Biggest Liar In The World Competition (Santon Bridge, Cumbria)

Kiruna Snowball Throwing Contest (Sweden)

Burning Tar Barrels (Ottery St Mary, Devon)

Australia Day Cockroach Races (Australia)

Annual Roadkill Cook-off (West Virginia, USA)

Tuna Throwing (Australia)

Goat Racing (Pennsylvania, USA)

World Worm Charming Championships (Nantwich, Cheshire)

World Shovel Race Championships (New Mexico, USA)

Penny Farthing World Championships (Tasmania)

The Great Mushroom Hunt Championships (Illinois, USA)

Annual Bat Flight Breakfast (New Mexico, USA)

Bognor Birdman Competition (Bognor Regis, West Sussex)

The Great Tomato Fight (Spain)

Summer Redneck Games (Georgia, USA – includes spitball bug zapping, hubcap hurling, watermelonseed spitting, bobbing for pigs' feet and the mud pit bellyflop)

World's Championship Duck Calling Contest and Wings Over The Prairie Festival (Arkansas, USA)

Annual World Elephant Polo Association Championships (Kathmandu, Nepal)

Scarecrow Festival (Wray, Lancashire)

GEOGRAPHY

The oldest exposed surface on earth is New Zealand's South Island.

England is smaller than New England.

The Eiffel Tower has 2.5 million rivets, 1,792 steps and can vary in height (according to the temperature) by as much as 15cm (6 inches).

If the earth were smooth, the ocean would cover the entire surface to a depth of 3,700 metres (12,000 feet).

The earth's surface area is 197,000,000 square miles.

2,000 pounds of space dust and other debris lands on earth every day.

The forests on Kauai in Hawaii are fertilized by dust from the deserts of China, 9,660 miles away.

It would take about 3,085,209,600,000 rolls of wallpaper to cover the Sahara.

The name of Spain

comes from

DEBERNY

The African baobab tree is pollinated by bats and its blossom opens only to moonlight.

A sizeable oak tree gives off 28,000 gallons of moisture during the growing season.

The national anthem of the Netherlands, the 'Wilhelmus', takes the form of an acrostic. The first letters of each of the fifteen verses represent the name 'Willem Van Nassov', or William of Orange. It is also the oldest anthem in the world.

Olympus Mons on Mars is the largest volcano in our solar system.

In May 1948, Mount Ruapehu and Mount Ngauruhoe, both in New Zealand, erupted simultaneously.

The Indonesian island of Sumatra has the world's largest flower: the *Rafflesia arnoldi*, which can grow to the size of an umbrella.

South Africa produces two-thirds of the world's gold.

The Angel falls in Venezuela are nearly 20 times taller than Niagara falls.

'the land of rabbits'.

Words

The word 'had' can be used eleven times in a row in the following sentence about two boys, John and Steve, who had written similar sentences in their essays: John, where Steve had had 'had', had had 'had had'; 'had had' had had the higher mark.

The word 'and' can be used five times in a row in the following sentence about a sign being painted above a shop called Jones And Son: Mr Jones looks at the sign and says to the painter, 'I would like bigger gaps between Jones and and, and and and Son.'

The words loosen and unloosen mean the same thing.

'Hippopotomonstrosesquippedaliophobia' is the fear of long words.

 We get the expression 'nosy parker' from Matthew Parker who was Archbishop of Canterbury in the 16th century. He had a very long nose and was extremely inquisitive – hence Nosy Parker.

The first letters of the months July to November spell the name JASON.

The word 'samba' means 'to rub navels together'.

Cerumen is the technical term for earwax.

The oldest word in the English language is 'town'.

The word 'coffee' came from Arabic and meant 'excitement'.

The word 'voodoo' comes from a West African word that means 'spirit' or 'deity' and has no negative connotations.

'Crack' gets its name from the crackling sound it makes when smoked.

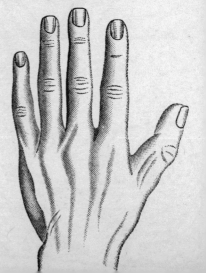

'Alma mater' means 'bountiful mother'.

The youngest letters in the English language are 'j', 'v' and 'w'.

The word 'diastema' describes a gap between the front teeth.

The stars and colours you see when you rub your eyes are called phosphenes.

No word in the English language rhymes with pint, diamond or purple.

The magic word 'abracadabra' was originally intended for the specific purpose of curing hay fever.

John Milton used 8,000 different words in *Paradise Lost*.

The word 'monosyllable' has five syllables.

The names for the numbers 'eleven' and 'twelve' in English come from the Anglo-Saxon for 'one left' (*aend-lefene*) and 'two left' (*twa-lefene*). They represented going back to your left hand and starting again after reaching ten counting on your fingers.

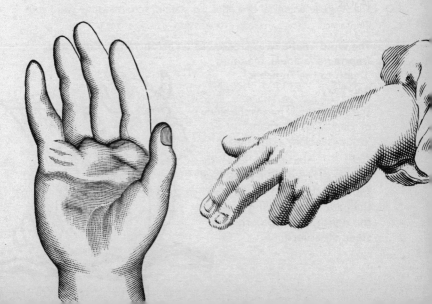

The phrase 'sleep tight' originated when ropes round a wooden frame were used to support a mattress. Sagging ropes could be tightened with a bed key.

Ten human body parts are only three letters long: eye, hip, arm, leg, ear, toe, jaw, rib, lip, gum.

The word 'lethologica' describes the state of forgetting the word you want.

The word 'mafia' was created as an acronym for *Morte alla francia italia adela*, meaning 'Death to the French is Italy's cry'.

The suffix 'ology' means the study of something. The shortest 'ology' is 'oology' – the study of eggs.

The word 'starboard' is derived from the Old English word for the paddle that Vikings used on the right side of their ships to steer: *steorbord*.

PEOPLE WHO HAVE SUFFERED FROM DYSLEXIA

Salma Hayek, Keira Knightley, Ozzy Osbourne, Jamie Oliver, Ruth Madoc, Lord Michael Heseltine, Duncan Goodhew, General George Patton, James Hewitt, Brian Conley, Sid Owen, Sir Steve Redgrave, Sonique, Richie Neville, Princess Beatrice

THE MOST BEAUTIFUL WORDS IN THE ENGLISH LANGUAGE?

In 2004, to mark its 70th anniversary, the British Council polled seven thousand people in 46 countries to ask them what they considered to be the most beautiful words in the English language. There was also an online poll that attracted over 35,000 votes. Here are the top 20:

1 mother	11 peace
2 passion	**12 blossom**
3 smile	13 sunshine
4 love	**14 sweetheart**
5 eternity	15 gorgeous
6 fantastic	**16 cherish**
7 destiny	17 enthusiasm
8 freedom	**18 hope**
9 liberty	19 grace
10 tranquillity	**20 rainbow**

PANGRAMS

The quick brown fox jumps over a lazy dog

Xylophone wizard begets quick jive form

Wet squid's inky haze veils sex of jumping crab

Jackdaws love my big sphinx of quartz

Pack my box with five dozen liquor jugs

The five boxing wizards jump quickly

Quick wafting zephyrs vex bold Jim

Mr Jock, TV quiz PhD, bags few lynx

Six plump boys guzzling cheap raw vodka quite joyfully

XV quick nymphs beg fjord waltz

PALINDROMES

Some men interpret nine memos

Star comedy by Democrats

We panic in a pew

Won't lovers revolt now?

Step on no pets

No, it is opposition

Live not on evil

Was it a car or a cat I saw?

Never odd or even

Sex at noon taxes

Able was I ere I saw Elba

Nurse, I spy gypsies – run!

Pull up if I pull up

Madam, I'm Adam

A nut for a jar of tuna

A Santa lived as a devil at NASA

A Toyota

Race fast, safe car

A slut nixes sex in Tulsa

Desserts, I stressed

Doom an evil deed, liven a mood

Not New York, Roy went on

Rot can rob a born actor

**Sit on a
potato pan,
Otis**

People who've been 'inside'

James Brown (carrying a gun and assault in 1988 – served 2 years; he had also served 3 years for theft when he was a teenager)

Ozzy Osbourne (burglary – 2 months in 1966)

Glen Campbell (sentenced to 10 days for drink-driving in 2004)

Don King (manslaughter in 1966 – served 3 years 11 months)

Zsa Zsa Gabor (slapping a cop – 3 days in 1989)

Kelsey Grammer (drugs – 2 weeks in jail for not doing the community service imposed for his offence in 1988)

George Best (drink-driving – 12 weeks in 1984)

Sean Penn (assault and violation of a probation order for an earlier assault – 32 days in 1987)

Chuck Berry (violating the Mann Act by taking a girl across state borders for 'immoral purposes' – 2 years in 1962)

Ryan O'Neal (brawling – served 51 days in 1960)

Stephen Fry (stealing credit cards – spent 3 months in a young offenders' institution in 1975)

Sir Paul McCartney (drugs – 9 days in Japan in 1980)

Evel Knievel (assault in 1977 – served 6 months)

Christian Slater (attacking policemen under the influence of cocaine – 3 months in 1997)

Oliver Stone (drugs – 2 weeks in 1969 while waiting to be tried for possession of marijuana)

Taki (drugs – served 3 months in 1984/5)

Robert Downey Jnr (drugs – sentenced to 6 months in 1997)

Nick Nolte (reckless driving – 30 nights in jail while at college, though he was released during the day to practise his football)

Stacy Keach (drugs – sentenced to 6 months in 1984)

Gregg Allman (drink-driving – served 3 days in 1986)

Jimmy Nail (GBH – 6 months in 1977)

Hugh Cornwell (drugs – 5 weeks in 1980)

Wilson Pickett (drink-driving and causing injury – served a year in 1992)

Mark Morrison (threatening a policeman – served 3 months in 1997, and sentenced to a year in 1998 for getting an impostor to do his community service)

David Crosby (drugs and possession of an illegal weapon – sentenced in 1983 to 5 years but served about a year and a half)

Johnny Vaughan (drugs – 4 years in 1988)

Anthony Newley (served a month in jail for driving while disqualified)

Muhammad Ali (one week in jail in 1968 for driving without a licence. He was sentenced in 1967 to 5 years in jail for refusing to serve in the army, but he challenged the verdict, it was overturned and he didn't spend any time in jail for it)

Ricky Tomlinson (served 2 years for conspiracy to intimidate other builders during picket-line violence in 1972)

Tim Allen (served 28 months in jail in 1978 for attempting to sell cocaine)

Mark Wahlberg (convicted at the age of 16 for his part in a robbery in which 2 Vietnamese were beaten – he served 45 days in jail)

Barry White (at the age of 16, for stealing tyres)

David Dickinson (at the age of 19, for mail-order fraud)

Jeffrey Archer (sentenced to 4 years in 2001 for perjury and perverting the course of justice)

Isaac Hayes (in 1989 for failing to pay alimony and child support)

Paris Hilton (in 2007, 45 days reduced to 23 for good behaviour for driving her Bentley without a licence which was a violation of her probation terms for a drink-driving offence)

CELEBRITIES WHO SHOPLIFTED

Michael Winner ('I stole from shops and from pupils at school')

Nick Ross (admitted shoplifting at his local Woolworth in Wallington, Surrey)

Farrah Fawcett (was twice arrested for shoplifting in LA before she was famous and was fined £280 – although she claimed that she was acting in revenge because the stores in question refused to take back defective goods)

Liam Gallagher (spent a volatile childhood shoplifting – as disclosed on a TV documentary)

Noel Gallagher (in the same documentary, Noel pointed out where he got nicked for shoplifting)

Tracy Shaw (stole from stores in Belper without realizing what she was doing. Was caught three times – including once with 99p-worth of strawberries – but was let off with warnings. 'Shoplifting is associated with anorexia')

Quentin Tarantino (as a teenager, stole an Elmore Leonard novel from a local store)

Roseanne

Julie Burchill

Jeremy Beadle

Groucho Marx

Alan Davies (as a kid)

Hedy Lamarr

Steve Strange (caught stealing a £10.99 Teletubbies doll)

Bruce Oldfield (sweets in Woolworth)

Mark Lamarr (shoplifted in his hometown of Swindon. 'One of the older punks would say he needed a new T-shirt so I'd just walk into a shop and nick one')

Béatrice Dalle (in 1992, she was given a six-month suspended sentence for shoplifting £3,000-worth of jewellery in Paris)

Rufus Sewell (stole records in Woolworth and, as a starving drama student, was caught stealing food)

John Lennon (shoplifted the harmonica he used on *Love Me Do* in Holland)

Jill Clayburgh (caught stealing at Bloomingdale's)

Courtney Love (in her early teens, she stole a Kiss T-shirt from a department store and was sent to a juvenile detention centre)

Jennifer Capriati

Winona Ryder (she claimed she was trying out a role. So how does she explain the stories going around LA that she has been caught several times before – only by shops who were less keen to press charges against someone so famous?)

Patsy Palmer (she was once caught stealing toys from Hamleys. 'We was nicking all these toys and they caught us. They gave us a warning. I don't know how we got away with it.')

Fiona Phillips (given a police caution for stealing cosmetics from Boots when she was a schoolgirl)

Goldie (Burton's)

Tom Jones (he and his friends would nick singles from record shops: 'In those days, all the records used to be on display and, as a gang, we would buy one and come out with six or seven')

Zoë Ball ('I used to shoplift quite a lot – just chocolate and stuff like that. I still feel bad about nicking a Marathon bar from a baker's shop when I was eight or nine. A woman caught me, but my parents never found out about it')

Jade Goody

Chris Eubank ('from the age of 14 to 16, I was one of the best shoplifters in London')

Claire Sweeney (a chocolate bar from a shop when she was eight)

PEOPLE JAILED FOR TAX EVASION

Lester Piggott (1 year in 1987)

Al Capone (11 years in 1931)

Sophia Loren (17 days in 1982)

Chuck Berry (4 months in 1979)

Leona Helmsley (hotelier; 4 years in 1990)

Allen Klein (former Beatles manager; 2 months in 1979)

Marvin Mitchelson (American divorce lawyer; 2 years, 6 months in 1993)

Rev. Sun Myung Moon (14 months in 1984)

Aldo Gucci (fashion boss; 1 year in 1986)

Peter Max (artist; 2 months in 1998)

Maria O'Sullivan (Ronnie's mother; 7 months in 1995)

PEOPLE WHO HAD THEIR ROLEX WATCHES STOLEN

Britt Ekland, Alexandra Heseltine, Michael Green, Bernie Ecclestone, Jilly Johnson, Caprice, Steve Norris, Gary Mabbutt, Gwen Humble, Lesley Clarke (Mrs Nicky Clarke), Julian Clary, Ian Wright

PEOPLE WHO WERE ARRESTED

Hugh Grant (for performing a 'lewd act' with Divine Brown in 1995 – he was fined and given two years' probation)

Brigitte Bardot (for castrating a donkey that was trying to mount her donkey – later she was not only discharged but was also awarded costs against the plaintiff)

Johnny Depp (for trashing a hotel suite in 1994 – he agreed to pay for the damage)

Billy Preston (for drink-driving and cocaine possession – given a suspended jail sentence and probation in 1992)

Johnny Cash (for being drunk and disorderly many times in the early 1960s)

Jodie Foster (for possession of cocaine – given a year's probation in 1983)

Harry Connick Jr (for having a gun in his luggage at New York's JFK airport)

Brian de Palma (for stealing a motorcycle and for resisting arrest – he was given a suspended sentence in 1963)

Carlos Santana (for marijuana possession – community service in 1991)

Paul Reubens (aka Pee-Wee Herman; for 'indecent exposure' in a cinema – he was fined and ordered to do community service)

Sean P. Diddy Combs (for possession of a firearm after a shooting incident in a bar in 1999) and Jennifer Lopez (arrested in the same incident and held in jail for 16 hours before being released without charge)

Chrissie Hynde (for demonstrating for animal rights in 2000. She used a knife to tear into leather and suede clothes in a Gap shop window in New York)

Jason Priestley (for drink-driving)

Vanilla Ice (after being accused of attacking his wife during a row in a car in 2001; he spent a night in jail in Florida)

Jennifer Capriati (for possession of marijuana in 1994; she was arrested in a hotel room and spent 23 days in a rehabilitation clinic)

PEOPLE WITH FATHERS WHO HAVE BEEN IN JAIL

Matt Lucas (John Lucas – fraud)

Ronnie O'Sullivan (Ronnie O'Sullivan Sr – murder)

Keanu Reeves (Samuel Reeves – drugs)

Heather Mills (John Mills – fraud)

Woody Harrelson (Charles Harrelson – murder)

Steffi Graf (Peter Graf – tax evasion)

Tatum O'Neal (Ryan O'Neal – brawling)

Lorraine Chase (Charlie 'Scarface' Parsons – robbery)

Patsy Kensit (Jimmy 'The Dip' Kensit – pickpocketing)

Stella McCartney (Sir Paul McCartney – drugs)

Brittany Murphy (Angelo Bertolotti – a convicted mobster. After three jail sentences he's alleged to have said: 'I got friends who make Tony Soprano look like an altar boy')

Jade Goody (Andrew Goody – robbery)

PEOPLE WHO HAD COMPUTER VIRUSES NAMED AFTER THEM

Osama bin Laden, Avril Lavigne, Michelangelo, Leela Zahir, Tonya Harding, Adolf Hitler

THE BIBLE

The word 'and' appears in the Bible 46,277 times.

The longest name in the Old Testament is Mahershalalhashbaz.

The book of Esther in the Bible is the only book that doesn't mention the name of God.

The chapters in the New Testament weren't there originally. When medieval monks translated the Bible from the Greek, they divided it into chapters.

Scholars believe that what we now read as 'forty', in Aramaic meant 'many'. So that 'forty days', for example, simply meant many days.

THE HUMAN CONDITION

Your feet are bigger in the afternoon than at any other time of day.

The average talker sprays 300 microscopic saliva droplets per minute, about 2.5 droplets per word.

A foetus acquires fingerprints at the age of 3 months.

The Neanderthal's brain was bigger than yours is.

The human body has 600 muscles, which make up 40 per cent of the body's weight. We use 300 of these muscles to stand still. We need 72 muscles to speak. If all 600 muscles in your body pulled in one direction, you could lift 25 tons.

A nail grows from base to tip in about 6 months.

Every human spent about half an hour as a single cell.

Beards have the fastest-growing hair on the human body. If a man never trimmed his beard, it could grow to over 9 metres (30 feet) in his lifetime.

One human hair can support 3 kilograms (over 6 ¹/₂ pounds).

The average man's speed of sperm emission is 11 miles (18 kilometres) per hour.

Every square inch of the human body has an average of 32 million bacteria on it.

Six-year-olds laugh about 300 times a day. Adults laugh about 15 times a day.

The attachment of the skin to muscles is what causes dimples.

Kidneys filter about 500 gallons of blood each day.

One in every 2,000 babies is born with a tooth.

The largest cell in a woman is the ovum. The smallest cell in a man is the sperm.

The most common blood type in the world is type O. The rarest, A-H, has been found in fewer than a dozen people since the type was discovered.

The tendency towards ingrown toenails is hereditary.

The most sensitive finger is the forefinger.

Weight for weight, men are stronger than horses.

The digestive tract is more than 9 metres (about 30 feet) long.

The ashes of the average cremated person weigh 4 kilograms (9 pounds).

Blood makes up about 8 per cent of the body's weight.

Due to gravitational effects, you weigh slightly less when the moon is directly overhead.

Every year about 98 per cent of the atoms in your body are replaced.

The entire length of all the eyelashes shed in a lifetime is about 30 metres (100 feet).

Your skull is made up of 29 different bones.

Hair is made from the same substance as fingernails.

Each square inch (2.5cm) of human skin contains 20 feet (6 metres) of blood vessels.

During a 24-hour period, the average human breathes 23,040 times.

The sound you hear when you put a shell to your ear is not the sea but blood flowing through your head.

Jaw muscles can provide about 200 pounds of force for chewing.

The human brain has about 100 billion nerve cells. Nerve impulses travel to and from the brain as fast as 170 miles (274 kilometres) per hour.

If you unfolded your brain, it would cover an ironing board. The more wrinkles your brain has, the more intelligent you are.

Alcohol does not kill brain cells, but detaches them. Reattachment would require new nervous tissue, which cannot be produced after about the age of five.

Your skin weighs twice as much as your brain.

There are 450 hairs in an average eyebrow.

The human brain stops growing at about the age of 18.

Your foot is the same length as the distance between your wrist and your elbow.

The chemicals in a human body are estimated to have a combined worth of 6.25 euro.

It's physically impossible to lick your elbow.

A cough comes out of your mouth at about 60 miles (96.5 kilometres) per hour.

Stars and their first films

Dame Julie Andrews – *Mary Poppins* (1964)

Dan Aykroyd – *1941* (1979)

Lauren Bacall – *To Have And Have Not* (1943)

Drew Barrymore – *Altered States* (1980)

Ned Beatty – *Deliverance* (1972)

Warren Beatty – *Splendor In The Grass* (1961)

Hywel Bennett – *The Family Way* (1966)

Orlando Bloom – *Wilde* (1997)

Helena Bonham Carter – *Lady Jane* (1984)

Marlon Brando – *The Men* (1950)

James Caan – *Irma La Douce* (1963)

Nicolas Cage – *Fast Times At Ridgemont High* (1982)

Sir Sean Connery – *No Road Back* (1955)

Tom Cruise – *Endless Love* (1981)

Willem Dafoe – *Heaven's Gate* (1980)

Robert De Niro – *The Wedding Party* (1963)

Johnny Depp – *A Nightmare On Elm Street* (1984)

Danny DeVito – *Dreams of Glass* (1968)

Clint Eastwood – *Revenge of The Creature* (1955)

Jane Fonda – *Tall Story* (1960)

Richard Gere – *Report To The Commissioner* (1975)

Whoopi Goldberg – *The Color Purple* (1985)

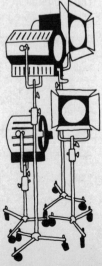

Jeff Goldblum – *Death Wish* (1974)

Hugh Grant – *Privileged* (1982 – credited as 'Hughie Grant')

Melanie Griffith – *The Harrad Experiment* (1973)

Gene Hackman – *Mad Dog Coll* (1961)

Goldie Hawn – *The One And Only Genuine Original Family Band* (1968)

Dustin Hoffman – *The Tiger Makes Out* (1967)

Sir Anthony Hopkins – *The Lion In Winter* (1968)

Holly Hunter – *The Burning* (1981)

William Hurt – *Altered States* (1980)

Anjelica Huston – *Sinful Davey* (1968)

Jeremy Irons – *Nijinsky* (1980)

Scarlett Johansson – *North* (1994)

Michael Keaton – *Night Shift* (1982)

Kevin Kline – *Sophie's Choice* (1982)

Keira Knightley – *A Village Affair* (1994)

Lindsay Lohan – *The Parent Trap* (1998)

Jennifer Lopez – *My Little Girl* (1986)

Rob Lowe – *The Outsiders* (1983)

Shirley Maclaine – *The Trouble With Harry* (1955)

Tobey Maguire – *The Wizard* (1989)

Steve Martin – *Sgt Pepper's Lonely Hearts Club Band* (1978)

Bette Midler – *Hawaii* (1965)

Sarah Miles – *Term of Trial* (1962)

Liza Minnelli – *Charlie Bubbles* (1968)

Eddie Murphy – *48 Hours* (1982)

Paul Newman – *The Silver Chalice* (1954)

Al Pacino – *Me, Natalie* (1969)

Sean Penn – *Taps* (1981)

Robert Redford – *War Hunt* (1961)

Keanu Reeves – *Youngblood* (1986)

Dame Diana Rigg – *The Assassination Bureau* (1968)

Julia Roberts – *Blood Red* (1986)

Cybill Shepherd – *The Last Picture Show* (1971)

Sylvester Stallone – *A Party At Kitty And Stud's* (1970)

Terence Stamp – *Billy Budd* (1962)

Sharon Stone – *Stardust Memories* (1980)

Barbra Streisand – *Funny Girl* (1968)

Meryl Streep – *Julia* (1977)

Donald Sutherland – *The World Ten Times Over* (1963)

Lily Tomlin – *Nashville* (1975)

John Travolta – *The Devil's Rain* (1975)

Kathleen Turner – *Body Heat* (1981)

Jon Voight – *The Hour of The Gun* (1967)

Orson Welles – *Citizen Kane* (1941)

Robin Williams – *Popeye* (1980)

Bruce Willis – *Blind Date* (1987)

Sir Norman Wisdom – *Trouble In Store* (1953)

Susannah York – *Tunes of Glory* (1960)

ACTORS WITHOUT A SINGLE OSCAR BETWEEN THEM*

Gene Kelly, Steve McQueen, Cary Grant, Glenn Ford, James Mason, Stewart Granger, Charles Boyer, Anthony Quayle, Montgomery Clift, Kirk Douglas, Greta Garbo, Agnes Moorehead, Carole Lombard, Barbara Stanwyck, Lana Turner, Judy Garland, Lee Remick, Natalie Wood, Rita Hayworth, Gloria Swanson
*Apart from honorary Oscars

ACTORS WITHOUT EVEN A SINGLE OSCAR NOMINATION BETWEEN THEM

Al Jolson, Tallulah Bankhead, Audie Murphy, Yvonne De Carlo, Errol Flynn, Hedy Lamarr, Sir Dirk Bogarde, Raquel Welsh, Boris Karloff, Veronica Lake, Olivia Hussey, Glenn Ford, Jacqueline Bisset, Martin Sheen, Dorothy Lamour, Peter Cushing, Brigitte Bardot, Roger Moore, Jane Russell, Harry Belafonte

ALL THE YEARS WHEN ENGLISH LANGUAGE FILMS WON THE PALME D'OR AT THE CANNES FILM FESTIVAL

2006 *The Wind That Shakes The Barley*

2004 *Fahrenheit 9/11*

2003 *Elephant*

2002 *The Pianist*

1996 *Secrets and Lies*

1994 *Pulp Fiction*

1993 *The Piano*

1991 *Barton Fink*

1990 *Wild at Heart*

1989 *Sex, Lies and Videotape*

1986 *The Mission*

1984 *Paris, Texas*

1982 *Missing*

1980 *All That Jazz*

1979 *Apocalypse Now*

1976 *Taxi Driver*

1974 *The Conversation*

1973 *Scarecrow and The Hireling*

1971 *The Go-Between*

1970 *M*A*S*H*

1969 *If...*

1967 *Blow-Up*

1965 *The Knack ... And How to Get It*

1957 *Friendly Persuasion*

1955 *Marty*

1949 *The Third Man*

PEOPLE WHOSE NAMES APPEARED IN FILM TITLES

John Malkovich – *Being John Malkovich* (2000)

Greta Garbo – *Garbo Talks* (1984)

Brigitte Bardot – *Dear Brigitte* (1965)

Bela Lugosi – *Bela Lugosi Meets A Brooklyn Gorilla* (1952)

Douglas Fairbanks – *F As In Fairbanks* (1975)

Fred Astaire – *The Curse of Fred Astaire* (1984)

Ginger Rogers – *Ginger And Fred* (1986)

James Dean – *Come Back To The Five And Dime, Jimmy Dean, Jimmy Dean* (1982)

Humphrey Bogart – *The Man With Bogart's Face* (1980)

Clark Gable – *The Woman Who Married Clark Gable* (1985)

Errol Flynn – *In Like Flynn* (1985)

David Beckham – *Bend It Like Beckham* (2002)

Pete Tong – *It's All Gone Pete Tong* (2004)

UNCREDITED MOVIE APPEARANCES

Paula Abdul (in *Can't Buy Me Love* – as a cheerleader)

Steve Buscemi (in *Pulp Fiction* – as a waiter)

Cyd Charisse (in *Ziegfeld Follies* – as a dancer)

Don Cheadle (in *Rush Hour 2* and *Ocean's Eleven* – both times as a criminal)

Phil Daniels (in *Bugsy Malone* – as a waiter)

Richard Dreyfuss (in *The Graduate* – as a student)

Kirsten Dunst (in *The Day After Tomorrow* – as a student)

Leif Garrett (in *Bob and Carol and Ted and Alice* – as the son of Dyan Cannon and Elliott Gould)

Charlton Heston (in the 2001 remake of *Planet of The Apes*)

Jason Isaacs (in *Resident Evil* as Dr Birkin)

Steve McQueen (in *Dixie Dynamite* as a motorcyclist)

Christian Slater (in *Austin Powers: International Man of Mystery* as a security guard)

Jaclyn Smith (in *Charlie's Angels: Full Throttle* as Kelly Garrett, her character in the original TV series)

ACTRESSES WHO SHAVED THEIR HEADS FOR ROLES

Persis Khambatta (*Star Trek: The Motion Picture* 1979)

Emma Thompson (*Wit* 2001)

Vanessa Redgrave (*Playing For Time* 1980)

Demi Moore (*G.I. Jane* 1997)

Sigourney Weaver (*Alien III* 1992)

Dervla Kirwan (*The Dark Room* 1998)

Alison Lohman (*Dragonfly* 2002 – though her scenes were cut)

Natalie Portman (*V For Vendetta* 2005)

PEOPLE WHO WROTE/CO-WROTE SCREENPLAYS

Jack Nicholson (*Head*)

Melvyn Bragg (*Isadora*)

Martin Amis (*Saturn 3*)

Erich Segal (*Yellow Submarine*)

John Wells (*Princess Caraboo*)

George MacDonald Fraser (*Octopussy*)

Roald Dahl (*You Only Live Twice*)

Christopher Logue (*Savage Messiah*)

Denis Norden (*Buona Sera, Mrs Campbell*)

Mike Sarne (*The Lightship*)

Paul Theroux (*Saint Jack*)

Clare Boothe Luce (*Come To The Stable*)

ACTRESSES WHO TESTED FOR THE ROLE OF SCARLETT O'HARA IN *GONE WITH THE WIND*

Lana Turner

Bette Davis

Norma Shearer

Miriam Hopkins

Tallulah Bankhead

Claudette Colbert

Katharine Hepburn

Loretta Young

Jean Harlow

Carole Lombard

PEOPLE WHO HAVE PLAYED GOD IN FILMS OR ON TV

Morgan Freeman (*Bruce Almighty* 2003)

James Garner (*God, The Devil And Bob* 2000)

Alanis Morissette (*Dogma* 1999)

Robbie Fowler (*Soccer AM* 1994)

Marianne Faithfull (*Absolutely Fabulous* 1992)

Robert Morley (*Second Time Lucky* 1984)

George Burns (*Oh, God!* 1977)

Groucho Marx (*Skidoo* 1968)

Valentine Dyall (*Bedazzled* 1967)

Martin Sheen (*Insight* 1960)

Pop/rock groups that appeared in films

All Saints – *Honest* (2000)

The Spice Girls – *Spiceworld The Movie* (1997)

Madness – *Take It Or Leave It* (1981)

The Sex Pistols – *The Great Rock 'N' Roll Swindle* (1980)

The Who – *The Kids Are Alright* (1979)

Led Zeppelin – *The Song Remains The Same* (1976)

Slade – *Flame* (1975)

T-Rex – *Born To Boogie* (1972)

The Monkees – *Head* (1968)

Gerry and The Pacemakers – *Ferry Cross The Mersey* (1965)

The Beatles – *Hard Day's Night* (1964) etc

Bill Haley and His Comets – *Rock Around The Clock* (1956)

THINGS SAID ABOUT TAX

'Income tax returns are the most imaginative fiction being written today.' (Herman Wouk)

'I have always paid income tax. I object only when it reaches a stage when I am threatened with having nothing left for my old age – which is due to start next Tuesday or Wednesday.' (Noel Coward)

'Next to being shot at and missed, nothing is really quite as satisfying as an income tax refund.' (F. J. Raymond)

'There's no such thing as a good tax.' (Sir Winston Churchill)

'In this world nothing can be said to be certain, except death and taxes.' (Benjamin Franklin)

'When they fire a rocket at Cape Canaveral, I feel as if I own it.' (William Holden)

'There should be no taxation without comprehension.' (John Gummer)

'The income tax has made more liars out of the American people than golf has.' (Will Rogers)

'The avoidance of taxes is the only intellectual pursuit that carries any reward.' (John Maynard Keynes)

'There's always somebody who is paid too much, and taxed too little – and it's always somebody else.' (Cullen Hightower)

'The wages of sin are death, but by the time taxes are taken out, it's just sort of a tired feeling.' (Paula Poundstone)

'Tax reform means "Don't tax you, don't tax me, tax that fellow behind the tree."' (Russell Long)

'Man is not like other animals in the ways that are really significant: Animals have instincts, we have taxes.' (Erving Goffman)

'Noah must have taken into the Ark two taxes, one male and one female. And did they multiply bountifully!' (Will Rogers)

THE LONGEST-SERVING BRITISH MONARCHS SINCE 1066

Queen Victoria (64 years: 1837–1901)

King George III (60 years: 1760–1820)

King Henry III (56 years: 1216–1272)

Queen Elizabeth II (55 years: 1952–)

King Edward III (50 years: 1327–1377)

Queen Elizabeth I (45 years: 1558–1603)

King Henry VI (39 years: 1422–1461)

King Henry VIII (38 years: 1509–1547)

King Henry I (35 years: 1100–1135)

King Henry II (35 years: 1154–1189)

King Edward I (35 years: 1272–1307)

ANAGRAMS

LESS IN HARMONY – Shirley Manson

TRASH IN AIMING – Martina Hingis

BELT MERITED – Bette Midler

CAMEL NOISES – Monica Seles

VERY COOL TUNE – Courtney Love

BOIL JELLY – Billy Joel

CHIEF CROWD ALARM – Michael Crawford

NEAT APPELLATION – Natalie Appleton

I'M LONE SNOB – Simon Le Bon

GOAL ANGER HELL – Noel Gallagher

ARTICLES TARNISH – Christian Slater

LOW BORE – Rob Lowe

EMERGE ANGRIER – Germaine Greer

HELL IS HER HAUNT – Ruthie Henshall

INHALE? CHEERS! – Charlie Sheen

WE'LL SEND ANYONE – Lesley Anne Down

CREEP DID WARN – Prince Edward

SUIT U WHOLE HEAP – Paul Whitehouse

EDIT WASN'T COOL – Clint Eastwood

I'M SENILE, SORRY – Neil Morrissey

RANDOM CAR LOVER – Carol Vorderman

MEANT TO CRUNCH MICE – Martine McCutcheon

NOW EVEN WIVES DO IT – Vivienne Westwood

AUTUMN HARM – Uma Thurman

DREARY MILD ACHE – Richard Madeley

BETRAY IN PRESS – Britney Spears

SEND MY OLD MAN – Desmond Lynam

NO! DO CENSOR! – Des O'Connor

DARN SAD MALE – Adam Sandler

MERRY WARDROBE – Drew Barrymore

GERMANY – Meg Ryan

A PRETENDER – Peter Andre

LIKES EASY MEN – Melanie Sykes

RAMPANT TOENAIL – Natalie Portman

LOWERS ULCERS – Russell Crowe

ME THIN MAN – Tim Henman

FINE TICKLE LADY – Felicity Kendal

A NIGHTMARE SELL – Leslie Grantham

VAST EGO ONCE – Steve Coogan

RANK LIES? CHAMPION! – Michael Parkinson

RENT RISES? WHOOPEE! – Reese Witherspoon

ONE'S NOT RASH – Sharon Stone

REVENUE SAKE – Keanu Reeves

TART JEERS TO REPENT – Janet Street-Porter

IS LASS INFLATED? – Lisa Stansfield

SARDONIC WHIRL – Richard Wilson

DOCILE FARTS – Fidel Castro

I DRAG ODD TRASH – Trisha Goddard

GOSH DREARY! – Gary Rhodes

INTO NEW LAD – Dale Winton

RESPECT MEANT – Terence Stamp

GIRLS' HEAVEN – Nigel Havers

THE THREE WISE MONKEYS

Mizaru (See no evil)

Mikazaru (Hear no evil)

Mazaru (Say no evil)

DEALING WITH COLD CALLS

Ask them if they're real or just one of the voices in your head.

Ask them to spell their name. Then ask them to spell the name of their company. Then ask them where the company is located. Then ask them to spell the company's location.

Tell them to talk very VERY S-L-O-W-L-Y, because you want to write down every single word.

If they're phoning from a kitchen company, tell them you live in a squat.

If they say they're not selling anything, tell them that that's a pity because you're in the mood for buying.

If they give you their name – 'Hi, I'm Sharon' – say, 'oh, Sharon, how ARE you?' as though they are a long-lost friend.

Tell them you're busy at the moment and could you have their home phone number to call them back later.

ADOLF HITLER (WITH EVERYTHING YOU ALREADY KNEW ABOUT HIM TAKEN OUT)

As a child, he was once beaten into a two-day coma by his father, Alois.

From 1925 to 1945, Hitler held the official title of SS Member #1. The man who was Member #2 wasn't Heinrich Himmler but Emil Maurice, Hitler's personal bodyguard/chauffeur and the man who is credited with founding the SS. Maurice, incredibly, was half-Jewish and, when this came to light in 1935, he was thrown out of the SS. However, he was allowed to retain all his privileges.

Hitler's suicide in 1945 was not his first attempt. In 1923, after the failure of his putsch, he was hiding out in the attic of his follower, Ernst 'Putzi' Hanfstangl. When the police arrived, Hitler tried to shoot himself, but a policeman managed to stop him before he could pull the trigger.

Hitler had Chaplin's *The Great Dictator* banned but he was curious to see the film himself and so he had a print of the film smuggled into Germany from Portugal, and watched it not once, but twice.

He collected pornography and used to draw it.

He had an affair with his half-sister's daughter who eventually killed herself.

Each of his two Mercedes Benz cars had a false floor fitted to make him look taller when he stood up.

Car manufacturer Henry Ford was the only American to get a favourable mention in Hitler's autobiography, *Mein Kampf*.

Myrna Loy, Bertolt Brecht and cartoonist David Low were all on Hitler's personal blacklist.

Hitler was awarded the Iron Cross after being recommended for one by a Jewish officer.

Hitler esteemed Clark Gable above all other actors, and during the war offered a sizeable reward to anyone who could capture and return Gable unscathed to him.

He was taking 92 different drugs towards the end of his life.

Four male descendants through his father's line were born between 1949 and 1965 in New York State. None of them had any children.

THE USA

About a third of Americans flush the lavatory while they are still sitting on it.

In Kentucky, 50 per cent of people getting married for the first time are teenagers.

The dollar symbol ($) is a U combined with an S.

Tennessee has more neighbours than any other state in the US. It is bordered by eight states: Kentucky, Missouri, Arkansas, Mississippi, Alabama, Georgia, North Carolina and Virginia.

Many businesses in Nebraska have the word 'Aksarben' in their names: such as 'Aksarben Five and Dime Store' or 'Aksarben Transmission Service.' Aksarben is Nebraska spelt backwards.

Deafness was once so common on Martha's Vineyard that all the people who lived there, both the hearing and the deaf, were fluent in their own dialect of sign language. No distinction was made in working or social life between those who could hear and those who could not. The gene for deafness was brought over in the 17th century by settlers from the Weald in Kent, and by the 19th century the rate of hereditary deafness on the island was 37 times the American average. Marriage to off-islanders eventually saw deafness disappear from the population; the last deaf islander died in 1952 (though deafness was still so unremarkable that her brief obituary in the *Vineyard Gazette* saw no reason to mention it).

In Alaska, it is an offence to push a living moose out of a moving aeroplane.

During the time the atomic bomb was being hatched by the United States at Alamogordo, New Mexico, applicants for routine jobs were disqualified if they could read. Illiteracy was a job requirement. The reason: the authorities did not want their papers being read.

The name 'California' was taken from a 16th-century Spanish novel, *The Exploits of Esplaidian*, by Garcia Ordonez de Montalvo. In the novel it was the name of an imaginary island, described as an Amazon kingdom ruled by black women.

The three US presidents who have faced real or impending impeachment – Andrew Johnson, Richard Nixon and Bill Clinton – also have in common that their names are euphemisms for the penis: johnson, dick and willie.

Every rise in the US divorce rate is matched by a rise in toy sales.

There are more plastic flamingos in the US than real ones.

The average American chews 190 pieces of gum each year.

Point Roberts in Washington State is cut off from the rest of the state by British Columbia, Canada. In order to get to Point Roberts from any other part of the state, you have to go through Canadian and US customs.

In the 1940s, the name of the Bich pen was changed to Bic out of concern that Americans would pronounce it 'Bitch'.

In Los Angeles, there are more cars than people.

Americans drink an average of 25 gallons of milk a year.

New Yorker magazine has more subscribers in California than in New York.

The main library at Indiana University sinks by several centimetres a year. When it was built, no one took into account the weight of all the books it would hold.

Ted Turner owns 5 per cent of New Mexico.

In 1976, a Los Angeles secretary 'married' her 50-pound pet rock.

In 1980, a Las Vegas hospital suspended workers for running a book on when patients would die.

Since 1 January 2004, the population of the United States has been increasing by one person every 12 seconds. Every 13 seconds someone dies, every 8 seconds someone is born and every 25 seconds an immigrant arrives.

In Vermont, there are 10 cows for every person.

72 per cent of Americans sign their pets' names on the greeting cards they send.

The United States consumes 25 per cent of the world's energy.

On a clear day, you can see five states from the top of the Empire State Building: New York, New Jersey, Connecticut, Massachusetts and Pennsylvania.

The largest living thing on earth (by volume) is the General Sherman Tree in Sequoia National Park. It is 275 feet tall (84m) and its trunk is 37 feet (11m) in diameter at the widest point.

Second Street is the first choice of street name in the US.

The US government keeps its supply of silver at the military academy in West Point.

The murder capital of the US is Gary, Indiana.

A party boat filled with 60 men and women capsized in Texas after it passed a nudist beach and all its passengers rushed to one side.

More than 8,100 US troops are still listed as missing in action from the Korean War.

All the earthworms in America weigh 55 times what all the people weigh.

The slogan on New Hampshire number plates is 'Live Free or Die'. The plates are made by inmates in the state prison.

There's enough concrete in the Hoover Dam to make a 4-foot/1.2-m wide belt around the equator.

In American there's a lawsuit every 30 seconds.

The average American walks four miles a year making the bed.

Every day, 7 per cent of the US eats at McDonald's.

NAMES

Kiefer Sutherland's full name is Kiefer William Frederick Dempsey George Rufus Sutherland

PEOPLE KNOWN BY THEIR INITIALS

W.H. (Wystan Hugh) Auden

A.J. (Alfred Jules) Ayer

J.G. (James Graham) Ballard

P.T. (Phineas Taylor) Barnum

J.M. (James Mathew) Barrie

H.E. (Herbert Ernest) Bates

A.S. (Antonia Susan) Byatt

J.J. (John Junior) Cale

G.K. (Gilbert Keith) Chesterton

J.M. (John Maxwell) Coetzee

e.e. (Edward Estlin) Cummings

F.W. (Frederik Willem) de Klerk

E.L. (Edgar Lawrence) Doctorow

T.S. (Thomas Stearns) Eliot

W.C. (William Claude) Fields

E.M. (Edward Morgan) Forster

W.S. (William Schwenck) Gilbert

A.A. (Adrian Anthony) Gill

W.G. (William Gilbert) Grace

D.W. (David Wark) Griffith

W.C. (William Christopher) Handy

L.P. (Leslie Poles) Hartley

P.J. (Polly Jean) Harvey

A.E. (Alfred Edward) Housman

P.D. (Phyllis Dorothy) James

C.E.M. (Cyril Edwin Mitchinson) Joad

k.d. (Kathryn Dawn) lang

R.D. (Ronald David) Laing

D.H. (David Herbert) Lawrence

T.E. (Thomas Edward) Lawrence

C.S. (Clive Staples) Lewis

A.A. (Alan Alexander) Milne

V.S. (Vidiadhar Surajprasad) Naipaul

P.J. (Patrick Jake) O'Rourke

J.C. (James Cash) Penney

J.B. (John Boynton) Priestley

J.K. (Joanne Kathleen) Rowling

A.L. (Alfred Leslie) Rowse

J.D. (Jerome David) Salinger

R.C. (Robert Cedric) Sherriff

O.J. (Orenthal James) Simpson

F.E. (Frederick Edwin) Smith

W.H. (William Henry) Smith

C.P. (Charles Percy) Snow

A.J.P. (Alan John Percivale) Taylor

B.J. (Billy Joe) Thomas

E.P. (Edward Palmer) Thompson

J.R.R. (John Ronald Reuel) Tolkien

P.L. (Pamela Lyndon) Travers

J.M.W. (Joseph Mallord William) Turner

H.G. (Herbert George) Wells

J.P.R. (John Peter Rhys) Williams

P.G. (Pelham Grenville) Wodehouse

W.B. (William Butler) Yeats

PEOPLE WHO DON'T APPEAR TO HAVE MIDDLE NAMES

John Major, Michael Howard, Lorraine Chase, Geoffrey Boycott, Lynn Redgrave, Jonathan Dimbleby, John Fashanu, David Hamilton, John Francome, Glenn Hoddle, Wendy Richard, Nerys Hughes, David Suchet, Keith Michell, Gerry Cottle, Ron Moody, Gary Barlow, Nasser Hussain, Elaine Paige, Annabel Croft, Mo Mowlam

UNUSUAL NAMES GIVEN BY CELEBRITIES TO THEIR CHILDREN

Dixie Dot – Anna Ryder Richardson

Pilot Inspektor Riesgraf Lee – Jason Lee

Seven & Puma – Erykah Badu

Tu – Rob Morrow (i.e. Tu Morrow)

Salvador – Ed O'Brien

Raven – Gary Numan

Ace Howlett – Natalie Appleton and Liam Howlett

Geronimo – Alex James

Deacon – Reese Witherspoon

Apple – Gwyneth Paltrow and Chris Martin

MaKena Lei – Helen Hunt (after a Hawaiian island)

Salome – Alex Kingston

William True – Kirstie Alley

Camera – Arthur Ashe

Jack Daniel – Ellen Barkin and Gabriel Byrne

J.C. – Jackie Chan

Erika, Erinn, Ensa, Evin and Ennis – Bill Cosby

Lolita & Piper – Brian De Palma

Brandi & Buck – Roseanne

Cruz – David and Victoria Beckham

Ross & Chudney – Diana Ross

Gib & Prima – Connie Sellecca

Jesse Mojo – Sam Shepard

China – Grace Slick

Weston – Nicolas Cage

Paris & Brielle – Blair Underwood

Rio – Sean Young

Lourdes – Madonna

Cuathemoc – Louis Malle

Shelby – Reba McEntire

Imani – Jasmine Guy

Atherton – Don Johnson

Paris – Michael Jackson

Paris – Pierce Brosnan

Libbi-Jack (daughter) – Gaby Roslin

Eja (boy) – Shania Twain

Kal-el (Superman's real name) – Nicolas Cage

Clementine – Claudia Schiffer

Bluebell Madonna – Geri Halliwell

Dusti Rain and Keelie Breeze – Vanilla Ice

**Vanessa Feltz, Tony Curtis,
John Huston, John Leguizamo,
Lord Byron and Donatella Versace
all named a daughter Allegra**

Good boy Eja.

PEOPLE WHO FOUND FAME WITH JUST A FIRST NAME

Jamelia (Davis)

Beck (Hansen)

Prince (Rogers Nelson)

Sinitta (Malone)

Madonna (Ciccone)

Dion (Dimucci)

Sade (Adu)

Caprice (Bourret)

Ann-Margret (Olsson)

Toyah (Willcox)

Cher (La Piere)

Yanni (Chrysomallis)

RuPaul (Charles)

Donovan (Leitch)

Melanie (Safka)

Nicole (Hohloch)

Björk (Gudmundsdottir)

Seal (Seal is short for Sealhenry and his surname is Samuel)

Taki (Theodoracopulos)

Arletty (Arletty was short for Arlette-Leonie and her surname was Bathiat)

Eusebio (da Silva Ferreira)

Heinz (Burt)

Charlene (Duncan)

Regine (Regine was a variation on Regina and her surname was Zylberberg)

Des'ree (Des'ree is a variation on Desiree and her surname is Weekes)

Fabian (Fabian is short for Fabiano and his surname is Forte)

Louise (Nurding/Redknapp)

Tiffany (Darwish)

Wynonna (Judd)

Dido (Dido Florian Cloud de Bounevialle Armstrong)

Aaliyah (Dana Haughton)

Brandy (Norwood)

Iman (Abdulmajid)

Jewel (Kilcher)

Kelis (Rogers)

Roseanne (Arnold/Barr)

Vendela (Thomessen)

PEOPLE WHO FOUND FAME WITH JUST A SURNAME

(Annunzio Paolo) Mantovani

(Stephen) Morrissey

(Chaim) Topol

(Harry) Nilsson

(Wladziu Valentino) Liberace

(Michael) D'Angelo

(Josip Broz) Tito

PEOPLE WHO FOUND FAME WITH JUST A NICKNAME/SOBRIQUET

Marilyn (Peter Robinson)

Capucine (Germaine Lefebvre)

Whigfield (Sannia Carlson)

Dana (Rosemary Brown)

Sting (Gordon Sumner)

Hammer (Stanley Burrell)

Pele (Edson Arantes do Nascimento)

Twiggy (Lesley Hornby)

Enya (Eithne Ni Bhraonain)

Suggs (Graham McPherson)

Martika (Marta Marrera)

Fish (Derek Dick)

Lulu (Marie Lawrie)

Yazz (Yasmin Evans)

2Pac (Tupac Shakur)

Twinkle (Lynn Ripley)

Fernandel (Fernand Contandin)

Aneka (Mary Sandeman)

Limahl (Chris Hamill – Limahl is an anagram of Hamill)

Falco (Johann Holzel)

Sabrina (Norma Ann Sykes)

Vangelis (Evangelos Papathanassiou)

Cantinflas (Mario Moreno Reyes)

Sonique (Sonia Clarke)

Bez (Mark Berry)

Coolio (Artis Ivey Jr)

Divine (Harris Glen Milstead)

Eminem (Marshall Mathers)

Flea (Michael Balzary)

Hergé (Georges Remi)

Saki (Hector Munro)

Molière (Jean-Baptiste Poquelin)

Sapper (Cyril McNeile)

Voltaire (François Marie Arouet)

Jordan (Katie Price)

Kool (Robert Bell)

Lemmy (Ian Fraser Kilminster)

Moby (Richard Hall)

Nena (Gabriele Kerner)

Nico (Christa Paffgen)

Pink (Alecia Moore)

Bono (Paul Hewson)

MEN WITH WOMEN'S NAMES

Dana Andrews

Gay Byrne

Kerry Packer

Val Kilmer

Marilyn Manson

Shirley Crabtree (original name of the wrestler Big Daddy)

Mandy Patinkin

Gert Frobe

Kay Kyser

Marion Morrison (original name of the actor John Wayne)

Lilian Thuram

By George

WOMEN WITH MEN'S NAMES

Leslie Ash

Sean Young

Michael Learned

Billie Piper

George Eliot

Cameron Diaz

Glenn Close

Jerry Hall

Charlie Dimmock

Daryl Hannah

George Sand

Teddy Beverley

Bye Mandy

PEOPLE WHO NAMED THEIR CHILDREN AFTER OTHER FAMOUS PEOPLE

Neneh Cherry: named daughter Tyson, after Mike Tyson

Dave Stewart and Siobhan Fahey: named son Django, after Django Reinhardt

Gyles Brandreth: named daughter Aphra, after the writer Aphra Behn

Woody Allen: named his son Satchel, after the baseball player Satchel Paige

Paul Young: named daughter Levi, after Levi Stubbs of The Four Tops

Demi Moore and Bruce Willis: named daughter Rumer, after the author Rumer Godden

Ricky Schroder: named son Holden, after William Holden

Nicky Henson: named son Keaton, after Buster Keaton

Mickey Stewart: named his son Alec, after Alec Bedser

Bryan Ferry: named son Otis, after Otis Redding

Will Self: named son Luther, after Luther Vandross

PEOPLE WHO WERE NAMED AFTER SOMEONE/SOMETHING FAMOUS

Nasser Hussain (after Colonel Nasser)

Penelope Cruz (after the song 'Penélope' by Joan Manuel Serrat)

Sadie Frost (after the song 'Sexy Sadie' by The Beatles)

Celine Dion (after the song 'Celine' by Hugues Aufray)

Paul Gascoigne (after Paul McCartney)

Jude Law (after the song 'Hey Jude' by The Beatles)

PEOPLE WHO CHOSE TO USE THEIR MIDDLE NAME AS A FIRST NAME

Christopher Ashton Kutcher

George Roger Waters

Patrick Ryan O'Neal

Lee Alexander McQueen

Robert Oliver Reed

Alexander Boris Johnson

John Anthony Quayle

Johan Jordi Cruyff

James Harold Wilson

Marie Dionne Warwick

Michael Vincent O'Brien

Henry Antony Worrall Thompson

Richard Geoffrey Howe

Ernestine Jane Russell

John Enoch Powell

Ruth Bette Davis

Alfred Alistair Cooke

Norvell Oliver Hardy

Isaac Vivian Richards

Sir Peter Norman Fowler

Georgina Davinia Murphy

Leonard James Callaghan

Robert Edward (i.e. Ted) Turner

Eldred Gregory Peck

Alexander James Naughtie

Mary Sean Young

Daniel Patrick Macnee

George Anthony Newley

Sir Edwin Hardy Amies

Arthur Nigel Davenport

Mark Trevor Phillips

Alastair Brian Walden

Thomas Richard Dunwoody

David Paul Scofield

Christopher Nicholas Parsons

James Paul McCartney

Michael Jeremy Bates

Mary Farrah Fawcett

Lord Michael Colin Cowdrey

William Clark Gable

Nigel Keith Vaz

Christopher Rob Andrew

Ernest Ingmar Bergman

George Richard Chamberlain

Terrence Stephen (Steve) McQueen

Sir Arthur John Gielgud

John Michael Crichton

George Orson Welles

Howard Andrew (Andy) Williams

Troyal Garth Brooks

Audrey Faith Hill

Nelust Wyclef Jean

Carole Penny Marshall

Margaret Jane Pauley

Isaac Donald Everly

Ellen Tyne Daly

Holly Michelle Phillips

Peter Marc Almond

Winnifred Jacqueline Bisset

Henry Ken(neth) Russell

NICKNAMES

Natalie Imbruglia – Jagger Lips and Frog Eyes

Benjamin Bratt – Scarecrow (because he was so thin)

Donna Air – Lego Legs

Macy Gray – Bum Jiggy

Lucy Liu – Curious George (her friends' nickname for her)

Nicole Appleton – Fonzie

Madonna – Nonni (family nickname)

Josie Lawrence – Big Bird ('I'm five foot ten inches tall')

Johnny Depp – Mr Stench

Kathy Bates – Bobo

Helen Mirren – Popper

Rachel Stevens – Ratz

J.C. Chasez – Mr Sleepy

Michael Vaughn – Virgil

Paris Hilton – Star (family nickname)

PEOPLE WITH UNUSUAL MIDDLE NAMES

Robbie MAXIMILIAN Williams

Anthea MILLICENT Turner

Richard TIFFANY Gere

Noah STRAUSSER SPEER Wyle

Courteney BASS Cox

Dom ROMULUS Joly

Hugh MARSTON Hefner

Bob XENON Geldof

Nick WULSTAN Park

Frankie ALICK Howerd

Spencer BONAVENTURE Tracy

Christopher CARANDINI Lee

Ludovic COVERLEY Kennedy

Chris LIVINGSTONE Eubank

Kenny MATHIESON Dalglish

Robin McLAUREN Williams

Donald McNICHOL Sutherland

Bob NESTA Marley

Sebastian NEWBOLD Coe

Robert SELDEN Duvall

Kurt VOGEL Russell

Alan WOLF Arkin

Peter WILTON Cushing

Billie PAUL Piper

FAMOUS SIBLINGS WITH DIFFERENT SURNAMES

Joan Fontaine & Olivia de Havilland

A.S. Byatt & Margaret Drabble

Emilio Estevez & Charlie Sheen

Warren Beatty & Shirley Maclaine

Keith Chegwin & Janice Long

Sheila Mercier & Lord Brian Rix

Lord Lew Grade & Lord Bernard Delfont

George Sanders & Tom Conway

Talia Shire & Francis Coppola

Peter Graves & James Arness

Gypsy Rose Lee & June Havoc

Ashley Judd & Wynonna

Beauty Culture

GENUINE NAMES FOR LIPSTICKS

Amour, Firecracker, Censored, Strawberry Fair, Corsaire, Nutmeg, Moon Beam, Neon Nude, Cool Candy, Passionate Pink, Mad Mauve, Risky Ruby, Portobello Plum, True Terracotta, Hot Honey, Barely Blush, Crazy Caramel, Too Truffle, Rolling Stone, Warm Platinum, Golden Spice, Chocoholic, Whisper, Fig, Parma Argent, Buttermilk, Sherbet Twist, Wine & Dine, Just Peachy, Hearts A Fire, So Cinnamon, In The Nude, Summer Daze, Let's Go Crazy

COUNTRIES THAT CHANGED THEIR NAMES

Rhodesia (to Zimbabwe)

Upper Volta (to Burkina Faso)

Aden (to Yemen)

Abyssinia (to Ethiopia)

Belgian Congo (to Zaire and back to Congo)

Dahomey (to Benin)

Siam (to Thailand)

Persia (to Iran)

Basutoland (to Lesotho)

British Honduras (to Belize)

Gold Coast (to Ghana)

Dutch Guiana (Suriname)

Nyasaland (Malawi)

The Afars and The Issas (Djibouti)

Portuguese Guinea (Guinea-Bissau)

Dutch East Indies (Indonesia)

New Hebrides (Vanuatu)

Bechuanaland (Botswana)

FICTITIOUS PLACES

Nutwood (Rupert Bear)

Walmington-On-Sea (*Dad's Army*)

Holby (*Casualty*)

Fulchester (*Viz*)

Llareggub (*Under Milk Wood*)

Erinsborough (*Neighbours*)

Gotham City (*Batman*)

Newtown (*Z Cars*)

Melchester (*Roy of The Rovers*)

St Mary Mead (*The Murder At The Vicarage* and all the Agatha Christie films and novels featuring Jane Marple)

WITCHES

In 2000, students at St Andrew's University tried to recruit 400 witches for a pagan coven.

Some years ago, Italian soccer was hit by a witchcraft scandal when it was revealed that the manager of the first division club, Pescara, had consulted a witch named Miriam Lebel. Apparently, this was just the tip of the iceberg and witchcraft is rife in the Italian game.

In New York, witches organized themselves into an 'Anti-Discrimination Lobby' in order to fight discrimination and to get a paid day off on Halloween.

In Gloucester in 1992, a new minister demanded his church be exorcised after he discovered that the organist, Shaun Pickering-Merrett, had been a practising witch for six years.

In 2001, villagers in southern India set fire to four women and a man they accused of witchcraft. The five were burnt alive.

Now that weddings can be held outside of churches and register offices, in 1996 a witches' coven in Worcestershire put in an application for a licence to carry out legal wedding services (or 'hamfasts').

HALLOWEEN

Lois Bourne is a 'white' (i.e. a good) witch from St Albans. When a friend complained that they hadn't been able to sell their house for four years, she cast a spell and the next day the house went under offer. Mrs Bourne modestly admitted that it could be a coincidence but anyway later said, 'Selling houses is very boring magic and I refuse to do it.'

In 1995, Susan Leybourne, 29, a witch who had been ordained a pagan priestess at the Circle University in Louisiana, became the first witch to become a chaplain at a British university after her (unpaid) appointment was requested by 40 members of Leeds University's Occult Society.

In 1978, the British writer Nesta Wynn Ellis visited a witch doctor in Zimbabwe who told her that in six months she would marry a man she hadn't yet met. She then went to another witch doctor, who told her the same. A month later, in Kenya, she met her future husband. Five months after that, they were married.

Iolanda Quinn, ex-wife of film star Anthony Quinn, is a self-confessed witch. When Quinn fathered a 'love-child', Mrs Quinn said, 'This baby is not his. You must believe me, I am a witch and I know.' Unfortunately for her, Quinn admitted being the father.

In Russia in 1995, Lyuba Lagutina, a publisher, went to a witch when her baby cried so much that he developed a hernia. The witch said a few spells and the baby was miraculously cured.

In South Africa, two so-called witches were recently burned to death after a bus crash killed 14 children. Speelman Matsipane and Mamiagabo Makwele were accused of being witches on account of their advanced age. They were dragged from their homes and murdered. This is not the only case of witches (or women who are accused of being witches) being blamed for accidents that had nothing to do

with them. Whenever someone is struck by lightning in parts of South Africa, it is said to be the work of witches, and old ladies suspected of being witches are driven out of their homes.

In 1989, Leicester Polytechnic had to cancel an 'exhibition on folk history' when 3,000 witches decided to descend on the college.

WISE WORDS FROM ALBERT EINSTEIN

'Only two things are infinite, the universe and human stupidity, and I'm not sure about the former.'

'I never think of the future. It comes soon enough.'

'The hardest thing in the world to understand is income tax.'

'An empty stomach is not a good political adviser.'

'Nationalism is an infantile disease. It is the measles of mankind.'

'I can't believe that God plays dice with the universe.'

WHAT PEOPLE DID IN WORLD WAR TWO

Jimmy Young served in the RAF as a physical training instructor with the rank of sergeant.

Baroness Barbara Castle was an administration officer in the Ministry of Food and served as an air-raid warden.

Sam Kydd was a private in the army but was captured and sent to a German POW camp. His book about his time there – *For You, The War is Over* – illustrated just how different POW camps were for officers compared to non-officers. He was also the POW adviser on the movie *The Captive Heart*.

Billy Wright was a corporal in the Shropshire Light Infantry and also made his debut for Wolves (as a winger) and for England (at right-half) in an 'unofficial' wartime international.

Lord Robert Runcie served with the Scots Guards and was a tank officer seeing action in Normandy and being awarded the Military Cross.

Lord Brian Rix served in the RAF and also down the mines as a Bevin Boy. (NB One in ten conscripts in the latter stages of the war were sent down the mines as Bevin Boys, named after the cabinet minister Ernest Bevin.)

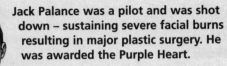

Jack Palance was a pilot and was shot down – sustaining severe facial burns resulting in major plastic surgery. He was awarded the Purple Heart.

Ray Lindwall served with the Australian army in New Guinea and in the Solomon Islands.

Eli Wallach served in the US Army Medical Corps and helped battle casualties in Europe.

Peter Sellers was in the Entertainments Division of the RAF and was attached to the Ralph Reader Gang Show.

Dame Vera Lynn raised morale for Britons everywhere with concerts and radio performances at home and abroad in Egypt, India and Burma.

Leslie Nielsen joined the Royal Canadian Air Force and trained as an air gunner but the war ended before he could see combat.

Michael Bentine served in the RAF as an intelligence officer.

Brian Johnston was a Grenadier Guards officer who was awarded the Military Cross for, among other reasons, his 'cheerfulness under fire' in Normandy.

Donald Swann was a Quaker and so registered as a conscientious objector but he still joined the Friends Ambulance Unit working with refugees in Greece and the Middle East.

Dora Bryan served with the army entertainment organization ENSA at home and abroad (Italy).

David Tomlinson served as a flight lieutenant in the RAF.

Aaron Spelling served in the US Army Air Force and was awarded the Bronze Star and Purple Heart with Oak Leaf Cluster.

Lord Home was an MP throughout the war but also saw active service as a major in the Lanarkshire Yeomanry before being invalided out with tuberculosis of the spine.

Arthur English served in the Army for six years, ending the war as a sergeant.

Lord Bernard Weatherill served in the 4/7 Royal Dragoon Guards & Indian Army and the 19th KGVO Lancers.

Sir Edward Heath served in the Royal Artillery, rising to the rank of major and getting a mention in despatches as well as being awarded a military MBE.

Bill Travers was dispatched to India's North-West Frontier to join a Gurkha regiment that was operating behind enemy lines alongside General Wingate's Chindits. He parachuted into the Malayan jungle in command of a small group of men to harass the Japanese.

Ian Carmichael served as a major in the 22 Dragoons in north-west Europe, gaining a mention in despatches.

Telly Savalas served with the US Army towards the end of the war and was injured in action.

Rossano Brazzi joined the Italian Resistance after his parents were murdered by the Fascists. He also continued to make films during the war.

Lord Roy Jenkins served in the Royal Artillery and then in special intelligence, where he reached the rank of captain.

George Cole served in the RAF but spent most of his time making films.

Dinah Shore travelled more miles than any other American entertainer to entertain the troops.

Robert Kee spent much of the war in a German POW camp. His book on his experiences – *A Crowd Is Not Company* – was described by *The Times* as 'arguably the best POW book ever written'.

Viscount Whitelaw served as a major in the Scots Guards, winning the Military Cross.

Leo Abse served in the RAF but was arrested for 'political activities' in 1944, which gave rise to a debate in Parliament.

Bob Paisley served in the Royal Artillery and fought in the North African and Italian campaigns, taking part in the liberation of Rome.

John Profumo served as a brigadier in the army and was mentioned in despatches. He also found the time to win Kettering in the 1940 by-election.

Robert Maxwell went from being a private in the Pioneer Corps to being a captain in the infantry. A marksman, he was awarded the Military Cross for storming an enemy pillbox in Brussels in 1945.

Jeff Chandler served in the army in the Pacific, rising from infantryman to First Lieutenant.

Raymond Baxter was an officer in the RAF flying Spitfires.

Rabbi Hugo Gryn was in Auschwitz extermination camp where he worked as a slave labourer.

George Bush was the US Navy's youngest ever fighter pilot. He flew 58 missions and was once shot down (and rescued). He won five medals.

Baroness Sue Ryder worked in the Special Operations Executive.

Sir Hardy Amies served in the Intelligence Corps and was head of the 1944 Special Forces Mission to Belgium. He rose to the rank of lieutenant-colonel.

Sir Fred Pontin worked for the Admiralty in catering and welfare.

Prince Philip served in the Royal Navy and captained a ship.

Anthony Powell served in the Welsh Regiment and the Intelligence Corps as a major.

Humphrey Lyttelton served with the Grenadier Guards.

Lorne Greene served in the Royal Canadian Air Force.

Martin Balsam served in the US Army Combat Engineers before transferring to the US Army Air Force.

George MacDonald Fraser served in the British army in Burma.

Robert Altman was a bomber pilot in the Pacific.

Johnny Carson served with the US Naval Reserve.

PEOPLE WHO WERE EVACUATED IN WORLD WAR TWO

Michael Aspel, Jack Rosenthal, Baroness Shirley Williams, Sir Michael Caine, The Beverley Sisters, Derek Jameson, Justin de Villeneuve, Sir Jonathan Miller, Jeremy Thorpe, Adam Faith, Harold Pinter, Bruce Forsyth, Barbara Windsor

SPORT

Jennifer Lopez was a high school star gymnast.

Jason Statham was a diver who represented Great Britain in the Seoul Olympics.

Kate Bosworth was a champion equestrian and played varsity soccer and lacrosse.

Suzanne Danielle represented her county at gymnastics while at school.

Joely Richardson attended a Florida tennis academy for two years.

Darren Day was a semi-professional snooker player.

Haydn Gwynne represented her county at tennis.

Martin Freeman was in the England junior squash squad.

James Alexandrou swam for his county and was ranked in the national top ten.

A baseball hit by a bat travels as fast as 120 mph – almost precisely the same (maximum) speed as the puck in ice hockey.

There are 108 stitches on a baseball.

Michael Parkinson was a good enough cricketer to play for Barnsley (with Dickie Bird and Geoffrey Boycott) and to have a trial for Yorkshire CCC.

Gary Lineker played second XI cricket for Leicestershire and once scored a century for the MCC playing at Lord's.

Terence Rattigan played cricket at Lord's, when he opened the batting for Harrow against Eton.

Eddie Charlton, the snooker star, appeared in the Australian surfing championship, played top-grade soccer, excelled at tennis and athletics, and carried the flag for Australia in the 1956 Melbourne Olympics.

Australian Rules Football was originally designed to give cricketers something to play during the off-season.

Celia Imrie threw the javelin for Surrey.

Sir Arthur Conan Doyle was a keen amateur cricketer who bowled the great W.G. Grace in 1900.

Lord Byron was an all-round sportsman who captained Harrow in their annual cricket match against Eton at Lord's.

It takes 3,000 cows to supply the US national football league (NFL) with enough leather for a year's supply of footballs.

Eminem is a keen darts player.

The average life span of a major league baseball is seven pitches.

A Costa Rican worker making baseballs earns around $3,000 per annum. The average American pro baseball player earns around $2,500,000 per annum.

At one stage in the 1920s Chelsea had three players who were medical students.

The bullseye on a dartboard must be precisely 5 feet 8 inches off the ground.

There are two sports in which the team has to move backwards to win: tug of war and rowing. (NB Backstroke is not a team sport.)

When Len Shackleton wrote his autobiography, he included a chapter entitled 'The Average Director's Knowledge of Football'. The chapter consisted of a blank page.

In 1972, an entire soccer team in Cordoba, Argentina, was jailed after the players kicked a linesman to death.

The Alexandra in Crewe Alexandra came from the name of the pub where meetings to set up the club were first held.

Dartboards are made out of horsehair.

PEOPLE WHO HAVE RUN MARATHONS

(London except where stated.)

Richard Dunwoody

Adrian Moorhouse

Jeffrey Archer

Nell McAndrew

Sir Ranulph Fiennes

Beth Cordingly

Charlie Brooks

Richard Herring

Kate Garraway

Andrew Morton

Major Charles Ingram

Brough Scott

Iain Duncan Smith

Lorraine Kelly

Donal Macintyre

Sean 'P. Diddy' Combs (New York)

Will Ferrell (Boston)

Jorg Haider (NY)

Oprah Winfrey (Marine Corps)

Phil Selway

Claire Goose (New York)

Scott Bakula (LA)

KEEN SQUASH PLAYERS

Tom Cruise, Mary Archer, Richard Dunwoody, Richard Wilson, Mike Atherton, David Essex, Anton Mosimann, Ian Balding, Michael Palin, Trisha Goddard, Nicole Kidman, Ian McShane, Nicky Clarke, Damon Hill

KEEN TENNIS PLAYERS

Mariella Frostrup, Gabby Logan, Tamzin Outhwaite, Alistair McGowan, Sir Cliff Richard, Robert Duvall, Terry Wogan, Des Lynam, Prue Leith, Gordon Brown, Les Dennis, Sam Torrance, Angus Deayton, Tony Blair, Roger Black, Rory Bremner, Martin Amis, Raymond Blanc, Roger Lloyd Pack, Sir David Frost, Sir Richard Branson, Chris Patten, Geoffrey Boycott, Loyd Grossman, John Francome, Christopher Martin-Jenkins, Dermot Murnaghan, Jeff Lynne, James Fox, Jung Chang, Trevor Eve, Alan Hansen, Peter Snow, Simon MacCorkindale, Sir Jackie Stewart, Nicky Clarke, Ainsley Harriott, Anthea Turner, Rosanna Davidson, Michelle Trachtenberg

KEEN ON SAILING

Jonathan Dimbleby, John Major, Michael Grade, Robbie Coltrane, Annabel Croft, Jeremy Irons, Valerie Singleton, Peter Skellern, Elle MacPherson, Alan Titchmarsh, Kelsey Grammer, Chloe Sevigny, Russell Crowe

KEEN TABLE-TENNIS PLAYERS

Steve McFadden (won competitions as a child)

Kevin Spacey (requests a ping-pong table in his room whenever he's on location)

Lord Norman Lamont

Chief Rabbi Jonathan Sacks

Roger McGough

Paul Gascoigne

Julian Bream

Michael Owen

Matthew Broderick

WOMEN WHO ARE KEEN GOLFERS

Catherine Zeta-Jones, Claudia Schiffer, Teri Hatcher, Felicity Kendal, Carol Barnes, Dame Kiri Te Kanawa, Mary Parkinson, Jo Durie, Rachael Heyhoe Flint, Dame Naomi James, Celine Dion, Cindy Crawford, Hazel Irvine, Caryl Phillips, Nicole Kidman, Jodie Kidd, Michelle Trachtenberg

KEEN SNOOKER PLAYERS

Steve Cram, Don Black, Sir Alex Ferguson, Robert Harris, Gary Lineker, Nick Faldo, Noah Wyle (plays billiards like a pool shark at the Hollywood Athletic Club), Kelsey Grammer (billiards), Finley Quaye (was a snooker hustler as a boy), Lisa Kudrow (plays pool like a pool shark and can perform trick shots)

IF …

If Holly Hunter married George W. Bush, she'd be Holly Bush.

If Iman married Gary Oldman, she'd be Iman Oldman.

If Cherie Blair married Oliver Stone, she'd be Cherie Stone.

If Ronni Ancona married Jason Biggs, she'd be Ronni Biggs.

If Minnie Driver married Alice Cooper, she'd be Minnie Cooper.

If Sandi Toksvig married Pauly Shore, she'd be Sandi Shore.

If Olivia Newton-John married Wayne Newton, then divorced him to marry Elton John, she'd be Olivia Newton-John Newton John.

JAMES BOND

'Who was the first person to play James Bond' is a famous trick question. No, it wasn't Sean Connery, even though he was the first movie James Bond (in *Dr No*). In 1954, James Bond was played by Barry Nelson in a one-hour US TV version of *Casino Royale*. Le Chiffre, the baddie, was played by Peter Lorre.

Since Barry Nelson, Bond has been played by Connery, George Lazenby, Roger Moore, Timothy Dalton and Pierce Brosnan (as well as by David Niven in the spoof *Casino Royale*).

Ian Fleming, the creator of Bond, took his hero's name from an ornithologist. Fleming was a keen birdwatcher and when he was looking for a name, he picked up a book by a distinguished American ornithologist named James Bond and decided to 'borrow' it.

Fleming also 'borrowed' the name of Bond's greatest enemy, Blofeld. Fleming had been pondering over a suitably nasty name for his villain when he chanced upon the name of Henry Blofeld, now a cricket commentator, in Boodles, the London gentlemen's club.

James Bond is renowned for his smooth talking. In *Diamonds Are Forever*, when Tiffany Case (Jill St John) asks him, 'Do you like redheads?', he replies, 'As long as the collars and cuffs match.'

For most people, Sean Connery is Bond, but Connery himself described the character as 'a Frankenstein monster I can't get rid of' and has said, 'I have always hated that damn James Bond: I'd like to kill him.'

James Bond has been going for so long that *Goldeneye* saw the first appearance by the daughter of a Bond girl. Eunice Grayson appeared in the first two Bond movies (indeed, it was to her that Bond first uttered the immortal words, 'The name's Bond, James Bond') and her daughter, Karen, 24, appeared in *Goldeneye*.

Bond's cars are almost as essential to the films' success as the villains and the girls. His most famous car is the Aston Martin DB5 with revolving numberplates, pop-up bulletproof shield and ejector-seat he drove in *Goldfinger*.

But if *Goldfinger* had the most memorable car, *Diamonds Are Forever* had the most memorable car stunt. That was the film when Connery (or his stunt man) two-wheeled a Ford Mustang down a narrow alleyway and then set it back on four wheels.

OTHER PEOPLE BORN ON CHRISTMAS DAY

1642 Sir Isaac Newton, English scientist

1899 Humphrey Bogart, American actor

1901 Princess Alice, British royal

1907 Andrew Cruickshank, British actor

1907 Cab Calloway, American musician

1908 Quentin Crisp, British writer and personality

1912 Tony Martin, American actor and singer

1918 Anwar Sadat, Egyptian politician

1923 Noele Gordon, British actress

1924 Rod Serling, American writer

1927 Alan King, American comedian

1934 Stuart Hall, British TV presenter

1936 Princess Alexandra, British royal

1936 Ismail Merchant, Indian film producer

1937 O'Kelly Isley, American singer

1941 Jim Bolger, British racehorse trainer

1942 Barbara Follett, British politician

1943 Hanna Schygulla, German actress

1944 Kenny Everett, British DJ

1944 Nigel Starmer-Smith, British rugby union commentator

1945 Noel Redding, British musician

1946 Jimmy Buffett, American singer

1946 Christopher Frayling, British playwright

1947 Kieran Prendiville, British writer and TV presenter

1948 Merry Clayton, American singer

1948 Barbara Mandrell, American country singer

1949 Sissy Spacek, American actress

1954 Robin Campbell, British musician

1954 Annie Lennox, British singer

1957 Shane MacGowan, British musician

1963 Ashley Metcalfe, British cricketer

1966 Stephen Twigg, British politician

1968 Helena Christensen, Danish model

1971 Lightning, British Gladiator

1971 Dido, British singer

1975 Marcus Trescothick, British cricketer

1978 Simon Jones, British cricketer

CHRISTMAS NOTES

Armenians celebrate Christmas on 19 January.

In the US state of Indiana, there is a town called Santa Claus where courses are held for department store Santas. Graduates become a BSc (Bachelor of Santa Clausing).

Christmas was officially abolished in England between 1642 and 1652 – thanks to the Puritans who hated the idea of anyone enjoying themselves.

Christmas cards had their origins in 15th-century Germany, and it wasn't until the mid-19th-century (and the advent of the postage stamp) that they were produced commercially in this country. Today, the most popular Christmas card is one depicting Santa Claus and his reindeer.

The *Mayflower* arrived at Plymouth Rock, Massachusetts on Christmas Day 1620.

THINGS SAID ABOUT CHRISTMAS

'Next to a circus there ain't nothing that packs up and tears out faster than the Christmas spirit.' (Kin Hubbard)

'Christmas is a holiday that persecutes the lonely, the frayed, and the rejected.' (Jimmy Cannon)

'What is Christmas? It is tenderness for the past, courage for the present, hope for the future. It is a fervent wish that every cup may overflow with blessings rich and eternal, and that every path may lead to peace.' (Agnes Pharo)

'There is no ideal Christmas; only the one Christmas you decide to make as a reflection of your values, desires, affections, traditions.' (Bill McKibben)

'Christmas waves a magic wand over this world, and behold, everything is softer and more beautiful.' (Norman Vincent Peale)

'Blessed is the season which engages the whole world in a conspiracy of love.' (Hamilton Wright Mabie)

'Christmas, children, is not a date. It is a state of mind.' (Mary Ellen Chase)

GENUINE PLACE NAMES FOR LOVERS OF DOUBLE ENTENDRE

Arsy (France)

Bald Knob (Arkansas, USA)

Balls Cross (West Sussex)

Bastardo (Italy)

Beaver (Pennsylvania, USA)

Bendery (Moldova)

Big Bone Lick (Kentucky, USA)

Blowing Rock (North Carolina, USA)

Bottom (North Carolina, USA)

Bra (Italy)

Broadbottom (Greater Manchester)

Burrumbuttock (Australia)

Buttock's Booth (Northamptonshire)

Climax (Michigan, USA)

Clit (Romania)

Cock Bank (Clwyd)

Cockermouth (Cumbria)

Comers (Grampian)

Condom (France)

Dildo (Canada)

Fertile (Minnesota, USA)

French Lick (Indiana, USA)

Fucking (Austria)

Hornytown (North Carolina, USA)

Humptulips (Washington, USA)

Intercourse (Pennsylvania, USA)

Knob Lick (Missouri, USA)

Knockin (Shropshire)

Lickey End (Worcestershire)

Loveladies (New Jersey, USA)

Lover (Wiltshire)

Muff (Northern Ireland)

Neck City (Missouri, USA)

Penistone (South Yorkshire)

Petting (Germany)

Phuket (Thailand)

Root (Switzerland)

Semen (Indonesia)

Shafton (Yorkshire)

Shag Harbour (Canada)

Thong (Kent)

Titz (Germany)

Twatt (Orkney)

Twin Humps Park (Australia)

Undy (Gwent)

Upper Dicker (East Sussex)

Wankers Corner (Oregon, USA)

Wide Open (Tyne and Wear)

Marriage etc.

Hugh Dennis met his wife Kate, a sound engineer, when Hugh was playing a talking fromage frais in a Soho voiceover studio.

Four of Mickey Rooney's weddings took place in Las Vegas.

Couples who celebrated their Diamond Wedding Anniversary

Lord Longford & Elizabeth, Countess of Longford

Perry & Roselle Como

Sir Donald & Lady Jessie Bradman

Anthony & Lady Violet Powell

Bob & Dolores Hope

James & Frances Cagney

Sir Alec & Lady Merula Guinness

Karl & Mona Malden

Lord James & Audrey Callaghan

Fred Zinnemann & Renee Bartlett

Sir John Mills & Mary Hayley Bell

Michael Denison & Dulcie Gray

The Duke and Duchess of Devonshire

Lord Richard Attenborough & Sheila Sim

George & Barbara Bush

Charlton & Lydia Heston

COUPLES WHO CELEBRATED THEIR GOLDEN WEDDING ANNIVERSARY

Dame Catherine & Tom Cookson

Jack & Florence Haley

Dame Thora Hird & Jimmy Scott

Sir Matt & Lady Jean Busby

Ray & Gwendolyn Bolger

Lord & Lady Lew Grade

Hammond Innes & Dorothy Lang

Robin & Patricia Bailey

Walter & Ruth Pidgeon

Hume Cronyn & Jessica Tandy

Pat & Eloise O'Brien

Carl & Emma Jung

Queen Elizabeth II & Prince Philip

Dick & Mary Francis

Lord & Lady Yehudi Menuhin

The Rev. W. & Margaret Awdry

Sir Harry & Lady Myra Secombe

Googie Withers & John McCallum

Federico Fellini & Giulietta Masina

Marlene Dietrich & Rudolf Sieber

Eli & Anne Wallach

PEOPLE WHO WERE/ARE MARRIED TO THEIR MANAGERS

Cilla Black, Neneh Cherry, Joe Bugner, Clodagh Rodgers, Celine Dion, Pam Ayres, Charlotte Rampling, LaToya Jackson, Anthea Turner, Judy Garland, Randy Travis, Vanessa Williams, Victoria De Los Angeles, Ozzy Osbourne, Luke Goss, Caron Keating, Paula Radcliffe, Faith Evans, Susan Chilcott, Michael Barrymore, Anita Harris, Lynda Carter, Ronnie Spector, Rita Hayworth, Mary Black, Dolores O'Riordan

PEOPLE WHO MARRIED THEIR MINDERS

Roseanne Arnold, Patty Hearst, Princess Stephanie of Monaco

PEOPLE WITH SPOUSES IN COMMON

Sonny Bono & Greg Allman – Cher

Peter Sellers & Slim Jim McDonnell – Britt Ekland

Fiona Fullerton & Susan George – Simon MacCorkindale

Liam Gallagher & Jim Kerr – Patsy Kensit

Gary Oldman & Martin Scorsese – Isabella Rossellini

Dudley Moore & Pinchas Zukerman – Tuesday Weld

Gary Kemp & Jude Law – Sadie Frost

Mia Farrow & Ava Gardner – Frank Sinatra

Henry Fonda & William Wyler – Margaret Sullavan

Sir Rex Harrison & Richard Harris – Elizabeth Harris

Artie Shaw & Lex Barker – Lana Turner

Humphrey Bogart & Jason Robards – Lauren Bacall

Mimi Rogers & Nicole Kidman – Tom Cruise

Ursula Andress & Linda Evans – John Derek

Vivien Leigh & Joan Plowright – Sir Laurence Olivier

Catherine Deneuve & Marie Helvin – David Bailey

Brigitte Bardot & Jane Fonda – Roger Vadim

Peter Sellers & Sir David Frost – Lynne Frederick

Charlie Chaplin & Burgess Meredith – Paulette Goddard

Michael Jayston & André Previn – Heather Jayston

George Sanders & Ronald Colman – Benita Hume

Laurence Harvey & Michael Wilding – Margaret Leighton

Clark Gable & William Powell – Carole Lombard

Germaine Greer & Maya Angelou – Paul de Feu

THINGS THAT SIMPLY DISAPPEARED

Deelybobbers

Pet Rocks

Clackers

Hai Karate After-Shave

Cabbage Patch Dolls

Broomball

Gonks

Paper Knickers

Hairstyles such as the Elephant's Trunk, Argentine Ducktail, Flat-Top, Conk, Spike-Top, Suedehead and Flop

WOMEN WHO DIED IN CHILDBIRTH

Jane Seymour (wife of Henry VIII, while giving birth to future Edward VI)

Two of Joseph Chamberlain's wives (one of whom was Neville Chamberlain's mother, and died when he was six)

James Watt's wife

Mary Shelley's mother (Mary Wollstonecraft)

Liz Smith's mother (when she was two)

Eric Sykes's mother

James Goldsmith's first wife

John Donne's wife

Charles Babbage's wife

Kenneth Grahame's mother (when he was five)

Fred Archer's wife (precipitating his suicide)

Princess Charlotte

Haing Ngor's wife (the Khmer Rouge's hatred of professionals meant he was unable to reveal that he was a gynaecologist and needed medical supplies to help her)

Al Jolson's mother (when he was eight)

Walter Pidgeon's first wife

Franz Liszt's daughter

Robert Johnson's first wife (aged 16)

Three of Jane Austen's sisters-in-law

Kim Il-Sung's first wife

Emperor Haile Selassie's daughter

Dan Maskell's mother (when he was 14)

Young Tom Morris's wife

Catherine Parr

MEN WHOSE PENIS WAS PRESERVED AFTER DEATH

Napoleon Bonaparte (it was eventually sold at auction where it fetched £2,500)

Grigori Rasputin (according to his biographer, 'it looked like a blackened overripe banana, about a foot long...')

PEOPLE WHO DIED OF LUNG CANCER

Steve McQueen, Jacques Brel, Yul Brynner, Joe DiMaggio, Roy Castle, John Wayne, Buddy Adler, Duke Ellington, Roddy McDowall, Ray Harford, Stubby Kaye, Buster Keaton, Desi Arnaz, Tex Avery, Bruce Cabot, Art Blakey, Cantinflas, King George VI, Lon Chaney, Andy Kaufman, Alec Clunes, Chuck Connors, Frank Loesser, E.G. Marshall, Franchot Tone, Gary Cooper, Walt Disney, Dick Haymes, Fernandel, Harry Guardino, Moe Howard, Eddie Kendricks, Warren Zevon, Doug McClure, Ray Milland, Robert Mitchum, Forrest Tucker, Boris Pasternak, Lloyd Nolan, Jesse Owens, Robert Preston, Carl Wilson, Vincent Price, Eddie Rabbitt, Alan Jay Lerner, Nicholas Ray, Robert Taylor, Sir Stanley Baker, Michael Williams, Gilbert Becaud, Nat 'King' Cole, Albert Collins, Rosemary Clooney, Betty Grable, Melina Mercouri, Agnes Moorehead, Jennifer Paterson, Carmen Silvera, Jacqueline Susann, Sarah Vaughan, Nancy Walker

CELEBRITY BEQUESTS

Two days before her death in 1970, Janis Joplin amended her will to provide $2,500 'so my friends can get blasted after I'm gone'. She also left a guest list. The all-night party duly took place at a Californian tavern where she had often performed.

In 1964, Ian Fleming, the author of the James Bond novels, left £500 to each of four friends with the instruction that they should 'spend the same within twelve months of receipt on some extravagance'.

In 1962, Marilyn Monroe left all her 'personal effects and clothing' to Lee Strasberg, her acting coach, 'it being my desire that he distribute these, in his sole discretion, among my friends, colleagues and those to whom I am devoted'. She also left Strasberg most of her estate.

In 1998, author Hammond Innes left his London home to the actress Celia Imrie, whom he'd befriended towards the end of his life.

In 1986, Cary Grant bequeathed all of his 'wearing apparel, ornaments and jewellery' to Stanley E. Fox on condition that

Mr Fox shared everything out among 14 specified people – one of whom was Frank Sinatra.

W.C. Fields's last requests, as listed in his will, were ignored. He wanted his body cremated without any religious ceremony. However, both his estranged Roman Catholic wife and his mistress held separate religious ceremonies before his body was interred in a mausoleum in 1946. Nor did anything come of the provision he had made for a 'W.C. Fields College for orphan white boys and girls where no religion of any sort is to be preached'.

P.T. Barnum, the famous American showman, drew up a will in 1882 leaving his daughter Helen $1,500 a year for life. When she left her husband, Barnum wrote her out of the will. Then, in an 1889 codicil, he left her a property in Colorado, which he believed was worthless. Two years later, he died and Helen inherited this property, which turned out to have mineral deposits that made Helen wealthier than all the other beneficiaries of Barnum's will combined.

In 1964, Cole Porter bequeathed his diamond dress stud to Douglas Fairbanks Jnr.

In his will, Noah gave the whole world to his three sons.

PAIRS OF CELEBRITIES WHO DIED ON THE SAME DAY

John Adams (second US President) & Thomas Jefferson (third US President) – 4.7.1826

Charles Kingsley (author of The Water Babies) & Gustave Doré (painter) – 23.1.1883

Franz Liszt (classical composer) & Frank Holl (painter) – 31.7.1888

Wilkie Collins (novelist) & Eliza Cook (poet) – 23.9.1889

Charles Stewart Parnell (Irish leader) & William Henry Smith (founder of W.H. Smith) – 6.10.1891

John Ruskin (social reformer, artist and writer) & Richard Doddridge Blackmore (writer of Lorna Doone) – 20.1.1900

Carl Bechstein (maker of the famous Bechstein pianos) & Gottlieb Daimler (motor car manufacturer) – 6.3.1900

Marshal Henri Pétain (French soldier and leader of the wartime Vichy regime) & Robert Flaherty (film-maker and explorer) – 23.7.1951

Josef Stalin (Soviet dictator) and Sergei Prokofiev (composer who was persecuted by Stalin) – 5.3.1953

King Ibn Saud (of Saudi Arabia) and Dylan Thomas (poet) – 9.11.1953

Ward Bond (actor) & Mack Sennett (film producer) – 5.11.1960

Michael Curtiz (film director) & Stu Sutcliffe (former member of The Beatles) – 10.4.1962

Jean Cocteau (playwright and film director) & Edith Piaf (singer) – 11.10.1963

Hedda Hopper (gossip columnist) & Buster Keaton (actor) – 1.2.1966

Billy Rose (Broadway producer) & Sophie Tucker (singer) – 10.2.1966

Che Guevara (revolutionary) & André Maurois (French author) – 9.10.1967

Mama Cass Elliot (singer) & Erich Kästner (author of *Emil And The Detectives*) – 29.7.1974

Steve Biko (anti-apartheid activist) & Robert Lowell (American poet) – 12.9.1977

Dame Gracie Fields (singer) & Jimmy McCullough (guitarist with Wings) – 27.9.1979

Joyce Grenfell (actress and writer) & Zeppo Marx (member of the Marx Brothers) – 30.11.1979

Thelonious Monk (musician) & Lee Strasberg (actor and drama teacher) – 17.2.1982

Muddy Waters (blues musician) & George Balanchine (choreographer) – 30.4.1983

William Powell (film star) & Tito Gobbi (opera singer) – 5.3.1984

Carl Foreman (film producer) & George Gallup (pollster) – 26.6.1984

Sam Spiegel (film producer) & Ricky Nelson (pop star) – 31.12.1985

Gordon Macrae (actor) & L. Ron Hubbard (creator of Scientology) & Vincente Minnelli (film director) – 24.1.1986

Wallis Simpson (Duchess of Windsor) & Bill Edrich (England cricketer) – 24.4.1986

Alan Jay Lerner (lyricist) & Jorge Luis Borges (writer) – 14.6.1986

Randolph Scott (actor) & Joan Greenwood (actress) – 2.3.1987

Mary Astor (actress) & Emlyn Williams (actor and playwright) – 25.9.1987

Arthur Marshall (writer and broadcaster) & Sir Thomas Sopwith (aviation pioneer) – 27.1.1989

Sugar Ray Robinson (boxer) & Abbie Hoffman (American activist and writer) – 12.4.1989

Tommy Trinder (comedian) & Mel Blanc (the voice of cartoon characters such as Bugs Bunny) – 10.7.1989

George Adamson (*Born Free* conservationist) & Diana Vreeland (fashion guru) – 21.8.1989

Graham Chapman (member of the Monty Pythons) & Norman Yardley (England cricketer) – 4.10.1989

Mel Appleby (of Mel and Kim) & Bhagwan Shree Rajneesh (guru) – 19.1.1990

Teddy Tinling (tennis dress designer) & Rocky Graziano (boxer) – 23.5.1990

Max Wall (actor and comedian) & Major Pat Reid (Colditz escaper and author) – 22.5.1990

Serge Gainsbourg (French singer and composer) & Edwin Land (inventor of the Polaroid camera) – 3.3.1991

Steve Marriott (rock star) & Don Siegel (film director) – 20.4.1991

Bernie Winters (comedian) & Jerzy Kosinski (writer) – 4.5.1991

Isaac Bashevis Singer (Nobel Prize-winning writer) & Freddie Brown (England cricketer) – 24.7.1991

Robert Maxwell (businessman) & Fred MacMurray (actor) – 5.11.1991

Stella Adler (drama teacher) & Albert King (blues singer) – 21.12.1992

James Hunt (motor racing driver) & John Connally (Former Texas governor and US presidential candidate, who was riding in the same car as President Kennedy when he was shot) – 15.6.1993

Elizabeth Montgomery (actress) & Elisha Cook Jr (actor) – 18.5.1995

Simon Cadell (actor) & Lord Douglas Jay (politician) – 6.3.1996

Ray Lindwall (Australian cricketer) & Andreas Papandreou (Greek Prime Minister) – 23.6.1996

Alfred Marks (actor) & Margot Hemingway (model and actress) – 1.7.1996

Mother Teresa (aid worker) & Sir Georg Solti (orchestral conductor) – 5.9.1997

Carl Wilson (Beach Boy) & Falco (singer) – 6.2.1998

Charles M. Schulz (*Peanuts* creator) & Screamin' Jay Hawkins (blues legend) – 12.2.2000

Sir John Gielgud (actor) & Dame Barbara Cartland (writer) – 21.5.2000

Perry Como (singer) & Didi (Brazilian footballer) & Simon Raven (memoirist) – 12.5.2001

John Lee Hooker (blues legend) & Carroll O'Connor – 21.6.2001

Chet Atkins (musician) & Joe Fagan (Liverpool FC manager) – 30.6.2001

Ken Tyrell (Formula 1 boss) & Aaliyah (singer) – 25.8.2001

Christiaan Barnard (heart surgery pioneer) & Troy Donahue (actor) – 2.9.2001

Milton Berle (comedian) & Dudley Moore (actor and pianist) – 27.3.2002

Sir Paul Getty (philanthropist) & Dr Robert Atkins (diet guru) – 17.4.2003

Robert Stack (actor) & Dame Wendy Hiller (actress) – 14.5.2003

Gregory Hines (actor and dancer) & Ray Harford (soccer boss) – 9.8.2003

Elia Kazan (film director) & Althea Gibson (tennis champion) – 28.9.2003

Alistair Cooke (broadcaster) & Hubert Gregg (performer and broadcaster) – 30.3.2004

Archibald Cox (Watergate prosecutor) & Jack Rosenthal (playwright) – 29.5.2004

Red Adair (firefighter) & Bernard Levin (newspaper columnist) – 7.8.2004

Hunter S. Thompson (writer) & Sandra Dee (film star) – 20.2.2005

Sir Edward Heath & Geraldine Fitzgerald (actress) – 17.7.2005

Elisabeth Schwarzkopf (opera singer) & Arthur Lee (blues musician) – 3.8.2006

Lord Lambton (politician) & Saddam Hussein (tyrant) – 30.12.2006

Alan Ball (footballer) & Bobby Pickett (singer) – 25.4.2007

PEOPLE WHO DIED IN POVERTY

Josephine Baker, William Blake, Mrs Patrick Campbell, Miguel de Cervantes, Christopher Columbus, Gustave Flaubert, Johann Gutenberg, William Hazlitt, Robert Johnson, Joe Louis, Herman Melville, Wolfgang Mozart, Thomas Paine, Edith Piaf, Rembrandt, Charles Rennie Mackintosh, Oskar Schindler, Gordon Selfridge (founder of the eponymous department store), Joan Sims, Anthony Steel, Laurence Sterne, Vincent Van Gogh, Vermeer, Oscar Wilde

FAMOUS PEOPLE BORN ON THE DAY OTHER FAMOUS PEOPLE DIED

Darren Gough – 18.9.1970 – Jimi Hendrix

Norah Jones – 30.3.1979 – Airey Neave

David Schwimmer – 2.11.1966 – Mississippi John Hurt

Lilian Thuram – 1.1.1972 – Maurice Chevalier

The Rock – 2.5.1972 – J. Edgar Hoover

Charles Wheeler – 26.3.1923 – Sarah Bernhardt

Pink – 8.9.1979 – Jean Seberg

Sophie, Countess of Wessex – 20.1.1965 – Alan Freed

Natalie Imbruglia – 4.2.1975 – Louis Jordan

Jim Dale – 15.8.1935 – Will Rogers

Derek Dougan – 20.1.1936 – King George V

Divine Brown – 9.8.1969 – Sharon Tate

Keith Vaz – 26.11.1956 – Tommy Dorsey

Barry Sheene – 11.9.1950 – Field Marshal Jan Christian Smuts

Suzanne Danielle – 14.1.1957 – Humphrey Bogart

Richard Littlejohn – 18.1.1954 – Sydney Greenstreet

Joe Haines – 29.1.1928 – Earl Haig

Charlotte Rampling – 5.2.1946 – George Arliss

Peter Purves – 10.2.1939 – Pope Pius XI

Helena Sukova – 23.2.1965 – Stan Laurel

Sinead O'Carroll – 14.5.1978 – Sir Robert Menzies

Ben Okri – 15.3.1959 – Lester Young

Ornette Coleman – 19.3.1930 – Arthur Balfour

Tim Yeo – 20.3.1945 – Lord Alfred Douglas

Teddy Sheringham – 2.4.1966 – C.S. Forester

John Hartson – 5.4.1975 – Chiang Kai-shek

Dennis Rodman – 13.5.1961 – Gary Cooper

Mary-Kate & Ashley Olsen – 13.6.1986 – Benny Goodman

Bill Withers – 4.7.1938 – Suzanne Lenglen

Oscar De La Renta – 22.7.1932 – Florenz Ziegfield

Louise Fletcher – 22.7.34 – John Dillinger

Ruthie Henshall 7.3.1967 – Alice B. Toklas

Monica Lewinsky – 23.7.1973 – Eddie Rickenbacker

Dino DeLaurentis – 8.8.1919 – Frank Winfield Woolworth

John Gorman – 16.8.1949 – Margaret Mitchell

Matt Aitken – 25.8.1956 – Alfred Kinsey

Derek Fowlds – 2.9.1937 – Baron Pierre de Coubertin

Savo Milosevic – 2.9.1973 – J.R.R. Tolkien

Michael Feinstein – 7.9.1956 – C.B. Fry

Karl Lagerfeld – 10.9.1938 – Charles Cruft

Stephen Gately – 17.3.1976 – Luchino Visconti

Holly Robinson – 18.9.1964 – Sean O'Casey

Eamonn Martin – 9.10.1958 – Pope Pius XII

Roger Taylor (the tennis player) – 14.10.1944 – Erwin Rommel

Melanie Blatt – 25.3.1975 – King Faisal of Saudi Arabia

Jenny McCarthy – 1.11.1972 – Ezra Pound

GENUINE I.T. HELPDESK EXCHANGE

CUSTOMER: My keyboard is not working.

HELPDESK: Are you sure it's plugged into the computer?

CUSTOMER: No. I can't get behind the computer.

HELPDESK: Pick up your keyboard and walk 10 paces back.

CUSTOMER: OK.

HELPDESK: Did the keyboard come with you?

CUSTOMER: Yes.

HELPDESK: That means the keyboard is not plugged in.

LASTS

The last letter George Harrison ever wrote was to Mike Myers asking for a Mini-Me doll.

19.11.1999 was the last date before 1.1.3111 when all the digits in the date were odd.

After Custer's Last Stand, Sioux Indian leader Chief Sitting Bull became an entertainer and toured the country with Buffalo Bill's Wild West Show.

The last time a First Division/Premier club had two players scoring more than 30 goals in a season was Sunderland in 1935–36 when Raich Carter and Bob Gurney each scored 31 goals.

EPIGRAPH

**'If a little knowledge is dangerous,
where is the man who has so much as
to be out of danger?'**
(Thomas Huxley)

ACKNOWLEDGEMENTS

For the past twenty years, I've been collecting weird and wonderful facts which I've been storing on bits of paper and, more recently, on my computer.

The result has been a series of books which I'm now delighted to have published in a single volume.

Most of what you will read has been acquired organically. However, I am happy to acknowledge material culled from the internet – especially in the sections insects etc., the human condition, fish etc., geography, birds etc., history, animals etc.,and science.

These three books required ingenuity, cleverness, and talent. Fortunately I had the help of a group of people who possess such qualities by the bucket-load. First and foremost was my publisher and editor, Doug Young. The other principal players (in alphabetical order): Hugh Adams, Luigi Bonomi, Penny Chorlton and Mari Roberts.

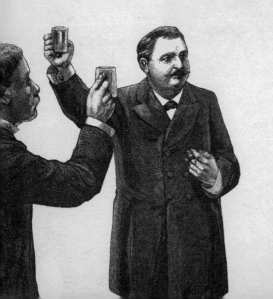

In addition, I'd also like to thank the following people for their help, contributions and/or support: Gilly Adams, Russell Ash, Paul Ashford, Alison Barrow, Jeremy Beadle, Marcus Berkmann, Jeremy Clarkson, Paul Donnelly, , Jonathan Fingerhut, Jenny Garrison, Rachel Jane, Patrick Janson-Smith, Sam Jones, Andy Kay, John Koski, Richard Littlejohn, Tricia Martin, William Mulcahy, Emma Musgrave, Bryn Musson, Amanda Preston, Nicholas Ridge, Simon Rose, Molly Stirling, Charlie Symons, Jack Symons, Louise Symons, Chris Tarrant, David, Thomas, Martin Townsend, Katrina Whone and Rob Woolley.

As ever, if I've missed anyone out, then please know that – as with any mistakes in the book – it's entirely down to my own stupidity.

Mitchell Symons
thatbook@mail.com

Fin